James B Lawrence

China and Japan, and a Voyage Thither

An account of a cruise in the waters of the East Indies, China, and Japan

James B Lawrence

China and Japan, and a Voyage Thither
An account of a cruise in the waters of the East Indies, China, and Japan

ISBN/EAN: 9783337003593

Printed in Europe, USA, Canada, Australia, Japan

Cover: Foto ©Andreas Hilbeck / pixelio.de

More available books at **www.hansebooks.com**

Yours Truly,
James B. Saunner.

CHINA AND JAPAN,

AND

A VOYAGE THITHER:

AN ACCOUNT OF A CRUISE

IN THE

WATERS OF THE EAST INDIES,

CHINA, AND JAPAN.

By JAMES B. LAWRENCE, U. S. M. C.

HARTFORD:
PRESS OF CASE, LOCKWOOD & BRAINARD.
1870.

Entered according to Act of Congress, in the year 1870, by

JAMES B. LAWRENCE,

In the Clerk's Office of the District Court of the United States, for the District of Connecticut.

TO

MY GALLANT SHIPMATES AND COMPANIONS

OF THE

Asiatic Squadron,

AND

THOSE "DEAR FRIENDS AT HOME,"

WHO EVER REMEMBERED US WITH INTEREST IN ALL OUR WANDERINGS,
THIS VOLUME IS AFFECTIONATELY DEDICATED,

BY THE AUTHOR.

PREFACE.

There have been times in the lives of almost every one, when they have stood with a group of friends, as some bright day closed into evening, and watched with admiration its varied pictures of colored and golden cloud-scenes. At such times one could not have failed to have remarked that each one saw scenes unnoticed or unrecognized by others. What would appear to one to be the figures of persons, would as clearly be recognized by another to be animals; and while one would be struck with astonishment at a very clearly defined picture of contending armies, or a noble tower with lofty battlements, to others these same scenes would appear but a confused and unshapen mass.

In like manner, no one beholds the same thing precisely alike, and in some cases there is a direct contradiction in describing the same object, and yet both may be correct so far as they go; as in the case of the two knights contending over the material of which the shield was composed. The fault was that one did not see the whole; and in no case yet has the multiplied descriptions of different countries and people either exhausted the subject, or made us accurately acquainted. There is ever an opportunity for "one more" to bring something new to our notice, or present the most familiar subject in some new and interesting aspect.

This must be the writer's excuse for saying something

regarding countries, people, and other topics that may appear familiar to many; but the most of his gatherings are from remote regions, which, while any information respecting them is intensely interesting, there is yet comparatively little known. In these gatherings the writer has endeavored to collect the most interesting, to be as comprehensive as his opportunities would allow, and to describe and narrate all in as concise a manner as ease would permit. He feels assured that the reader will find in these pages some new and interesting items regarding the remote regions of which he writes; and yet is at the same time conscious that they will not be missed from the vast mass left for other observers and future years.

As a public ship is always an object of national interest, and therefore cannot be uninteresting for her republican parents to know of her wanderings, the writer has given in connection with these gatherings the most important facts respecting the "cruise" of the vessels with which he was connected. He has also endeavored to notice some great evils which exist in an important national institution, and which do not seem to be in harmony with our national character. It should be the aim of all to produce a reform in this institution, and to show to the world in our Navy an example of correct American principles.

Respecting his style, the writer makes no pretensions, although he is well aware that so much depends upon it, that the simplest incident is embellished by it; and the most trifling item from the pen of some are by it so expressed as to possess all the fascinations of a romance. Still the writer feels assured that the simplest account of a voyage has such indiscriminate popularity, that he may safely rely upon the interest of his subject, without particular reference to style. Something, however, should perhaps be said in respect to the form in which the book has been written.

The writer has chosen the form of "letters" because this is less didactic and stiff than any other, and also, while he has found greater freedom and ease in writing as from one friend to another, he hopes that the reader will derive deeper pleasure from the perusal. To the charge of egotism, which some might bring against him, he would say in defence, that this form necessarily occasions a considerable use of the first person; and after all, what is history or the account of anything but the aggregate of individual experiences and emotions?

It might have been better in some respects had the writer followed more closely the directions of good Master Bayle in his prescriptions for description and invention. Although his sage rules have not been taken as a guide, yet whenever he had a statement to make in connection with his subject, that belonged to the common stock of history and science, or has had views and sentiments to convey which another has better expressed than himself, he has not hesitated, without further acknowledgments, to use such materials, in part or entire, and to blend them with his own into a kind of mosaic, in which he admits that his part is little more than the cement.

However, this has not been carried to any great extent by him; and the reader need not expect to find the history of each place run back to primeval dates, including an elaborate treatise on Mineralogy, Botany, and all other sciences of every place; for the writer has mainly noted the objects and topics which interested him at the moment; and provided that the perusal of these gatherings impart to the reader one-half the interest and pleasure that the writer experienced, he will be content.

JAMES B. LAWRENCE,

SANDISFIELD, MASS., *July 1st*, 1870.

CONTENTS.

LETTER I.
BOSTON HARBOR. - - Page 9.
On board—A glance at the Wachusett—The Berth Deck.

LETTER II.
UNDER WEIGH. - - Page 15.
"Down by the Run"—Preparing for Sea—Presidential Rejoicings—The Pains of Parting.

LETTER III.
AT SEA. - - - Page 20.
Stationing—Amusements—Sunday on board Ship—Treatment of Seamen—Our Officers—Preparations for Port—Land Ho!—Emotions—Dominica and Martinique—Beautiful scenery of the latter—Fort de France Harbor—The Town—Tropical Fruits—Cheering Strains.

LETTER IV.
MARTINIQUE, WEST INDIES. - Page 29.
"Putting on Ship's Harbor Dress"—Introduced to the Inhabitants—"Coaling Ship"—Ship's Rations—"Boxing the Compass"—Rambling Ashore—Mistaken Kindness—Fort de France—The Streets—Buildings—"Quarter Deck Guard"—Aground—Afloat Again—Go 'round to St. Pierre—A glance at the Town.

LETTER V.
MARTINIQUE TO CAPE VERDES. - Page 40.
"General Quarters"—Scrubbing Hammocks and Washing Clothes—Divisional Routine—Daily Routine—Relative Position and Duties—"Cleansing Ship"—Meeting Vessels—Sight the Cape Verdes—St. Antonio and St. Vincent—Porto Grand Harbor—"Bird Rock"—"Washington's Head"—The Town from the Ship—Inhabitants—Our Flag.

LETTER VI.

CAPE VERDES. - - Page 47.

News from Home—Mourning for President Lincoln—Target Practice—On Shore—A word about Sugar—Leave for Porto Praya—St. Jago—Porto Praya Harbor—The Town—Money—Fresh Provisions—Result of One's Misdeeds—A False Alarm—Visitors—A Fair One—Reminiscences—The Lost Anchor.

LETTER VII.

PORTO PRAYA TO ST. CATHARINE. - Page 54.

Rough Weather and Sea-sickness—Jib Bogue—Neptune's Visit—Becalmed—"By the Wind"—Half Rations—Off Rio Janeiro—Scenery—"Sold"—Steer for Montevidio—The Pampero—First Storm at Sea—A Fearful Night—In the Vortex of the Hurricane—Trying Moments—"About Ship"—"Land Ho!"—Put into St. Catharine.

LETTER VIII.

ST. CATHARINE. - - Page 66.

Coal and Provisions—Hard Bread—More News from Home—An Oranging Expedition—"Fourth of July"—"Dressing Ship"—Depart for Rio—Chess—Preparations for entering Rio—Entering the Bay—Sugar Loaf—The Scenery of the Bay of Rio Janeiro—The Bay—Coaling Ship—Healing the Breach.

LETTER IX.

RIO JANEIRO. - - - Page 76.

Ceremonies for the Emperor—Holidays—The Susquehanna—"Ship Visiting"—Money and "General Liberty"—A Defaulter—Murder of a Messmate—The Funeral—The Ceremony—Wedding of "Mary and John"—At the Landing—Royal Chapel—Paintings—Rua do Ouvridor—Rua do Ouvris—Don Pedro Square and Cafe—Coffee—Rio Janeirians—Praya Grande—A pleasant Acquaintance with Strawberries and Cream—The French Theatre—Navy Yard and Iron Clads—New Use for Window Blinds and Shutters—The Intuitive Portuguese Jealousy—"Mooring Ship"—Visit to Botafogo and Botanic Gardens—Repairs.

LETTER X.

RIO JANEIRO TO "THE CAPE." - Page 92.

Weighing Anchor—Good-bye to Rio—That Dutchman—Mending—A New Personage introduced with New Uses, etc—What a Band!—

Africa Sighted—Good Hope—An Arrival in Port—Simon's Bay, South Africa.

LETTER XI.
CAPE TOWN, SOUTH AFRICA. - Page 99.

Fishing at Simon's Bay—Toad Fish—Cape Town and Table Mountain—On Shore—A glance at the City—Castle—Barracks—Wine with good advice from Mr. Bacchus—Market and Fair Venders—Government Grounds and Colonial Museum—Curiosities—An Excursion to Wynberg—Constancia Vineyard—Result of Treading on Toes—Visitors and Comical Description of "de Rible Gun"—Our Ball—Death of Ryan—The Yeoman—The Hartford—Castle Building.

LETTER XII.
BATAVIA, JAVA. - - Page 112.

Coffee and Spices!—Leave Cape Town—Theft—A Narrow Escape—Sailors' Superstitions—Christmas—Sick at Sea!—Becalmed—Routine; Oh how Monotonous and Tiresome!—"Fair Wind, with our Engines"—Java Head—Anjer Point—Javanese and Boats—Harbor—Batavia—Sail Ashore—Government Grounds—How we Rode and what we Saw—Native and Foreign Quarters—Botanical and Zoological Gardens—The George Green—Onrust—Preparations for Departure.

LETTER XIII.
MANILLA, LUZON. - - Page 126.

From Batavia to Manilla—Waterspouts—Target Practice—Borneo—Fruitless Search for "Wild Men"—Luzon—Manilla—Inhabitants—Dress—The Town—Earthquakes—Cigars and Manufactories—Visit the Cathedral—La Plaza—Native Quarter—"Washington's Birth day"—Garroting.

LETTER XIV.
HONG KONG, CHINA. - - Page 134.

Manilla to Hong Kong—Sight Hong Kong—The Irate Admiral—First Introduction to Chinese—Appearance and Costumes—Hong Kong Harbor and Island—Victoria—News from Home.

LETTER XV.
MACAO, CHINA. - - Page 141.

Passage from Hong Kong—Picturesque Appearance of Macao—"General Liberty"—"Fast Boats" and Tanka Girls—Experience with them going ashore—The Cathedral—Chinese Quarter—Barbered—Costumes—Foreign Quarter—Palanquins—Chinese Theatre—Camoens and Chinnery—Humanity, Swapping Black Skins for Yellow ones.

LETTER XVI.

CANTON. - - - Page 150.

Leave Macao—Canton River Scenery—Chinese Graves—Features in Landscape—Approaching the City—Varieties of Boats—"Factories"—Arrival of Admiral—Importunities of Tanka Girls—Curiosity Street and Curiosities—Silks—City Walls—Bird's-Eye View—Houses—Streets—Business—Execution Ground, etc—Honan Side—Visit of Governor—Mandarin Costumes—Beggars and Curious Law.

LETTER XVII.

HONG KONG. - - Page 165.

Leave Canton—Whampoa Anchorage—A shore view of Hong Kong—Queen's Road—"Old Sam"—Incident Illustrative of Chinese Imitation.

LETTER XVIII.

SHANGHAI. - - Page 170.

Hong Kong to Shanghai—"A Man Overboard!"—Run a Junk Down—Woosung—Shanghai from Forecastle—A Shore View—Sampans—Native City—Taeping Monument.

LETTER XIX.

NEWCHWANG. - - - Page 179.

Leave Shanghai—Shantung Promontory—Yingtse—Hu—"The Long-Knife Man"—His Band and their Depredations—An Unsuccessful Expedition—Our Midnight Sortie and Success—Tortures and Executions—Chinese Currency—Drowning of Breems—Surveying the Bar—The Tautai's Visit—A New Pet—Incidents of Stay—Independence Day.

LETTER XX.

CHEFOO AND TUNG-CHOW-FOO. - Page 189.

Leave Newchwang—The Great Wall—Takoo—Chefoo—Go up to Tung-chow-foo—The Difficulty—Another Expedition—Turns into an Excursion—Return to Chefoo—On Shore—A Mandarin Traveling—The Cemetery—General Liberty—The Corean Difficulty.

LETTER XXI.

SHANGHAI AND ON THE YANGTSE KIANG.   Page 201.

Chefoo to Shanghai—Depart for Hankow—Yangtse Kiang and Scenery—Golden and Silver Islands—Chinkiang—Heat, Sickness, and Death—Death of Captain Townsend—Return to Shanghai—Funeral of Captain Townsend—Obituary Notice.

LETTER XXII.

SHANGHAI.   -   -   -   Page 212.

Fever—Ramble about Shanghai—Chinese Prisons—Tea Gardens—Tea.

LETTER XXIII.

A LOOK AT JAPAN.   -   -   Page 215.

A Death and Burial at Sea—Yokohama—Japanese—Dress—Courtesy and Salutations—Yokohama Harbor—Land at the *Hettlebar*—Hamora Street—Bird's-Eye View of Town—Drying Tea—Native Quarter—Incidents of Way—Curiosities—Go up to Yeddo—Escort our Minister—What we encountered in our march through the city—Minister's Residence and Grounds—Ventilation—Yeddo—The New Captain—General Court-Martial—Return to Yokohama—S——. bids us " Good-bye "—Depart for Nagasaki—Oosima—The Typhoon—Enter Inland Sea—Divisions—Scenery, etc.—Nagasaki Harbor—The Town—Japanese Currency—Horseback Ramble about Nagasaki—A few words about Japanese.

LETTER XXIV.

HONG KONG.   -   -   -   Page 236.

Nagasaki to Hong Kong—Arrival—Go up to Macao for Fête—Cruising after Pirates—Description, Mode of Attack, etc.—A Sad Incident—Visit an Opium Saloon—" Take a Whiff," and Effects—Central Market—Public Gardens—Kowloon Shore—The Fire—Cool.

LETTER XXV.

HONG KONG.   -   -   -   Page 243.

Cruising Northward—Tsing Hoy—Swatow—Amoa Straits—Tung Sang—Salt Works—Sweet Potatoes—Off Amoy—Scenery—Amoy—On Shore—Chinese Cemetery—Graves, etc.—White Stag Hill—Picturesqueness of Kulang-soo—Sunday Services with Attractions—Return to Hong Kong—Thanksgiving—Lose Dr. Page.

CONTENTS.

LETTER XXVI.
WHAMPOA. - - - Page 253.

Go up to Whampoa—In Dock—Repairing—A Sad Death—Curiosities—Summary Punishment for Stealing—A Word on Chinese Government—A Ramble into Interior—Music and Wine—New Town—In the Country—Bananas—Pagoda Eminence—The View—Inside the Pagoda—Old Whampoa—Chinese Ploughing—Grinding—Printing early known, Manner of, etc.—Parsee Burying Ground—Chinese Funeral—The Joss Tower—Return to Hong Kong—Christmas Festivities—A Sad Parting.

LETTER XXVII.
CHEFOO. - - - Page 269.

Depart for the Northward—In Linchan Bay—A Typhoon—Shanghai—Powder Explosion—Loneliness—A Novel Combat—Depart for Chefoo—Arrival—Cold, but Pleasant—Shooting and Skating—The General Sherman Affair—Description of Chinese Written Language and the Spoken—Learning in China.

LETTER XXVIII.
COREA. - - - Page 277.

Depart for Corea—Approaching the Land—Nein-Fo—Coreans—Dress, Appearance, etc.—Communications sent to King of Corea and Chief of Province—Survey and Nomenclature of Bay and Inlets—The Chief's "Winter Cap"—Filthiness of Coreans—A Tough Yarn—Corean Version of Gen. Sherman Affair—Unsatisfactory Reply to Communications—A Vindictive Savage—Go to Port Hamilton (Nanhoo)—The Harbor—Islands—Villages—Houses—General Remarks upon Coreans.

LETTER XXIX.
SHANGHAI. - - - Page 285.

Passage from Corea—At Shanghai—Chinese New Year's Holidays—Customs—Calls—Dress—Visit of Catholic Missionaries—Ship Visiting and Pleasant Acquaintances.

LETTER XXX.
SECOND TRIP UP YANGTSE-KIANG. - Page 289.

Summary of Past Year with us—Delightful Weather—Depart from Shanghai—The Grand Canal—Scenery and Sights up the River—

Chinese Landscapes—Floating Farms—Hankow—Size of, form, defenses, etc.—Scene on Han River—Sailing through a Crowded Thoroughfare—A City on the Water—" Laws of the Road "—Visit Wuchang—International Sports on Shore.

LETTER XXXI.
Down the Yangtse. - - Page 297.

Rebels and Refugees—Origin of " Land Pirates "—A Brutal Deed—Kiukiang—Burning Cities—Courage—Chinese Military—A Battle—Porcelain—Tea—A Large Story—Nankin—Notorieties—The Porcelain Tower—A Sham Battle—Return to Shanghai.

LETTER XXXII.
Foochow and Ningpo. - . Page 306.

To Foochow by Inland Passage—Scenery of the Min—Pagoda Anchorage—On the Pagoda—Foochow—Soap Stone Carvings—Foochow to Chinhae—" Joss-House Hill "—Chinhae—Approaching Ningpo—Suburbs—" Heaven-conferred Pagoda "—The Mohammedan Mosque—A " Sing-Song House " and Female Temple—The City—Houses—Courts, etc.—Services and Attractions—The Confucian System.

LETTER XXXIII.
Shanghai. - - - Page 319.

Passage from Ningpo—The Fire—The Captain's Speech—Our Church—" For to go and see the Races "—Firemen's Muster—A Desirable Acquaintance—Taou System of Religion—A Ride under Difficulties—Cremorne Gardens—Sik-a-wai, and Incidents of Ride.

LETTER XXXIV.
Shanghai. - - - Page 336.

The American Arms at Formosa—A Horrible Execution—Small Feet—The " Glorious Fourth "—Boat Racing—Christianity in China—Outline of Chinese Government—Kites and Kite-flying.

LETTER XXXV.
Pootoo. - - - Page 347.

Cruising for Sanitary Purposes—Ningpo and Passengers—Chusan—Tinghai—" Chickens for Sailors !"—Beauties of Pootoo—Temples, Services, Devotions, and Duties—Prayers—Introduction of Buddhism—Doctrines—Present Condition—Sacred Flowers—Genii's Well—Surf Bathing.

CONTENTS.

LETTER XXXVI.
HONG KONG. - - - Page 362.

Pootoo to Shanghai—"Homeward Bound"—Excitement—Hong Kong—Our Fleet—Typhoon Season.

LETTER XXXVII.
HONG KONG. - - - Page 368.

Transferred to United States Flag Ship Hartford—The Wachusett and Wyoming go—A glance at the Hartford—Another Typhoon.

LETTER XXXVIII.
NAGASAKI, JAPAN. - - Page 375.

Hong Kong to Nagasaki—"Winter's Coming Again"—Rumors—Japanese Traditions, Basis and Form of Government, Laws, Etc.—Death of the Admiral's Secretary—Piracy, and arrival of Shipwrecked Party.

LETTER XXXIX.
HIOGA, JAPAN. - - - Page 380.

Leave Nagasaki—Simonosaki—Wonderful Dwarfs, Etc.—Hioga—A sad Christmas—More Rumors—"Opening the Ports"—Prospects of Japan—Go over to Osaca—The City—Tycoon's Palace—"The Barge has Capsized!"—Bringing off the Living and the Dead—Our Drowned Shipmates—A House of Death—Return to Hioga—The Funeral—To Osaca by Land—Laws in regard to Christianity—Perfection of Japanese Police—Pagoda, with its Temples, Inn, Etc., in Outskirts of Osaca—In the City—"Necessity the Mother of Invention."

LETTER XL.
HONG KONG. - - - Page 396.

Return to Nagasaki—Transferring—Nagasaki to Hong Kong—Gambling—An Adventure in Canton—The "Feast of Lanterns"—Go up to Whampoa—Chinese mode of Printing and Manufacture of Books—Diet of Common People—A Chinese "Tea Drinking"—A Glance at Chinese History—Boundaries and Extent of China—Population—Ready for Home.

LETTER XLI.
SINGAPORE, EAST INDIES. - - Page 411.

"Homeward Bound"—Passage from Hong Kong—Singapore—Mahometans—A Charming Ride—The Lorcha—"Humbugging"—Arrival of the Piscataqua—Fruits, Etc.

LETTER XLII.

CAPE TOWN, SOUTH AFRICA. - Page 422.

"Homeward Bound" Again—Anjer Point—A Blow—Hole-in-the-Wall Simon's Town—Cape Town.

LETTER XLIII.

ST. HELENA. - - - Page 425.

Cape Town to St. Helena—"The Fourth"—Ladder Hill—Jamestown —"The Briars"—Plants and Stones—"Willow Cottage"—The "Cabbage Tree"—The Tomb of Napoleon—Old Long House— Hutt's Gate—Superficies, &c., of St. Helena.

LETTER XLIV.

NEW YORK. - - - Page 435.

Our Last Passage—Home Again—Farewell.

LIST OF ILLUSTRATIONS.

	PAGE.
J. B. LAWRENCE,	frontispiece.
MACAO, CHINA,	140
STREET BARBER,	146
SHANGHAI, CHINA,	174
SMOKING OPIUM,	238
WHAMPOA REACH,	254
PAGODA ANCHORAGE, FOOCHOW,	306
HONG KONG, CHINA,	365
TYCOON'S PALACE, OSACA,	386

ر

LETTERS.

LETTER I.

U. S. S. WACHUSETT, Boston Harbor, }
March 1, 1865. }

MY DEAR R.:

At last my long cherished desire is about to be attained—that of going to sea. You know how strong that desire has been, how long and eagerly I have striven to attain it, and now that success is about to crown my undertakings, you can better imagine my feelings than I can describe them. It was your earnest request that I would write you at length concerning what I might see, hear, or think, that might savor of interest to you, leaving me to select such matter as I might deem interesting. At the same time you promised that whatever should fail to awaken the interest anticipated should be as thankfully received as though it had accomplished the desired end, in short, promising in all cases to take the will for the deed. In view of such a request, so favorably conditioned, I could not do less than I did,—cordially promise that so far as it should lie within my power, I would gratify you.

About a week ago I learned that the Wachusett would soon be ready for sea, and that she was bound for China. That country, above all others, I have ever been anxious to visit, and, as a favorable account of the Wachusett officers had been given me by a friend who was acquainted with them, I was induced to volunteer for her. So many of my applications to be sent to sea having been refused before, I was a little apprehensive that this one might share a similar fate, but when the Marine Guard was detailed for the Wachusett this morning, I found myself to be one of the number. There were fifteen of us in all; one sergeant, two corporals, and twelve privates, constituting what is called a "Sergeant's Guard."

With one exception, I have no acquaintance with any of them, but so far as appearances go, I should call them an intelligent body of men, such as know their duty and will not hesitate to perform it, and among whom I shall find some worthy and congenial associates. In the close relationship that we, of necessity, must sustain, I shall know them thoroughly ere long. We were ordered to have everything in readiness to go on board that same forenoon, and although the command came unexpectedly to us all, we set to work packing and making the many necessary preparations for the change from barrack life to shipboard existence, and long before noon all were ready.

Then came the leave takings—parting with the friends and acquaintances that we had made whilst together in Barracks. One and all were agreed that we were fortunate in being selected for the "Wachusett's Guard," and "a pleasant cruise—an interesting cruise—you are going to have," were their words as we shook hands and said "good-bye."

A final inspection under the "Arcade!" then we slung knapsacks, and, to the sound of the fife and drum marched to the lower end of the Navy Yard, where the Wachusett was lying alongside the wharf. But one regretful face did I see in the "Guard," and I do not wonder at its being *regretful*, for H. has but a few months longer to serve, and already has had nearly forty months' sea service. Arriving at the wharf we marched on board the Wachusett, over planks thrown out from her after pivot port—the Wachusett, which is to be our home for the next thirty months at least. Not very attractive or home-like did it appear to us—everything in uproar and confusion, and dirty—awful dirty!

We found the crew on board before us, which numbers about one hundred and seventy-five men, of almost every color, shade, and nationality. Some of them were dressed in citizen clothing, some in the regular man-of-war-man's suit, and others with a part of each. It was an easy matter to determine that they had just come from the "Guard O," by their dirty appearance, and in the way that they kept all their possessions about them; seated on a dirty box, black-bag (for clothing) between their knees, and tin-pot, pan, and spoon, either held in their hands, or fastened to a belt about the waist. Many of them were intoxicated, and were exhibiting the usual phenomena of such a condition,—singing, shouting, and fighting.

After an inspection by the executive officer, we were permitted to go below, and, after finding our quarters, we set to work cleaning them up and preparing a place for our baggage, which arrived shortly after, and was stowed away. It was now dinner time, but owing to the confusion which everywhere prevailed, no dinner had been prepared; but we managed to satisfy the cravings of our appetites with sundry slices of cold meat and bread which we had had the forethought to bring with us from the Barracks.

Immediately after coming on board three sentries were posted and a corporal placed on guard, whose duties are to see that no one leaves the ship or comes on board without permission from proper authorities, that no liquor is brought on board, and that good order everywhere is maintained throughout the ship. These are the prominent duties of the Marine Guard, but in addition, there are numberless other less important ones which they are required to perform, so that, although they have nothing to do with the managing and cleaning of the ship, they can boast of no more ease or leisure than the seamen.

The unoccupied moments that I have had to-day have been spent in a survey of the ship, in which I was accompanied by a boatswain's mate, who, being well versed in everything about the ship, was able to impart much valuable information.

The Wachusett is a screw propeller, of one thousand and thirty tons burden; bark-rigged, carrying top-gallant sails; is two hundred and thirty-seven feet length of keel, and about forty feet beam; and carries a battery of ten guns, one one-hundred, and two thirty pound Parrot rifles, on pivot; two one-hundred pound rifles, and four thirty-two's—smooth bore—on broadside, and a twelve pound boat-howitzer. Her tall, slender spars; long, low, beautifully modeled hull, and the gracefulness with which she sits upon the water, have compelled all competent judges to pronounce her to be one of the finest vessels in our navy. All are already disposed to be proud of her, and provided that her sailing qualities prove to be equal to her outside appearance, none could ask for a better ship.

The to'gallant forecastle is an unusually large one, extending nearly to the foremast. Underneath is a fine, roomy place, where the men can find shelter in cold or stormy weather. There is the scuttle-butt (in which water for drinking is kept), the Captain's galley, and cable compressers. There are also hooks for about twenty-five to swing their hammocks underneath this forecastle. Just forward of the foremast is a hatch, with two ladders leading down to the berth-deck, and another one just abaft the foremast. Continuing on aft to the upper cabin bulkhead, come successively the capstan, hundred pound rifle on pivot, fire-room hatches and smoke-stack, the four thirty-two's on broadside, main-mast, engine-room hatch, steerage and ward-room hatches, two one hundred pound rifles on broadside, ward-room sky light, mizzen-mast, cabin hatch and sky-light, binnacles, and helm. The poop is about twenty-five feet in length, underneath which is the upper cabin. One of the thirty-pound rifles is mounted on the poop, and the other on the forecastle. The bulwarks are about four feet high—very thick and strong: on top of them, extending from the forecastle to the poop, are square troughs, about eighteen inches wide and deep—the hammock nettings; in these the hammocks are stowed every morning——protected from the weather by a thick, painted, canvas covering.

Leaving the spar-deck and going down to the berth-deck by the ladder at the foremast one finds himself in a dark crowded, dirty, ill-ventilated *hole*, and, at present, in the greatest confusion imaginable. Just picture to yourself such a place, and then consider, that although barely seventy-five feet in length, it is the place where nearly two hundred men must eat, sleep, and in a great measure *live!* About ten feet of the forward part of the deck is partitioned off, and is used as an apartment for prisoners—in naval *parlance* denominated the "Brig." Close by this are two apartments, two feet square—the "sweat-boxes," and near these are two reals containing large hawsers. The "galley" occupies a central position on the deck, and is said to be an uncommonly good and convenient one. Extending along the sides of the berth-deck are iron rods about four feet high, called "jackstays," to which the black-bags are fastened. Ranging up and down on either side of the deck are the mess-chests, four feet long and two feet wide and deep, in which are kept the dishes and some articles of food. In the after corner, on the port side, is the Paymaster's Issuing-room, and in the opposite corner are two small rooms, one of which is the Sergeant's Store-room, and the other the Surgeon's Dispensary. Between these rooms are two coal-shutes, and a reel holding an eleven-inch hawser, leaving a narrow passage-way behind them, in which is a table, at which I am now sitting and writing to you. The berth-deck is separated from the fire-room by a double-walled partition of wood and iron.

Underneath the forward part of the berth-deck are several

store-rooms, the Yeoman's room, and the powder magazines. Underneath the after portion are the holds, chain-lockers, and water-tanks.

The berth-deck is lighted by means of small, round apertures in the ship's sides, which are closed by thick circlets of glass, set in iron frames, and called "dead-lights." If these were but cleaned of the dust and cob-webs that now cover them, the ship would be far lighter than it now is—*lighter* in both acceptations of the word.

Of the remaining parts of the ship I will make mention in some future letter, when I have had more time and better opportunities for examining them, and am better acquainted. I have had as yet no good opportunities for forming an opinion of the crew, and should I narrate my experiences thus far, with them, there would be nothing but what you might see and hear every day around any rum-selling tavern. So I shall wait for something better.

Now, provided your patience, even, has held out thus far, I imagine that I hear you saying to yourself—"I think that L. really needed all the promises that I made him; I shall have to take the will for the deed, and if all his letters are going to be of this stamp, I am afraid that they will fail to awaken the interest and pleasure that I hoped and expected to derive from them."

Have patience, my dear R., I know that the most that I have written thus far, must seem dry and uninteresting to you; but yet, exercising that liberty of selection which you so kindly granted me, I thought best, in the first place, to give you some description of the place that for so long a time I must call my home, and some little insight into my duties: then, I shall be the better able to devote my whole time and space to the narration of the interesting incidents of the cruise. So I have devoted this introductory letter to the aforesaid description and insight, and now I think that I can promise you, that in my next letter you will find a change for the better.

LETTER II.

U. S. S. WACHUSETT, Boston Harbor,
March 4, 1865.

MY DEAR R.:

A cold, drizzling rain has baptized our first three days' stay on board the Wachusett—the beginning of from two to three years of such existence. Of course you wish to know how our time has been employed, so I will tell you. One and all have been as busy as bees, and hard at work from morning till night in making the thousand and one necessary preparations for sea.

In commencement I must narrate to you my first night's experience. Leaving barracks in such haste as we did, I was not sufficiently careful in slinging my hammock, as I found out by an unpleasant occurrence. I was very tired and sleepy, and was folded in the embrace of Morpheus almost as soon as I had got into my hammock, but had been in this agreeable situation but a very few minutes when "down I came by the run," the clews having slipped out from both ends of the hammock. I was so seriously injured by the fall, that I have been unable to do any duty since.

Did you ever sleep in a hammock? If not, you have missed one of the greatest discomforts there is in the world. Before trying to impress upon your mind wherein that discomfort consists, I must first endeavor to give you some idea of the construction of a hammock. Take a piece of canvass or strong cloth, six feet in length and three in width, and make ten or twelve eyelet holes in each end; then, in these holes fasten—*securely*, mind you—strong cords, about two feet long; and the other extremities of the cords, at each end, fasten to a ring; by means of the rings, hang up the hammock on hooks, so placed that it will be stretched nearly as much as possible; now place in it a mattress to lie upon, a blanket for covering, and the hammock is ready for use. Be very careful, now in getting into it, else you will meet with the same mishaps that I met with in my first attempts. First I tried getting into it the same as though I was getting into a bed. The result was, I went completely over it, striking head foremost on the deck on the opposite side. Next, I made the attempt from a camp-stool, but that plan ended like the first, by my being on deck. The third trial, I took hold of two hammock hooks overhead, and finally managed to swing myself into the hammock, but had to keep firm hold of the hooks to prevent my falling out; and there I lay, not daring to let go, or move even. To make this more impressively disagreeable, you need to be slightly sea-sick, feel miserably in general, and have the ship rolling and pitching about wildly.

But to return, you are now in your hammock, and find yourself describing an arc of a circle, with your head and feet elevated at an angle of about forty-five degrees, whilst the sides of the hammock are drawn up around you, so that it would not take a great stretching of the imagination for you to imagine yourself in a bag. In this undertaking you would have great assistance could you only be situated as we are—each man's "billet," or sleeping room being but fourteen inches wide. Seven men sleeping in a bed eight feet wide affords the best comparison that I can make. When one turns or moves, the motion is communicated to all; consequently we are ever pleased when a neighbor is called to go on post. This for the past few days has had its drawbacks, for, when he would return after his two hours of guard duty were over, just as we were beginning to enjoy the luxury of "more room," we had a wet bed-fellow. Besides this, we can never count upon having more than two hours of continuous sleep, for, not yet acquainted, the "corporal of the Guard" often wakens the wrong man—usually, *the right man last.* Still, notwithstanding all these many discomforts, old sailors would prefer a hammock to sleep in, to the best bed; and I haven't the least doubt but that I shall turn to it as the source of one of my greatest enjoyments during the cruise. The "old salts" had a hearty laugh this eve, at the expense of a landsman who was searching for his hammock on the "East Boston side of the ship," saying that he placed it there this morning. After he had searched the hammock nettings on that side many times over in vain, and was about concluding that the hammock was lost, some one told him that the ship had swung with the tide since then, and he would probably find it on "the Boston side;" and so he did.

A few words now about mess arrangements. The crew is divided into messes of from ten to twenty persons, and one of the number is called the "cook of the mess. He does not cook, but receives from the purser's steward the daily ration allotted to his mess, ties the various articles together in bundles and marks them with a stick or talley, on which is cut the number of the mess, and takes care of the mess chest, the mess pots, pans, dishes, and other articles belonging to the mess in common. The rations are always served out on the day preceding that to which they belong. Each mess cook delivers his share to the ship's cook, who, with an assistant, prepares it all in the "coppers" under his charge. Just before noon he takes a sample to the officer of the deck to show that it is properly done, and if so the mess cooks receive the "grub" again from the ship's cook. At noon they spread painted cloths upon the deck, place the "grub" and dishes upon them, and then the boatswain's mates pipe all hands to dinner. The same ceremonies are observed at breakfast and supper, with the exception that the only articles received from the ship's cook is her water for coffee and tea.

All the messes have contributed greater or lesser amounts with which to purchase extra stores and conveniences for their messes, and the berth-deck is now fairly lumbered up with barrels of flour, potatoes, and such like articles which they have purchased.

What I have mentioned refers exclusively to the men or crew, each division of officers having its own apartment, its own cooking apparatus and special cook. Of these divisions there are four—the starboard, steerage, or "gun-room," the engineer's steerage, the ward-room, and the Captain's.

To-day "Old Abe" takes the Presidential chair for another four years, over which the firing of cannon and the ringing of bells indicate that the city, in common with the whole nation, rejoiceth. God grant that the acts of his administration may be tempered with wisdom and justice, and some means be devised soon to bring this bitter civil war to a close.

Sunday March 5th.—This morning the outside world brightened up a little. During the forenoon the Captain came on board, and after a thorough inspection of the ship, etc., we were pronounced to be ready for sea. Accordingly at 3 P. M., we weighed anchor and slowly steamed down the bay in charge of the pilot. About an hour later we passed Fort Warren, and the soldiers there stationed came down on the beach and gave us three hearty cheers as we passed.

I have just been up on the forecastle, taking a farewell look at Boston, and now but the dim outline of the land can be seen. A farewell look, and for how long? Some of the most sanguine say for only two years, others say thirty months, while there are many who think we will be fortunate if we see the United States again within three years. So think I. But some there are amongst us who have taken their last look of country, friends, home, and all they hold most near and dear. We are all hoping that we may not be of that number, but Death, the tyrant, ever disregards our wishes, and takes us, ready or not. No, it is not probable that the Wachusett will prove an exception to the general rule, but it carries out many that have bid home and friends " good-bye" forever.

But all at this time are not sad; a large number of the crew are far from being so; while many of us are scarcely able to keep back the tears from our eyes, at the thoughts of the long separation from home and friends, and the possibility of never beholding them again, there are many " poor Jacks" who have no deeper feeling than that they are leaving a hospitable place where they have whiled away a few jovial hours, in a social way. He may think of the changes that will occur before he returns, but all that kind of gratuitous boding will be little more than a flash across Jack's mind and if it finds utterance at all, the following stanza may give it full vent:

> " The sea bird wheels above the mast,
> And the waters fly below,
> And the foaming billows flashing fast,
> Are leaping up the prow.
> Hurrah! hurrah! the shores we quit,
> And those who are within,
> May they be safe and standing yet,
> When *we cross these* waves again!"

LETTER III.

U. S. S. WACHUSETT,
Fort de France, Martinique. West Indies.
March 16, 1865.

MY DEAR R.:

I will now get a letter in readiness so as to be able to mail it at the first opportunity. I left you in my last letter just as we were taking a farewell look at the United States. But we had only a few minutes given us for the sad thoughts which were fast overcoming the most of us, when the boatswain and his mates piped "all hands to muster." All crowded aft on the lee side of the quarter deck, and then the executive officer gave all their stations at the battery, divided the crew into watches, and appointed them to different parts of the ship: forecastlemen to the forecastle, foretopmen to the foretop, maintopmen to the maintop, and afterguards to the after part of the ship. Over each division two captains were appointed. The marines and firemen were not included in this division, they having their peculiar duties to perform.

One watch—composed of one-half of the seamen—is kept on deck all of the time at sea, to manage and take care of the ship, and is relieved by the others every four hours. The watch from 4 to 8 P. M. is divided into two watches of two hours each, for, otherwise one portion of the crew would have the same hours every day. These are denominated the "dog-watches." When "all hands" are called to loose or furl sail, get up anchor, or any other business that requires "all hands," then no one is excused unless on duty at the time that will not admit of being left.

Other musters a few days later, gave all their stations at

loosing and furling sail, and fire-quarters. The marines have the thirty-pound rifle on the poop, are stationed at the main try-sail in loosing and furling sail, and at the boats' falls, in fire-quarters, with instructions to allow no one to lower a boat but by the orders of the commanding officer.

Our course after leaving Boston was easterly, steaming along against a light head wind, until Wednesday morning, when it was altered to the southward, and we set fore and aft sails. Our destination was a *dead secret*, of course: many knowing conjectures were made as to the first port we would make, but no one knew excepting the Captain and Sailing-master; because, if we all knew, the Captain would be no wiser than ourselves, and the profound humbug of mysteries would be lost to our wonder.

The first two or three days out were spent by the crew in holystoning the decks, ladders, and gratings, with sand, scrubbing the paint-work, cleaning the bright-work at the guns and cleaning and polishing up, and putting everything in order generally. In all this they had such good success that at the end the Wachusett appeared like an entirely different ship from the one that first met our gaze lying alongside the wharf at Charlestown Navy Yard. Removing the dust and cobwebs from the "dead-lights," made the berth-deck much *lighter*, as I supposed that it would do.

Monday evening we crossed the Banks of Newfoundland. The night was very dark, and we came very near running down a fishing schooner which was "lying to" there. As it was we carried away her jib-boom. She had not a single light displayed, and if there was any one on "look-out," he must have been asleep—certainly he was not attending to his duty, else he would surely have seen our lights. I should think that their narrow escape would make them more careful in the future.

A few days out, and the crew showed some signs of arousing themselves out of that lethargy in which they had been since leaving Boston, and showed themselves to be a smart, lively, fine-looking body of men. But what a variety of color, shade, and nationality, they present! If Adam should look down upon them from the windows of heaven, he would hardly recognize them all as members of his family. One evening I had just finished "posting my Journal," when hearing the sounds of mirth on deck, I went up to see what was going on. Before leaving Boston the crew purchased a variety of musical instruments, boxing-gloves, and foils, with which to enliven the dullness and monotony of shipboard existence. But to return: arriving on deck I found that the sounds of mirth which I had heard, proceeded from a party dancing to the sound of the violin and guitar. A performer was soon found for the banjo, one for the flute, another for the tamborine, and yet another for the bones. After a few minutes employed in *tuning*, all struck up together, and then one and all joined in a "good old-fashioned breakdown," and with such zest and gusto as to fairly make the Wachusett tremble. Many of the officers came forward, and although the sense of their dignity forbade them from joining, they appeared to enjoy the sports but little less than the actual participants, as was manifested by their cheers, and cries of "keep it up."

When all were tired of dancing, the music struck up some familiar home airs, and then the sports of the evening were varied by singing. What a purifier and elevator of the mind and thoughts is music! How much it tends to draw forth the higher and better feelings of one's nature! This is true, wherever found or under what shape. Some excellent songs were sung that night, and well sung, too, and I, for one, was never more impressed with the power and influence of music, than I then was impressed. All felt more cheerful and happy for these few hours' pleasure, and so far as possible, have repeated the sports thus inaugurated, with some variations, every night. Sometimes we were too tired for sports, as the greater portion of each day was taken up in exercising with the battery, and making ourselves acquainted with our several duties. We have yet hardly become accustomed to the great change in the weather, which daily grew warmer as we proceeded further to the southward, and even before the first week had passed, the last overcoat and muffler were stowed away, awaiting some future need.

The first Sunday out, I was for the first time introduced to the manner in which the Sabbath is regarded and kept on board of a man-of-war. It is regarded by nearly all, more as a day for rest and recreation than anything else. There is some faint attempt made outwardly to acknowledge the Sabbath, to be sure, but then it is obvious to all that it is done only because the law so requireth, and the Captain wishes to conform to the requirements of the law in this respect. Many, I found, were seriously questioning and doubting in their minds whether or no it was really Sunday, but finally concluded that it must be, as rice was served out the day before, and "rice is served out only for Sunday dinners."

It being decided that it *was* Sunday, all set to work cleaning, polishing, and dressing the ship and themselves for the Captain's inspection at 10 A. M. Then all assembled at their stations at quarters, dressed in their best, and with their arms cleaned and brightly polished. Could one only stand on the forecastle during a Sunday inspection, when everything is so neat and clean, and previously knowing nothing about a man-of-war, the sight would impress that one, that a sailor's life was elevated above that of common mortals. But one short week's experience would thoroughly dispel that illusion.

After inspection "all hands" were called aft on the quarter-deck to muster, whilst the sea-service of the Episcopal Church was read by the Captain. This is omitted on many men-of-war, and done on the Wachusett, as I said before, because the Captain *wished* to fulfill the requirements of the law in this respect. I express the feelings of many when I say, that I should like very much to be so situated as to be able to attend church every Sunday. Without this privilege, and surrounded by the ever attending influences of a man-of-war, we will find it extremely difficult, sometimes, to make Sunday appear like Sunday to us. But many months, years in fact, will intervene before that time comes again.

After service, the remainder of the day, by the kindness of the Captain, is given to the crew to smoke, write, read, and do such-like things for themselves, as they may choose. But once a month, on these sacred Sabbath mornings, we have "general muster," when the articles of war are read to us in all their thundering terrors, and the often recurring penalty which closes so many sentences, " Death, or such other punishment as a court martial shall adjudge "—the halter and the bullet.

In speaking of this, the remark of an eminent surgeon in our Navy is brought to my mind. " There seems to be a strange overlooking, or inconsistent view of human nature, or Navy nature is not human nature. In the first place there is an expectation that every one who goes on board of a man-of-war, is to hold all sorts of deaths—by hanging, shooting, or drowning—in utter contempt. Indeed it seems as though he is to seek them as the natural end of existence, and to be hung or shot for avoiding them; and yet these are the official threats

'To haud the wretch in order,'"

and once a month, on sacred Sabbath mornings, they are ferociously shaken over our heads, begetting no other feelings than contempt or defiance.

Another statement by the same surgeon is very truthful: "The assembled wisdom of the nation, by slow and painful processes, got a kind of inkling that terror and threats were not the most expedient means of governing the American seamen; and they devised a code which, in pay, privileges, and honorable testimonies, offers a reward for fidelity and obedience. But this ray of sunshine was not permitted to gleam through the death penalty and the gloom of the articles of war. It was a mistake. How many beside the Chinese are befogged by 'ola custom!'"

Since leaving Boston, I have been on duty as one of the captain's orderlies, and in this capacity I have been able to see and know much about our Captain. Those acquainted with him can but agree with me in saying that he is a thorough seaman, a perfect gentleman, and one of the most polished scholars ever met with. He is a very firm, intelligent looking man, of about forty-five years of age, and, although my acquaintance with him is short, I have no hesitation in saying that the appearance is but typical of the man. After serving through the Mexican war, he resigned, and was spending a quiet life at home at the outbreak of the rebellion. He promptly offered his services, and was accepted, his old rank of Lieutenant being given him. He was at the passage of Forts Jackson and Philip, and the capture of New Orleans. Afterwards he did good service on the coast of North Carolina, and was rewarded by the rank of Commander in the regular service. His latest services were rendered while in command of the iron-clad Essex, and he is spoken of as being "one of the best fighting men on the Mississippi and Red rivers." Commander Colvocoresses, was first appointed to the command of the Wachusett, but Captain Townsend subsequently received the appointment upon his making the request. It is rumored that at the end of this cruise he intends to resign and return to citizen's life again. With him as Captain, I am certain that we shall have a pleasant and interesting cruise.

Lieutenant John W. Philip is the executive officer. He is a fine looking, well formed young man, of twenty-five years of age, and, judging by his appearance and actions thus far, is a man of great determination, and an almost indomitable will. He is a graduate of the Naval Academy, and although so young, has seen much service. The other officers I have seen but little of as yet, and therefore am unable to introduce them to you. Will only say that as yet, I have had no occasion to disagree with my friend in his good account of them.

From the thorough cleansing of the ship yesterday, as well as the polishing down, the crew augured that we would soon make some port, and in this surmise, they proved to be correct; for, when I went on deck this morning, I found that we were "lying to," and had been thus since midnight. Many anxious eyes were looking out for land, and soon their search was rewarded, and the joyful cry heard "land ho!" A little later, and the high, dark line off our starboard quarter, resolved itself into two parts, looking like blue clouds in the distance, but which were soon known to be the islands of Dominica and Martinique. Both of these islands are very high and mountainous. Mt. Solferino on Dominica, attains to the height of 6,075 feet above the level of the sea, and Mt. Peeler on Martinique, to 4,430 feet.

Our run from Boston was characterized most of the time by clear, pleasant weather, a smooth sea, favorable winds, and little, if any, sea sickness. To-day is certainly one of the most beautiful days I ever saw, just such as one would desire on which to behold a foreign shore for the first time. Soft and balmy is the air, blue and gently rippling the sea, and everything in nature apparently striving to make all things appear beautiful to us, and to create in us fit thoughts and feelings to enjoy whatever is beautiful.

As soon as it was daylight, we got up steam and started ahead again, leaving Dominica on our starboard bow, and Martinique on our port. The islands are situated about forty miles apart, but they are so high and mountainous that it appeared to be barely one-third that distance as we passed between them.

Dominica presented to our view nothing but a huge mass

of barren rock, but, on the other hand, the prospect was entirely different. More than one I heard to exclaim, " how beautiful !" as they gazed upon the shore of Martinique. Indeed it was truly beautiful, its beauty enhanced no doubt by the great contrast it presented to the last view of the country we had left so recently. There the ground was covered with ice and snow, and everything barren and dead. Here everything is fresh and green, the hills clothed with verdure, the trees covered with leaves and fruits, and the air warm and balmy as that of our summer. The change seems almost wonderful; 'tis like going to sleep in mid-winter, and not waking again till mid-summer.

At such a time, and in such a scene one may be excused a little poetical emotion—nay, would not one without it have that unpoetical soul which the master of the human heart has told us, is " fit for treason, stratagem, and spoil?" It has been remarked that, " islands, all islands, are poetical existences in themselves: their philosophy is poetry, mysterious in their sea boundaries, cut off from the grave, solid, unchanging character of the mainland ; they grow gradually from the deep sea depths, by the microscopic labors of the coral, insect, or thrown at once into the upper air amid earthquake throes, and volcanic convulsions, shaking the earth to its centre. They are the abodes of pirate heroes, and goat skin clad Cruisers." Nothing of this kind, however, is the story that Martinique has to tell. It simply has to boast that here Josephine, the first wife of Napoleon, was born, and that here her early childhood was passed.

But to return to where I was before this digression, nearing Martinique, whose shores we were all admiring so much. Deep gullies cut the mountainous sides—beautifully wooded glens, through which charming rivulets could be seen tracing their course by the flashing and sparkling of the waters in the sunlight as they leaped over some miniature precipice. Between these wooded glens were patches of sugar cane, grain, and vegetables, the whole dotted here and there by a dwelling, embowered in a grove of orange trees.

I was on duty at the time, and perhaps I did not conduct myself exactly *a la militaire*, standing up in the after pivot port, and with my little glass taking a view of everything that we passed, in short, utterly unconscious that I was not on some pleasure trip, instead of being under the rigid discipline of a man-of-war. But no one said me "nay," and I can but think that the Captain kindly permitted it all, for several times I noticed him smilingly watching my enthusiastic observations. Let it be as it may, I enjoyed it all, and was not reproved, so *I* am satisfied. One of the principal benefits which I am to derive from my being in the Navy, is to see foreign countries, and to learn something of the manners, customs, and other points of interest about the people. So I shall gratify my curiosity, and benefit myself, whenever an opportunity offers itself, so that it can be done consistently.

Farther on, and leaving the high lands, we next sailed along the shores of a low, level section of the island, and which was in a high state of cultivation. Thus alternating, at one time having the country nearest us high and mountainous, then low and level, and our course constantly changing as we followed the shore line, we finally entered a large indentation of the coast on the southern side of the islands, and at noon dropped anchor, about half a mile from the pretty little town of Fort de France, situated at the innermost point.

The harbor here is large, and, although merely an indentation in the coast, it is said to be very secure, as the wind seldom blows from the direction of the open sea during a storm. There is but little shipping here, two or three merchant vessels, two English and three French men-of-war, with a few schooners and smaller craft comprising the whole.

The town stretches along a slightly sloping pebbly beach,

and as viewed from the ship, it is exceedingly neat and quite picturesque, with its small whitewashed, tile-roofed houses, and, scattered here and there, fine large mansions situated in beautiful gardens and fairly embowered in trees. To the left of the town is a bold, rocky eminence, on the summit of which stands a large stone fortress, from whose tall flag-staff floats the tri-color—Martinique belonging to the French. Behind the town the land rises abruptly so as to form quite a high mountain. About half way up its side, a small cottage is pointed out to me as the one in which Josephine was born.

I should like very much to go on shore this afternoon and sit awhile under the trees of the pretty little park, near the middle of the town, and which looks so charmingly cool and inviting from the ship. Although but little more than two weeks ago I was on shore, it actually seems as though it was more than as many months. Oh for a good ramble in the country! To fully realize this great deprivation, one must have a nature which leads him from the trammels of city life, must to the fullest extent be susceptible to the charms of country life—in the country finding what is most congenial to his nature. This is the better, the holier, the happier solitude to which the poet invites. It is to the wilds and groves of Nature.

> "God's first temples ere man learned
> To hew the shaft and lay the architrave
> And spread the roof above them,—ere he framed
> The lofty vaults, to gather and roll back
> The sound of anthems."

There indeed may the lonely ones

> "Go forth, under the open sky, and list
> To Nature's teachings, while from all around,
> Earth and her waters and the depths of air,
> Comes a still voice."

For those having such natures, it will take a long time, if it is ever done, to become fully reconciled to this close confinement of shipboard existence.

As soon as we were anchored, numerous small boats came hurrying off from the shore with washerwomen, and other persons desirous of our patronage and of supplying us with the many comforts which sea-worn people are apt to require. The most attractive articles to us were those oranges, pineapples, bananas, cocoanuts, and other fruits peculiar to a tropical clime. Those of us who were so fortunate as to have some of the *rhino*, rapidly invested it in that inviting stock. We *tasted* tropical fruits for once. Most of the crew have a good supply of "stamps," but those are almost worthless here. Many times have I seen a silver dollar refused to be given for a five dollar greenback.

As I sit here engaged in writing, the soul-stirring strains of the "Star Spangled Banner" are wafted to my ears through the open port, from the French "Liner's" band played out of compliment to us. The air has ever been a favorite one of mine, but doubly dear and impressive does it now seem to me, as I hear it in a foreign land, from foreign sources. Near me one is accompanying the air, with the words, and more deep, more heartfelt than ever before is the wish now uppermost in my mind that ever

"The Star Spangled Banner in triumph may wave,
O'er the land of the free, and the home of the brave."

LETTER IV.

U. S. S. WACHUSETT, St. Peirre, Martinique,
April 2, 1865.

MY DEAR R.:

My last letter to you, left us anchored at Fort de France, after an eleven days' passage from Boston. The two days succeeding our arrival were employed by the crew in cleaning up the ship and " putting on her harbor dress," so that she was in proper trim to receive the numerous visitors who came Sunday afternoon.

The French are the ruling race here. Beside them there are a few English merchants, and also a few Americans, but the great mass of the inhabitants are negroes. In every respect these are an exact counterpart of those in our own country. As you have doubtless become fully acquainted during the war with the characteristics of the negro, and the many phases of slavery, I will not weary you by a lengthy account of them as seen here.

Tuesday, March 21st, we hauled alongside the coal-wharf, and in the afternoon commenced " coaling ship." We began at two o'clock, and in less than four hours the bunkers were all filled, more than two hundred tons having been taken in. The celerity with which this coaling was performed, excelled that of any which I ever saw or heard of where manual labor alone was employed. To me it presented an exceedingly novel and interesting spectacle. The forward and after pivot ports were both let down, and planks thrown out from them to the wharf. The *workmen*, were almost exclusively *women*, and they carried the coal in little shallow baskets, (each holding about three pecks,) upon their heads. Once having commenced, they kept up a continuous stream— coming in through the for'ard port with the full baskets, and passing out through the after port with the empty baskets. One out of every twenty of the baskets was weighed, and record of the number carried in, was kept by an apparatus somewhat resembling the smaller size of Fairbank's platform scales, which made a mark every time the platform was stepped upon. I watched the human stream passing in and out, during the entire time that it was engaged in coaling, without tiring, and, although "coaling ship" is ever an unpleasant, dirty time, I could'nt help feeling a little regretful that it was so soon finished. The ship was "washed down," and we returned to our old anchorage that same night.

An altercation just now between the purser's steward and some berth-deck cooks, determines me to say a few words about government rations. One and a quarter pounds of fresh or salt beef, or three-fourths of a pound of pork, twenty-two ounces of soft bread or flour, or sixteen ounces of hard bread to each man; eight quarts of beans, or ten pounds of rice, eight pounds of roasted coffee or a pound and one-half of tea, and fifteen pounds of sugar to one hundred men is the daily allowance. In addition to this there is an allowance of six pounds of butter to one hundred men twice a week, and salt, vinegar, pickles, and molasses, almost as much as desired. The only articles the government furnishes us for breakfast and supper, are hard bread and coffee, or tea. Mondays, Wednesdays, and Saturdays, we have pork and beans for dinner. The pork that we have had thus far, if not "still-fed pork," bears a striking resemblance to it, and decidedly is not fit to be eaten. The beans are boiled with the pork, thus making a soup. Tuesdays and Fridays we have for dinner "salt horse and duff." The latter is a sailor's plum pudding with musty dried apples for the *plums*. Yet if it is well made, and one is hungry, the "duff" is quite palatable. To get some idea of the "salt horse," take a piece of *sole leather thoroughly impregnated with salt-petre*, and chew it. It may seem almost incredible to you, nevertheless it is true, that nearly all the salt beef we as yet have received, has been nearly as tough, tasteless. and devoid of nutriment as the piece of sole leather with which it has been compared. Thursdays, we have canned meat and dessicated potatoes. Very few like the beef, and I must confess that sometimes I have had serious doubts of its *being* beef. The potatoes bear a close resemblance to *sawdust*, before they are cooked, nor does the resemblance *cease* with the cooking, for then they have scarcely any more taste and nutriment than the sawdust would have. I have seen dessicated potatoes that *were* good, but I am convinced that those furnished us are but the refuse of starch factories. Sundays, we have canned beef and rice. The rice is boiled in water with a little salt thrown in, and eaten with molasses; we find it quite palatable, especially when *half-starved*, as we usually are on Sundays. The hard bread resembles soda biscuit in outward appearance, but there the resemblance ceases, for it is made simply of flour and water, and, as the name implies, is very hard Not only this, but the bread we have is very old, musty, and fairly alive with weevil. Of the coffee, tea, butter, and other articles, I will not attempt any description, and will only say. that not a single article do we have served out to us that I would not be ashamed to offer the meanest beggar at home.

I have not told you all this about our rations to weary you with unhappy complaints; but to deal justly by you, and to present you in my letters, not only with the scenes before my eyes, but also with the spirit which looked out upon them, and to show, I hope, for the good of those who come after me, how many *gratuitous annoyances* are added to those *necessarily* incident to a Naval life. The government pays enough for these articles of food to have those of the very best quality, and so I suppose it *thinks* that they are. The contractors are the ones that in the main are blamable for the unwholsome, unpalatable food that we receive—men of such *small despicable souls*, that for the sake of adding a little more to their wealth, do not hesitate to bring years of discomfort and suffering upon thousands of those very ones who are devoting their lives to protect them and their ill-gotten wealth. For such persons there could be devised no punishment *too severe*, or but what *they* would *richly* deserve. The government and especially the heads of the Navy Department are by no means entirely freed from blame, because they provide means enough to procure good, wholesome food; it is their *duty to see* that that food *is* procured. By so doing they would have more efficient, better contented seamen, and this, too, without any extra expense.

One day as I was on duty shortly after our arrival at Fort de France, Mr. Philip came aft and speaking to several "messenger boys" that were standing there, said, "Boys, I presume you all wish to go on shore. Now you may go just as soon as you are able to 'box the compass.'"

Of course I was longing to go on shore, too, so after a moment's hesitation, I went up to him and said, "Mr. Philip, will you rank me with the 'boys' in this promise?"

To this request he smilingly replied, "yes, Orderly, I will."

"Well then," I said, "I will do it now," and thereupon I began and going around both ways, "boxed the compass" to his satisfaction. So much for having studied Trigonometry before "going to sea."

When I had finished he said, "Well, you may go ashore as soon as your duty will suffer you."

One beautiful afternoon, a day or two after this occurrence, accompanied by two or three friends, I sat out for the shore upon my promised liberty.

A pull of about five minutes brought us to the little pier at the foot of the park near the middle of the town, and then, leaping from the boat, I, for the first time placed my foot on foreign soil. All the others in the party had been in many foreign countries, and were not a little amused at my enthusiasm. One remarked, "you will delight more to place your foot on the shore of your own country, after you have been absent two or three years, than you now are to place it on those of a foreign country." Doubtless this may be true, but even supposing that it may be so, I cannot on that account, see any reason why I should not take as much pleasure as possible in what I now have. The desire for this privilege has been strong with me from my earliest recollections, and now I have hopes of its being gratified.

Several negroes were lounging about the pier, and under the trees of the park, and *those* were the specimens of humanity to whom we were first introduced. As we landed, off went the hats of more than a dozen of them, and every mark of politeness and courtesy in their power was shown us as they came forward, either soliciting alms, or offering their services as guides, each one urging that one's respective merits or needs. To some of the most wretched looking we gave a few coppers, but soon were forced to desist from all such intended acts of humanity, as we found that *we* only *increased* the number of the needy and suffering. The importunities of the applicants for the position of "guide," were at length quieted by the selection of one of the most intelligent appearing of the number. The park we found shorn of many of its apparent beauties as viewed from the ship—being but a barren common, unfenced, and whose only attractions were a few locust trees, and a fine monument near its center, erected to the memory of Josephine.

Now for a look at the streets—queer streets you would call them, who have walked on brick side walks, with broad carriage ways intervening. They are for the most part mere alley-ways, and, except when there are shops or stores, alleys between drear walls, with here and there gateways and doors opening into the grounds and houses behind the walls. The pavement is composed of small stones, in many places set in regular figures, squares, diamonds, etc., and sometimes lined off by white stones. It looks very prettily, and the streets are very neat and clean, for, being inclined planes, they are thoroughly washed by every rain, and besides, through most of them a stream of water is constantly flowing.

The houses are for the most part very small, kept scrupulously neat and clean, and in general whitewashed on the outside. But besides these, there are many fine looking mansions, situated in fine, deep yards, filled with flower-beds, and groves of trees peculiar to a tropical clime. The better class of stores are tended by fair French dames, but those are few in number, being by far outnumbered by the small, insignificant shops, kept by some aged or decrepit negress. At almost every turn of the street we encountered venders of cakes, fruits, etc., either having their wares exposed for sale on tables and stands by the sides of the streets, or carried in baskets on their heads. At the back of the town is a fine, large, granite reservoir, from which the town is supplied with water. A visit to the cottage in which Josephine was born completed the list of "sights" to be seen at Fort de France. Everything there we found to be plain and unassuming, with no special attraction excepting the fine portrait of Josephine, taken in her youth, and which hung against the wall in one of the rooms.

Whilst lying at Fort de France, the " Guard " had their first introduction to "quarter-deck guard." Would you know who or what that might be? It is simply to stand on the quarter-deck from morning until night, dressed in full uniform, cross-belted, and with muskets at hand ready to be paraded at a moment's notice, for any person of distinction that may choose to come on board. I know that it presents a fine, showy appearance, this parading in our gay, showy uniform coats and hats, white pants and belts, and with everything bright and shining; but if those who delight in such performances could be obliged to stand for a few hours, thus coated and belted, in the hot sun, I am sure that they would be less zealous for such empty displays. An animated running commentary was kept up during the day.

"I wonder what we are kept up here for, like so many fancifully dressed monkeys," says one.

"To show what they can do, and that the Americans can be as foolish and silly as either the French or English," answer three or four.

"Well, I wish that whoever is the cause of our being here, had to stand with us in this hot, broiling sun," says the first speaker.

"If I had only thought that we would be obliged to use this monkey rig, I would certainly have thrown mine overboard before we came in here," says another.

"I wish that it was time to go on post," says a third, and all echo the wish. Yes, we all used to feel relieved when the time came for us to go on guard, for then we might get some shelter from the melting rays of the sun.

Now don't think that in speaking of all this I am finding fault with our officers, for I am not. Why! did they desire it ever so much, they are powerless to demolish such great mountains of ancestral humbuggery as these, so strongly are all nations bound by, and so completely under the sway of, "ola custom." During our stay at Fort de France, a French frigate and an English line-of-battle ship came into port, and for three or four days we were kept on the quarter-deck all of the time in readiness to honor their officers whenever they might choose to come on board. During the day I would wish that these vessels had not come in, but when evening came and we, after being dismissed, had had our supper, and had gone up upon the forecastle for our evening chat and smoke, then these ships' bands would cheer and enliven us with some good old home air, or those of their own country; and, in the enjoyment of the present, we would forget the annoyances of the past. O, Music! what better tribute can I give thee than that thou ever callest to mind the sweetest pleasures of life, and ever awaken'st in my heart purer and nobler thoughts?

Wednesday, March 29th, we intended coming up here, and with this intention, at 4 P. M. we got up steam, weighed anchor, and started in *high* style. But in striving to excel ourselves, our *grand sweep* brought us out of the deep water of the harbor, and soon we found ourselves hard aground on a ledge of rocks close under the fort. Boats from the French and English vessels were immediately dispatched to our assistance; hawsers were passed from us to these vessels, but all our united efforts were ineffectual to haul us off. After an hour or more spent thus, Captain Townsend, turning to Mr. Philip, said in his calm, quiet way, "It is evident that we are aground and unable to get off at present. I think that you had better give the men their hammocks and we will see what can be done in the morning." Fortunately it was low tide when we ran aground, and in the morning at high tide we were easily hauled off. The next day a couple of divers from the French frigate came and thoroughly examined the bottom of our vessel, rejoicing us by the report that no damage had been done with the exception of tearing off a part of a sheet of copper. This they repaired the following day.

With everything as good as it was before we ran aground, yesterday we got under way and the second time started for St. Pierre. Without any accident we arrived here, a distance of twelve miles, in less than an hour.

The harbor of St. Pierre is an open roadstead, affording no protection against the storms which are frequent in these latitudes, and consequently it has scarcely any shipping. Fort de France is the seaport of the island, but St. Pierre is by far the largest town, and is the capital. It is very prettily situated on both sides of a small ridge which extends back from the sea. A large portion of the houses are elegant mansions, situated in beautiful and extensive grounds—the abodes of the foreign residents, the Consuls, and the wealthy. The streets are narrow, but the same order and neatness prevail here as at Fort de France. I was on shore yesterday evening, but saw nothing worthy of special note more than what I have already mentioned.

Some time during the night the U. S. S. Connecticut came into port, and is now lying near us. Dame Rumor told us to-day that one or more piratical vessels were cruising about these islands, and that the Wachusett with the Connecticut were to cruise about for them. Another story that the Dame told us is in the opinion of all more probable. We have a roving commission for one year, to cruise after piratical vessels, more especially in the East India waters, and at the expiration of the year, are to report at Macao, China.

Yesterday terminated our first month on board the Wachusett, and all seem to acknowledge that it has been fraught with more pleasure and interest than was anticipated. It truly has been a good commencement to the cruise, and if it prove typical of the whole, I, for one, shall be satisfied.

LETTER V.

U. S. S. WACHUSETT, Porto Grande, Cape Verdes,
April 29, 1865.

MY DEAR R.:

On the 4th of April we sailed from St. Pierre, bound for some point on the coast of Africa. The first few days out were very unpleasant—the wind blowing strongly from the northwest, the sea running very high, and all accompanied by frequent showers of rain. The sixth day out, it cleared off, and during the remainder of the passage we had delightful weather and everything as pleasant and favorable as we could reasonably expect or even desire. We were under sail alone during the greater portion of the passage, and had such good breezes that we logged on an average more than six knots per hour, and arrived here this morning, having made the passage in twenty-five days.

The first incident of interest during the passage was "general-quarters." At these we were exercised the same as if we were in action—calling away boarders, repelling boarders, fishing and securing masts that had been shot away, securing rigging, putting out fires, working the battery, and acting out everything that might be necessary to be done in an actual engagement. Considering that this was the first time that the most of the crew had witnessed anything of the kind, they did very well. The Captain and Mr. Philip both warmly commended us for our creditable performance.

The second noticeable incident of the passage was presented in our scrubbing hammocks for the first time. As yet I have had no duty assigned me since on board the Wachusett which I dislike more heartily than I do this scrubbing hammocks. Shall I give you some insight into the performance? Well, unsling your dirty hammock, (that is, take out the bedding and remove the clews,) and with the rest of the crew spread it down upon the deck. A good stiff brush, a bucket of water, and a piece of soap, are essential requisites. Rolling up one's sleeves and pants, (of course you are barefoot,) are not only indications that one is in earnest in one's work, but also that there is a desire of keeping the clothes clean, which otherwise cannot be done. But we had everything prepared to commence operations. After wetting the hammock, soap it over thoroughly, and then, down on your hands and knees, take the brush and scrub away with all your might and main for half-an-hour or more. I can promise that you will find it about as tiresome a task as you have ever undertaken. I scrubbed upon my hammock for more than an hour, and *then* stopped, not because I had got it as clean as desired, but that I was completely exhausted.— When I was ready to hang it up, the only vacant space was close by the newly tarred stays, so that when it was taken down it was *nearly* as clean as when I commenced to scrub. Several were in the same condition, and when hammocks were presented for inspection, the order was, " Scrub them over." In washing clothes nearly the same process is gone through with as in the scrubbing of the hammocks, and like them the clothes are hung up on lines extending from one mast to another, or between different parts of the "standing rigging." There are four ." wash-mornings" in a week at sea, and two in port, when the washing must be done.

As we are now fairly settled down into the regular routine of "man-of-war life," I will give you the divisional routine for exercising. Mondays, general quarters. Tuesdays, 1st Division exercise with the battery, 2d Division and marines with small arms, and 3d Division with single-sticks. Wednesdays, 2d Division and marines exercise with the battery, 3d Division with small arms, and 1st Division with single-

3*

sticks. Thursdays, 3d Division exercises with the battery, 1st Division and marines with small arms, and 2d Division with single-sticks. Fridays, battalion drill with small arms and fire-quarters, or, if it is in port, man and arm all boats. Saturdays, cleaning, and Sundays, inspection and rest. Occasionally the Powder Division and the Engineer's Division exercise with the battery or small arms.

Now, perhaps our "daily routine" would interest you. At daylight in port, or at seven o'clock at sea, "all hands" are called. Only five minutes are allowed for dressing, lashing hammocks, and stowing them in the "nettings." If more time is taken, scraping shot or some similar punishment is inflicted. The first business of the morning is to "wash the decks down" and clean up generally. Go to breakfast at 8 A. M. After breakfast clean the bright-work and go to quarters at 9 A. M., when the battery, men, and arms are inspected. After quarters the divisions have their exercises for the day, and which occupy the greater portion of the forenoon. Go to dinner at noon; "turn to" at 1 P. M., and do whatever work may be required. Go to supper at 4 P. M., with the usual "meal hour" for eating and smoking. The hammocks are "piped down" soon after sunset, and then the crew are permitted to smoke and do whatever they may choose until 9 P. M., when those not on duty are supposed to be in their hammocks and to keep quiet. This is the routine when lying at anchor, but when at sea there are some variations. A portion of the crew are on deck all of the time, and they perform the whole of the work. Instead of nine o'clock they "pipe down" at eight.

All this that I have spoken about—scrubbing hammocks, and daily routine, refers exclusively to the enlisted men. The several divisions of the officers have each a large room in common, and each officer has either a bunk or a stateroom, small to be sure, but thus dispensing with all need for hammocks as well as the vexations attendant upon the possession of them. At quarters one or more officers are attached to a division, who superintend the working and taking care of the battery, etc., themselves under the general superintendence of the executive officer, who is in turn under the commands of the Captain. At all times there is an officer on watch, called the officer of the deck, who, during the time he has the deck has full charge of everything about the ship, subject only to the orders of the Captain or executive officer.

Last Thursday was devoted to a thorough cleansing of the ship. This was imperatively called for, as the lice and other vermin usually attendant upon the early part of a ship's " commission," instead of lessening in numbers seemed to be alarmingly on the increase. Every one's clothes were inspected, and those that were found to be infested with the hostile vermin, the clothes were thrown overboard and the possessors "scrubbed." Next, all the hammocks and blankets were washed and rinsed in hot water and, lastly, the ship was washed down fore and aft with boiling hot water. Thus the vermin received a "foretaste of that which is to come." We have not been troubled with any signs of them since "the cleaning," nor do I think that we will be troubled again this cruise.

During the passage we both met and passed many vessels, several of which we " spoke." 'Tis very pleasant thus to meet and converse with those similarly situated—far out in the midst of the ocean, to learn one another's ports of departure and destination, to exchange greetings, to learn the most interesting incidents of each one's passage, and send messages to those we have left behind. Yes, 'tis very pleasant, and a pleasure known only to those " who go down to the sea in ships and do business in the great waters."

It has been well expressed by a familiar writer, that " in a common voyage, if one be asked what he has met, he may answer, ' Waves! waves! waves!'" since all else that might attract or be noted—the many nameless associations upon the ocean—these must be seen and felt to be known:

> "For who can tell, save he whose heart has tried
> And danc'd in triumph o'er the waters wild,
> The exulting sense—the pulses mad'ning play,
> That thrills the wand'rer o'er the trackless way?"

When I went on deck at four o'clock this morning, to take my watch, I ascertained that we had been "lying to" since midnight, on account of our proximity to the land. At daylight we started ahead again, and a few minutes later we heard the welcome words "Land ho," sung out from the mast head. Soon we were able to see the land from the deck, looking like a thick cloud just rising above the horizon. Now get down the map, my dear R., and unless you have the whole world dotted and spotted geographically in your eye, look out the little islands of St. Antonio and St. Vincent in the Cape Verde group, on the coast of Africa just a little north of the line. The first mentioned of these islands was the earliest sighted by us, but we did not approach near enough to examine it very closely—only saw that it was very high, mountainous, and sterile. There is a volcano on the eastern side which had an eruption about six months ago, and another is daily expected.

About noon we rounded the southeastern point of St. Antonio, and then sighted St. Vincent, some twenty miles distant—our destination. This island presented the same physical characteristics of surface and soil as those given of St. Antonio. We passed between these two islands, and after numerous alterations of our course, at length we entered the mouth of Porto Grande harbor, and finally dropped anchor about half a mile from the shore. The harbor here is a large indentation of the coast, nearly semi-circular in form and affording a secure anchorage. The mouth of the harbor is between four and five miles wide, nearly three-fourths of which is occupied by a high, narrow island, which protects it from the northwest winds. About midway from shore to shore, just inside of this island, is a large conical shaped rock, about one hundred feet high, and called "Bird rock," from the number of birds which used to resort there yearly to deposit their eggs and rear their young. I think that "Target rock" would be an equally appropriate name, as it has been used as a target for centuries by the men-of-war visiting the harbor, and many hundred tons of metal have been hurled against it. A closer view of the land only confirmed the first impressions of its physical characteristics—that it is high, bold, and mountainous. Upon the starboard side in entering the harbor is a succession of peaks, whose outline bears a striking resemblance to the profile of Washington, and is designated as "Washington's Head" on this account. Possibly I might not have noticed the resemblance had it not been suggested to me; but then, it did not require a great stretch of the imagination to mark the resemblance. Experimentally I asked a man standing near me, if the outlines of these peaks resembled the profile of any one that he could think of, and was almost immediately answered "yes, Washington's." I am sure that the man had never heard of the resemblance being noticed before. Certainly I never saw a country so barren and desolate as that of St. Vincent. Not the least sign of vegetation can be seen, not even the green moss so commonly seen upon rocks. The whole vista is naught but one barren, rocky, brown waste.

The town of Porto Grande lies on a sandy strip, which circles around the inner point of the bight or indentation which forms the harbor. It is a small, insignificant looking town, and with one or two exceptions the houses are all small wooden huts. About midway up the mountain, behind the town, is a small, dilapidated, brick fort, mounting two or three guns, and over which floats the Portuguese ensign, St. Vincent belonging to the Portuguese. The fort is worthless as a defense for the harbor or town, but I think that it answers every purpose; in fact, I cannot conceive why they should need any defense to retain this barren island.

There are a few European residents at Porto Grande, representations of almost every nationality. By far the greater portion of the inhabitants however are African negroes, all bearing the usual stamp of ignorance, sensuality, and the more low and debasing vices by which man is liable to be enslaved. All of the water consumed by the inhabitants has to be brought here from a distance of about fifteen miles, and sometimes much suffering is occasioned by its scarcity, when stormy weather prevents their procuring a supply.

There is but little shipping in the harbor at present—some five or six small merchantmen, two Portuguese war schooners, with a few schooners and small craft comprising the whole. I was pleased to see the glorious stars and stripes floating from the peak of one of the larger vessels—a sight seen by us for the first time since leaving the States, excepting on the Connecticut and our own vessel. It hardly seems possible that two or three rebel privateers could have damaged our commerce as they have done. Although a fact to be lamented, yet it is a true one that there are few merchantmen *bold* enough to fly the stars and stripes away from the immediate protection of our navy; so that now there is hardly one to be seen where before the war there was a score. I hope the day is not far distant when the glorious emblem of liberty can be borne with safety and with *pride* to the most remote corners of the earth. I have never doubted that that day will some time come, and only hope that *soon* again we shall see our country occupying a higher and prouder position than it ever occupied before.

LETTER VI.

U. S. S. WACHUSETT, Porto Praya, Cape Verde, }
May 26, 1865.

MY DEAR R.:

May, thus far, has been an interesting and eventful month to us; prominent among whose items of interest are the news of the capture of Richmond and the surrender of Lee's army —thus virtually ending the war—and the cowardly assassination of President Lincoln. We received the news by a French mail steamer, May 6th, which brought us English papers containing the full particulars. After inspection the following day the Captain called us aft and read to us the "news from home." Over the first portion of the news one and all were much rejoiced, and I do not think that there was one but that was saddened by the latter. How much there is, in those few words that were repeated so many times that day, "The war is over and President Lincoln is dead!" Yes, the war is over and the "unholy, wicked rebellion" is now a thing of the past. Such *good news* yet seems almost incredible, almost too good to be true. But our source of information was so reliable that there does not remain the least doubt of the truthfulness of the report. I *wish* that I might hear that the report of President Lincoln's death was a *canard*, but the news of that as well as the other comes to us *too well authenticated* to admit of doubt. The particulars of the assassination that we received, as well as those of the plot to assassinate the most prominent men throughout the country, were very fully given to us, but as you are doubtless better informed of them than I am, I will not repeat them here. We all hope that all future plans and attempts of this description may be frustrated.

There were traits in President Lincoln's character, and points in his administration, which many would have changed, if possible, but methinks that all good, loyal persons will uphold me in this—that he always had the welfare of the country at heart in his every action, to the best of his ability doing what he thought was right and proper; and, by his wisdom and firmness of command he has brought this great and terrible civil war to a successful termination, as well, and better perhaps, than any other one in the country could have done. We could all have desired that he might have lived to see the country in the garb of peace again, thriving and prosperous as she was before the war. Still, after all, perhaps it is for the best that he should have been removed by death, for now henceforth he will be remembered with honor and respect, if not as a martyr.

The day following that upon which we heard of his death, the flag was kept at half-mast, and half-hour guns fired all day, out of respect to the memory of President Lincoln. At muster that day, an order from the Captain, in conformity with the order from President Johnson, was read, that every officer should wear crape on his left arm for a period of six months.

While lying at Porto Grande we had our first target-practice with the battery. We fired six rounds at that ancient and common target, "Bird Rock," from which we were distant about two miles. The first three rounds fired were with percussion shell, about half of which struck the rock, exploding the instant they struck it. For the last two rounds, solid shot were used, about two-thirds of which hit the rock. For the first time, the Captain said that the firing was uncommonly good, and warmly commended the captains of the guns. But the greater portion of these had filled that position before, so that in reality it was not their first practice. Still they will be able to do much better when they become accustomed to the guns.

I went ashore but once while we were at Porto Grande— there being nothing in the place to tempt me to make a second visit. The town consists of about forty small, mean-looking, wooden buildings, the greater portion of which are situated on one street, which runs parallel with the beach and close to it. We did not derive much pleasure from our ramble about the town, for we not only saw nothing worthy of note, but at every step we would sink ancle-deep in the sand. Consequently we did not devote much time to this ramble, but spent the day in walking along the beach searching for shells, and in playing billiards in the small, low-roofed building near the landing.

It may seem but a trifling incident to you, but to us, the getting of six barrels of sugar was one of the most interesting incidents of our stay at Porto Grande. For more than two weeks previous we had had none in the ship, and had been obliged to use molasses for our coffee. Coffee and tobacco are necessaries of a sailor's life. Give him those as he wants, and almost anything will be borne; but you if interfere with these necessaries, either by lessening the amount or by a deterioration of the article, you are injuring him more than in any other way could be done. To the uninitiated it is almost like taking so much nauseous medicine, to drink a cup of coffee as it is usually made in the service; but, by degrees they become accustomed to it, and at last, think of it as one of their greatest luxuries.

We made preparations early in the morning of Tuesday, May 9th, for leaving Porto Grande, but it was late in the evening before we were under way. The night was clear, the moon at its full, the wind favorable and strong, the sea smooth, and the passage of that night was certainly the most pleasant we had thus far had. Our course lay much of the time in a channel between numerous small islands, and in many places this channel was quite narrow and circuitous. With a navigator less skillful than our sailing-master, Mr.

Grove, and on a less clear and pleasant night, with the attending favorable circumstances, it would have been hardly wise to attempt to go through there in the night-time. About 9 A. M. the next day, we sighted the extreme northern point of St. Jago, our destination, and distant from Porto Grande about one hundred and fifty miles. Two hours later we came very near the northern coast of the island, along which and the eastern side we sailed some thirty or forty miles. The land was hilly and broken, but not rocky, and looked as if the soil were quite fertile. Just now everything is sere and dry, owing to the long-continued drought. It was a few minutes before sunset when we entered the harbor of Porto Praya and dropped anchor about a mile from the town—near the old anchorage of the Constitution. It was here that she was lying during the war of 1812-15 when the English sloops-of-war Cyane and Levant appeared off the mouth of the harbor. As she started to go out in pursuit of them the fort which defends the town fired upon her. She for the time paid no attention to the firing of the fort, but went out and captured both of the English sloops, and then returning, she demolished the fortifications.

The harbor here is an open roadstead, facing the east, and when the wind blows from that direction, it is said to afford a very poor anchorage. The shipping here is less even than at Porto Grande.

The town is situated on a bluff about one hundred feet high, near the innermost point of the harbor. It contains some fine buildings, but on the whole presents an ancient, decaying appearance. To the right and front of the town is the fort, built of stone and brick, and mounting some fifteen or twenty guns. Near the northern outskirts of the town is a wide, deep ravine, filled with orange, banana, and cocoanut trees, which are now covered with their ripe fruit. The inhabitants here, like those at Porto Grande, are for the most part negroes, with comparatively few Europeans. The latter are principally Portuguese. St. Jago, with the rest of the Cape Verde group, belongs to Portugal, and Porto Praya is the capital of the group.

Have you any idea that it is a very difficult thing for us to get money? By the rules of the Navy we are not supposed to receive any of our wages until the end of the cruise. However, the advancing of money is left to the discretion of the commanding officer to a certain extent; but he is restricted to "special and necessary wants." This rule applies only to those "for'ard of the mast," the officers drawing their full pay every month. If one of the crew asks for money it almost always results like the following application of an aged seaman, which I heard this forenoon: going up to where the Captain was standing, and doffing his cap, he said:

"Captain, will you be so kind as to give an order to the Paymaster to let me have a little of my wages?"

The Captain replied, "Well, B., how much do you want?"

"Five dollars, sir."

"What do you wish to do with it?"

"Well, sir, I am getting to be so old that I can't eat the government rations as well as I could thirty years ago, when I entered the Navy, and I would like a little money with which to get me some 'extras.'"

"Of course nothing but specie will be of any use to you. Now every dollar in specie costs the government more than two dollars in currency, and what is given you can only be charged dollar for dollar. The government is deeply in debt, and every means of economizing must be employed. I am really sorry in your case, but I can't let you have any."

Notwithstanding all this reasoning there are over thirty officers in the ship drawing on an average more than one hundred dollars each, in specie, every month, and which is so invested by the greater portion of them, as to more than double their pay. It does seem strange that the government should thus pet and pamper a few, who have nearly everything that could be desired, and who undergo comparatively few hardships or fatigues, while at the same time the small sum of five or six dollars of their hard-earned wages is denied to those who make up the "bone and sinew" of the Navy. I do not speak thus from any personal grievances, for thus far I have had all my requests for money granted me. But where there is one thus fortunate, there are twenty that are not so.

Since we have been lying here we have had "fresh provisions" for the first time since leaving Boston. The cook of each mess receives a piece of meat—varying in size according to the number of men in his mess—which he tallies and puts in the "coppers." Some rice, potatoes, cabbage, and other vegetables, are then *sparingly* added, and the whole boiled together. At dinner time each cook draws his own piece of meat, and also a certain portion of the soup. The meat, from being boiled so long and in a large quantity of water, becomes nearly tasteless, but the soup is excellent. The Purser's steward tells me that fresh provisions are far less expensive to the government than salt ones are. They certainly give better satisfaction to the crew, and I don't see any reason why we should not receive them altogether whenever we are in port. But I suppose that it is in this as in almost everything else connected with the service, however much it may be better for the government and for the men, if those to whom such matters are left are put to any trouble or inconvenience by any act, that act is seldom performed.

The day that I was intending to go on shore for a visit to the old town of Porto Praya—which is situated about five miles back from the sea, the American Consul sent off word to the Captain, protesting against any more liberty to the men being given him. His reason for so doing was because some of our crew, while under the influence of liquor, had made some disturbance among the citizens. This is too often the case—some poor worthless character taking away the good name and the privileges of a large number by his misdeeds.

Some time in the early part of May we had news that England had declared war against the United States. This statement came so well authenticated that we had scarcely a doubt of its truth. Knowing this you will not be surprised to learn that when an English war-vessel appeared off the mouth of the harbor about a week ago, the greatest excitement prevailed among us; boats were hoisted up and secured, steam got up, the battery loaded, and every preparation made for action at a moment's notice. But with no apparent hostile intent the vessel came in and quietly dropped anchor near us. A boat was sent to her, which brought the report that it was the English corvette Zephyr from Cape Town, South Africa, and "homeward bound." Her latest advices from home made no mention of there being any hostility between England and the United States, nor of the prospect of there being any war. We have since had many a good laugh with their crew over *our* "false alarm."

Ever since we have been lying here we have had a great number of visitors from shore, of almost every age and nationality, and of both sexes. With one of the fair visitants, a young lady of about eighteen, a large number of our officers and crew have become quite deeply *smitten*, and in one case, a more serious affair than love is rumored. "Breach of promise" and "twenty paces" are the common reports, but however true the former may be, I have my doubts of the latter, on account of the *timidity* of one of the parties. I must confess that she is certainly one of the most lovable of the female persuasion that I ever saw—almost perfect in form and feature. She has a more speaking eye, and a more sweet, winning expression than the generality of womankind possess. Now you must not think that I am smitten at last by female charms because I am thus enthusiastic in my account of this particular fair one. I trust that I can see and appreciate true beauty and loveliness without getting *spoony* (to use a very expressive word) over the possessor. I was not a little amused a few evenings ago at the remarks of a conceited *younger* officer who had had the privilege of being her escort and guide in showing her the items of interest about the ship that afternoon. He said, "I was more than half seriously revolving in my mind the *pros* and *cons* for remaining here and winning her heart and hand. But when I came to sum them all up, I found that the *cons* by far outnumbered the *pros*, so I have concluded that not yet would I 'give up the ship.'"

In relating a personal experience, I express that of several shipmates. On board ship there are many leisure moments, and these we have largely devoted to study. We find that the benefits resulting therefrom are two-fold. On the one hand we are increasing our store of useful knowledge, and on the other we are weaving about us one of the most effectual defenses against the many temptations and moral dangers of man-of-war life. We are so constituted that in order to keep our minds in some degree of moral purity we must be surrounded by correspondingly pure influences—certainly by enough to balance the bad and impure. Woman, whenever she is worthy to be called by that name, has an influence to ennoble and purify the mind and thoughts. The truth of the assertion may be seen by comparing those that have been under this influence with those that have been deprived of it, even if they have been surrounded by other minds noble and good. Probably in no place in the world is this influence more completely lost or needed more than on a man-of-war. As I said in the first place, the employment and diversion which study gives, may do much to counterbalance the bad influences.

Last Friday, May 19th, we made every preparation for getting under way, intending to take our departure from Porto Praya that day. But when we came to heave up the port anchor, the cable came in with no anchor attached to it, the cable having parted and left the anchor at the bottom. "So much for intending to sail on Friday," the superstitious "old salts" said. All preparations and intentions of departure were indefinitely postponed, the cutters called away, and searching for the lost anchor commenced. After two days spent in dragging, two divers from shore were employed; but, after one day's fruitless labor, they became discouraged, and would come no more. Two of our own crew next attempted to find the anchor by diving, but they gave out before the first day was over. Yesterday we tried steaming about the harbor with the starboard cable "hove short," so that the anchor would just touch the bottom, hoping that it would catch hold of the missing one. But like the others this plan proved unsuccessful, and the missing anchor is missing still. This evening the Captain said that it was useless to continue the search longer, and that we would leave here to-morrow. We all hope that he may not alter his determination, for we are heartily tired of Porto Praya.

LETTER VII.

U. S. S. WACHUSETT, St. Catherine, }
June 28, 1865.

MY DEAR R.:

Dame Rumor was truthful, for the next day saw us take our departure from Porto Praya. We found the sea to be very rough, and many of us were *just a little* sea sick. But I remember one that was not sick in the least—the steerage cook, a big, burly negro, " black as the ace of spades," and who rejoices in the *sobriquet* of " Jib Bogue." His *loud* singing, and side-splitting " haw, haw" could be heard as usual while cooking the dinner, doing much to enliven the spirits of all. He is decidedly the happiest man in the ship.

Friday, June 2d, 1865, will long be remembered by many of us, for.that was the day on which we were presented to Neptune the Monarch of the ˙Deep. For this ceremony, preparations had been made before leaving Boston, but so quietly had all been conducted, that every one except those in the secret were taken by surprise. This ceremony is not so common as it was formerly, but, whenever the assent of the commanding officer can be obtained, the " old salts " seldom miss the opportunity of enjoying the sports of the occasion. The Captain, with characteristic desire of affording pleasure and amusement at all proper times, assented to the request of the leaders, but imposing reasonable restrictions upon what should be done.

At 4 P. M., all were startled by the hail off our starboard bow, " Ship Ahoy !"

The officer of the deck (who was in the secret) answered, "Aye, aye, sir."

"What ship is that?"
"The United States Steamer Wachusett."
"Where are you from, and where are you bound."
"From the United States, bound to China."
"I am Neptune, the Monarch of the Deep; bring the ship to so that I can come on board."

The orders of his Majesty were obeyed, and he came on board—through the hawse-pipe, I suppose; for after a few minutes' delay, the curtain (which had been hung up at the break of the forecastle ever since noon) was removed, and there issued forth from the forecastle his Majesty, Neptune He was seated on his chariot of state (the howitzer carriage fitted up for the occasion) with that ancient matron, Mrs. Neptune, by his side, drawn by ten men, preceded by a band of music, and accompanied by all his attending train. On either hand were his two barbers, the one bearing a huge tin razor full of notches and rust, and the other a huge swab. Around him were about thirty faithful retainers armed with swords. They marched down the port gangway—the band playing "Lo! the conquering hero comes"—as far as the wardroom hatch, then crossed over to the other side of the deck, and came to a halt by the starboard gangway. Formal permission having been granted to his Majesty by the Captain to have all the novices among the crew presented to him, preparations were made for the ceremony. A studding-sail was got up, its corners raised and the sail kept filled with water by the steam pumps. Then, a platform was erected between this and the throne.

Everything being in readiness, His Majesty sent his retainers to bring to him all the novices (that is those that had never crossed the Line) and then the ceremony began. The novice was seated on the platform, blindfolded, and then well *lathered* over with the swab, which had been dipped in a preparation of tar and grease. The knight of the razor then performed his duty, utterly regardless of the cries and groans of his victims; and, whenever they would open their mouths to complain, they were treated to a cup of salt water. This part of the ceremony finished, the victim is requested to rise a moment, the seat removed, and then when told to sit down again, barkward he tumbles into the vat of water and the hose is turned upon him. Sore, half sick, half blinded, and half drowned, after numerous fruitless attempts he at length emerges from the vat, escapes from his tormentors, and can console himself by looking upon the other victims undergoing the same treatment. The "shaving" continued for upwards of two hours, until all were initiated excepting the marines who resisted, and the officers who paid the forfeit with wine. Thanks were then given by his Majesty to the Captain, for his courtesy and kindness; and after wishing the Wachusett a pleasant cruise and the safe return of all to their homes and friends, he departed as he came. The whole affair passed off pleasantly and was much enjoyed by all. The grotesque costumes, the cries, groans, and *appearance* of the victims occasioned many a side-splitting peal of laughter, and "Neptune's visit" will long be remembered by all.

Up to this time our course had been southwesterly, the wind westerly, and with all sail set we had been sailing along at the average rate of five or six knots per hour. But that day the wind left us and for three days we lay on the equator, becalmed, under the hot, scorching rays of the sun. Hardly anything in a sailor's life is more unpleasant than to be becalmed, the sails flapping idly against the masts, and the vessel not moving a single knot during an entire day. One and all seemed disposed to echo the boatswain's prayer "Blow, Good Devil, blow, and take the lower studding-sail."

June 5th we got up steam, and with awnings spread, we were more comfortable and in better spirits. In the evening a strong breeze sprung up, so that we stopped steaming and proceeded under full sail again. For a week our course was variable, sailing "by the wind," which took us well to the westward. Our destination when we left Porto Praya was said to be Cape Town. Everything, however, seemed to indicate that Rio Janeiro was to be our next port; and thither we would have thought that we were destined, had we not had positive orders from the government, that under no consideration whatever, should we call at any Brazilian port. This order was given on account of the existing hostile feeling of the Brazilian government towards the Wachusett, which vessel seized the rebel steamer Florida in the harbor of Bahia about a year ago.

Going "by the wind" in the variable, or "horse latitudes," is far from being pleasant. Occasionally we would steam for a few hours, then proceed under sail alone, or for days lie becalmed. At last we received a steady breeze, and although it was not as favorable as could have been desired, obliging us to "tack ship" frequently, we all hailed it as a godsend, so much did its coolness refresh and enliven us.

Soon after crossing the Line there were a great many rumors afloat regarding the amount of provisions in the ship—some asserting that there was barely a sufficiency to last a week. Soon all were startled by another rumor to the effect that we were to be placed on half-rations; this caused the most intense excitement. First the sugar gave out and we were obliged to substitute molasses again for our coffee and tea. A day or two later, and we not only had no sugar for our tea, but had no tea for the sugar. Tuesday, June 13th, the climax was reached when the Captain gave orders that the crew should be placed on "half rations." The greatest excitement then prevailed, and, after numerous consultations, the crew deputed the petty officers to represent them at the "mast" and endeavor to get the order countermanded. An increase from one-half to two-thirds rations produced a momentary lull. It was, however, only momentary, and at noon nearly every man in the ship, taking his diminished ration in his pan, went to the "mast" and asked to see the Captain. He came, and, after listening to their complaints, he acceded to their request for full rations, but to their request that the ship might be put into some port nearest us, and a fresh supply of provisions obtained, he said that he had received positive orders to call at no Brazilian port, and there was no other nearer than Cape Town. So we had full rations again, but *full* only in name, not having any sugar, but little molasses, and half rations of bread, pork, and beans. The officers' messes were but little better provided for than those of the men; and, for a barrel of flour which our mess had, they offered more than five times its original cost. When one is hungry, money is no equivalent for food, so the flour was not sold. The details of the sufferings from hunger during the time that we were on half rations would be but a repetition of what too many have endured during the war, and with which you are doubtless well acquainted. June 16th we boarded several vessels, hoping to be able to procure supplies from them. We were unsuccessful in every case, their cargoes being railroad iron.

Monday, June 19th, "Land Ho!" shouted out from the mast head thrilled all with the deepest delight, for we thought that the Captain had finally decided to enter some Brazilian port. But this pleasure was short lived, for about noon we came to anchor a little to the eastward of the entrance to the harbor of Rio Janeiro. Our anchorage was a little westward of a lofty, naked cone, called "False Sugar Loaf," in contradistinction to one very similar, about eight miles to the westward of it, which marks the entrance to the harbor of Rio. We lay within two or three miles of the shore, surrounded by scenery of great splendor and beauty. At least, so it seemed to us; but, perhaps our discoveries of beauties were owing in a measure to the long time that it had been since we had seen the land. Nothing, I find, so much enhances the beauty and worth of anything, or calls forth such pleasure from its sight or possession, as the deprivation of it for a time when ardently longed for. But to return to the scenery near our anchorage. Before us, at the distance of a few miles, was the wild range of mountains immediately south of the channel into Rio, the most striking feature of which is known to sailors by the name of " Hood's Nose," from a supposed strong resemblance to that appendage of his lordship's face. " Indeed," it has been remarked, " the whole range presents the outline of a colossal figure in as near conformation to the human shape, as the effigies on many tombs of the fifteenth and sixteenth centuries—lying on its back, with its head towards the sea."

On our right, and very near, was a beautiful beach of snowy whiteness, stretching in a long curve to the east, beyond the beach stretched a narrow interval of low land, covered with grass, backed by abrupt hills and mountains, of various and beautiful outline; the center of the sweep rising much above the rest, and forming a kind of crown to all around; the whole beautifully wooded and still in the luxuriance of nature.

Grand was the view in front, with a sail or two in the foreground; on our right stretched the white beach, green hills, and mountains before described; while behind, and on our left, in the east, rolled the ocean; all forming such a scene as will for a long time remain stamped upon my memory with the most pleasing remembrances.

But our object in stopping off the mouth of the harbor, was not to admire the beautiful scenery; it was to endeavor to procure provisions, from vessels bound either in or out of Rio, or to send in word and have the provisions brought out to us. We boarded three vessels, but without procuring what we wished—all of them being loaded with coal. From one of these vessels, the caterer of the ward-room mess bought a barrel of flour, or what he supposed to be flour, for which he gave thirty dollars in gold, but having brought it on board and opened it, the flour proved to be oatmeal. Meantime the vessel had entered the harbor and was out of sight.

I had heard much said about "the rolling grounds" at the mouth of Rio harbor, and my experience in this instance told me that the report had not exaggerated. Certainly I never saw a vessel roll and pitch about more wildly in a storm. Its effects were plainly marked in the great number that were made sea-sick.

Whatever may have been the intentions of the Captain, the evening of that same day saw us leave our anchorage, and start for Montevideo. We were all much disappointed in not going into Rio, and there was scarcely one in the whole crew, that would not have been willing to have fought our way in, if necessary.

Our course for Montevideo was southerly, and for the first three or four days, we sailed along finely with a favorable but very light breeze. On the evening of Saturday, June 24th, everything betokened the approach of a storm, and the prospect of that evening was verified in the "pampero," or hurricane that followed. Early Sunday morning it began to rain, pouring in torrents, and accompanied by occasional gusts of wind. After each lull in the wind, it would commence to blow again with increased fury. Just after dark that evening, the wind hauled to about two points abaft the beam, and we then close-reefed the top-sails, and took in all the remaining ones except the fore-topmast stay-sail, and the main top-sail. When I went on deck at midnight to take my watch, I found that the barometer was falling rapidly, and the storm steadily increasing, which it continued to do, from that time until 3 A.M. The wind was then blowing a regular hurricane and "coming from all points of the compass." After a few minutes' lull, the storm with its gathered strength burst upon us, sweeping everything before it. First the main sheets parted, and in a few minutes the sail was fairly torn into ribbons. Next the fore-top-sail gaff was carried away, and before the sail could be brailed up, it had several large holes torn in it, and a number were severely injured by the sheets as they flapped about. While they were at work in securing it, a noise like the booming of a cannon was heard, and upon inquiry, I learned that the fore-topmast staysail had burst in half a dozen places. The sail was soon hauled down and secured. Attention was next paid to furling the main-top-sail which was done without much difficulty, during a few minutes' lull. But we paid dear enough for that lull, for the men had barely laid in from the yard when the storm again burst upon us, with greater fury than ever. The fore top-sail was the only one now left set, and every moment we expected to see that carried away. Volunteers were called for to go up and furl it. Five or six were found willing, but the rest hung back. It seemed almost a fool-hardy undertaking, for the topmast had been sprung early in the evening, and it swayed to and fro with a heavy thump, at every roll of the ship. Beside all this the cold was so intense as to benumb one and make it extremely difficult to hold on. But the sail was clewed up as well as possible, and then the volunteers, now increased to fourteen, went aloft to furl it. As there was now no sail on to steady her, the ship rolled and pitched about worse than ever. The mast went from side to side with a thump, that could be distinctly heard on deck, above the roar of the gale; the sail was wet and heavy; the men soon benumbed with the cold, and a full hour elapsed before the sail was furled. And an hour of the most intense anxiety it was to us all; for every moment we expected to see the mast carried away, or some one lose his grasp and go overboard, not daring to hope that we should see them all safe on deck again. And as they came down and unharmed stood by our side once more, there was a deep breath of relief drawn, and a silent clasping of hands which spoke more eloquently than words could have done.

The officer that had the deck during the mid watch, proved himself to be decidedly incapable of managing a ship during a storm, getting nervous and excited, giving wrong orders, and even losing entire command of himself. For more than two hours we lay in the trough of the sea, the seas breaking over the sides, and splintering four inch oaken planks as if they had been so much paper. Some of the guns got adrift and went from one side to the other with a thump that fairly made the ship tremble, and for a time the greatest imaginable confusion prevailed. About 2 A.M. Mr. Philip came on deck, all hands were called, and the hatches battened down fore and aft.

It was about 4 A.M. when the fore-top-sail was furled, and the storm staysails and spanker " got up " and set. Meanwhile the Captain had sent forward to his cook and had a couple of kettles of good coffee made, and so when the work was done we each had a pint of coffee. I don't think that anything ever tasted better than that coffee did then.

When I went down on the berth deck, what a sight met my gaze! mess chests, kettles, dishes, provisions, etc. were, piled up in heaps, or scattered about the deck in glorious confusion. But one and all were too tired to put things to rights and threw themselves down wherever they could find a place and slept until 8 A.M. In fact, some slept the greater portion of the day, hammocks not being piped up at all.

Going on deck at 8 A.M. I found that we were in the vortex of the hurricane; that all around us not a breath of wind was stirring, and everything was as still as death, while in the distance on every side could be seen the dark raging hurricane, and the murmur of its fury be heard. The spectacle could not fail to impress one with feelings of sublimity and awe; and that imprint I shall vividly remember to my dying day. I was not the only one who for a time little expected to see land or friends again.

Despairing of being able to reach Montevideo, the Captain determined to put the ship about, and steam off out of the hurricane. Accordingly we got up a full head of steam and with everything prepared as well as possible we started. We were about two hours in getting out, and I hope never to endure another moment of suspense such as was crowded into every minute of those two hours. Every instant it seemed as if the next would be our last, and I verily believe that had the Wachusett been a less staunchly built vessel, or been less skillfully handled, we should never have seen port again. Through some mismanagement of the man at the helm, she pooped a sea, which made her tremble like a leaf from stern to stern, and for a moment it seemed as if the flood of water on her deck would break her. She could not have stood another such sea. However, with the exceptions of some holes torn in the storm sails, which were up, and a portion of the hammock nettings carried away, we experienced no injury while standing out of the hurricane.

The sailors, many of whom have been following the sea for the last twenty years, all agree that they never experienced a worse gale than this "pampero" was. Yesterday we proceeded farther to the northward. The storm abated and the sea grew less rough, but still the waves ran very high, and we rolled and pitched about so much as to make all of us a little sea sick.

The weather this morning still continued cloudy, cold, and unpleasant, but the sea was quite smooth in comparison with that of yesterday.

About 10 A.M. we heard the welcome, joyous words, "land ho!" shouted out from the mast-head. This we soon ascertained to be the long, narrow island of St. Catherine, which lies off the coast of Brazil, about four hundred miles to the southward of Rio Janeiro. About noon we arrived off the mouth of the harbor. For about a mile the entrance is very narrow, reminding one very much of a river. The land on either hand is very uneven, but with no considerable emi-

4*

nences. The scenery is exceedingly wild and picturesque, no signs of civilization to be seen, and the whole surface as far as the eye could reach, covered with groves of orange trees, and a dense and luxuriant growth of vegetation. Emerging from this narrow entrance, we saw a broad and beautiful bay before us, stretching away almost as far as the eye could reach, the waters of which were as smooth as a mill pond.

We steamed about five miles up this bay, and then came to anchor about one mile from the shore, opposite a small village, whose name, or whether it has any, I as yet have been unable to learn.

The town of St. Catharine lies about six miles farther up, around a bend of the bay, and not in sight from where we are lying. We draw too much water to go up any farther, a fact which is regretted by all.

Scarcely any signs of civilization are to be seen; here and there an occasional clearing, but the surface for the most part covered with forests. I will give you some further description of the place, as soon as I shall learn about it.

How long we are to remain here I am unable to conjecture, but suppose we shall stop long enough to take in stores, if they can be procured here. I should not be sorry if none were to be had, for then I think we should be obliged to go to Rio Janeiro, and I am very anxious to see that place.

LETTER VII.

U. S. S. WACHUSETT, Rio Janeiro,
July 10, 1865.

MY DEAR R.:

For once my wish has been granted. Provisions were not to be obtained at St. Catherine, and we were compelled to come to Rio Janeiro for them. That same afternoon that we dropped anchor at St. Catherine, Mr. Philip and the Paymaster went up to the town to see about getting coal and provisions. The next morning a lighter came down, bringing some fresh provisions and some hard bread, but with the news that coal and salt provisions were not to be obtained. The hard bread that was brought fully merited its name, for, in every sense of the word, it was decidedly the *hardest* that I ever saw. In appearance it resembles a loaf of brown bread, baked in a quart basin, and which had *raised down* instead of up, so that it was about an inch in thickness. I tried some of it for breakfast the next day. It was somewhat *harder* than flint, and to eat it without soaking was a matter of impossibility. On account of so many of them being broken, the gunner entered a protest against our using the battle-axes to break the biscuits up into mouthfuls, and we had to resort to the heels of our brogans. Fortunately I was not as hungry as some others, so that I waited until mine could soak, and did not insanely attempt to eat it without, as they did, breaking their teeth, getting choked, &c. Beside all that has been said, it is really affecting to think that at every mouthful one is destroying the homes of thousands—of weevil, bugs, &c.,—and with the homes, the inmates.

Saturday morning the crew holystoned the decks, ladders, and gratings, scrubbed the paint work, and shifted into white clothes, so that we were fully prepared, after the most approved man-of-war fashion, to take in the two lighter loads of coal which came down that morning. Mr. Philip and the Paymaster returned that morning and brought with them some late American papers. The most interesting news was that of the capture of Jeff. Davis in female clothing, while attempting to escape across the border into Mexico; also, that Booth, the assassin of President Lincoln, had been killed. Mr. Philip also brought us word that two American men-of-war were lying at Rio.

While lying at St. Catherine, bumboats used to come along side bringing the largest and most luscious oranges that I ever tasted. These were sold very cheap, four or five for a cent. Sunday afternoon, a number of us went to Mr. Philip and asked permission to take one of the cutters and go ashore after a load of oranges. This request was granted after a moment's hesitation, and about fifteen of us, armed with baskets and bags, set out upon our "oranging expedition." The place chosen was the hill to the right and rear of the village before mentioned. The slope was covered with a forest of orange-trees, whose ripe fruit fairly made the hill look yellow in the distance. We found a good place for landing, and, leaving bags and baskets under the charge of the boat-keeper, set out for a ramble. As we drew near the hill, we paused a moment to feast our eyes upon the trees fairly groaning under their load of ripe, yellow fruit, while the ground was covered with that which had fallen off.

There were thousands and thousands of bushels of the largest and finest oranges that I ever saw, all to be had for the taking of them. As I stood there feasting my eyes, (and mouth, too,) upon them, I wished that I could have had all my friends there to enjoy the feast with me. In sweetness and delicacy of flavor, those oranges by far surpassed any that I ever before tasted. In fact, it is impossible to procure as good ones at home; for, in order that they may be preserved until they can be carried there, they must be picked when green. Oranges will keep but a very short time after they are fully ripe, and that rich, delicious flavor is not to be had unless they are allowed to mature on the tree. Beside the ripe oranges, there were blossoms, and the green fruit in nearly every stage of its growth, on the same tree. After eating our fill and rambling about for two or three hours, we went down to the boat, procured and filled our bags and baskets with the largest and ripest fruit, and, with our boat deeply laden, returned to the ship. There arriving, the oranges were divided out to the messes, and so one and all rejoiced over our "oranging expedition."

Monday we took in about fifty tons of coal from an English bark, which was lying near us. In the evening the Captain returned from St. Catherine, whither he had gone the Saturday previous, and gave orders to have everything in readiness to start for Rio Janeiro the next morning.

Tuesday, July 4th, was a "glorious day," as far as the weather was concerned, so soft and balmy the air, not a cloud to be seen, and the temperature just right for comfort. We "dressed ship" at sunrise in honor of the day, as did also the three Brazilian corvettes, then lying at anchor in the harbor. This was done by hoisting an American ensign at the fore, main, and mizzenmast-heads and peak, and the jack on the jack-staff out on the bowsprit. One nation "dresses ship" for another by hoisting that nation's ensign at the foremasthead, and their own ensigns at the other mentioned places. In the morning, after the work was finished, the crew shifted into white frocks and cap-covers; permission was granted them to smoke all day, and no unnecessary work set them to do—a man-of-war-man's holiday. I wish that we had been into some port where we could have procured the materials to celebrate the day in a more appropriate manner.

From the senior Brazilian naval officer at St. Catherine, Captain Townsend had the assurance that the Florida affair had been satisfactorily settled, and that now we could go into any Brazilian port we wished without fear of being molested. At 11 A. M. we were under way; at 2 P. M. we had cleared the mouth of the harbor and were standing northwardly with all sail set, and with a good fair wind we were averaging nine knots per hour. The following two days were occupied by the crew in cleaning and painting the ship, painting boats, and making everything as neat and trim as possible, in order to make a fine *debut* at Rio.

For some time I had been watching the boatswain's mate, of whom some mention has been made, and the surgeon's steward, as they were engaged in playing chess, and endeavoring, in vain, to get some insight into the game. One morning, on our passage from St. Catherine to Rio, A. came to me and said that if I had any leisure time, and felt so disposed, he would endeavor to initiate me into the mysteries of chess. Of course I had time, and wished to learn; so the apparatus was procured and the initiating commenced. That day and the following were taken up by this teaching, and at the end, I had become quite skillful at the game. To me it is quite fascinating, and I promise myself much pleasure and profit from its acquisition, as it will serve to while away some of the long and tedious hours of the cruise. This feeling is common to all.

Thursday evening, July 6th, we sighted land, which we knew to be some islands off the mouth of the Bay of Rio Janeiro, so we "lay to" the greater portion of that night, as we were afraid that we might run aground should we attempt to proceed in the night time. The crew were quite merry that night over the prospect of going into Rio the next day, and singing and dancing were kept up until a very late hour.

Going on deck the next morning, I found that the promise of the previous evening of our having a fine day to go into

Rio had not been verified, for the rain was pouring in torrents. As soon as it was daylight we started on our way again for Rio, then about twenty-four miles distant, and at 8.30 A. M. we began to "open" the bay. Two or three pretty inlets, with rocky bases, enveloped by thick shrubbery and brush-wood, lie at the entrance of the channel.

Among the first points of interest which demanded notice and admiration, were the magnificent cone of the Sugar-Loaf, on our left, and the fortress of Santa-Cruz, with its floating banner, on a gently swelling hill on our right. From these points, on either side, the shores of the bay, lined at the water's edge with the cottages and hamlets of the fishermen, sweep widely around; while behind, hills, in the richest cultivation, sprinkled with farm-houses and villas, and crowned with churches and monasteries, all in purest white, rise abruptly on every side, till two or three miles inland, they terminate in ranges of mountains of the boldest and most varied beauty.

At the distance of about three miles from the entrance, a small castellated island rises from the water, over which a tower, here and there, with a forest of shipping adjoining, designated the location of the city. A little to the right, a succession of low, green islets, studding the smooth waters of the bay, showed the direction in which it penetrates far into the interior, till, at a distance of forty or fifty miles, the lofty and fantastic peaks of the Organ mountains closed the view.

The Sugar-Loaf is a strikingly unique and imposing object, a gigantic rock, a thousand feet high, singularly of the form which its name indicates, and inclining slightly over its base southward. It is entirely naked, excepting a little tufting of moss and bushes in some of the crevices indenting its sides, and on its top. Apparently, it is utterly inaccessible on every side; but it is said that a British officer succeeded in reaching the top and planting there the flag of his nation.

The story adds, however, that he paid for his venturesome deed with his life; whether perishing in the descent, or by the dagger of an assassin, is not known; but the latter is thought most probable.

A party of Austrian officers accomplished a similar feat; and an American, also, is said to have left the stars and stripes waving from its summit—a report as well founded, probably, as either of the former; for our countrymen, in whatever part of the world they are found, are not, to say the least, behind any that they meet, when boldness and intrepidity are in requisition.

The distance from the Sugar-Loaf to the city, in a direct line, is about five miles; but the shores on either side sweep from the channel into several bays, making the route by them much more circuitous. Botafogo, the largest and deepest of these inlets, first meets the eye. The entrance to it is very narrow, and almost entirely shut out from the sight. Encircled by wild and lofty mountains, it exhibits, at almost every point of view, the characteristic features of a fine lake. In the momentary glance as we passed, with the vapors of the morning still hanging upon the mountains, but for a cottage here and there, with the boat of a fisherman along the shore, it might have been thought still a haunt only for the numerous sea-fowl seen hovering around its waters, or soaring among the inaccessible crags above.

Next to Botafogo, and forming a kind of outer bay to it, comes the widely-curving Praya de Flamingo, or "Beach of the Flamingoes," lined with a range of fine houses. Immediately adjoining is the Gloria Hill, a place of great beauty, and forming one of the most conspicuous points in the panorama of the whole bay. Upon its brow stands the first public building attracting particular notice in approaching the anchorage—the church "Nossa Señora de Gloria," of our lady of glory. The building is a small octagon, with lofty towers of neat and well-proportioned architecture; the whole beautifully white, ornamented with pilasters, cornices, and casemates of brown freestone. It is delightfully located and overhung with trees and shrubbery of splendid growth.

Beyond the Gloria is another indentation, over which is seen a long stone causeway, lined with houses on the inner side, and above and beyond, a section of a lofty and massive aqueduct, running from the mountains to the city. Then comes another hill, surmounted by a monastery—a gloomy pile, and in poor repair—immediately beneath which, on a low piece of level ground, lies the greater portion of the city, with its numerous steeples and towers, the most conspicuous being those of the imperial chapel and cathedral.

The imperial residence fronts the water, and, with the public square adjoining, is in full view from the anchorage; while the episcopal palace stands on a hill, some two hundred feet high, in the center of the city. This is a fine building, and finely located, but of heavy and monkish architecture. Near it, on the west, is another hill and convent; and, closely adjoining the imperial navy-yard, from which a small rocky and fortified island runs into the harbor, and completes the outline of the sketch on this side of the bay.

With these leading objects, surrounded by masses of building for a foreground, backed by verdant hills in high cultivation, having cottages and villas embowered in bloom and beauty, scattered over them,—the whole terminated by a splendid range of mountains, with the shaft of the Corcovado, two thousand feet in height, rising in the center like a pinnacle against the sky,—you will have some conception of the magnificence of the scene.

At the city, the bay is about three miles wide. The opposite shore, on the north, is called Praya Grande. It is less wild and lofty in its general features, but equally rich in the varied beauty of hill and dell, wood and lawn—of plantation in all the luxuriance of artificial improvement, and mountain forest, standing, as for ages, in perennial verdure, undisturbed by the inroads of civilization.

There may be scenery in the world that equals this, but there can scarce be any that surpasses it. As a whole, it is sublime; while every distinct section would, in itself, make a picture. Whether viewed in mass or detail, it exceeds in beauty and variety everything that I have as yet seen.

Now to generalize a little. Rio Janeiro, the capital of the Brazilian empire, ranks as the largest and most flourishing city of South America. It lies on the western side of the bay, which is some seventy or eighty miles in circumference, forming one of the most spacious and secure receptacles for shipping in the world. In comparison with all others, travelers have pronounced the bay of Rio Janeiro to surpass them all in beauty. It is studded with upwards of one hundred islands; the ships of all nations are constantly seen passing in and out of its channels, and innumerable small boats are ever flitting about. Some thirty-five or forty men-of-war, and several hundred merchant vessels, representing almost every nationality, are now in the harbor.

The town is tolerably well built, much in the European style, the houses being three or four stories high, though the streets are quite narrow. The place where we anchored was nearly opposite the Emperor's chapel, about a mile from shore. The French, English, and Portuguese flag-ships saluted us as we came in, their bands playing "Hail Columbia."

Saturday morning, July 8th, we got under way at an early hour, steamed across the bay to the coal-wharf, and for once, regardless of man-of-war custom, we "coaled ship" before cleaning up. Commenced work at 9 A. M. and finished at 4 P. M., having taken in about two hundred tons. Two large American clippers were lying alongside the coal-wharf, discharging coal. I made the acquaintance of the second mate of one of them, who took me on board, shewed me about the ship, introduced me to his wife—a very pleasant and quite pretty young woman of about twenty-five—kept me to dinner, and when I was coming away gave me an armful of books and papers, making my visit an exceedingly pleasant and profitable one. At 4.30 P. M. we got under way again, and steamed back to our old anchorage, washing down and cleaning the ship while on our way there. That same evening we saluted the Brazilian flag with twenty-one guns, thus forever healing the breach made by the Wachusett in taking the Florida out of Bahia, upwards of a year ago.

Sunday was stormy, or we doubtless would have been thronged with visitors; as it was, but few came. This morning it cleared off, and it has been a lovely day. The crew have been hard at work all day in painting, scraping spars, setting up rigging, tarring down, and polishing up generally. They have sufficient employment of this description to keep them busy all this week.

I have not the least idea how long we shall remain here, but everything now betokens a long stay. I hope that this may be; for I hardly think that we shall find another place where there is so much to excite and interest, or that we shall like as well.

LETTER VIII.

U. S. S. WACHUSETT, Rio Janeiro,
September 19, 1865.

MY DEAR R.:

The prospect of a long stay in Rio has been verified, and the anticipated pleasure has been more than realized by nearly all. Yes, our stay in Rio has been a very interesting and exciting one.

Tuesday, July 11th, all the men-of-war in the harbor "dressed ship," "manned yards," and fired a salute of twenty-one guns, for the Emperor of Brazil who passed down the harbor on a Portuguese corvette. He was starting for Paraguay to visit his forces there, now engaged in war with the Paraguayans. It was a splendid sight, thus to see upwards of fifty men-of-war all dressed out, with their yards manned, and to hear the salutes thundered forth.

Thursday we "dressed ship," with the Brazilian flag at the main, and fired a salute of twenty-one guns in honor of the birth of a princess. Upon more than one-half of the days that we have been lying in this harbor we have "dressed ship," and fired salutes for some nation's holidays. Every nation, except the United States, has had one or more. In one week the Brazilians and the Portuguese had each two holidays, and it does seem as if these two powers had as many as all others here represented. The most of us, however, would not object to having every day a holiday; for they ever bring some excitement, thus enlivening a long stay.

For a long time the Wachusett was the only representative of the United States in the harbor. During the early part of August, the Mohongo came into port, and remained long enough to go into the dry-dock and have her bottom cleaned. She then continued on her way around the Horn to join the North Pacific squadron. About two weeks later the Susquehana, flag-ship of the South Atlantic squadron and bearing the flag of Rear Admiral Gordon, arrived at Rio Janeiro. All were rejoiced at her presence; for, since her arrival, it has seemed as if we had held a higher position with the other nations here represented, all of which have one or more large vessels. Then, too, among the salutes fired at almost every hour of the day, the stars and stripes have sometimes been seen at the foremast-head.

Since that time the squadron has received further addition in the shape of two or three gunboats, so that the officers and crews have had much pleasure in their intercourse with each other and in "ship visiting." It is customary when two or more vessels of the same nationality are lying in port together, to allow a number of the crews to visit each other Sunday afternoons. All avail themselves of this privilege, those of the same department or rank visiting each other as old friends, although they may be from different States, and have never met before.

For a long time after our arrival, the Wachusett was daily thronged with visitors, all of them anxious to see the vessel that seized the Florida. Being made the "Lion of the harbor" was somewhat different treatment from what we expected; but it really seemed as if they couldn't see us enough or show us enough respect and courtesy. I am sure that we are all better satisfied that it was so than that they should have harbored enmity for what is now past. Personally, however, I cannot say that I greatly admire this lionizing, for, nearly every day we are paraded in full uniform, on the quarter-deck to receive some distinguished visitor.

Soon after we came into port, the crew received their first allowance of money, and had "general liberty" given. As there was not a sufficient amount of silver in the ship, a large number of the crew received their allowance of five dollars in ten milrea bills—a milrea being equal in value to a silver half dollar. In the afternoon when the dingy was sent on shore, many of those that had received bills sent them ashore by the coxswain to have them changed into specie. When the dingey returned late in the evening, the coxswain was missing. The boat's crew said that he left them as soon as the boat touched the shore and they had not seen him since then, nor has any subsequent search revealed anything regarding his whereabouts. He had about two hundred dollars, and has doubtless returned to the States.

The following morning our watch went ashore on "general liberty." When the boat returned the next day with the liberty men, three of the marines were absent. Towards evening word was brought off from shore, that one of them, a man named Lee, had been found dead in the street that morning, and that the remaining two were in gaol. In the evening they came off, bringing the following particulars.

After reaching shore the day previous, they strolled about the city for a time, making a few purchases, and drinking pretty freely. About dark they went into a hotel at the upper part of the city kept by an Irish-American with whom one of them was acquainted. There they remained about two hours, rolling ten-pins and drinking until supper time.

As there was to be a dance at the hotel that evening, and they could have lodgings, they concluded to remain there over night. In the course of the evening all of them drank very freely, but Lee was the most intoxicated of the three. About eleven o'clock he retired; but, half an hour later he came out of his room, and said that he was going out for a walk. Before he came back the others retired, and it is not definitely known whether he returned or not.

They were awakened the next morning by a policeman, who broke into their room, told them that their comrade had been found dead in the streets, and wanted to know if they knew anything about it. They told him about his going out the evening previous, but supposed that he had returned. The policeman then took them to the dead house to identify the body of their comrade, and after that to a magistrate, who having heard what they had to say concerning the affair, released them. The only mark to be seen on Lee's body, was a small purplish spot over his left temple, which bore evidence of his having received a blow there.

By some it is thought that he was murdered by some of the old crew of the Florida, many of whom were at the hotel that evening, and with whom Lee had some angry words. Others accuse the landlord of committing the murder, but I can't see for what reason he should do it. Not that I think he would hesitate, if there was a sufficient inducement for so doing, but he had no trouble with Lee, and he certainly could not have done it for money, as Lee at the time of his death had not more than two or three milreas.

'The sleeping apartments of the American house are on the second floor, opening upon a balcony, which overlooks the street. Now by some it is thought that he returned after going out, and wishing to go out the second time, instead of going down stairs, walked over the balustrade, which is very low, and was killed by the fall. The latter I think is the most plausible explanation; more so, after seeing the scene of the affair. The body was found but a short distance from where he would have fallen. He might not have been instantly killed, but lived long enough to get that distance.

Early the next morning, Monday, Captain Townsend sent his clerk ashore to make preparations for the funeral. About noon he returned with the coffin, and a few minutes later the body was brought on board. At 2.30 P. M. all hands were called to bury the dead, and the funeral service of the Episcopal church was read by the Captain.

The body was then taken ashore for burial, accompanied by several of the officers and crew, and a firing party of eight marines. The cemetery to which we conveyed the remains lies at the western extremity of the city, and is the most beautiful one that I ever saw. It is very large, and very tastefully laid out in lovely walks and drives; the roads and paths on either hand shaded by splendid trees, or bordered with beds of the most beautiful flowers of almost every variety. On the whole it appears more like some beautiful garden, than the resting-place of the dead. For this I give the Brazilians credit; thus, leaving grim-visaged death shorn of some of his terrors, so that one could almost be content to die, if one could only rest in such a lovely spot as this.

In the corner set apart for the Americans, under the shadow of a beautiful weeping willow, we laid him down. At the grave the usual services were read by the surgeon, and, when all was over, we fired three volleys over his grave, and returned to the ship.

Robert Lee was an Irishman by birth, but had lived in the United States ever since he was a small boy, for the most part in the neighborhood of Boston, and in thought, word, and external appearance was a thorough American. Naturally of a quiet, retiring, kind-hearted disposition, he was without an enemy in the ship. He served all through the war in the army of the Potomac. It seems hard that, after escaping all the dangers there, he should die such a death far away from home and friends, in a foreign land. He leaves a motherless little girl about twelve years of age, with some friends in Roxbury.

Oh! I came near forgetting to mention "the wedding of Mary and John," which was celebrated on board the Wachusett, Saturday evening, July 22d, the mate and stewardess of the American steamer A———, being the happy couple. The A——— is chartered by the Brazilian government, and by it used in transporting troops and supplies to their forces in Paraguay.

In the forenoon of that day the mate came on board and asked the Captain if he could and would marry him. He said that the steamer was to leave in three days, and that he wished to get married before she started. By the Brazilian laws, the marriage would be illegal, unless the bans were published for three weeks previous. Of course Captain Townsend could and would tie the knot for them, and with his usual generous accommodating disposition, and a desire to see everything done with as much *eclat* as possible, he set his cook at work to prepare refreshments, sent his steward ashore for fruits, flowers, and other decorations, and had the cabins and quarter-deck finely and tastefully decorated. The couple came aboard about 8 P. M., but the ceremony was delayed about an hour in waiting for the captain of the steamer.

The bride was either very timid or opposed to the wedding, for she kept her face buried in her handkerchief nearly the whole time, and appeared as if she were crying bitterly. She was richly attired, but in a manner entirely devoid of good taste. As far as I was able to judge by an occasional glimpse of her face, I considered her a very plain, unattractive woman. John, a tall, broad-shouldered, good looking young man, with a frank, open, honest expression, tried every means within his power to soothe her, but without success.

As soon as everything was in readiness for the ceremony, all hands were called aft on the quarter-deck to witness the marriage ceremony. Mary and John took their place, and then the Captain proceeded to marry them. Mary still kept her face buried in her handkerchief, only uncovering it to answer in a low tremulous voice the questions asked her. The captain of the steamer gave the bride away, John slipped a ring on her finger, and the twain became one flesh.

After the ceremony they repaired to the upper cabin, and partook of the refreshments there prepared, and where all the officers were presented to them. After they had taken their departure, the captain summoned a large number of us into the cabin where we drank to the health of the bride and groom in a glass of the Captain's wine. Three days later the A——, started for Paraguay, and two smiling faces waved their handkerchiefs to us in passing.

Doubtless you begin to think that I have been a long time in Rio without getting ashore. My first *cruise* on shore was in company with a friend who has been in Rio many times before, and was almost as well acquainted with all the places of interest, as with those of his native city.

We landed at a narrow quay in the middle of Palace Square, one of the busiest quarters of Rio. This square is quite neat and pretty for a Portuguese city, although without any attractive ornament, and built without order or taste. After passing the prison-like granite building near the center, dignified by the name of palace, we entered Rua Direita at its rear, passed under an arch which connects the palace to a range of chambers on the opposite side of the street, and stopped before the Royal Chapel near by. This is very plain and simple without, but very rich within, as we found upon entering. The most attractive thing to be seen there, is the painting of the Crucifixion, which hangs against the wall opposite the entrance, and which is so well executed, that one needs to lay his hand upon the canvass before he fully convinces himself that it is not a *living* reality. So perfect is it, that one feels sure that he beholds the blood trickling down from the spear-thrust in His side and the prints of the nails in His hands and feet. On His countenance one distinctly sees the expression of pain together with that seraphic smile, which could only belong to one very near to Heaven and God. It seems incredible that the skill of man could execute anything so perfect as this. The roof or ceiling of the Chapel is high and vaulted, and upon it is the finest fresco painting that I ever saw. There are represented " the angels of God ascending and descending upon the Son of man."

From the Rua Direita we turned up into Rua do Ouvredor,

a narrow street, filthy and badly paved, but the Broadway of Rio. This street is lined on either hand by attractive shops of fancy goods, colored silks and cloths, and flowers and feathers. Among the most attractive curiosities to us were the large number of strange and brilliantly colored bugs and insects, either seen in large collections in suitable frames, or tastefully set in some article of jewelry. The greater number of the last mentioned we saw on Rua do Ourives, or the jewelers' street, which crosses the middle of Rua do Ouvridor. This street is upwards of two-thirds of a mile in length, and is occupied throughout by jewelers and silver-smiths.

The head of Rua do Ouvridor opens into Don Pedro Square, near a noted Café. We were somewhat faint when we reached the head of this street, so we entered the Café and called for coffee and cakes, throwing down the usual price, three cents. The Portuguese and their descendants, as well as the Spaniards, are very fond of this beverage, as is shown by the almost numberless little saloons or cafés which are found on almost every corner of the streets of their cities and towns, and these always filled with customers. The quantity of the coffee obtained is small, but the strength of a large cupful is condensed into that of a small one. I remember one saloon in particular where the cups in which they brought us the coffee, would not hold more than two table spoonfuls, and were emptied at a single draught. The sensation then experienced has been aptly compared to "that of a slight electric shock." But to return to the Café, and the coffee and cakes that were soon brought. There we remained upwards of an hour *a l'espagnole*, eating cakes, sipping our coffee, and listening to the songs of a quartette of little boys and girls, who accompanied their songs with the sound of the flute, violin, harp, and guitar. The sweetness of their childish voices, as they sang for us the Star Spangled Banner, I had never heard equaled, and it tempted me to many subsequent visits to this café.

The French use brandy as an addition to their coffee, and their example is followed to some extent by the Brazilians. Whenever coffee is called for, in many saloons, a decanter filled with brandy and finely graded is placed upon the table; then, when the bill is called for, the bottle is examined and one charged according to the amount used. I tried the experiment, but don't think that brandy is any improvement to coffee.

After leaving the café the attractions of Rua do Ouvridor, induced us to turn our steps thitherward again. A prominent reason, that this street has been the principal rendezvous during our stay, for our jolly tars, even of the finest cloth, is that there they would meet, either in the shops or on the street, the most attractive specimens of womankind to be found in Rio. The man spake from experience who said that, "it is the sailor alone, after being absent as he often is, for weeks and months from the presence of endearing woman, who can fully appreciate her cheering attractions. To him woman is a new creature, the fairest object he can meet with in a voyage; and, when contrasted in his mind with his gross companions of the ruder sex with whom he has weathered the seas, he is enraptured, and the first fair one, in whatever garb, that meets his eye, appears to him like a perfect houri, and he eagerly gazes at her and at all of her sex, with an open soul of admiration swimming in his eyes."

The females, those that are of Spanish or Portuguese descent, are generally of a pale complexion, but have a certain delicacy of feature which renders them very pleasing objects; and the affability of their manners heightens the agreeableness of their personal attractions. The proverbial Portuguese jealousy still exists among the many in Rio, not only to mar, if not to deaden their own social pleasures, but also to prevent a stranger from forming any extended acquaintance. During our stay here, however, I have formed many pleasant acquaintances among both sexes, and the moments passed in their society will ever be remembered as some of the pleasantest of my life.

A large proportion of the inhabitants of Rio are miserable half-naked blacks and mulattoes. Although the greater number of these are slaves, if at any time they become free, they are from that time, nearly, if not quite the white man's equal. They may vote, hold slaves, hold civil or military offices, or even become members in the House of Assembly. The degree of familiarity existing between the whites and blacks is disgusting to a newly arried American. It is no uncommon sight to behold a refined, intelligent looking white lady promenading the streets, arm in arm with a coarse looking, coarse appearing negro.

In the evening we went to the French theatre. This differs from any previously seen by me as regards the internal arrangements, and closely resembles a German bier garden. At short intervals about the parquet, dress circle, and galleries, tables were placed and chairs set around them. We went in and seated ourselves at one of these tables, and hand-bills were immediately brought us by pretty waiter girls. On one side of the bills was the programme of the evenings' performance, and on the other a list of liquors, cigars, fruits, coffee, and cakes, with prices of the several articles attached. We called for coffee, cakes, and cigars, and there we sat in true Brazilian style, sipping our coffee, smoking, and conversing between the acts, calling for a fresh supply of articles when required.

The piece enacted was an amusing comedy, and although intelligible to no one of the party but myself, yet we had many a hearty laugh over what I could understand, and translate to them. Several songs were sung with piano accompaniment, and there was a great deal of dancing, separately and intermixed with the play, that all could understand and appreciate. The Brazilians appear to be very fond of ballet dancing, judging by the manner in which every such dance was *encored*.

Another day when we were on shore, we decided to pay a visit to Praya Grande, which is opposite to the city, across the elliptic bay, and about three miles distant. Having procured tickets at the office near the landing, we stepped aboard the ferry-boat and after a pleasant ride of fifteen minutes, we were brought to the opposite side. Arriving there, we found Praya Grande to fully answer our expectations in regard to elegance of mansions and beauty of surroundings; a happy commingling of city and country. There were large palatial mansions, situated in large, beautiful gardens, fairly embowered with trees; wide streets, smooth and beautifully shaded, and everything, in short, as lovely and charming as one could wish.

One garden above all others attracted our attention, not only on account of its size and beauty, but also because we there saw growing many home plants and flowers. From the gardener, who was standing near the gate, we obtained permission to take a walk about the grounds. While commenting upon a bed of strawberries, many of which were then ripe, a pleasant, middle aged lady came along and asked us if we did not belong to the American man-of-war in the harbor. We replied that we did. She told us that both her husband and herself were from Connecticut, and many of her friends were now resident there. They left the states about ten years ago and had not returned since; but they hoped to go there again ere long. She, seeing the longing looks that we were casting toward the strawberry-bed, asked us if we would like to have some strawberries. We replying that we would very much indeed, she said that if we would wait a few minutes she would have some prepared for us. In the meantime she invited us to seats in a charming little summer-house, near by, and then entered into conversation with me, I having told her that I too was from Connecticut. In about half an hour, a servant came, bearing a dish of strawberries smothered in cream, accompanied by another bearing short-cakes and a pitcher of milk. We then had such a feast as we had not tasted for many a day, and one which we enjoyed as only those can that have been similarly situated. About five o'clock we told her that we must return. She picked, arranged, and presented each of us a beautiful bouquet of flowers, and invited us to make her another visit should we remain long enough in Rio Janeiro to come ashore again. She said that it was so seldom she ever saw one from Connecticut, or from the United States even, that she prized such visits very highly, ever considering them as a great favor to herself. We told her that we had not enjoyed ourselves so much since we left home, and should by no means deny ourselves the great pleasure of another visit to her, if practicable, especially when we had every reason to believe that our visit would be received with pleasure.

A visit to the Navy yard reveals no great wonder or attraction, with the exception of the dry dock, which is spoken of as being the finest in the world. It is about three hundred and twenty feet long, and seventy-five feet wide, cut out of the solid rock. On the stocks and nearly ready for launching, when I visited the yard a month ago, were two iron clads, the first attempts of the Brazilians at establishing an iron clad navy. About a week ago one of them was completed and started for the seat of war in Paraguay. The Brazilians have great hopes of these iron clads, but they appear to me to be weak opponents for our monitors. Their finishing shops for shot and shell were much better conducted than I expected to find them; but then we, with ideas that there are no people in the world equal to the Americans, would attribute this circumstance to the fact that the superintendents of the shops are Americans.

In traversing any of the more fashionable streets of Rio, one cannot fail to notice the great number of blinds that are left partially open, and mirrors placed upon the inside of them. For a long time I was puzzled to know for what purpose this was done, and at last, I requested a friend to tell me. He said that the mirrors were so placed that the occupants of the rooms could perceive whoever was passing in the streets, or what was being done there. If one wanders from the business part, to the rear of the city, he will find many pleasant squares containing public fountains, and will see the humble dwelling of the lowly side by side with the palatial mansion of the noble and wealthy. The former are seldom more than one story high, and the windows are screened by lattice blinds which swing at the top. Upon pleasant evenings, these blinds will be seen opened a little way, and in the coverts, bashful lovers who meet there to whisper their soft endearments. This is said to be the custom for all their courtships, a custom derived from the mother country. The mansions of the noble and wealthy are usually surrounded by high, strong walls, the entrances to which are secured by massive double doors. The Portuguese jealousy of females may there be observed in the closed blinds and iron bars for the windows.

On another excursion to the city, we found all the churches, stores, and houses decorated. It was a religious holiday. All were attired in their best garments, and all places of business were closed. Before the principal churches in the evening, there was a very fine display of fireworks, prominent in which were rockets and fire-balloons. The people appear to attach supernatural power to these fireworks, as aiding in the banishment of evil spirits, and there is always a grand display on every church holiday, or celebration of high mass.

Once while lying here we filled our tanks with shore water. The consequence was that several of the crew were taken sick and some of them have not yet recovered from the effects of the change of water. It is a well known fact that much sickness and many deaths are occasioned by the change of water in going from one country to another. Probably there is no water in the world as pure or as healthy as good condensed water. Not only this, but when a vessel condenses all the water used by her crew, it obviates all the sickness occasioned by the change in going from one country to another.

After we had been at Rio upwards of two months, it was one morning called to mind that we had not " moored ship," and that it would be an excellent idea to do so. This is done by dropping the anchors some distance apart and then attaching both of the cables to a large swivel, so that when the ship swings around with the tide, the chains do not become twisted. The principal object in mooring ship, is that she may take up less room in swinging, than when lying with a single anchor down. It is usually considered a very short and simple performance, but whether we had no superintendent, or whether we had too many, I can't say, I only know, that we made a long tedious job of it, using up the greater portion of the day.

For a visit to Botafogo a number of us set out a few days ago on foot. We arrived there after an hour's delightful walk, having stopped frequently to examine and admire the unusual beauties of a residence and its surroundings. It was a charming sunny morning, and the undulating smooth road, now skirting the water side, and thence winding around the base of a range of hills, was hemmed in by the hedges of gardens, or lofty walls of masonry, above which hung the rich fruits of palmate and other tropical trees with flowers of the jessamine and honeysuckle, scenting the air. At Botafogo many of the wealthy business men of Rio have their residences, and some of them are almost perfect paradises, with their beautiful and extensive grounds attached.

A short distance from the principal quarter of Botafogo, the Botanic Garden is located. This comprises from seventy-five to one hundred acres plotted off into groves and flower-beds, artificial mounds, and broad avenues meeting at a pretty fountain near the center. In the grove were the dark olive, the crotons, the crescentia, which bears a great calabash; the carambola, which bears an excellent arid fruit, the cinnamon, red pepper, and clove trees. The avenues are shaded by the dense foliage of the mango tree; the bamboo and plantain; and the coffee, orange, and other trees peculiar or indigenous to South America. But in the variety of flowers, or in their beauty and rarity, the garden that we visited at Porto Praya would fully equal, if not surpass this place. The scenery all around is remarkably picturesque and beautiful, and the effect is heightened by the shaft of the Coocovado which rises immediately behind the town of Botafogo.

There has been so much else to write about, of apparently more interest, that I have entirely neglected to speak of the repairs which were entered upon soon after our arrival here, and have been the occasion of our long stay. Upon an examination of the engine, a crack some seven or eight inches in length was discovered in one of the crank-pins. For a month the engineers were engaged in putting a band around it, and making some other necessary repairs. We have had a bridge put up just abaft the smoke stack, and resting on the bulwarks. This I think is a decided improvement.

Another improvement was the extension of the poop about five feet, so as to cover the wheel, and underneath having a little room on each side; one for the armory, and the other for the signal locker. This also makes a good shelter for the orderly on watch, and then gives us more room to work the gun.

This was finished about three weeks ago, and the carpenters have since been busy in repairing the decks, getting new spars in place of those destroyed or injured by the gale, etc.

We have had a great number of desertions since we have been lying here, more than thirty in all, and but two or three of the runaways have been captured. With a few exceptions, those that have deserted were excellent seamen, among the best that we had in the ship. These we find make quite a lessening in our effective force.

To-morrow we leave here for Cape Town, so that to-night we will look upon the lighting up of the convents on the hills, and of the churches on the oblong plain beneath, of rockets, and other signs of a religious holiday; hear the sweet sounds from the bands of the English, French, and Portuguese frigates near us, and hear the many other evening attractions and pleasures of our stay at Rio, for the last time in many months or years.

LETTER X.

U. S. S. WACHUSETT, Simons' Bay, South Africa,
October 2, 1865.

MY DEAR R.:

> "All hands unmoor! unmoor!
> Hark to the hoarse, but welcome sound,
>   Startling the seaman's sweetest slumbers,
> The groaning capstan's turning round,
>   The cheerful fife's enlivening numbers;
> And lingering idlers join the brawl,
> And merry ship-boys swell the call,
>   All hands unmoor! unmoor!"

Nearly all had become wearied with our long stay at Rio, so that when the orders were given to get under way September 20th, all sprang to the call with alacrity, and cheerfully assisted in all the many necessary preparations. Early in the morning two of our number bade us "good bye," and were transferred to the Susquehanna, there to await transportation to the States, their period of enlistment having expired. It was nearly 5 P. M. when the shrill whistles and gruff voices of the boatswain and his three mates piped "all hands up anchor." Up from below, through every hatch-way, like trains of ants, to their several stations came the interminable throng,—all longing to be at sea once more.

The shrill whistle piped again on deck, and from stem to stern the word was passed,—the fifes and violin struck up a well-timed quickstep—and tramp, tramp, stepped the centipeded train over the deck. In a moment the helm was up, around went the propeller, and the ship moved slowly and gracefully down the Bay from her anchorage, dipping her colors in return to those of the vessels she passed, and to the playing of Hail Columbia by their bands. As soon as we had steamed out of port, so that we could shape our course, the fires were put out, the clanking of the engine ceased, and sail was made on the ship.

Our month's run from Rio Janeiro to the Cape was characterized by strong, favorable winds, no very severe storms nor rough seas, and everything considered, it was as speedy and pleasant a run as we could reasonably expect. The only damages done to the ship was the springing of one top-mast and carrying away the jib-boom.

The man that we received in exchange for the two we transferred to the Susquehana, falls far short of filling the place of one of them. He is a short, thick-set, thick-headed, ill-featured Dutchman, and decidedly the *meanest* man in the "Guard." As soon as he came on board he was made acting-corporal, and the first night he commenced operations by reporting three or four of the guard for some trifling misdemeanor. Reporting one of our own number is never done unless absolutely necessary. So when he commenced in reporting every one for unnoticeable misdemeanors, discord and enmity were soon created in the "Guard." Our number is small in comparison with the rest of the ship's company, and any division is to be feared and avoided as much as possible. It seems strange that we should have allowed such an one to have brought discord into the "Guard." And yet he did bring it. Another example of the maxim—"Great results oftimes spring from trifling causes." One night he reported a man for sleeping on post, and about half an hour later he himself was found asleep on watch. So some of the crew fastened a halyard to his feet, and then from the other side of the deck, they triced him up by the heels, and left him hanging about six feet from the deck. He was half an hour in releasing himself from this predicament, and was fortunate in not being discovered by the officers.

As captain's orderly I had enjoyed all the privileges that I wished, and was so well satisfied with my duties that I was not pleased with the promotion to corporal, and duty in the gangway assigned me. But there was no use in remonstrating, so I accepted of the change with the best possible grace. To be sure I have more leisure, and there are some other advantages gained, but still, in my estimation, the *cons* more than outnumber the *pros*.

On this passage my *wardrobe* was found, upon examination, to be in such a condition as to compel me to relinquish all other duties and pleasures, and to devote several days to mending and repairing. At first it was slow and awkward work, but, by patience, and spurred on by necessity, I soon became quite expert with the needle. I can safely say now, that I do not prick my fingers more than once a minute, on an average, and quite often am not compelled to do my work over the second time. What prizes we will all be in the matrimonial market when we return home—able to cook, wash, sew, and do many other things to lighten the labors of all the future Mrs.!—but I will not anticipate. Yes, necessity has compelled me to learn many things which I will find useful and advantageous in after life. How often have I seen the time, when, if I had known how to sew, some sorrow or mortification would have been spared me!

One personage we have on board which I think I have not yet introduced to you; that is a large, dog-faced monkey, which we purchased at St. Catherine. He is decidedly the most knowing, and most comical monkey that I ever saw, and scarcely a day passes but that he is the occasion of much mirth to the crew. The sailors have taught him so that he will sit up and smoke a pipe, dance, and perform an immense number of interesting feats and tricks. Whenever the crew are all aft on the quarter deck, at muster, then Jocko is in his glory. He will go down on the berth deck, and woe be to the ditty-box that is left unfastened, or anything that he can injure left within his reach, for he will surely seize upon it. He tried his hand at bread-making for us several times, (a pan of flour having been left by the cook where he could get at it,) to the ruin of the flour and the injury of whatever might be lying near. In Rio we procured some little Guinea-pigs which Jocko evidently thought were going to supplant him in the affections of the crew. · Instead of killing or injuring them, which he easily could have done, he used to carry them up to the pendant-tackle block, when he would leave them and then descend to the deck and watch for them to fall. Fortunately all were rescued, with one exception, before his intentions were fully carried out.

At other times poor Jocko has been the medium of communicating the dislike which the crew had for certain officers. On this passage a great deal of merriment and no small excitement was created, by dressing him up in a uniform resembling S.'s, and then sending him aft to where he was standing in the midst of a group of other officers. They greeted his advent by a roar of laughter, while S. was fairly purple with rage. Immediately he rushed into the cabin and reported the circumstance to the Captain, saying that it was the greatest insult he ever had in his life, comparing *him* to a monkey! The Captain ordered Mr. Philip to find out who the perpetrators were, but all his investigations were without success. No one knew anything about it. So the affair was dismissed with orders that the uniform should be altered, and that nothing of this kind should occur again. It will be a long time, however, before the affair will be hushed up, and many will yet be the hearty laugh had about " S—— and Jocko."

For the past two or three months, the sergeant has been at *work* upon a duo of American citizens of African descent, training, or attempting to train them for the "ship's drummer and fifer." By dint of explaining, coaxing, promising, threatening, together with sundry raps with the drumsticks,

> "A spur
> To prick the sides of his intent,"

he at length forced so much *music* through their unusually thick skulls, that he pronounced them far enough advanced to beat to quarters. Accordingly three or four evenings ago they were brought up to make their *debut*. They played so near the appropriate air that about one out of every ten knew what they meant, and went to their quarters, but the rest stood and looked at them in blank amazement, wondering what in the world they were attempting to do, or what was meant. Finally a resort to the boatswain's whistle was necessary, before all came to their quarters. After retreat was beaten, Mr. Philips called all hands aft on the quarter-deck to muster, and told them that whenever they should hear that *noise* again we might know that it was for quarters.

Friday, October 20, 1865, will ever remain a white day in my geographical calendar, for it was then that I, for the first time, rested my eyes upon that black continent "whose people have given the world more political and religious trouble than their physical strength has ever given it aid." The truth of this remark is painfully evident in the experiences of our own country. It was then also a white day beyond this geographical wonder, in that after thirty days of sea rolling, and ship dietetics, we were to have the quiet repose of port, to taste shore fruits, and once again to place foot on good solid mother earth.

When I went on deck this morning, there were the great rocky buttresses, and ragged mountains of South Africa, jutting away out into the sea, which rolled in upon them from the South Pole, or, at least, the Antarctic continent. Table Mountain, and all the individualized and named peaks of this renowned Cape were in sight as we ran along the shores of "Good Hope," rounded its promontory and entered the smooth green waters of Simon's Bay. There are a few neat looking English houses clustered on the beach, at the foot of the gray, naked mountain which towered behind them. About noon we cast our anchor in front of Simon's Town, a pretty, quiet, little place of about one thousand inhabitants.

The anchor down, then came all the bustle and preparation of an arrival in port. In full uniform, with everything bright and shining, we were ordered to hold ourselves in readiness to be paraded at a moment's notice to receive any distinguished visitor that might come on board. The boats were lowered and Mr. Grove despatched to wait upon the authorities and arrange about the salutes. Various boats were hurrying off to us. One was that of the health officer and harbor-master, before whose visit we must not communicate with the shore; another, with the United States flag flying, brought the American Consul; a third, with a pennon in the bow and an English ensign in the stern, brought us a Lieutenant from the English senior officer's ship—the Valorous.

The salutes over, the string of small boats, which had been lying astern to be out of the way of the guns, now pull up to the gangway, and the occupants, each striving to get up before his neighbor, climb up the ship's side, and step on board. There are provision dealers, grocers, tailors, bumboatmen, washerwomen, all zealous to show their cards and recommendations from previous ships and secure the patronage of the various messes. To the ship's company the bumboatman is the most useful of these merchants. He may be all in one. His boat is their corner grocery store. At meal hours he comes alongside the ship with his fresh fruits, fresh bread, cooked fish and meats, and a tempting variety of articles, peculiar to the port in which the ship is lying. He is a convenience, also, for communicating with the shore, making purchases, bringing off small packages and such like things. All avail themselves of his services, preferring them to the *ifs* and *ands*, the mighty concession which so often attends the getting ashore, and nine chances out of ten not getting ashore when the article is most required. Of course, a man in such close association with the people of the ship, must have a certain amount of reputable character. or else he may do much mischief by smuggling liquor, and other important articles on board. The choosing of a bumboatman, Mr. Philip has ever left to the sergeant and master-at-arms. On this occasion a tall, slender, neatly-dressed Malay with a red handkerchief around his head won their favor.

Simon's Bay owes its existence as a place of note to the fact that it is sheltered from those fierce south-east winds which roll the Atlantic in before Table Bay and Cape Town, where, from May to September it is very dangerous for vessels. It is the site of the government dockyard and the place for the anchorage of the government shipping. Near the entrance of the harbor is a small island on which stands a lighthouse. How long we will remain here I can't say, but Dame Rumor hath it, that in a few days we are to go around to Cape Town. But she is a fickle jade, and not always to be relied upon.

LETTER XI.

U. S. S. WACHUSETT, Cape Town, }
South Africa, November 22, 1865. }

MY DEAR R.:

Dame Rumor was right. We remained but a few days at Simon's Bay and then came around to Cape Town.

We had one pleasant occupation while we were lying at Simon's Bay, and that was, fishing. A line over the side with a bit of pork attached for bait, and an abundance of mackerel, salmon, and two or three other varieties of fish would reward the fisherman. While on watch in the evening, I used to catch fish enough for breakfast for our mess. At the same time with mine, there would be lines out all the way from the forecastle to the poop, and nought was heard but the exultant cry of some fortunate fisherman, the thump of the fish as it was detached from the hook and cast on deck, and the flapping of it as it lay there. Upon our first arrival the harbor-master placed in the Surgeon's hands the following printed paper:

NOTICE.

"There is a fish in Simon's Bay, commonly called 'Toad Fish.' It is about six inches long, back dark, with deep black stripes; belly, white with faint yellow patches. It swims near the surface, and is a constant attendant upon the lines employed in fishing. When taken from the water it puffs out considerably. Should any portion of this fish be eaten, *death ensues* in a few minutes."

From curiosity to see the fish we all tried to catch one and at last were successful. We found it to exactly answer to the description given.

We remained at Simon's Bay long enough to make some repairs on the top-mast and take in coal, and on Friday, October 27th, we came around to Cape Town. The sailing distance is about forty miles, and we steamed it in a little more than three hours, beating the Valorous' time by about half an hour. We anchored about a mile from the shore.

Cape Town, the capital of Southern Africa, and the most important European settlement on the continent, is situated near the isthmus of a peninsula, formed by Simon's Bay on the east, and Table Bay on the west, on which last the city itself is built. Immediately behind, rises precipitously Table Mountain, 3,582 feet high, above the level of the sea, and consisting chiefly of steep cliffs of naked schist and granite The Devil's Hill, 3,315, and Lion's Head, 2,160 feet high, rise on each side. The triple summit forms a very conspicuous object from the sea, over which these spots command a very striking prospect.

Cape Town being the only good place of refreshment for vessels between Europe and America on one side, and India, China, Japan, and Australia on the other, it must ever remain a place of great commercial importance. The country itself affords for exportation, wines, hides, skins, and a great variety of minor articles. The population is estimated at 35,000. It was settled by the Dutch in 1650, and among the European residents here, the Dutch element greatly predominates. In the war between England and Holland, in 1795, Cape Town was taken by the English, but at the time of the peace, it was restored. Upon the renewal of hostilities, it was recaptured in 1806, and since that time it has been retained by the English.

Table Bay affords accommodations for a great amount of shipping, but from the month of May until September it affords a very insecure anchorage, being exposed to the fierce southeast winds which prevail at that season of the year. During the gale which prevailed last May, it is estimated that seventy ships and smaller craft were beached, and upwards of fifty lives lost. It was the worst gale that has visited Table Bay for many years. They are at present engaged in constructing a breakwater which shall protect the anchorage from those long, heavy swells which make the anchorage so dangerous during the prevalence of those gales from the southeast. At this season of the year the harbor is considered safe, only on rare occasions some little annoyance is caused by the sea being so rough, that boats and men on shore are compelled to remain there several days before they can return to their ships. One time when the Captain and a large number of the crew were ashore, our bumboatman—pointing to Table Mountain—said "The Minzenburg has its cap on, and we will have a storm before morning from the southeast." And so we did. We dropped another anchor, and our communication with the shore for several days was interrupted, difficult, and dangerous. 'Tis said, that whenever the cloud gathers on the top of Table Mountain, the wind blows from the southeast. The winds of southern Africa are very fitful, changing from the northwest to the southeast without a moment's warning, more than the gathering of the cloud-cap on Table Mountain.

There is much less shipping in port than I expected to find; a couple English men-of-war, half a dozen steamers, and some thirty or forty merchant vessels and smaller craft are about all.

In its general appearance, Cape Town reminds one of a New England city, and viewed from the ship, nestled as it is at the base of Table Mountain, with its many church spires and fine buildings, the substantial farm-houses on the outskirts, the cars arriving and departing, all together form a picture that will forever remain imprinted upon my memory, ever to be looked at with pleasure.

My first ramble about Cape Town was when on general liberty and accompanied by one of the orderlies. After landing and purchasing what articles we wished, we set out for a stroll about the city. The site of Cape Town is an inclined plane, gently sloping from northeast to southwest. Long street, extending from the landing in a northwest direction through the town, is the principal street. It is very wide, smooth, and level, and on it are located the court house, post office, and principal church, hotel, banks, and stores in the city. Other streets run parallel with this, connected with each other by numerous cross-streets. After walking for a short time we agreed that it was much easier and more pleasant to ride. Accordingly we procured a cab,—"Hansoms" they call them, light, two-wheeled, basket concerns, with a seat perched up behind for the driver, just room enough for two, and very easy, very nice to ride in we found them. Everything arranged, away we started along central wharf, next the sea, our first object being to visit the Castle. Our pony was smart and active, and we were brought to our destination in a short time after we started, stopping a few minutes at the barracks on our way, for the purpose of seeing the soldiers drill.

The Castle is an ancient Dutch structure, built in the early years of the colony. It has heavy stone walls, and surrounding it is a wide, deep moat now disused and filled with rushes and long grass. We passed over a draw bridge, entered through an archway (which is closed by a heavy iron gate,) and stood in a square some forty or fifty feet across. Stone staircases lead to the top of the walls on each side, one of which we ascended and stood on the summit of the fortress. A few heavy ancient pieces of ordnance on the side facing the sea, were the only defenses. Below are casemates and beds for mortars. Around the walls, inside, are rooms where the married soldiers, their wives and families, of the troops stationed at Cape Town reside. A guard is daily detailed from the barracks for duty here.

"Will you not come up to the barracks," said a sergeant,

as we were about leaving. After a moment's hesitation we replied " certainly," and having dismissed our carriage, we went there with him. "The barracks" is a fine large brick building on the southern outskirts of the town. It is situated some little distance back from the street, with a small parade-ground in front, within the walls, and a fine large one in the park, between them and the street. Entering, we found the barracks turned topsy-turvy, and everything at variance with the usual cleanliness and good order of a military station. "You must not wonder at not finding us in better order," said the sergeant, "for the place has just been vacated by the ninth, and we, the tenth, arrived here only two days ago; but, come with me to the 'Canteen' and taste our Cape wines."

We had heard much said in praise of the Cape wines, and after tasting we were disposed to add a good word of our own. Among others, there were placed before us the several kinds of Constancia, which had been presented our host by his friend—the superintendent of the vineyard. Such delicate, fine flavored wines it had never been our good fortune to taste before, and I fear that we did not strictly follow the very good advice of Mr. Bacchus, who says:

" Let them three parts of wine all duly season,
 With nine of water, who'd preserve their reason;
 The first gives health, the second sweet desire;
 The third tranquility and sleep inspire:
 These are the wholesome draughts which wise men please
 Who from the banquet home return in peace.
 From a fourth measure insolence proceeds:
 Uproar a fifth; a sixth wild license breeds;
 A seventh brings black eyes and livid bruises;
 The eighth the constable next introduces;
 Black gall and hatred lurk the ninth beneath;
 The tenth is madness, arms and fearful death.
 For too much wine poured in one little vessel,
 Trips up all those who seek with it to wrestle."

Mindful to some degree of this advice, with many thanks to our English friends for their hospitality, we at length bade them " good-bye," and continued our ramble about the town.

Nearly opposite the barracks is the new market—a fine, large brick building, built and owned by the government. The stalls within are rented from the government, and are, for the most part, tended by fine-looking, buxom English girls. At a subsequent visit, in the evening, when the building was lighted up, I was charmed by the fine display of fruits, wreaths, flowers, and not a little by the fresh beauty of many of the venders. Captivated partly by some luscious looking pears, closely resembling our Bartletts, and partly by the winning looks and tone of the vender as she said "sixpence" to my inquiry as to their price, I was led to invest somewhat largely in them, and I must confess that I am unable to decide which I enjoyed most, the pears or the conversation which I had with the vender whilst tasting them. The greater number of these venders are farmers' daughters who come in from the country to dispose of their produce. Many of them are quite intelligent, witty and lady-like, as well as quite pretty in appearance.

Leaving the market and ascending the eminence at the rear of the town on which the signal-station stands, we had a splendid bird's-eye view of Cape Town. Hardly could a checker-board be laid out with more regularity, and everything looked so exact, so neat and so clean, that I stood for a long time enjoying the view. Our lodgings for the night were at the Central Hotel, kept by a middle-aged, matronly English lady with whom I spent several hours very pleasantly in conversing. We had as good accommodations as one could desire, and I would recommend the Central Hotel to any one visiting Cape Town, and desiring "food and lodgings." In the evening I went out with one of the gentlemen boarders for a walk, and to make some calls. As a class, I was far better pleased with the English than I expected, and I have formed many pleasant acquaintances among them at Cape Town.

The head of Long street opens upon the Government grounds, through which extends the mile long oak avenue, a thousand old oaks, with seats underneath for visitors to rest and refresh themselves. Upon the right, a short distance from the entrance, in a small but beautiful garden, (by some called the Botanical, by others the Governor's garden,) stands a fine large granite building, the Colonial Museum. This I visited several times. A hall extends through the middle of the building, on the right of which is the Public Library. Opening the door and entering this room, one is confronted by a large, splendid oil painting of Queen Victoria. I never visit the museum without stopping awhile and enjoying this lovely painting. 'Tis said that when Prince Alfred visited Cape Town a few years ago, after an absence from home of several years, and saw this portrait of his mother, he was affected to tears, so true to life is it executed. On the left of the hall, before mentioned, is the museum, containing stuffed specimens of most of the animals of South Africa, and also a valuable collection of shells and other curiosities peculiar to the country. Many specimens here found are not in any other museum in the world. Nearly opposite the museum is the residence of the Governor of the Colony, Sir Harry Woodhouse.

Here many of us have made a commencement to the collection of curiosities which we intend to gather this cruise. I have a few shells, porcupine quills, and ostrich eggs. There are many other articles which we would purchase if the ship were now "homeward bound," but which we think we had better postpone until that time.

Of the incidents of our stay at Cape Town, there is none that will be remembered with more pleasure by me than the excursion which a number of us made to Wynberg, a very pleasant country town some eighteen or twenty miles from

Cape Town. Being on shore one day on an invitation to dine with an English gentleman, and after dinner having a few hours to invest in sightseeing, we concluded that the most profitable investment would be an excursion to Wynberg. We went thither in the cars, Wynberg being connected with Cape Town by railway. A word or two now about the cars. They are some twenty-five or thirty feet in length and divided off into apartments large enough to accommodate four persons each. According to position and furnishing they are denominated first and second class. They are entered by doors on the sides, and as soon as one is in and seated the door is shut and fastened on the outside by the conductor who rides on a little platform at the rear of the car. After leaving Cape Town, our road for two or three miles was along the beach, through pleasant, fine looking farms, with neat, cosy farm-houses attached, the prospect varied here and there by a wind mill. I will here mention that all the grinding done at the Cape is by wind power, there being, as yet, no steam or water power employed.

After riding two or three miles along the beach, the road turned off into the interior, running all the way through fine farms and vineyards. We were about an hour in going to Wynberg, stopping at five stations on our way there. From the conductor we learned that we would have two hours in which to look about the place before the train returned; A. and myself, therefore, agreed that we would make the most of those two hours. We took our way over a smooth, wide, and beautifully shaded road, flanked on either hand by elegant mansions situated in wide, beautifully laid out grounds. We walked slowly, that we might the better enjoy so much beauty, filling our souls with deep copious draughts, so that our two hours passed by almost like some beautiful dream. Perhaps you may think that I am indulging in some such ecstasies as are incident to sailors on shore, over rural charms and prettily embowered houses; but I may be excused in this, for the beauties of Wynberg are of no common order. We extended our walk a short distance out from the village of Wynberg to the Constancia estate where are made the celebrated Constancia wines. The vineyard is only a few acres in extent, but there, and in no other place, is raised the genuine, original Constancia. It is difficult for any one familiar with the spirituous taste of most wines, to believe that any such rich, syrupy fluids can be produced from the grape alone, without the addition of sugar. But such is the fact. The grapes are permitted to almost wilt upon the vines before they are plucked, and to facilitate this process the leaves are thinned from the vines. One accustomed to the mode of raising grapes with us would scarcely recognize a Cape of Good Hope vineyard.

At a little distance, he could hardly distinguish it from a potato field, the vines not being over three feet high, bunches of fresh shoots supported on old knotty, venerable, gray looking stalks, many of which are as old as the vineyard. This is about two hundred years of age, having been planted by one of the first governors, and gallantly called after his wife, "Constancia."

Leaving Constancia and Wynberg we took the cars and returned to Cape Town. We had agreeable companions on this return trip, in the shape of an old English merchant and his daughter, a lovely young lady about sixteen or seventeen years old. A blunder made in treading upon the old gentleman's corns introduced us, and long before we reached Cape Town, we were quite good friends, and had invitations to visit them at their home.

Since we have been lying here, the ship has been fairly thronged with visitors, ladies and gentlemen coming off from shore by lighter loads. At one time there were over a hundred on board, all anxious to see an American man-of-war, which, according to their accounts, is quite a curiosity to the Cape Town people. There were so many visitors that almost every one of the crew had some one to whom he was "showing the ship." 'Twas laughable to see some almost ignorant *land lubber*, conceited enough to strive to explain the managing of a vessel in a storm or the working of the battery in action to one who doubtless knew much more about the matter than he himself did. But the most laughable incident of all was the explanation of the rifle gun on the forecastle, given by " Jib Bogue," and how he expatiated upon its virtues, to a nicely dressed, intelligent, and fine looking English lady. He said, " Madam, dis am de rible gun, what carries de comical skell, which kills de men, cuts up de riggin and, and——kicks up de d—l generally." To have seen the astonishment of the lady and to have heard the roar of laughter with which this speech was received would have made the most sedate person smile.

Wednesday evening, November 16th, the officers of the Wachusett gave a ball to the Cape Town people, which proved to be a very successful, very fine affair. Guns were run forward, awnings spread, the quarter-deck hung round with flags, and in short, transformed into a very good and tastefully decorated ball room. At dark the deck was illuminated, and before seven o'clock the guests had all arrived and the dancing commenced. I cannot speak very highly of the band, but the music that they discoursed was much better than would be expected from their appearance. There were twenty-six ladies present, about the same number of civilians, three or four English officers, and a few of the Hartford's, beside our own. When the dancing commenced aft, sets were also formed among the men forward. All went on nicely for a time, but too frequent visits to the decanters set out on the ward-room tables and free of access to all, helped along by sundry flasks of " Cape smoke," brought off from shore, at length began to take effect, and then the "*ruxions*" commenced. Several not satisfied with dancing forward, must go aft to dance with the ladies. Being refused by these a disturbance was made, but they were soon confined, and with a few slight exceptions, the ball passed off very quietly and very pleasantly, and I think gave perfect satisfaction to all.

Friday, November 10th, another was added to the number of those who have bid home and friends "good-bye" forever. James Ryan, captain of the forecastle, died that day, after a painful and lingering illness. He was buried on shore here the following Sunday with military honors. He was a thorough seaman, a good shipmate, and well liked by both officers and men. He was about thirty years of age, a native of New Bedford, Massachusetts, and it is said, leaves no family.

While we were lying at Rio the master-at-arms, and one or two others, accused the yeoman to the executive officer of having a candle lighted in his room until late one night, and, at the same time, the yeoman was drunk, having come off from shore about two hours previous. Accordingly he was disrated and put on deck as a landsman. After this, he grew morose, down-hearted, and, as some would have it, "out of his head." One day, when ashore in a boat, he deserted. Just before leaving Rio he returned, and in the most pitiable plight; barefooted and bareheaded, clothed in rags, half starved, and without a cent in his pocket. A few days after he came on board, his feet commenced paining him, and showing them to an old sailor, who had spent several years in Brazil, he was asked where he had been while ashore. He answered, "To the mines." The man then told him that he had got "jiggers," or chegers, in his feet from going barefoot on the sand, and unless they were taken out they would multiply indefinitely, and eventually cause his death. So to work he went and cut out all that were visible, and so continued day after day, until they were all gone. The jiggers bear a striking resemblance to the small maggots sometimes found in cheese. From that time he suffered almost untold torments, being confined in the brig and sweat-boxes, having his head shaved and blistered, and every conceivable indignity heaped upon him, alike by officer and man. A day or two ago a gentleman came off from shore and inquired for him. After a few moments' conversation with him, he went to the Captain and by paying the amount that he was indebted to the ship procured his discharge and took him on shore; and I, with a few others, was glad that at last he was free from his tormentors. I thought at the time, and have since been convinced that the master-at-arms himself lit the candle in his room when the yeoman was asleep, so as to get him reduced, and get some one of his friends appointed in his place. In this undertaking he succeeded but too well.

I have narrated this circumstance to you, my dear R., in order that you may see what men there are in the navy, and to what extent the jealousies and envyings of men will sometimes carry them, trampling under foot every feeling or sense of honor, respect, or pity. This was done, too, against a ship mate, who ought in these respects to be second only to relatives and friends.

The morning of the same day that the ball took place, the U. S. S. Hartford came into port bearing the flag of Rear Admiral Henry H. Bell, and now on her way to join the Asiatic squadron, over which she is to be flag-ship. I have heard that the Admiral is not very much pleased with our long stay at Rio and Cape Town, and that we had not joined the squadron on the station ere this. His first order was that we should be ready for sea in twenty-four hours; but he afterwards extended the time to six days, so that to-morrow we expect to leave here. The Hartford is one of the class designated as "second-rates," of something over 1,800 tons burden, ship-rigged and carrying a battery of twenty-one heavy guns. Everything about her looks like a man-of-war, a long, low, black hull, a beautiful model, and something about her spars truly majestic. I intended to have visited her, but had the afternoon watch on visiting day, and so could not go very well. .

To-day has been the most lovely one that we have had in a long, long time. It has not been without clouds, but what there were, were light, airy things which seemed to enhance instead of detracting from the beauteousness of the day. A day it has been on which a person could sit for hours, watching the clouds, and building castles in the air, resigning for a time all the cares and anxieties of the present, and in perfect happiness and contentment, residing in those castles which his imagination has constructed. It has been said "perfect happiness is not to be found in this world," but as I sat this afternoon in the gangway, and watched those light, fleecy clouds as they passed overhead in their rapid flight, meanwhile building a magnificent castle, of which a some one was to be the chief garniture, I experienced what I call almost perfect happiness. Yes, methinks the happiness I then felt might be called "perfect" with more propriety than can two-thirds of that which passes undisputed for such. I was disturbed in my castle building by the announcement that supper was ready, so forthwith I had to descend from my lofty elevation to a bowl of coffee and ———— common place words and thoughts. I was not a little inclined to be provoked at the interruption, and exclaim with Ecclesiastes, "Behold, everything is vanity and vexation of spirit." I am glad that to-morrow we start again on our way to China.

LETTER XII.

U. S. S. WACHUSETT, Batavia, Java,
January 26, 1866.

MY DEAR R.:

Coffee and spices! In my childish thoughts the name of Java was always associated with coffee, while her sister islands were similarly suggestive of spices of various kinds. The fact may perhaps be accounted for by the close study which I was wont to bestow upon certain gaily colored labels which decorated packages of these articles.

In mentioning these islands a writer has remarked that "Bishop Heber's beautiful missionary hymn has so associated the fragrance of spices and poesy with these islands, that one feels reluctant to break the bonds of genius which have thus bound them together;" but true it is, the "spicy breezes" are wafted only by the poet's imagination.

My last letter left us at Cape Town. When I went on deck at six bells the following morning, I found that we were under way and under steam alone, following the lead of the Hartford, steaming out to sea.

> "Through ocean's perils, storms, and unknown waters,
> Speed we to Asia."

We had to keep slackening our speed to avoid running into the Hartford, but as soon as we were clear of the land, stopped steaming, and made all sail; then matters changed. She carries more than double the amount of sail that we do, her propeller trices up, and she can sail almost as fast again as we can. She lowered her topsails two or three times, for us to come up, but a little before dark she hoisted them up, and lowered them for us no more. The next morning she was out of sight and we have not seen her since. She arrived here about fourteen days before we did, and after remaining about a week, started for Hong Kong, the Admiral having concluded that we were not coming to Batavia.

Shortly after leaving Cape Town we had our second court-martial; this time, for theft. The court acquitted the prisoner of the charge, and scarcely one in the ship believed him to be guilty of the crime of which he was accused, although the missing article was found in his bag. Stealing is one of the worst crimes that can be committed on board ship; for, where there are so many, in such close connection with one another, and with so little room that we can call our own, clothes, valuables, and money even are often placed within the reach of a would-be thief. I have noticed one good thing in this respect, in this ship's company, that when any person has been detected taking anything not his own, let it be ever so trivial, or from whoever taken, one and all have made it their province to bring the affair before the proper authorities. By them all such acts have been severely punished. These stringent measures have been attended by the best results, and it is now no unusual thing to see money publicly placed in some one's ditty box, and then the box left for days unlocked about the decks; and very seldom is a man heard to complain that he has lost anything.

On this passage T—— and I had a very narrow escape from death. While standing in the gangway and talking together, one of the men who was working aloft at the time, carelessly let fall a heavy marline spike, which passed close to my face and buried three inches of itself in the deck. Scarcely a second before that time, I was standing in that exact spot, and had been moved back by the roll of the ship. I must confess I was a trifle frightened when I considered what a narrow escape I had had, and what would have been the consequences had the spike struck me. We can never be

6*

too thankful to Him who holds us in the hollow of his hand, and preserves us from the many dangers which constantly surround us, and this too, when we so richly deserve his displeasure.

One day the Surgeon knocked one of the little monkeys which we got in the Cape Verd's overboard for some mischievous prank which it had been playing upon him. It was interesting to note the expressions of the old sailors at this conduct. They consider it a great crime to maltreat any animal, thinking that storms, head winds, and everything that is bad result from such treatment. So when the monkey was thrown overboard that evening, they were loud and deep in their imprecations against Dr. King, and prophesied a storm before many days. Sure enough, the very next night, about midnight, the wind rapidly increased in force, and in less than an hour it was blowing quite a gale. This lasted seven or eight hours. Fortunately, we took in the to'gallant sails, and fore and aft sails, and reefed topsails in time, else the consequences might have been quite serious. As it was, not much damage was done, only a few rents in the sails, ditty-boxes capsized, and the decks flooded a few times. This circumstance, of course, strengthened their superstitious belief. As I am speaking about sailor's superstitions, I will make mention of one or two other matters which have come under my notice. When we were off the Cape there was a great number of birds around the ship which are called " Cape Pigeons." Several of the officers amused themselves by catching these birds with a hook and line, a bit of bread being attached, for bait. Several old sailors stood watching the proceedings, growling and swearing about the deed, and prophesying all sorts of evil, that would result therefrom. But, at last, when one of the officers proposed killing some of the pigeons, and stuffing them to preserve for curiosities, they could contain themselves no longer, and went to the "mast" and requested Mr. Philip to put a stop to the proceedings, which he laughingly promised that he would do. Nothing will provoke an old sailor quicker than to commence to whistle near him. He will tell you that it will bring head wind and unfavorable weather.

But we had some fishing which no one disapproved of, and that was in catching porpoises, or sea-hogs as they are sometimes called. We caught several on the passage, and an agreeable change we found them, after having salt food so long. In appearance and flavor their flesh bears a close resemblance to veal. They are so large that one made two meals for the whole ship's company.

The day before Christmas the crew had double rations of whatever they wished served out to them, and the cooks were busy from morning until night in making preparations for the Christmas dinner. After hammocks were piped down, they were piled up upon the hatches, and the berth-deck brilliantly illuminated. The band were then collected and, seated upon the hammocks, they discoursed sweet and *feet-stirring* music to all that were of a dancing turn. This together with singing and other sports, was kept up until nearly midnight, one and all enjoying themselves "hugely." I did not feel very well, and consequently did not join in the festivities to any great extent; still, I enjoyed myself very much in looking at the rest. Christmas was made as much of a holiday as possible, having no quarters, and no more work than was absolutely necessary, with the privilege of smoking all day, which is granted only on rare occasions. Then the dinner! It was the best we had tasted for many a day, and much better than I thought it was possible to get up under the circumstances. There were plumb puddings, chicken pies, mince pies, cakes, and any amount of ale and wines which were sent forward from the ward-room.

This Christmas, however, was far from being a merry one to me; for up forward in the sick bay, swinging in a cot, I was tossing restlessly about, with the pains of scarlet fever.

Up to this time the holidays had been associated in my mind with snow, sleigh rides, and certain frozen ears and noses, but this Christmas will ever be remembered in connection with sweltering heat, as the thermometer stood in the neighborhood of 100° above zero on that day and for many days afterwards. During this time the wind entirely died away, so that it was almost suffocating on the berth deck.

It is unpleasant to be sick under the best of circumstances, but how much more sad it is thus to be far away from home, in a foreign country, or in foreign waters, amongst strangers, with no one caring whether you live or not; more than that, "I hope the poor fellow will get well, but I am afraid he never will;"—a passing remark from some Jack Tar, the subject of the remark speedily dropping from his mind. Sick at sea! No one can know the force of those words, unless he has had the experience, has been sick on a man-of-war, out at sea, where those many little delicacies that a sick man naturally craves cannot be obtained, without the comforting and tender care of mother, sister, or some female friend, and surrounded by the discomforts and unpleasantnesses which are hard enough to bear when one is in the best of health. But I would not have you think that I was neglected or treated ill, for that was by no means the case. There was not one of the crew that would not have done almost anything to have eased my pain or added to my comfort—more, perhaps, than they would have done for many others. The truth is, a sailor in a little while learns to look upon sickness and death with contempt, or utter indifference, and to expect the sickness and death of some near friend as a matter of course. I am sure that I have no reason to complain, for I had as good and tender care as could be expected under the circumstances; yes, and far better. It was then that I learned the value of the friendship of my associates, for they did everything within their power to alleviate my sufferings and make me comfortable. Often they sat for hours beside my cot and fanned me when I was feverish, or talked and read to me when I was restless. Yes, notwithstanding my strong determination to get well, I fear that I should not have done so had it not been for the constant and devoted care of these two friends.

From December 28th, 1865, until January 10th, 1866, we lay becalmed, the sails flapping idly against the masts, the sea as smooth as glass, and the vessel hardly logging a knot in twenty-four hours. Occasionally, a little puff would spring up, but would not last long. We had beautiful weather, but oh! so tiresome. There we lay, day after day, in the same place, with plenty of coal in our bunkers, a smooth sea, through which our engines could urge us without impediment; our port only three or four days off! The same daily routine: rise at six bells, seven o'clock—breakfast at eight—quarters for inspection at two bells, nine o'clock—this lasts ten minutes; then the Doctor prescribes, and every one goes to what he has to do, some to duty, and others to reading, sleeping, smoking, or walking the deck. There is no further break in the day until the master gets an observation of the sun at meridian, when he tells us that it is twelve o'clock, and what the latitude is, and the men are whistled or piped to dinner. Then they read, sleep, and walk again, until four o'clock, when they are piped to supper; after which the same routine over again until the drum beats for evening quarters. The Doctor does the evening prescribing—we have our hammocks piped down, and then smoke and spin yarns until eight o'clock, which puts out the smoking lamp and lights on the berth-deck; nine o'clock extinguishes those in the steerage, ten those in the ward-room, and the day is done. These, with a daily exercise of the divisions at the battery, or with small arms, and twice a week general quarters for a grand battle exercise, make up the routine of our existence. This is occupation enough—leisure enough—but, as it has been aptly expressed, "'The occupation is an unvarying form, the leisure, a weary interval of unvarying pursuits. No freshness, no change, no novelty."

"Lovely seemed any object that should sweep
Away the vast, salt, dread, eternal deep."

There we lay upon its bosom in a calm—the winds lulled, the engines and engineers rusting, the occupation of firemen and coal-heavers gone. We pity and mourn for everything and everybody, but, most of all, we mourn for our pent up selves, and grieve that we are not rich enough to refund to the National Treasury the cost of the coal which would take us into port.

"Lay aft all the firemen and coal-heavers and hoist the smoke-stack!" was almost the first word that I heard passed by the boatswain's mates, Friday morning, January 10th.

"We are going to get up steam at last," cried out many voices as they started up in pleased emotion, from listlessly pursuing some occupation, or from dozing, apparently infused with new life.

Early in the forenoon, we sighted a high point of land off our starboard bow, which we subsequently discovered to be Java Head, the most western extremity of the island. About an hour later, we sighted land on our port bow, the most southern point of the island of Sumatra. At noon we were between these two islands—in the entrance of the straits of Sunda. The straits at this point are from sixty to seventy miles in width. They kept narrowing gradually as we proceeded, until about five o'clock we were off Anjer Point, the narrowest part, and there they are about fifteen miles in width. Anjer Point has attained a world-wide celebrity,—not on account of any commercial importance, or from the size or beauty of the place, but from the fact that all the vessels trading with China, Japan, and the many islands of the eastern and southeastern coasts of Asia, pass through these straits within sight of the Point, and almost invariably stop there on their passages to and fro. From there a telegraph extends to Aden, and a list of the vessels sighted at Anjer Point is telegraphed to Aden, and from there to Europe, and the whole commercial world. When we were off there a bumboat came alongside, from which we procured some fruits. We did not stop, but proceeded about ten miles farther and then came to anchor for the night in a beautiful little bay, at the northeastern extremities of the straits. It was so dark that night that I was unable to get a good view of the surrounding country, and we left there the next morning before daylight for Batavia. The distance, about sixty miles, was steamed in a little more than six hours, and about noon we dropped anchor off Batavia, about three miles from the shore—the shallowness of the water preventing our nearer approach. It appeared a quiet, lovely spot to us, and there were but few vessels at the anchorage.

As we ran in, however, the harbor became suddenly alive. A fleet of canoes, thronged with bronzed Javanese, announced their rapid approach to us by the confused clattering of many voices. The boats were ticklish, wabbling affairs, but managed with great skill and dexterity. From the boats our glance was turned to the chattering, scolding, jabbering, quarrelling human beings on board of them.

Their costume is attractive, and has been thus described: at Galle a little book has been published called " A Guide to Galle," in which, alluding to a portion of these countries, it says: "The rainy season extends from December to May, and from May to December it is wet." And so, in describing the costume of our new acquaintances, one might say, that "from the head to the hips there are no clothes, and from the hips to the heels, about the same." Their principal article of clothing is a white or bright colored "come-boy"—a shawl folded as a petticoat about the waist, and worn alike by the more respectable of both sexes. The women, however, wear a short jacket dropping over the breasts, leaving the skin bare between that and the "come-boy." The lords of the lower class indulge in no such waste of clothing, but are content with that amount of clothing which is a bare sufficiency. All have black teeth and bloody mouths, from the use of the betel-nut mixed with lime and pepper leaves. From the bumboats which came alongside, we got an abundance of excellent oranges, bananas, pineapples, cocoanuts, and a great variety of other fruits peculiar to a tropical clime.

Well, I have been speaking about some of the people and usages of Batavia, without getting into the place. I will commence with the harbor; very wide and spacious, water shallow a long distance out from shore, and scarcely anywhere going beyond fifteen fathoms. An old Dutch line of battle ship is the only man-of-war in the harbor except the Wachusett. Some few steamers, and fifty or sixty merchant vessels, make up the rest of the shipping. Seaward is quite a large island, named Onrust, on which stands the navy-yard, coal wharves, dry-dock, and a pretty little village, all guarded by a heavy Dutch frigate,—Java belonging to the Dutch.

The town—where is it? Tall cocoa-nut trees, here, and there, and everywhere, waving their graceful branches in the breeze, and promising to sea-parched throats the sweet refreshment of the sparkling water of the young fruit—a promise which is fully kept—are the most that we can see. Some three miles distant lies the shore, and there stands the tall form of a light-house, at the entrance of the canal which leads up to the city—some two miles farther. Hidden behind these groves are the houses, churches, shops, hotels, and clean, quiet streets, of a population of one hundred and thirty thousand—Dutch, Germans, English, Americans, Chinese, Javanese—and a mixture of all—Protestant, Catholic, Mohammedan, and Buddhist.

Batavia is the seat of Government of the Dutch settlements in the East Indies. It is of great importance in the commercial world, being the emporium in which all the merchandise of the Dutch company in India is deposited; so that here you may find the various spices from the Molucca or Spice Islands; gold dust and diamonds from Borneo; coffee and pepper from Celebes and Sumatra; bees-wax and dye-woods from Timor; tin from Banca, etc. But you must accompany me in a ramble ashore if you would learn more about the place. I have been several times, and have always enjoyed myself very much. We should liked to have had you with us when I went about a week ago, accompanied by a friend. The wind was favorable, so that the men were spared the labor of pulling the boat until we arrived within about a mile from the city, where a beautiful cocoa-nut grove shut off the wind, and near the edge of which grove a second light house stands. The canal, which I mentioned as leading from the harbor to the city, is about one hundred feet wide and deep enough to float large schooners. From the second light-house to the city, it is completely thronged with boats and small craft of almost every Eastern nation. Chinese junks with their confused mass of red painted wood-work, with great goggle eyes painted on their bows, East India boats, close by a half European half native built schooner on which floats a red flag with a white elephant painted on it—the emblem of Siam, whilst every intervening nook is filled with the small boats of the natives.

Landing, we found ourselves in a high-walled enclosure containing about one hundred acres—the government grounds. Within are the store-houses, forts, barracks, a hotel, ship-chandlery, and a few private residences. Several carriages were in waiting near the landing, and we had barely left the boat before some native had us by the button-hole, persuading us to take one. This of course we did, as no one thinks of going any distance on foot in Batavia. Could you but have seen us, you, with your notions of traveling, would have thought that we were supporting considerable style for persons in our position—a comfortable two-seated carriage, drawn by two small, but spirited little ponies, with a driver, footman, and interpreter, as attendants—but the whole establishment, with attendants, cost us only three guilders—one dollar and twenty cents—for the whole day. After leaving the government grounds, we found ourselves in a small park, from which branched off two streets. We took the one on the right, and a few minutes' drive brought us to the native quarter. Here we alighted, bidding the driver to wait for us, thinking that we could the better pursue our explorations on foot. A short ramble about showed us that the streets were very narrow, and very dirty; the houses, for the most part small, filthy, and very close together; and the whole densely populated. In the shops, the principal articles for sale are, fancy straw baskets and boxes, coarse articles of lacquered-ware, grass-cloths, &c. The better portion is occupied by Chinese, and these for the most part are money-changers, bankers, and merchants. Reëntering our carriage and returning to the park, we took the road to the left, over a smooth wide street, shaded on either hand by elm, locust, and other trees. And how very different is this quarter of the city from that we had just left! Here are elegant mansions, situated in the most beautiful grounds, and fairly embowered with trees,—sufficiently removed from each other to satisfy one whether he prefer the city or country. And this street extends nearly five miles. On it are some seven or eight hotels, and two or three churches. Running parallel with the principal streets, are canals, on which can be seen the magnificently decorated barge of the wealthy, floating side by side with the rude boat of the native. Fruits of every kind peculiar to this clime, can be seen, growing not only in private gardens, but also by the roadside.

Not to visit the Botanical and Zoological Gardens, is not to visit Batavia. Fully impressed with the truth, and with the importance of such a visit, after we had had dinner, we directed the driver to turn the horses' heads thitherward. The gardens are some two miles from the upper extremity of the city, but it is certainly one of the most enchanting drives in the world. Our ponies were uncommonly smart, the roads smooth and level, and we reclined in the carriage in the greatest ease and comfort imaginable, enjoying the ride, enjoying the fruits which we obtained, and above all, enjoying the beautiful scenery, which is unrivaled in this part of the world.

An hour's drive brought us to the Gardens. At the entrance are directions for visitors, in Dutch, German, French, Spanish, and English. The admission fee, one guilder each, we paid and then entered. The Gardens comprise about one hundred acres, beautifully laid out in charming walks and drives, and containing specimens of the different species of plants, trees, shrubs, birds, and animals, peculiar to this part of the world.

After entering, one first passes through the portion devoted to the various plants and flowers with the many shrubs surrounding the beds, and lining the walks. To the right of this are the cages containing lions, tigers, panthers, leopards, and other wild beasts, while still further on are the cages of the feathered tribe, from the tiny sparrow to the huge bird called the East India Ostrich. Some birds of paradise attracted our attention, and drew forth much admiration by their gorgeous plumage. Near the center of the gardens is a large, magnificent building containing but one principal room, magnificently, yet withal tastefully decorated, and chiefly used as a banqueting hall. Beyond this building is the shed and yard of the elephant. With him we amused ourselves a while, by giving him fruits. Close by is the collection of monkeys, every variety and of every size, from the wee little thing no larger than a rat, to the large, fierce, ugly baboon as large as a good sized calf. A lovely little grotto, which a number of the little ones had, interested and amused us very much. Near these were the parrots, hundreds of them of every variety of size, form, and hue. Tastefully interspersed over all the grounds lining the walks and drives, are trees of every species. Back of all is a wild and picturesque glen, the more noticeable there, because there are scarcely any other irregularities in the surface for a long distance around. What a glorious place this would make for excursions and pic-nic parties! After spending about three hours in examining the many interesting objects we picked some flowers and returned, much pleased with our visit to the gardens, and well assured in our own minds that if we had not visited them we had not seen Batavia.

A few mornings ago we noticed the flag on the American bark George Green hoisted with the Union down—the signal of distress. A few minutes later a boat came to us from her reporting that the crew refused to "turn to." The second cutter with an armed crew, Mr. Grover, Mr. Kelly, Corporal A—— and myself with our side arms were sent aboard of her. We found the crew in the forecastle, and from one of them I learned the cause of their dissatisfaction. The Captain, with whom they shipped, died just before the vessel arrived here, and then the first mate assumed command. He said that the Captain was a kind, humane man, and beloved by all the crew ; but that the mate, the present captain, was cruel and severe, and hated as much as the former was beloved. For this reason they wanted to be paid off and discharged, which the mate refuses to do. They were all called aft to muster, and, after speaking a few words to them, Mr. Grover asked if they would "turn to." Fifteen out of the crew of seventeen refused, and were taken by us aboard the Wachusett. Three of them have shipped with us, and the remainder have been sent aboard the Dutch frigate, there to await the disposal of the American consul.

Monday, January 22d, we weighed anchor and steamed up to the island of Onrust, and hauled alongside the coal wharf. The next day while the crew were engaged in coaling ship,

A—— and I went out for a stroll about the island, or islands, there being two of them. The one on which is the coal wharf is small, being only about an eighth of a mile in circumference. A wide channel, which is crossed by a rope ferry, intervenes between this and Onrust. Onrust is a lovely island about two miles in circumference, and is for the most part covered with groves of orange, banana, and cocoa-nut trees. The inhabitants of the latter did not give a good name to the crew of the Hartford, saying that when she was up there for coal, some of the crew went ashore, broke into a store, and destroyed and stole goods to the value of several hundred dollars. I have no doubt that it was all done by three or four unprincipled scamps who had neither any respect for themselves, nor for the good name of their shipmates. And thus it is, three or four such individuals will frequently, by their lawless deeds, injure the reputation of as many hundreds of honest, honorable individuals, with whom they are associated. Our search along the beach for shells was rewarded by finding several rare and curious specimens. After having taken in over two hundred tons of coal in about five hours, we returned to our old anchorage off Batavia, that afternoon.

Yesterday the crew were busily employed in getting in stores, both public and private, and to-morrow we expect to start for China. On some accounts I am sorry that we are to leave Batavia so soon, for our stay here has been a very pleasant one. Although the weather has been rather too warm for comfort, there is ever a good, cool, sea-breeze, which enables us to support the heat without experiencing much suffering. Fruits of all kinds are abundant, good, and very cheap. But then, on the other hand, I am anxious to get to China and once more be in communication with friends near and dear, which I have left behind, and from whom I have not heard in so long a time.

LETTER XIII.

U. S. S. WACHUSETT, Manilla, Luzon,
Philippine Isles, Feb. 27, 1866.

MY DEAR R.:

We left Batavia the following morning, after the date of my last letter, as I expected. We steamed along all that day and night, and following day, on a northerly course, the next night coming to anchor at the southern entrance of the Straits of Banca. The next morning at day-break we got under way and steamed through the Straits. In many places these are very narrow, the island of Banca on our starboard beam, and the island of Sumatra on our port, both being plainly visible. Islands of various sizes stud the Straits throughout, and on the whole our passage through them was a very pleasant one. January 31st, we crossed the line, but there was no such excitement over it as there was when we crossed it before. That same day we saw a water-spout some nine or ten miles away from us. In the distance it looked like a huge tunnel, with the nose downwards. It approached nearer and nearer us, and when about a mile distant, we fired a shot from the howitzer, and it instantly broke. For five minutes, the water fell upon us from it, as if we had been in a severe thunder storm. I tasted of the water, and was surprised to find that it was fresh, for I had always supposed that the water of which they were formed was drawn up from the sea. We saw another water-spout later in the evening, but it did not approach within six or seven miles of us.

Three days later we sighted the island of Borneo, along whose shores we sailed for three days, at times so close that we could observe human beings walking along the beach. In all that time we did not see the least sign of cultivation, nothing but high mountains and dense forests. Our object in sailing so close to the land was to find the Dutch island of Amboyna which we knew to be somewhere along the coast, but did not know the exact locality. Monday evening, February 5th, we thought that we had discovered it, and accordingly came to anchor some little distance off from the shore; but the next morning when we got under way, and approached nearer we discovered our mistake. Nevertheless, we came to anchor there, and some thoughts were entertained of having a boat expedition to the island. After lying about half an hour we again got under way, and steamed toward the mainland. Just before noon we again dropped anchor, in as secure and as lovely a little bay as I ever saw.

Not a boat nor vessel of any kind was in sight, nor on shore was there the least sign of civilization or inhabitant The surrounding country was mountainous and covered with forests and a thick growth of underbrush, everything wild and picturesque in the extreme. In the southeastern corner, a small river emptied itself into the harbor, from which, about half an hour after we anchored, three boats filled with natives, came into view and approached the ship, making signs that they were friendly. When about two boats' lengths distant, they stopped, evidently viewing us with a great deal of wonder and curiosity, and mingled with unmistakable signs of fear. After considerable coaxing we finally induced them to come alongside. They were all Malays, clothed in the garb of the lower class, showing that with them the fashions had not changed since the times of our first parents. They had a few green cocoa-nuts in their boats which they readily exchanged for hard bread and tobacco. Everything about the ship and ourselves was viewed with a great deal of wonder and curiosity by them, and I doubt very much if they had ever seen a ship or an European before. One of our crew, a Malay, tried to converse with them, but was unable, as they spoke a different dialect from his. After remaining on board a short time, they took their departure.

Sometime in the afternoon the second cutter and gig, with armed crews, several officers, and a number of the men—in which I was included—went ashore on an exploring expedition, and with some *faint* hopes of being able to find and bring on board some of the "wild men" to add to our stock of curiosities. We penetrated some two or three miles into the interior, but without finding the remotest signs of inhabitant more than the three or four huts near the beach, where resided those natives that visited us. By signs and by drawing a rude representation of an ox on the sand, Captain Townsend tried to make them understand that he would like to purchase one from them; but without making them comprehend what he wanted. Birds, somewhat resembling robins, were numerous, and not in the least shy of us. We shot several of them with our carbines. We picked up a few curious stones and shells on the beach, and returned to the ship taking off with us a little puppy, more resembling a bear than a dog, which we named "Borneo," after the name of the island. We remained there that night, getting under way at daylight the following morning.

That day we had our first target practice with small arms. The target was suspended from the fore yard arm, and we stood on the poop to fire at it. The distance was only about one hundred yards, but we found it a very difficult target to hit, on account of its swaying to and fro, and on account of the rolling and pitching of the ship. Not one out of every six shots fired hit it. The prize of two and a half dollars each, repaid two of us for dirtying *our* muskets.

Sunday we sighted some islands belonging to the Philippine Group, and during that and the following day we had a number of them in sight. On some, we saw several active volcanoes, which are very numerous in this group. Monday morning, we sighted the island of Luzon on which stands Manilla, our destination. In the evening we came to anchor just inside the entrance of Manilla Bay. This Bay is very large, being some ten or twelve miles in length by seven or eight in width, and would afford a secure anchorage for all the navies in the world. At each side of the entrance is a large island which narrows it down to less than a mile in width. At daylight we left our anchorage and after an hour's steaming we again came to anchor about a mile from the town. During the day the usual business of an arrival in port was gone through with, such as saluting the flag of the nation to which the port belongs, engaging a bumboat-man-compradore, washermen, &c.

Luzon, with the greater portion of the Philippine Group, belongs to Spain, whose domains here are said to extend over 50,000 square miles. Manilla, the capital of the Spanish Possessions, is situated at the northeastern extremity of the bay of the same name, on the southwestern side of the island of Luzon. It is a very ancient city, and contains a population of 140,000 inhabitants, according to the census of 1860. A large proportion of them are Malays. The remainder are, for the most part, Spaniards, with a sprinkling of Portuguese, Dutch, English, and Americans. The town is subject to earthquakes and was nearly destroyed by one three years ago.

But come, let us take a ramble on shore and examine everything of interest about the town. As we put foot on shore at the substantial and convenient jetty, we find ourselves in the midst of a picturesque crowd—Malays, Hindoos, Chinamen, Europeans; a mingling of bright colors, white and crimson predominating. The first noticed are the Chinamen, with all the head shaved but the crown and the hair from this depending in a long plait, or queue, to the ground, or wound in circles about the head. White or red striped petticoats or savongs fell from the waists of some

7

and a few more bright colored jackets, but many encumbered with no more clothing than would meet the demands of decency. We must not walk, so we go with a bright-eyed little native boy, (who speaks good English, and whom we have engaged as a guide,) to the stables and procure a carriage for which we pay two pesos, (two dollars,) for all day. First we will have a ride through the town for the *sake* of the ride, and then we will examine the many places of interest more minutely. The streets are wide and smooth, the carriage easy and commodious, the ponies smart and lively, the sights varied and interesting, and you cannot fail of enjoying the ride.

The houses are none of them very large or elegant in appearance, with the exception of a few in the eastern suburbs of the town, where the more wealthy and influential reside. There may be seen some elegant mansions situated in beautiful grounds. The houses of the main portion of the city are seldom more than one and one-half stories high, are built of brick, and have tiled roofs. About one-third of the town is in ruins, destroyed by the recent earthquake; but the inhabitants are now fast re-building it. The larger buildings suffered most, and consequently nearly all the churches were destroyed. Only one was left entirely uninjured. Two others escaped with only a small portion of the walls demolished. The falling of the bell from the steeple of one of them killed about twenty-five of those who had taken refuge in the church during the earthquake. "There," said the guide to me, pointing to a heap of ruins, "is where the hospital stood, which buried in its fall over five hundred of its inmates." The loss of life during the time of the earthquake is variously estimated at from two to ten thousand. A more definite number will probably never be known.

The town is divided into two unequal portions by a small river which runs through it from north to south. This is spanned by a fine bridge, which has a draw in it to allow vessels to pass up and down the river. That portion which is situated on the left bank is almost entirely included in the walls of a large fort, which is upwards of two miles in circumference. Within these walls are situated the residences and places of business of the greater portion of the European residents at Manilla, also the government buildings, the hospitals, principal churches, etc. Among the chief celebrities of Manilla are its cigar manufactories. To visit these a pass is required from the Governor. Fortunately, a number of us found sufficient favor in the eyes of a Spanish gentleman for him to interest himself in our behalf and procure the required pass, and with us paid a visit to the principal manufactory. There we saw every stage in the process of the manufacture of a cigar, from the dressing of the leaf, to the packing in boxes ready for exportation. Upwards of five thousand persons, of every age, sex, color, and nationality, are employed in these manufactories, besides there being a great variety of machinery made use of. The cigars here manufactured are in every respect equal to the best Havannas, and can be bought for $8.00 per thousand.

Among other places of interest, I paid a visit to the only Church which was left entirely uninjured by the earthquake. It was built upwards of two hundred years ago, and has successfully withstood the many earthquakes by which the city has since been visited. It is very rich in massive adornments of gold, silver, and precious stones. To the rear of the Church and attached to it, is a fine picture-gallery, containing many valuable fine old paintings by Michael Angelo and by two or three others of the first masters. An old monk shewed me about, and our only means of communication was by Latin. With what knowledge I had of the language, and with the assistance of a dictionary, aided by certain impressive shrugs and signs, we made out to understand each other very well. Upon leaving I made a present to the Church and received the old monk's blessing.

In front of this walled town is a fine water battery, and to the left is "La Plaza," a beautifully shaded park, with charming walks and drives, where on pleasant evenings can be seen the wealth, beauty, and fashion of Manilla, enjoying themselves *a l'espagnole*.

Now let us cross over the bridge and enter the native quarter of the city. We find dirty alley-ways for streets, which every few steps are constantly changing in direction,— the whole town laid out in the greatest possible irregularity. The houses are for the most part constructed by making a floor elevated some three or four feet from the ground, supported on stakes driven into the ground, and then a semicircular covering made of bamboo reeds and thatched with mats, straw, or leaves. Others have only the earth beaten hard for a floor. These huts have each but one room, which serves for kitchen, dining-room, bed-room, and all, and where reside from five to thirty persons. Greater filth, and more squalid misery, accompanied by fewer redeeming traits, are seldom to be found.

I expatiated somewhat largely upon the virtues of the coffee which is to be obtained in Rio Janeiro; and I might do the same upon the chocolate which is to be procured in Manilla. I have drank chocolate many times, but I never could say that I really loved it until I drank it here, and I never go ashore without making two or three calls at the stand of an old Spanish lady who *knows* how to make delicious chocolate.

Thursday, February 22d, we "dressed ship" and fired a salute of twenty-one guns at noon, in honor of Washington's birth-day. Out of courtesy to us, nearly all of the vessels in the harbor also "dressed ship."

My collection of curiosities has received a valuable addition in the many rare and curious shells which I have obtained here. I have also procured a few cloths, and fancy articles in grass, and a number of new coins.

The past few days have been spent by the crew in "coaling ship and taking in stores," and to-morrow, I hear, we are to leave this place and not anchor again until we reach China. A few days ago we invalided one of our men home in a clipper bound for New York. The Captain has been on shore sick nearly all the time that we have been here, and for a time, it was rumored that he would not recover; but this morning he came on board, rejoicing us all by his comparatively healthy appearance.

A little after daylight this morning three Malays were garrotted on shore, for the murder of a policeman a few days ago. The place of execution was in front of the fort and in full view of the ship. The victims were seated upon a scaffold erected for the purpose, and chained to their seats. A leathern thong was passed around the neck of each one, and then twisted tight until the breathing was stopped and death ensued. As is usual upon such occasions, the execution was witnessed by many thousand spectators. Garroting is a favorite mode of execution with the Spaniards. The executioner has it in his power to end the sufferings of his victim by an almost instantaneous twist of the thong, or he may prolong the sufferings by tightening and loosening the twist. I am told that it is customary with those who are thus to suffer death, to bribe the executioner to release them from suffering as speedily as possible.

LETTER XIV.

U. S. S. WACHUSETT, Hong Kong, China,
March 5, 1866.

MY DEAR R.:

At last we have arrived on the station; have reached China—just one year from the day when we steamed down Boston Harbor, bidding home, friends, and country "goodbye" for a time, and started upon this long cruise. It has been a year full of interest and event to me; more so than any similar period of my life. In this year I have traveled over twenty thousand miles, visited twelve different ports, seen the manners and customs of many different people, and here the close finds me seventeen thousand miles from home by the nearest sailable route, among strangers, without an old friend or acquaintance near me, or even a good opportunity of hearing from those whom I have left behind.

About eight o'clock on Friday morning, January 28th, we heard the welcome words, "All hands up anchor," and in less than fifteen minutes the anchor was up and we steaming down Manilla Bay. One and all worked with a will then, anxious to get to Hong Kong as soon as possible; for there awaited us our letters of one year's accumulation, with all the incidents of joy and sorrow which, in a changing world, might in that time occur. These furnished the principal theme of conversation during the entire passage, and were seldom absent from our thoughts. With what anxieties, hopes, and fears, did we look forward to the time when we should arrive at Hong Kong, obtain our letters, and receive news from our friends at home! But I will not anticipate. Our passage was a remarkably pleasant one, course northwesterly; winds favorable, but light; sea smooth, and we steaming along pleasantly at the rate of seven or eight knots per hour.

At nine o'clock yesterday morning, we sighted the high, mountainous island of Hong Kong, with the numerous small, jagged, rocky islands near it; and at four o'clock in the afternoon we entered the northeastern passage to the harbor of Hong Kong. After proceeding about half a mile in this passage we came to anchor in as quiet and lovely, as it was secure, bight, some five or six miles distant from the city.

Our reason for anchoring, some asserted, was because it was wanted to clean and polish up the vessel, so as to present a fine appearance when we should go into port; whilst others would have it, that it was done so as to be exactly one year in reaching the station from the day of our departure from the States. For my part, I think that both of the explanations are correct. To guard against a surprise, or any attack by the many pirates which infest these waters, the lookouts went on last night with loaded carbines, and twenty rounds of ammunition.

Early this morning it commenced raining, and has continued to rain steadily all day. Yet, notwithstanding this, all hands were called early, and great preparations made for going into port. At eight o'clock we weighed anchor, and after steaming about fifteen minutes, the city of Hong Kong, and the harbor with its immense amount of shipping and many thousand junks and sampans, burst upon our view. Half an hour's steaming brought us along side the Hartford, but when we signaled to know if we should come to anchor, a negative was returned; the Admiral seemingly displeased at our long delay in getting on the station. An intense excitement was created in the ship when it became rumored that we were not to be permitted to come to anchor, but had to go out for a week's cruise as a punishment for our long delay. Captain Townsend, however, with his customary *nonchalance*, ordered his gig to be called away and manned, and said that he would go on board the Hartford and see what could be done with the Admiral. His mission was successful, for in a few minutes the signal was made for us to come to anchor, which we did, and moored ship.

Our first contact with the Chinese introduced us to their indomitable energy, perseverance, and industry. An enterprising Chinese pilot had picked us up far out at sea, and another had been on the lookout for us since the arrival of the Hartford, about a month ago, and as we ran up to our anchorage we encountered a Chinese invasion. A fleet of boats, propelled by mat sails, by sculls and oars, bore down upon us. The principal object of competition was to get the office of compradore—the privilege of supplying the various messes,—and of being the ship's bumboat. Then there were tailors, shoemakers, painters, washermen and washerwomen, peddlars, besides aspirants for the honorable position of "fast boat"— the boat which, being the home and dwelling-place of the proprietor and family—wives and children—is employed instead of the ship's boats in taking us to and from the shore.

As one has so aptly described an arrival at Hong Kong, "on came the competing fleet, regardless, apparently, of being run down by us. We were not then familiar with the dexterity with which these boats are managed—being suddenly turned and their course changed just as they appear to be running upon an object. Stimulated by the prize before them and confident of their skill, they paid no attention to the orders to keep off, if, indeed, these could be heard above the clamor and screeching of their own tin-toned throats. Some of the greater tacticians had small American ensigns flying, as if they thought that by so doing they would be more favorably noticed by us.

"Up alongside the ship they dashed, and despite their skill, not without some damages to their bamboo spars. Men and women clambered up the ship's sides, and thrust forth bundles of certificates from their former patrons in our service, and at the same time assuring us that he or she was No. 1, in their respective vocations."

A portion of these boats, those usually employed to carry passengers, are European-built gigs, have canvass sails, and are also propelled by from two to six oars. Of this class is "our fast boat." The *sampans*—Chinese-built boats—are rude, clumsy-looking affairs. In shape they are triangular, with the apex cut off, and that at the bow. The stern is the most elevated. About two-thirds of the after portion is roofed over with two or three matting semicircles. They are propelled by sculls. In these, families of ten or twelve are sometimes seen.

Judging by looks, size, or dress, a newly arrived foreigner can barely distinguish the males from the females; both look and dress so nearly alike. Wide, loose, nankeen pants and sacks, sometimes of a dark, and sometimes of a light-blue color, the bottoms of the pants encased by the stockings reaching nearly to the knees, and secured by fancy-colored garters; the shoes, thick-soled, flat-bottomed, turning up a little at the toes, with tops made of silk or velvet. In stature the Chinese are comparatively short, with thick-set bodies; complexion, of a light-yellowish cast; features, closely resembling those of a negro; hair and eyes black as jet, and teeth remarkably regular and white. The males have the head shaven, except a circular spot on the crown, about three inches in diameter, where the hair is allowed to grow long. This is plaited, and with the addition of some dark-colored silk, the "tail," or queue, reaches nearly as low as the heels. On their heads they wear close fitting skull-caps, made of eight sections, with a colored knot on the top. The women do not shave the head, but wear the hair done up on a frame somewhat resembling the handle of a large plane, at the back of the head, and adorned with pins, tassels, and other ornaments.

7*

This is the dress of the middle class—merchants, tailors, and those of similar occupations. The lower class—boatmen and coolies, or laborers, have a deep, dark bronzed complexion, seldom wear any covering on their heads or feet, and wear clothes made of some coarse cotton material.

Further particulars of their dress, manners, and customs, I will give you, as soon as they are brought to my notice. A few words now about the Harbor and City of Hong Kong, as far as I have been able to see for myself, and learn from reliable sources.

The harbor is an irregular, oblong sheet of water, some six or seven miles in length, and from one to four in width, lying between the island of Hong Kong and the mainland· It is said to afford a very secure anchorage for shipping, except during the typhoon season, when vessels are compelled to anchor for safety in the large bight on the western side of the harbor, and which from this fact is called "Typhoon Bay."

The harbor is at present filled with men-of-war, steamers, and merchant vessels of almost every nationality, impressing one with the great commercial importance of the city. Besides these, there are many thousand Chinese junks and smaller craft.

The island of Hong Kong, or Hinkeang, (i. e., The Fragrant Streams,) is nine miles long, eight broad, and twenty-six in circumference, presenting an exceedingly uneven surface, consisting for the most part of ranges of barren hills, with narrow intervals, and a little level beach land. The highest peak, Victoria Mt., is 1,825 feet high. Probably not one-twentieth part of the island is available for agricultural purposes. It was ceded to the Crown of England in 1842. The town of Victoria lies on the north side of the island. On the south side are the government buildings and dry-dock, the whole called Aberdeen.

"The city of Victoria may be said to extend from Happy

Valley on the extreme east, to West Point on the extreme west, a winding road of about three miles in length, the Queen's Road, skirting the bay and winding along the foot of the mountains washed by the waters of the bay. The mass of the city lies within the central two miles of this space, straggling settlements linking in the remainder. Indeed, nearly a mile beyond the eastern point I have named, separated from the rest of the city, are the extensive buildings of the great commercial firm of Jardine & Co., which seems to be an independent, though allied sovereignty, firing its morning and evening gun, keeping its own police force, and running an individual line of steamers to the East Indies. After the city begins to leave the Queen's Road with any lateral aspirations, there is nothing for it but to climb the mountain's side; and so it does, with angular, dark-green, granite-knobbed mountain spurs, along which wind terraced roads, fringed with shrubbery and gardens. High up on these elevations stand the pretentious palaces of the successful merchants and high officials. Also, standing out to catch the breeze, with the union jack flying in its front, is the yellow-washed castle of the Governor; the residence of the Bishop of Victoria, and the Cathedral, with fortifications and military quarters, lying to the right and front. Over all, from an elevation of eighteen hundred and twenty-five feet, looks down Victoria peak, on city and bay, man-of war and merchant vessel, sampan, lorcha, and junk; and on its summit is the signal-station." There, also, is mounted a gun, the firing of which announces that a mail-steamer has been sighted. On the opposite, or Kowloon shore, stand the military store-houses, prisons, and hospitals. When the city of Victoria is lighted up at night, it presents a beautiful sight, and is said to bear a striking resemblance to Gibraltar.

Through the courtesy of the house of Thomas Hunt & Co., the accumulated letters of a year's absence from home were sent on board soon after we anchored, and then the hopes, fears, and anxieties of that time were to be realized or dispelled. Only the later portion of our mail, however, was received, the earlier having gone to Macao, and not yet sent down. From that which we did receive we could gather what we were most anxious to learn—the welfare of our friends at home. I was rejoiced to ascertain that my own were all in good health, as were most of my old acquaintances. Some few births, marriages, and deaths, were made mention of, but none of them of special interest with the exception of a little brother added to the family circle at home. What a glorious feast I had in perusing the bundle of letters which fell to my share! And how happy I felt after I had read them all, and had every doubt, fear, and anxiety dispelled, and my best hopes realized! I had not felt so lightsome and joyous for many a day. One cannot fully appreciate the worth of good letters from friends near and dear, unless he has been similarly situated. Like myself, the greater portion of the crew had good news from their friends; and many were the smiling faces seen, and many a laugh was heard, as the last letter was read, and the continued good health and prosperity of those left behind was there mentioned, with the assurance that the absent ones were still remembered in love and friendship. Verily, "Good news doeth good like a medicine," and "As water to a thirsty soul, so is good news from a far country." We then realized the truth and force of these two passages of Scripture. All the letters, however, did not bring good tidings, and there were many sad hearts and tearful faces, as some read of the loss of friends, near and dear friends, whom they would never behold again in this life. Thus is it ever in this world; while some are enjoying every pleasure and blessing which earth can afford, there are others whose lot it is to endure the bitter pangs of sorrow and adversity.

Macao, China.

LETTER XV.

U. S. S. WACHUSETT, Macao, China,
April 2, 1866.

MY DEAR R.:

We have been nearly a month in China, and begin to be tolerably familiar with the manners, customs, and excentricities of the Chinese; and yet scarcely a day passes without revealing some new and interesting trait, or something to excite our wonder and curiosity.

You see we have shifted our anchorage since I wrote you last. We remained at Hong Kong only eleven days, and on Thursday, March 15th, we got under way, and started for Macao. As we were obliged to follow the lead of the Hartford, we were seven hours in steaming the distance of forty-five miles, and came to anchor about two miles from the shore, the water being too shallow to admit of our approaching any nearer. We found the Store Ship "Relief," from which we are to take stores, in the harbor, and she will soon start for home. An English gunboat, a few coolie ships and merchant vessels, two or three river steamers, and a number of Chinese junks and smaller craft are the only vessels beside our own in the harbor.

There is a charming repose, heightened by contrast, in such a quiet old town as Macao to one who, but a few hours before left the fussy, upstart pretensions of Hong Kong, where everybody is trying to be somebody, and nobody believes anybody else to be anybody. The natural site of Macao is picturesque. The city climbs up the sides and through the ravines of a group of hills, the summits of which are crowned with old castles and convents. Conspicuous amongst the ruins of Macao on the hill-tops, is the front wall of an old church, standing out sharp and clear upon its elevation. Only this front wall remains, its rugged edges and window-openings cushioned with moss and wild foliage which time has planted. Such old towns as Macao, made up of massive old houses, surrounded by grounds darkened by trees, and tangled in shrubbery, which, with the crabbed independence of age has a will of its own above all trimmings or trainings, are very pleasant to me. The inhabitants present the picturesque in the social scene, as the crumbling tower, touched by the setting sun does in the natural.

"The stone faced mole, or praya, which curves in front of the city, was in former days the scene of bustling commerce, but is now the pleasant, quiet promenade of those who have nothing better to do. Besides this Portuguese and foreign Macao, there is a dense mass of a Chinese town."

As a sea-port for Canton before Hong Kong sprang up, Macao had a day of commercial prosperity. For over three hundred years it has been a foreign settlement. The general impression is that it was given to the Portuguese as a reward for their having suppressed piracy on the coast; but there is no evidence of there ever having been any relinquishment of authority on the part of the Chinese. The Portuguese claim seems to be that of possession, at first, tolerated; then, permitted, and now, acknowledged, in fact if not in name.

Provisions at Macao are abundant and good, the climate healthful and pleasant, and it is the chosen retreat of business men, merchants of Hong Kong, and the refuge of those whose fortunes have been broken. These various elements unite to make up an agreeable society, and their sole occupation and amusement is social intercourse. The combined population, Portuguese, Foreign, Chinese, Malay, and mixed, is variously estimated at from twenty-five to forty thousand.

A few days after our arrival here we had general liberty given us. The usage is to keep the men on board ship for months while the officers, officers' servants and a few privileged ones are permitted to go ashore in every port. This tantalizing and provoking contrast, increases the discontent arising from so long a confinement in their floating prison; and when they are permitted they go ashore in large gangs, for a twenty-four or forty-eight hours' debauch. The idea of those in authority is that a sailor will have this debauch, and, in their ignorance of man nature, they overlook the fact that it is by their treatment, that he has been brought to this condition.

When our legislators produced the act to "provide for the more efficient discipline of the navy," in their simplicity they assumed some natural human rights to exist on board a man-of-war, for they say: "Section 3. And be it further enacted, that it shall be the duty of commanders of any vessels in the navy, in granting temporary leave of absence and liberty on shore, to exercise carefully a discrimination in favor of the faithful and obedient;" and among the penalties is "deprivation of liberty on shore in foreign stations." Instead of this there ought to be a law enacted that in no case, except one of absolute necessity, should men be deprived of liberty at stated periods of time.

The first touch of the foot to the shore after such an estrangement is an intoxication. All have felt this after a long sea voyage; then to this is added the excitement of numbers, and the tendency to outrage which arises from the physical power of numbers turned loose for indulgence in a weak community. Now, instead of this management of the crew, suppose that when in port, such as behaved themselves were permitted to go ashore in small parties daily, as they could be spared from their duties. The frequency of visiting the shore would lessen the excitement, the small numbers would diminish the probabilities of disturbance, and in every respect, the most beneficial results to all would be obtained. Some commanders have tried this method, and have always found it to be attended with good benefit.

Our "fast boat" was used here to convey the liberty men on shore instead of the ship's boats; but when I went ashore with a number of others a few days ago, I found that our large boat could not approach the land, the remainder of the passage being made in small sampans. Quite a novelty are these sampans—Tanka boats they are called—as are also the girls who, I was about to say, *man* them; and as these girls really do the hard work of the men, I might let the nautical term remain. These picturesque, white teethed, laughing mouthed, bandana-kerchiefed nymphs live on the water and make their living by landing passengers from the steamers which ply between Macao, Hong Kong, and Canton, and from the large junks, and in rowing to the bathing-places the business men and dissipated wretches who retreat to Macao for a few weeks to recruit. The Tanka boat people are said to be of an unknown race, distinct from Tartar or Chinese. They have their own customs; the females never contract their feet, and they marry among themselves. Where the men live and how, I have not been able to ascertain. Three pretty girls won our favor so much that we made use of their services and gave in return, a shilling each—more than five times the regular fare. Such is the influence of beauty, found here among the Chinese as well as at home among the highest.

Landing on the praya, and passing up a narrow alley-way towards the center of the town, we soon came to a large stone cathedral which bore evidences of great antiquity in all its surroundings. This stands on one of the eminences upon which the city is built. As we landed the matin bells sounded, and called forth the stanza from one of our number.

"The convent bells were ringing,
  But mournfully and slow;
In the gray square turret swinging,
  With a deep sound, to and fro.
Heavily to the heart they go!
  Hark! the hymn is singing——."

As we approached the Cathedral the sweet tones of the low chant fell upon our ears, inviting us in. We entered, and after crossing ourselves with holy water, took seats. The congregation numbering some three hundred Portuguese, foreigners, Chinese, and mixed, were on their knees and the choir was chanting our Saviour's Passion—it being Annunciation Day. The service was very finely and very impressively conducted, but as it was in the Portuguese tongue it was intelligible to none of us. The building was like any other catholic cathedral, but it was very rich in gold and silver adornments and in fine old paintings.

Leaving the Cathedral, we walked through the Chinese quarter, where we were presented many things of interest, and shown a great variety of races, and some of their occupations and habits. At stands by the sides of the streets, or in little shops, the mechanics were busily at work, as well as numerous braziers, tinmen, and blacksmiths. On every hand the barbers were to be seen shaving, shampooing, plaiting queues, and cleaning out ears, noses, and eyes. They use small triangular razors, the apex fastened to the handle. We seated ourselves in a small corner shop to get "barbered." Without using any lather, the barber commenced to shave us. We remonstrated but were told that lather did no good, that its use would make the hair coarse and stiff, and was never employed by the learned. The beard was removed almost in a twinkling, and then with little hoe-shaped spoons the barber examined our nose, ears, and eyes, removing little bits of dirt and wax that had been accumulating there for ages. We thought that with this act our torments would cease, but in this we were doomed to disappointment. After twisting our necks about in every conceivable direction to all our cries of "Hold on!" the barber replying "me no hurt you," he next fell to beating our backs, breasts, and sides, until we began to think that we were to be pounded to a jelly, and forced him to desist. The last operation, I have been told, is performed to drive away bodily pains. I am sure that I am unable to see the virtue of it, and know that I did not recover from the effects of that "barbering" for many days. The price for the whole was only about two cents, but I would not undergo the torments of the operation the second time for twice as many dollars.

Well, leaving this we have the market shops. The pork-dealer is dealing out his slender cutlets, the fruiter his pines, bananas, oranges and other fruit. Next to these are masses of green salad, cabbage, pears, beans, radishes, etc. There are dried fish and fresh, and ducks split open and pressed flat, as if they had been under heavy weights for a long time.

An excellent description of the dress of the Chinese is given by Surgeon Wood, in narrating what he saw in a ramble along the streets of a Chinese city.

"The laboring coolies with their burden-sticks across their shoulders, fill the streets, all dressed in much uniformity, with broad-brimmed, sharp-peaked hats made of palm leaves, blue cotton shirts or frocks coming down to their hips, trowsers of the same, reaching half-down their legs, with either bare or straw-sandaled feet. The women wear precisely the same costume except that the outer garment hangs loose, and the trowsers reach the feet. Even among the lower class a few small footed women are seen tottering along like children on short stilts; but the most of them are barefoot or wear a shoe with a sole an inch thick and shaped like a rocker skate. Mothers are seen tottering along the streets, with their infants bound to their backs by a square piece of cloth. When you would meet the better class of Chinese another style of costume varies the streets. Black satin or velvet embossed shoes, with thick white soles, white leggings reaching to the knees, and meeting blue silk breeches which are fastened by silk garters, or the breeches may descend the leg fitting it closely and secured by ribbons. The outside garment is either a figured silk or woolen robe, or a long

STREET BARBER.

robe loose and flowing, figured or trimmed with furs. Although there is a general costume, it admits of as much variety as may be seen on some of our principal streets in the States. Rain or shine, cloudy or clear in the daytime, every Chinaman has an umbrella and at night a lantern." During the entire day the streets are thronged with people, both afoot and in sedan-chairs, traveling confectionery and cake-shops. Cobblers in old shoes, workers in leather, menders of broken China, with their implements of trade, are among the moving occupants of the streets, while coolies are seen carrying their heavy burdens and bales to and fro.

The Chinese have attained great eminence in the manufacture of silk and cotton cloths. They are also noted for their skill in the carving of ivory, tortoise-shell, mother of pearl, and other ornamental articles, and also for the taste they display in the arts of embroidery, dyeing, and the making of artificial flowers and papers of fine tissue.

Leaving the Chinese and entering the foreign quarter of the city, one finds himself in a comparatively desolate place, with its solemn stillness, and decaying old mansions, churches, and theatres. The streets are very narrow and uneven, except the one which winds around the praya. No wheeled vehicle is to be seen, all the transporting being done by coolies, and the traveling done on foot, on horseback, or in palanquins carried on the backs of coolies. These palanquins are square, upright boxes, about four feet high and two square, trimmed with silk or green baize, and with a seat on the inside. It is supported by two poles, some ten or twelve feet in length, slightly curving from the middle to the extremities where they are joined by a cross-bar. I took a short ride in one of them, but the jolting, unsteady motion produced by the bearers was not very agreeable to me. Those, however, that have become accustomed to this method of traveling, say that it is a very agreeable one.

In the evening I went out from my lodgings for a stroll

around the Chinese quarter. As I approached it I heard the discordant noise of the gongs, and tom-toms, and the screeching of the Chinese fiddles. Following these sounds until they became louder and more intolerable, I found myself among a motley crowd, over whose faces glared the lights from a covered platform in an open space before the principal temple. It was a Chinese theatre, supported by a subscription of the Celestials, for public performances. All that I could make of it was this confounding noise of all imaginable discordant instruments, a crowd of people moving about the stage in various Chinese costumes, including silken royal robes—with masked faces, and in the pause of the instruments screeching to each other in voices no less discordant. A Chinese play often lasts for months, commencing at the births of the principal characters—which takes place publicly upon the stage—following every important event of their lives, and terminating with their deaths, which also takes place upon the stage. A stay of some five or ten minutes was enough for me.

Macao is celebrated as being the spot where were spent the last days of Camoens, the writer of the only great poem which the Portuguese have produced—the refuge of the poverty stricken bard, and the locality of the lonely cavern where he nursed his muse. A victim, he was, of thwarted first love, was born noble, and in his early life enjoyed nearly every felicity which birth, wealth, and talent could bestow. Early in middle life, with shattered fortunes and dearest hopes dashed to the ground, he left his native country, came to Macao, sustained his existence by the begging of his negro slave, and ended his life in a hospital. Since his death—as is the case generally—the Portuguese have discovered his great talents, worth, and merits, and done much to honor his memory. The cave of Camoens is in the grounds of a private residence. It has been so perverted by art as to lose all that is romantic or picturesque.

Associated with the fame of Camoens is that of Chinnery, who died at Macao, alike celebrated with his pen and pencil. He was an eccentric genius, who loved the productions of his talent better than fame or money, and parting with them for neither.

A terrible incident has associated itself with our stay at Macao. A few days ago, a Spanish bark left here for Cuba with a load of coolies, "humanity swapping black skins for yellow ones." Soon after leaving the harbor, the coolies rose, murdered the crew, and then after plundering the vessel of everything that was valuable, abandoned her. The vessel was discovered this morning by a merchantman bound into Macao, drifting about. Thinking that something must be the matter on board, they sent a boat to ascertain. They found the officers and crew lying about the decks where they had fallen, and everything that was of value removed from the ship.

LETTER XVI.

U. S. S. WACHUSETT, Canton, China, }
April 13, 1866.

MY DEAR R.:

Tuesday, April 3d, we left Macao, and started for Canton, the Hartford taking the lead with bumboat and compradore's boats in tow, and we following with the Relief and our boats. As soon as we were clear of the mouth of the harbor we all made sail and stopped steaming, proceeding thus until we arrived at the mouth of the Canton river.

The Chu-kiang or Pearl river, more commonly called the Canton river, is formed by the union of three rivers, the West, North, and East rivers, the two first of which unite west of the city of Canton, and the East river joins them at Whampoa. Beside these there are numerous other smaller rivers, creeks, and canals which pour in their waters. After a course of about five hundred miles it passes out to sea through several mouths, the best known of which is the Boca Tigress. The delta into which the East, West, and North rivers fall might be called a gulf, if the islands in it did not occupy so much of the area. This, together with the country drained by these rivers and their tributaries, is said to form the most fertile portion of the province of Canton, and this is one of the most extensive estuaries of any river in the world—being a rough triangle about one hundred miles on each side. The Bay of Lintin—so called from an island of the same name where the opium and store-ships formerly anchored—is the largest sheet of water within the estuary, and lies below the principal mouth of the river called *Fu Nun*,

i. e., Boca Tigris, or Bogue. From Macao to the Bogue, we came up Lintin Bay in a northeasterly direction, a distance of about forty miles. Few rivers can be more completely protected than the Pearl. At the Bogue—through which we passed—it is very narrow, and on each side are high hills, admirable positions for defenses.

The ruins of three Chinese forts—two on the left bank, and one on the right, are visible. They were all powerful with their guns against their own shipping, but of little avail against the power and skill of their enemies during the late war. Some ten or twelve miles farther up the river, on the left bank, we saw the ruins of another fort, while on the opposite bank, on a hill back from the river, solitary and alone stood an ancient pagoda.

Just before reaching Whampao—about thirty miles from the Bogue—there is a sharp bend in the river, and our course, which hitherto had been northerly, was changed to the westward, continuing thus until we reached Canton, some twelve or fifteen miles farther on. There the river contains many islands, the small ones of Whampoa, French, and Danes, and the large one of Honan. At the lower extremity of Dane's island we parted company with the Hartford, she drawing too much water to proceed up to Canton, and so going up the Junk river, or passage to Whampoa, while we proceeded up the Whampoa to the city. On the Junk river about midway between Whampoa and Canton are the Barrier forts, reduced by the Americans in 1856.

Our way up the river presented us with the interest of varied scenery. The waters, reddish yellow in color, were rolling, flowing around and between rocky islands, some of them clothed in green. The banks were a succession of lofty mountains, hills with intervening valleys, dotted with Chinese villages. 'Tis strange that any one of observation should have spoken of these river borders as uninteresting or thinly populated. Every cove has its populous town or village, and where there is a fertile spot on the hill-side there life is planted.

Some of the green hill-sides are sprinkled with large-sized white semicircles. These are the Chinese graves. They have been spoken of as resembling a large old fashioned, oval-backed sleigh, high behind, and low in front. There are two semicircular or horse-shoe shaped enclosures of masonry, one within the other. The outer one is three or four feet high at the back, and some ten feet in diameter.

After passing the Bogue, the hills recede, and the river is lined with a series of paddy fields, in some places so low as to require an embankment to prevent them from being overflowed. By means of gates in these embankments the fields can be flooded when desired. When the banks of the river are higher the irrigation of these fields has to be done by hand, and some of the methods employed are quite curious, and interesting to observe. Pumps worked by treadmills are the most common, but occasionally two will be seen with a bucket to either side of which a cord is attached, by means of which they lower the buckets into the water, and then by suddenly tightening them by pulling in opposite directions, the water is thrown to a considerable distance. Their apparatus for fishing, as seen located along the river's banks, or in bows of boats, is quite a novelty. Nets attached to bamboo frames, and then fastened to the end of a long pole, which rests upon an upright frame, somewhat after the style of an old fashioned well-sweep are principally employed. In using, the end to which the net is attached is lowered down into the water where it is shallow, and then after remaining there a short time, it is raised by means of a cord attached to the other end of the pole. We saw several successful fishermen with from one to a dozen fish, caught at one time. The banks along the wide delta of the river are frequented by immense flocks of wild geese, duck, teal, and other wild fowl.

The most animated scene, however, is the river itself, as one approaches the city. The stream is fairly thronged with ships, steamers, and junks lying at anchor. The mass of them lie between the city and a small island about a mile and a half below it, on which stands a small circular fort called the "Bird's Nest," to which it bears a striking resemblance on account of the concave form of its interior. Some of the junks are enormous masses of timber, and almost defy description. The bottom is a large, square scow upon which are built sides of heavy plank. The bow end of each side is rounded off like a sled, but all the square bow is left open, as it is said, to the winds, waves, and water-gods. Here lies the anchor usually made entirely of wood, with one or two flukes, and almost as heavy as iron. In the sides are openings to take in the cargo, which are closed by doors, fitting into grooves water-tight. The rudder is a heavy mass of timber, seven or eight feet square, and is placed in a wide opening in the stern. Although they are usually bright with paint outside, they are ever filthy and dirty within. The stern is a confused mingling of gods and dragons in white, green, yellow or other bright colored paints.

Every junk has its own joss-house, where a light, by which to make offerings to their gods is kept constantly burning.

The stern is built up into platforms of cabins, and three or four heavy, naked sticks are the masts. Triangular sails made of thin strips of bamboo are used.

Lying near these are a number of armed junks, extraordinary looking vessels, with all sorts of cannon projecting from their sides. Closer in shore are the canal boats, long and roofed over, and their sails protected from the weather by varnished or painted matting. Then there are the smaller boats, tiny, graceful canoes, managed with almost wonderful dexterity, and the Tanka passenger boats, roofed over with wattled straw matting, and made water-tight by paint, the back closed by a wooden partition, containing a window, and the front having a bamboo screen which can be removed at pleasure. Sometimes instead of the matting coverings there is substituted a small wooden house with green blinds, making a decided improvement. The numerous varieties of boats to be seen here would take a week's writing to describe, for they are of every variety of form, size and color, (but those that I have mentioned are the most prominent varieties,) from the tiny canoe to the huge junk, and from the wretched dugout of the beggar to the floating palace of the mandarin. Then there are market boats, confectionery shops, and, in short, almost every vocation carried on upon the water that there is upon the land. It is estimated that there are seventy-six thousand boats in and about Canton, with an estimated population of five hundred thousand, who are born, live, and die upon the river and are buried in its waters. At almost any hour of the day, dead bodies may be seen floating down the river, and instances are recorded of vessels being obliged to clear the dead bodies away from their bows before they could proceed up the river.

On the right bank of the river and almost hidden by the forest of masts, lies the old city of Rams-Kwangtung-Canton, associated in the minds of old ladies and merchants with teas and silks, and of all juveniles with fire-crackers, and Christmas. For a city so renowned, it makes but little show in approaching it, and one would never imagine that it contained over one million and a quarter inhabitants within its seven miles of wall, over the tops of which its low, tiled roofed houses are just to be seen.

In the western suburbs of the city are the "Factories," the name given to the only spot where, formerly, foreigners were allowed to reside. They occupy a river frontage of seven or eight hundred feet. In front of them, on the river side, is a wide, park-like street, containing many fine trees, and affording a pleasant promenade for the foreign residents. As we rounded the point just above the Bird-Nest, we saw them all out for their evening promenade, and as I stood on the forecastle watching them, home was brought more forcibly to my thoughts than by the sight of any place previously visited. From that moment I took a great liking to Canton. It was about five o'clock when we dropped anchor opposite these Factories, about one hundred and fifty yards from shore.

The Factories were destroyed by the flames of war in the attack on the city in 1856, and since then have been rebuilt, much after the old plan, but on a more extensive scale. They are built of brick, stuccoed, with granite foundations. Some of them are three stories high, but the most of them are only two. Within a park-like enclosure, near the middle of the town, stands the pretty chapel of the Episcopal church. Besides the foreign residences and their *hongs*—store-houses and ware-houses—there is quite an extensive Chinese town, included under the general name of " Factories."

The, following Friday the Admiral and staff came up in his barge, and remained several days on board us, so that for a time we were flag-ship.

Our stay here has been characterized by almost incessant rain-storms, there having been scarcely a single pleasant day since we arrived. I would have preferred having a fine day for my ramble and tour of sight-seeing on shore, but after waiting a week in vain, and hearing that we were to remain here but a day or two longer, I concluded it was best to go while there was an opportunity. Accordingly, one rainy morning, a number of us started. Travelers at home are constantly annoyed by the ferocious importunities, and deafening cries with which hackmen assail them. All this is scarcely equal to the Tanka girls of Canton. These girls do all the boating on the river—such as carrying passengers and messages between the shipping and shore. Their boats, roofed over with matting, are kept scrupulously neat and clean, not a speck of dirt visible anywhere, and everything in its proper place. Order and system are necessary to this neatness, as the boat is the permanent dwelling of its three or four inmates—their kitchen, dining-room, and bed-chamber.

I will now give you the appearance of the inmates as seen by me on my way to the shore; two young women and two little girls. The women wore loose Chinese trowsers and short frocks of dark blue silk, with heavy ear-rings, anklets, and bracelets of a pearl-colored stone or of silver. The young ones were uncommonly good-looking, with cheerful faces framed in bright-colored handkerchiefs thrown over their heads and fastened under the chin. In the merry animation with which they urged, and finally persuaded, me to employ their boat, they displayed beautifully regular and white teeth.

At the landing I was joined by a friend, and together we proceeded to the American Consul's, persuaded his compradore to procure a guide for us, and then set out upon our ramble about Canton. Our first visit was to the western suburbs of the city, the principal streets of which are "Old China" and "New China" streets, and the one which is, as its name implies, "Curiosity" street. The latter is by far the most fascinating to a newly-arrived European. In the shops—scarcely more than boxes—what tempting wonders meet the eye! All the elaborate carvings and curious workings of ivory, sandal-wood, tortoise-shell, mother-of-pearl, ebony cabinets and tablets, curious bronzes, brightly-painted porcelain, jetty lacquer-ware—so smooth and so bright as to reflect everything around like so many mirrors; work-boxes and tables, chess-men and chess-tables, and toys of almost every conceivable kind! Some of the carvings seem almost the work of a magician. Ivory balls, one in the other, to the number of seven or nine, all exquisitely carved, we could not believe were cut out of one solid piece, and not cunningly introduced by some imperceptible opening, until we had visited the shops where carving was done, and seen that originally they were but one piece, and cut from the various apertures which the balls contained, until one after another was dislodged and turned, and then carved like the first. The skill of the Chinese in carving is only equaled by the rapidity with which the work is performed. There were little ivory and sandal-wood boxes, scarcely six inches in length, the carving of which took many days' labor, and yet they could be bought for from one to five dollars.

There were other little, gloomy shops, where the passerby could see scarcely anything to attract his attention, more than that everything, as about the other shops, was scrupulously neat and clean. Respectable old Chinamen, as neat and tidy as their shops, sat behind the counters as if they had nothing to do, nor wished for anything. These, the guide told us, were the silk merchants, and that they were accustomed to fill orders for from fifty to one hundred thousand dollars worth of silks. Upon entering and enquiring for these articles, chests were opened, and rolls of elegant silks, plain, figured, and embroidered, of nearly every hue and pattern, were displayed. Lacquered boxes, too, would be opened, containing elegant crape shawls. Any number of these were taken out for us to look at and examine, and then folded and put back again with as much neatness as if they had not been disturbed. Although we kept the merchant busy for an hour or more in unrolling and unpacking, and then left with purchasing only a few articles, we were *chin chinned* away with as much politeness as if we had purchased a cargo.

The manufacture of silk has long been established among the Celestials. Many years ago, when the people of Europe were going about with naked bodies, the very lowest of the Chinese were clothed in silks. They are still celebrated for the abundance of their silks, as well as for their variety and beauty, equaling any European manufactories, and in crapes, excelling them. The Chinese are a well-clothed nation. They are as frequently seen clothed in silks and satins, as Europeans are in woolens.

An hour or so spent in viewing the many wonders in the shops, along the street, finally brought us to the walls of the city. The suburbs approach so close to the walls, that we would not have noticed them, had it not been for the long, low archway, underneath which we passed in entering the southeastern gate of the city, and the thick, heavy, iron ribbed gates or doors by which it is closed. The foundations of the city walls are of sandstone, and the upper part of brick. They are about twenty feet thick and from twenty-five to forty feet high, having an esplanade on the inside and pathways leading to the ramparts. The part of Canton inclosed by walls is about six miles in circumference, having a partition wall running east and west, which divides it into two unequal parts; the southern and smaller of which is called New Town, and the other Old City. There are twelve outer gates, four in the partition wall, and two water gates, through which boats pass from east to west across New City. A ditch once encompassed the walls but it is now dry on the northern side. On the other three, and within the city it, together with most of the canals, are filled by the tide, and all present a revolting mass of filth at the bottoms, when the retiring waters expose them. The gates of the city are all shut at night and a guard is constantly stationed at them to preserve order. Among the names of the gates are, Great Peace Gate, Eternal Rest Gate, Bamboo Wicket Gate, Five Genii Gate, &c.

.After entering the gate, we crossed the greater extent of New City from west to east, and then passing through one of the gates in the partition wall, we traversed the Old City from south to north, visiting the principal places of interest on our way. A little after noon, we stood on the high ground at the northern part of the city where the English planted their batteries after scaling the walls. The appearance of the city and its surroundings as viewed from that elevation was very interesting, and as I stood there enjoying the view, I thought of you and how much you would enjoy the prospect, if you could have been with me. It was one vast expanse of reddish tiled roofs, relieved by a few tall trees and interspersed by pairs of high, red poles, used for flag-staffs, to point out the residence of some official, public building or Joss temple. To the north were the White Cloud Hills at the foot of which the city stands. The river, however, is the prominent feature in the landscape, with its myriads of boats of all sizes, forms, and colors, some stationary, others moving, and all resounding with the mingled hum of laborers, sailors, musicians, marketers, children and boatmen pursuing their several sports and occupations. A small island in the river on which was the fort called Dutch Folly, or Sea Pearl, by the Chinese, with its fanciful buildings, and beautiful trees, with the quietude reigning over it, contrasts agreeably with the liveliness of the waters around. The hills to the north rise twelve hundred feet above the river, their sides covered with graves and tombs, the Necropolis of this vast city. On the points nearest the town are the ruins of three or four forts.

The streets of the city are very narrow, scarcely more than six or eight feet in width, rudely flagged, underneath which are the sewers which are washed out by the tides of the river. Considering the enormous masses of people crowding these alleys, they are kept much cleaner than I should think possible. We heard continually behind us, as we passed through them, the cries of coolies bearing sedan chairs or heavy burdens, supported on sticks across their shoulders. The streets are not wide enough for the coolies bearing these burdens to pass without the foot passengers giving way, and as they proceed at a rapid pace, half trot, they clear their way of all obstacles, as I learned to my bitter cost, being nearly knocked down two or three times with the end of their poles. The houses are built of wood or brick, with tiled roofs. The fronts of them present a curious appearance with their many projecting curiously carved roofs and cornices. The long vista of these narrow alley-ways presents a very gay and animated appearance. The shop signs, about one foot wide by four or five feet in length, are suspended vertically by the sides of the doors. They are of bright vermilion or jet black colors, finely varnished, and lettered in gold. Besides these, suspended over the streets from lines or bamboo poles stretching from the tops of the houses on one side to those on the other, are various gay banners, flags, and cloths. The apothecary shops, with their ornamental labeled jars, and the hat-stores, with their plumed and ornamented mandarin hats, also present a gay appearance. In Canton, as is said to be the case in most large Chinese cities, those following different occupations confine themselves to different streets, thus shoemakers and their shops are to be seen on one street, tailors and their shops on another, and so on. The number of the streets is estimated to be over six hundred. Among their names are Dragon street, Martial Dragon street, Pearl street, Golden Flower street, New Green Pea street, Physic street, and Spectacle street. There are four prisons in the city, all of them large establishments. All the capital offences of the province are brought to Canton for trial, and this makes it necessary to provide spacious accommodations. The execution-ground is a small yard near the southern gate of the city, between it and the river. There had been an execution of a number of pirates a day or two previous, and their heads were exposed in a rack near by the block on which they had been beheaded. Suspended on a post was a placard relating the circumstances attending the affair, in Chinese characters, which the guide translated for us.

After leaving the city, we crossed over the river to the Honan side, on which are located several European buildings, and a large number of Chinese. A little farther down is a large settlement of Parsees. After a short ramble there, visiting the more prominent curiosity-shops, and temples, commonly known as the Honan Joss-House, about dark we returned to the ship.

I have been thus particular and minute in my description of Canton and its surroundings, because I am told its main points and features are common to most Chinese walled cities, so that, hereafter, as I visit and make mention of other places, I shall only speak of such additions and exceptions as may be brought to my notice, without wearying you with a repetition of the main features, which are the same in all.

It is only of late years that foreigners have been allowed within the walls of Canton, and now, even, women are prohibited from entering its gates. Only a short time ago, a lady, more curious and more venturesome than the others, went within the walls clothed in male attire. She was discovered, and would have been taken to prison, and doubtless suffered death, had not an influential gentleman been passing at the time and rescued her. In the whole time that we were within the walls we did not see a single European, a European article, nor a Chinaman with whom we could converse excepting the guide.

Canton has hitherto been known as the most truculent city of all China. Our principal object in coming here was to request an interview with the governor-general of the two quarantine provinces, in order to satisfy his own eyes that the United States have re-established their naval squadron on that coast, though in peace and good will towards the Chinese, who had honorably maintained their neutrality during the late rebellion in our own country. I have been informed that upon the visit of our admiral and captain to His Excellency a few days ago, he manifested the best disposition toward our country and countrymen.

A few days after their visit the governor sent word to us
8*

that he would "visit the admiral on board of the Wachusett." Accordingly every preparation was made to receive him with all due honors and attentions. The ship was clothed in her cleanest and brightest dress, as were also the officers and crew. An hour or more before his arrival an official came bearing complimentary cards, as is their custom.

"The civilization of the Chinese," it has been well remarked, "is shown by their courtesy and complaisance to one another. In no other heathen country do we see so much attention paid to ceremony, so many compliments exchanged, or such polish in intercourse with one another. The poorest or meanest will seldom permit a stranger to pass their door without inviting him to enter; and if he acquiesces, the pipe and cup of tea is immediately offered him, nor does the master of the house presume to be seated until after the stranger has been."

The governor's approach was announced by the beating of gongs and cymbals, and in a few minutes his barge—a large, long boat, with a wooden house built upon it, bright with paint, and decorated with pictures of dragons and gods, with his flag flying from a staff in the stern—came in sight, propelled by long poles and oars. Arriving alongside, he was received by the admiral and other officers in uniform, and by the Guard with presented arms; and, as soon as his barge could drop astern, a salute of seventeen guns was thundered forth. He is a large middle-aged man, and the most intelligent, finest looking Chinaman that I have yet met. He wore instead of the trowsers, or over them, close fitting leggins of heavily embroidered satin. The frock was of silk, thick, rich, heavily embroidered, and reaching almost to his heels. Over this he wore a cape of the same material, also embroidered, but of a darker color. His hat bore a striking resemblance to those of the continentals, the top surmounted by a transparent red stone or button as they are called, to which a plume sloping back was attached. On the back and breast of his robe a stork was embroidered, and his girdle-clasp was of prehnite set in rubies; all these showed him to be a mandarin of the first order. As only mandarins and high officials are permitted to do, he wore boots. Around his neck was a string of precious stones reaching half way down his back, and at his side he wore a dagger, the golden hilt of which was studded with jewels. He was accompanied by a large retinue of mandarins, officials, soldiers, and attendants. The former wore a dress similar to that of the governor, only less rich, and with different adornments according to the rank. Some of the officials wore flowered gold buttons as badges of their office. The soldiers wore conical-shaped straw hats, ornamented with red fringe, light blue nankeen robes and jackets, on the back and breast of which were Chinese characters, designating to what division they belonged. The governor was accompanied by one of the foreign residents, who acted as interpreter.

He remained on board upwards of three hours, examining every thing about the ship with a great deal of attention and interest, and upon his departure expressed much pleasure with his visit, and gave many thanks for the courtesy and kindness which had been extended to him. 'Tis strange and somewhat amusing to us to have a Chinaman salute us after their custom, which is, to shake their own hands instead of those of the one saluted. This is always accompanied by "Chin chin," which would answer to our "How do you do," "Thank you," or "Good bye."

During our entire stay here the ship has been thronged with boat-loads of beggars, the abject misery and squalid appearance of whom would defy description, soliciting bits of hard bread and any refuse article that might be thrown away. As a number of their boats were under our bow yesterday, one of the poor wretches fell into the water, and would have drowned had he not been rescued by some of our crew, although there were hundreds of boats near. The reason of none of his countrymen affording him assistance was explained to me by our bumboatman. He said that according to the laws of China if one rescued a poor man from drowning, he was bound to support him for the remainder of his life, should it ever be necessary.

LETTER XVII.

U. S. S. WACHUSETT, Hong Kong,
April 17th, 1866.

MY DEAR R.:

Before breakfast Sunday morning, April 15th, we "unmoored ship," got up the port anchor, and made the usual preparations for getting under way. After breakfast the crew shifted into mustering clothes, and at nine o'clock all hands were called to muster for church service. The Rev. Mr. Grey, rector of the Episcopal Church at Canton, officiated. This was the first sermon that I had listened to in over a year, and I enjoyed it, with the whole service, very much, and wish that we might have the same every Sabbath. To be deprived of attending church regularly is one of the greatest privations that I have experienced since I have been in the service, and especially since I have been aboard ship. On that account, if no other, I shall be glad when my period of enlistment expires.

As soon as service was over we got under way and started for Whampoa, coming down by the same passage as we went up. On this account we had to go to the lower extremity of Danes Island before we could turn and go up to the anchorage, thus making our sailing distance about twenty-five miles, while the river steamers, which go by Junk Passage, have to run only about ten miles. We came to anchor by the Relief, our object in going to Whampoa being to take in stores from her. The Hartford with the admiral, we heard, had returned to Hong Kong. We remained at Whampoa only about three hours, so I did not go on shore, and you will have to be content, for the present, with such observations of the place as I was able to make from the ship.

At Whampoa (*i. e.*, Yellow Anchorage,) is a reach in the river, four miles in length, where the shipping usually lie, above which it is impossible for large vessels to go. The old town of Whampoa, with its pagoda, lies on an island of the same name, north of the anchorage, and distant some four or five miles. Viewed from the ship, it presents a very interesting and picturesque appearance, being fairly embowered in trees. Near the water's edge, and, in fact, partly built upon the water, is New Town, the residence of the foreigners, which appears to be a small, dirty, insignificant place. Upon the opposite bank, on Danes Island, are the dry docks, the largest and principal ones to be found in China. On this side, stretching along the bank of the river for about a mile, is Bamboo Town, the houses for the most part constructed—as the name implies—of bamboo. These are chiefly the residences of the dock-laborers.

The country to the north of the anchorage is low and level —one vast expanse of paddy-fields nearly as far as the eye can reach. On the southern side there are several picturesque hills, covered with trees and beautiful verdure. The summit of the one rising immediately back of Bamboo Town, is crowned with the showy tombs of a Parsee burying-ground. The eminence itself is oval in form, covered with beautiful trees, shrubs, and verdure, and forms the most interesting and picturesque feature in the whole landscape.

That night we anchored just outside the Bogue, and came here early the following day. We had barely anchored when Dame Rumor brought us the news that we were to get ready as soon as possible, and proceed to the northward to investigate and settle some difficulties which American residents there are reported as having with the Chinese. Later advices strengthen these reports, and I have come to the conclusion that there must be some truth to this intelligence of Dame Rumor. The crew have been hard at work yesterday and to-day making the necessary preparations, and to-morrow we expect to start.

After dinner to-day, accompanied by a friend, I took one of the many passenger-boats which crowd about the ship, and set out for the shore. After a pull of about ten minutes we landed at the fine stone pier in front of Hunt & Co.'s buildings. A glance right and left showed a fine, wide street, with numerous piers and wharves—"*Bund*," it is called—fronting a long row of buildings; stores, warehouses, ship-chandleries, &c. In front was a short, wide street, finely shaded, leading to Queen's Road, while at the junction of the streets rose a tall, square, granite pillar, with a clock on each side near the top—The Clock Tower. Passing up the street to Queen's Road, turning the corner at the post-office, and going west, we found ourselves amid the large magnificent houses of business of the foreign merchants. These, with the better class of Chinese silk, ivory, and lacquer shops, extend along Queen's Road for about three-fourths of a mile, when the road, "both topographically and morally, makes a descent into Tae-ping-shan, the dense Chinese settlement proper, where, amid native trades, robbers, painted courtesans, opium and tea saloons, foreigners keep drinking-shops and sailor boarding-houses."

Retracing our steps and going east from the clock-tower, between more store-houses and places of business, we came upon a beautifully shaded park, in which are the parade and cricket grounds of the English troops, opening to the sea on one side, and overlooked on the other by the Episcopal church perched upon an eminence. Passing on through this our way led through long ranges of military quarters, with shady walks under rows of trees at their front, and with sentries posted at the gates. Here we saw specimens of the guardians of the place; European soldiers in close crimson jackets, or dark-skinned, curly-haired Sepoys in tight-fitting European dress. Beyond these we came to the Navy Yard, and public buildings, built of granite.

Instead of continuing on our walk to Happy Valley, we

decided to leave that for some future visit, and so after retracing our steps to the clock-tower, we ascended the hill for some two hundred yards to Hollywood Road, a street which runs parallel with Queen's Road. Following this west we passed many elegant mansions,—some of them set back in deep, shaded yards, beautified by fountains and statuary,—large banks and houses of business, hotels, the Catholic church, and again made a descent into Tae-ping-shan. To the eastward, Hollywood Road leads to the reservoir—from which the city is supplied with water—and also to several private residences, including the large, elegant mansion of the Governor, with its beautiful grounds, above which are the public gardens recently established. Above Hollywood road are several smaller streets, for the most part lined with private residences, and the extensive granite prisons and police station of the colony.

To one personage, interesting to all men-of-war's-men visiting China, I must devote a little space,—"Old Sam,"—the bumboat man. I don't suppose that an American man-of-war has visited China for the last ten or fifteen years, that every one on it did not know this personage. He is a dark-complexioned, withered, dried-up old Chinaman, with limbs shaking as if he had the palsy, and looks so thin and light that a breath of wind might blow him away. He is very keen and shrewd, and keeps the best bumboat that I ever saw, and which is said to be the best one on the station. "Hab got eberyting," he replies to all questions as to what he has, and this you find to be almost true; eatables of all kinds, and almost any knick-nack that a man aboard ship would require, while what he has not, by informing him, he will bring it off from shore if it is to be obtained. He is reputed to be very wealthy. Every man-of-war that comes into the harbor he supplies with a bumboat, always tending the Senior's ship himself, his son, "Young Sam,"—a tall, well-formed, good-looking, intelligent young Chinaman of about twenty—tending the next in rank, and some relatives the others. They always go with the vessels to Whampoa, Macao, and Canton, but never to the northward, so we shall lose them.

I must narrate an incident of our stay here, illustrative of the imitative faculties of the Chinese, and their lack of invention. As labor is very cheap, and Chinese tailoring good, many of the men have sent cloth ashore to the native tailors and had clothes made. They would seldom take the measure, but wanted a pattern. One man, wishing to have a pair of pants made, gave the tailor an old pair, adorned with several large patches, for a pattern. When the work was done and delivered, the new pants were a perfect imitation of the old ones, even to the size, form, and number of the patches which they contained, and what was better still, the tailor demanded extra pay for the extra labor.

LETTER XVIII.

U. S. S. WACHUSETT, Shanghai,
April 28, 1866.

MY DEAR R.:

Our six days' passage from Hong Kong to Shanghai was characterized by strong winds, a rough sea, and two lamentable incidents.

As I was standing on the forecastle Thursday morning, April 19th, conversing with the sergeant and enjoying the glorious sight of the waves rolling in their majestic swells, and the beautiful, many-colored rainbows formed by the sun shining upon the falling spray, our conversation and my pleasing meditations were brought to an abrupt termination by the ship making a deep plunge into a huge, coming wave, and at the same time shipping a sea over her bow, sweeping everything before it, and "piling us up" on the chicken-coops at the break of the forecastle. While struggling there, endeavoring to extricate myself, I heard the cry, that cry which no one hears without a feeling akin to horror, "a man overboard!" It was Charles Parker, captain of the forecastle; but whether he was swept off by the sea, or knocked overboard by the jib-sheet block, (as he was engaged in clearing the sheet at the time,) no one seemed to know. There was not time to investigate the case, but to turn to that which they did know, and see what could be done. A man overboard, and in such a sea as that! Everyone felt that something ought to be done, but what? It was not a time to order anyone out upon the water. But there was no necessity for such an order,—a crew of volunteers, headed by Mr. Wise— an ensign—sprang to the whale-boat, and with some difficulty, attended by no small amount of danger, managed to lower it and shove off. They had, however, proceeded hardly two boats' lengths from the ship when Parker was seen to sink to rise no more; making our first tribute to Chinese waters. From the time he was knocked overboard until he sank, not a cry was heard to escape him, and from this, it is thought that he was knocked off by the block and stunned by the blow. After waiting a few minutes for him to reappear, without seeing any signs of him, they returned to the ship. The sea was running so high, and the ship rolling so heavily, that their coming along side was attended with much difficulty and danger, and there were many narrow escapes from death getting aboard.

While they were preparing to secure the boat it got adrift, and the second cutter was lowered, manned, and sent after it. When she was returning, just as I was preparing to go below, there was heard another cry of horror. "The second cutter has capsized." Springing upon the hammock-nettings, I saw the boat overturned, and the men clinging to her bottom or to the gunwales. The other cutter was then lowered, manned, and sent to the rescue, but none of us expected to see more than two or three of the crew rescued, if any were. With deep interest and anxiety we watched that boat as it flew to the rescue under the careful and skillful guidance of the coxswain. The men were finally all picked up, and the boat returned in safety to the ship. We succeeded in securing the two cutters, but had to leave the whale-boat.

After a delay of three hours we again proceeded on our way, one of our crew and one boat gone, the two cutters badly stove up, and every thing in confusion about the decks.

That same evening, while passing through Formosa Channel, we narrowly avoided running over some of the many fishing junks which crowd the channel, they not showing any light until we were close upon them. A little after midnight the look-out on the forecastle reported a light right ahead;

but although "the helm was put hard up," we were too close to avoid running over the junk. Our flying jib-boom penetrated her mainsail, lifting it, mast and all out of her, and throwing the junk to one side. When the crew saw that we were about to run them down, instead of endeavoring to save themselves, they commenced to beat upon gongs and cymbals, burn joss papers, and invoke their gods. From the cry that they set up after we ran upon them, we thought they were in a sinking condition, and accordingly lowered a boat and went to their assistance, but found that they were all right, except that their mainmast and sail were gone—those had saved her. To add to our misfortunes our flying jib-boom was broken by the collision, and had to be cut away to clear us from the sail of the junk.

We "laid to" the night of the 23d, thinking that we must be near the light-ship at the mouth of the Yangtse-kiang River. We fired three or four guns, and sent up rockets for a pilot, but none came to us. As soon as an observation could be made the following morning, we found that we were then some twenty-four miles distant from the light-ship, towards which we then started. We arrived there about eleven o'clock, took in a pilot, and, after steaming about an hour, sighted land off both bows—the main land off our port, and Tsungmung Island off our starboard bow.

Tsungmung Island is where the Yangtse-kiang discharges its waters by two mouths into the Eastern Sea. At two o'clock we entered the mouth of the Woosung River, which is there about three-fourths of a mile in width. On the left bank stands the small, unwalled, Chinese town of Woosung, but it is a mere collection of low buildings, having nothing of interest about it, unless it be the long line of earth-works below it, now deserted and grass-grown, or the immense number of junks which throng the river before the town. Also lying there, I noticed two or three small steamers which the Chinese had purchased from the Europeans, and now used as revenue-cutters.

From Woosung to Shanghai the distance is about fourteen miles, nearly due south, up the Woosung River. The land on both sides of the river is low and level, and for the most part devoted to rice culture. Many clusters of houses and groves of fruit-trees are to be seen along its banks. A short distance above Woosung are the French store-houses, and opposite them a French frigate was lying at anchor. After proceeding about ten miles we passed around a small bend in the river, and came in view of the city of Shanghai, stretching along the left bank, with its immense shipping thronging the river before it. It was about four o'clock when we dropped anchor before the American Consul's, about one hundred and fifty yards from shore.

I was surprised at the size of Shanghai, for it is, as you might say, just born. At home we are used to the rapid growth of cities as seen at the west, but they had the modesty to start with the infantile existence of villages. But Shanghai, as a residence for foreigners, seems to have sprung at once into adult strength and glory. Fifteen or twenty years ago the place where the city now stands was a swamp, dotted over with filthy, bamboo-built Chinese houses, and there are some aboard the Wachusett that say when they were here ten or twelve years ago it was a small, insignificant town, in comparison with what it is at present. Now for upwards of two miles along the outer side of the horse-shoe curve in the river, by nearly a mile in width, is a city of large commodious mansions, many of them quite elegant ones, especially those fronting the river and in view from the ship. Several of them are situated in what is termed a "compound"—a well enclosed plat of garden and shrubbery—the walls forming the boundaries of the streets, which are opened upon by carriage-gates guarded by porters' lodges. The "Bund," a wide, pleasant promenade and carriage-drive, curves along the river's bank in front of the city, and is active during the day with business, and cheerful towards evening with equestrians, carriages, and promenaders.

The foreign city is divided, topographically, into three portions—the English, French, and American concessions—each flying their own national flag, and under the jurisdiction of their respective consuls. The American concession is the lower one of the three, and extends from about one-fourth of a mile to the eastward of where we are lying, to Su-chau Creek, about the same distance to the westward. Commencing at the lower extremity the eye rests first upon wharves, founderies, and warehouses, the principal of which are near Hunt's wharf. Next comes Captain Robert's ship-yard and his residence, and then another row of store-houses. At the head of a short street which leads back from the Bund, is seen the Episcopal chapel, with its square tower, a neat, tasteful, granite edifice, with green blinds, situated in a charming little yard filled with shrubbery. Further on, past a few fine residences, is a medical hall, and then comes the fine large building of the United States Consulate, with a pretty yard filled with shrubbery, in front of which stands the tall flag-staff, from which floats the stars and stripes. Continuing on, we pass a hotel, the head of Old China Street, the Exchange, another private residence or two, the Astor, another private residence, and come to the Su-chau Creek. In the rear of all, at the heads of the streets leading back from the Bund, are to be seen several elegant mansions, standing in beautifully adorned enclosures.

Leaving this and crossing the tile-paved draw-bridge which spans Su-chau Creek, our eyes rest upon the English settlement, by far the finest and most extensive portion of Shanghai. Where the Su-chau Creek forms its junction with the Woosung (or, as it is more commonly called, the Whang-po) River, is the most beautiful of the localities of Shanghai. Here, looking down the reach of the river, up the waters of

Shanghai, China.

the creek, and over the whole settlement, surrounded by large grounds and brick wall, are the showy buildings of the British Consulate. The consular buildings, court house, and post-office, are all near each other, with the union jack flying in their front.

After crossing Su-chau Creek the shore runs almost at right angles to its former course, southward to Yang-kin-pang Creek, upwards of a mile in front of the English concession, which, in reality, is the foreign city of Shanghai. It presents an imposing front of large, elegant mansions, many of them having beautiful yards in front, and over which fly the flags of several different nations, showing them to be the residences of consuls. At intervals can be seen fine, broad streets, leading back from the Bund, lined on either hand by stately buildings.

The Bund itself is lined with numerous wharves, where vessels are lying, taking in or discharging their cargoes. Towards the upper part of the English concession is an extensive pile of buildings—the Chinese custom-house.

From Yang kin-pang Creek to the eastern walls of the Chinese city—about half a mile—is the French concession, over which floats the tri-color. A few fine buildings, from the midst of which rises a lofty church spire, with the wide, busy Bund in front, is all that meets our view from the ship. Of the walled or Chinese town but the northeastern corner of the walls can be seen.

At the point where the Chinese and foreign cities of Shanghai meet upon its banks, the river, about three-fourths of a mile wide, makes a horse-shoe curve of two or three miles from northeast to southwest. A low, green plain lies in this bend, leaving the river to curve around it of uniform width. Near the extreme point there is an old signal-stand, not now used. Back a little are several *godowns*, or storehouses. Still farther back are several large, elegant mansions, standing in wide, deep yards, filled with large trees and fine shrubbery. Close by the river's bank, opposite our anchorage, is an extensive lumber-yard and machine-shop. To the whole is given the name of Pootung side, or simply Pootung.

The country around Shanghai, on every side, is a continuous flat, the only mountains in sight being about thirty miles distant in a northwest direction. The entire population of Shanghai is estimated at two hundred and fifty thousand. There is a large amount of shipping in the harbor, including some of the largest and finest clippers in the world. The greater portion of the vessels are lying at or opposite the wharves just below us, or those at the upper part of English Concession, or at French Concession. Such is the view of Shanghai as seen from our forecastle. Now if you will accompany me on a ramble ashore, we will see what the shore view will furnish of interest.

The hackmen at home, or the Tanka girls at Canton, are not to be compared to the sampanmen of Shanghai for brazen importunity. Curious triangular affairs are these sampans, bright-red, with an eye painted on each side of their blunt bows. They are propelled by grave-looking Chinamen, who, with blue cotton trowsers, no upper garments—or at the best a light cotton sack—shaved head, and broad-brimmed, conical hat, stand up, each alone, in his own boat, swaying himself to and fro as he slowly but steadily sculls his sampan. As we show ourselves at the gangway, the ship's side is thronged with these sampans, each man clamoring loudly for us to take his boat.

We land and spend some time in looking about American Concession, or Hong Que, as it is called. On the street running parallel with the Bund we find a few fair buildings, and a large number of drinking-shops and sailor boarding-houses, with a few miserable Chinese huts.

Crossing the bridge over Su-chau creek, we find a toll-gate at the opposite side, but as the keeper sees that we are in uniform, we are not called upon to pay. Passing along the Bund in front of English and French Towns, we find ourselves "amid bustling scenes and noisy cries—cries from the cargo-boats and others on the water; cries from the venders of fruits, cakes, and confectioneries on shore, but above all, on every hand, turning every corner, up and down every street, there comes upon our ears the wail, 'a-hoo! a-hoo! a-hoo!' the cry of the laboring coolies, who, with the bowed staff on their shoulders and a burden at each end, are hurrying along with tottering steps, with an expression in their cry as though the breath was being pressed from their bodies at every step. From the weight of these burdens, this might well be the case, for all cargoes are transported to and from the warehouses and wharves by men." The traveling of foreigners, and of most Chinese above the rank of laborers, is done in sedan-chairs, upon men's shoulders. No burden-horses or vehicles are to be seen, those on the Bund being mere displays of luxury. Human labor is cheaper than horses or machinery.

Adjoining the upper part of French Town, shut in by dark, gloomy walls some thirty feet high, is the old, or Chinese city. The walls are some three miles in circumference, and from them open six gates, into suburbs even more extensive than the city itself. A moat twenty feet in width and about the same in depth, surrounds the city. The approaches and entrances to the city are most repulsive. On each side of the street leading to it are grouped most disgusting, deformed, wailing, and howling beggars. The details of the condition and appearance of these wretches would be too repulsive for narration. One of the most common and repulsive deformities is that of losing the feet at the ancle-joint in attempting to bandage the feet into littleness. The gates are low arched channels about thirty feet in length, and look like the entrances to sewers. The streets are the sewers themselves, narrow and filthy beyond description. The houses are for the most part built of brick, with tiled roofs, and in no respect differ materially from those of any other Chinese city.

We will not penetrate further into the city to-day, but will leave it for some subsequent visit when we have a guide and more time, and will now take a look back into the English Concession. It is a mile wide, and in some places even more than that, well laid out in fine level streets, with large, commodious places of business, intermixed with large, palatial residences situated in lovely yards. Still further back are many fine Chinese stores and shops. The English chapel stands in a large, but at present not very attractive yard, inasmuch as it is covered with the materials from which they are constructing a new church, which promises to be a fine one. Coming out upon the Bund again, we behold a monument near the bank of the river, and upon examination find that it has been erected to the memory of those foreigners who fell in the Imperial cause during the late Taeping rebellion. General Ward—a native of Salem, Mass.—is at the head of the list.

Our ramble has necessarily been restricted, my dear R., and our view of the interesting sights but partial. At another time, however, when we have a better opportunity and more leisure, we will be more lengthy and minute.

LETTER XIX.

U. S. S. WACHUSETT, Newchwang, }
July 5, 1866.

MY DEAR R.:

Our stay here, which promised at first to be but a few days, has lengthened out to more than two months, and what then bade fair to be tedious and wearisome, has been enlivened by many interesting incidents. Although we leave here in a day or two, one and all hoping that we may never return, I shall ever revert to our time spent at Newchwang, as to by no means the most uninteresting period of our stay in these waters. But now return with me to Shanghai, where my last letter to you was mailed, Saturday, April 28th, and with me take notice of the interesting incidents in the order in which they have been noted down.

That same evening we were serenaded by some of the Wyoming's liberty-men, who came alongside in sampans, and discoursed sweet music—accompanied by some good singing—until nearly midnight. In my account of Shanghai, I neglected to mention the presence there of the Wyoming, a sister ship of the Wachusett. She left the States about two months after we did, and has been some three or four months on the station—having come directly hither.

Just before noon the next day our cutters were brought off from shore, where they had been sent for repairs. This completed the repairs made for the damages done on our passage from Hong Kong, and as all other preparations—such as taking in coal and provisions—had been completed the day previous, at two o'clock we got under way and proceeded down the river under the charge of the pilot. We left him at the light-ship, and then altered our course to the northward, steaming along at the rate of seven or eight knots per hour against a light head wind. The next day our port boiler gave out, so that our speed was lessened to five or six knots. The morning of the third day out we sighted land off our port bow, which proved to be Shantung Promontory, a high peak on the mainland of China, at the straits which connect the Gulf of Pechele with the Yellow sea. About noon we rounded this point of land and altered our course to nearly due west. The following morning we entered the Gulf of Liautung, again altering our course to the northward. In the evening, thinking that we must be near land, we came to anchor. We got under way again at daylight the next morning, and after an hour's steaming we sighted a low, level tract of land right ahead, in which there was an opening some three-fourths of a mile in width—the mouth of the Liau river.

On approaching nearer to the land we saw a vast plain, stretching away as far as the eye could reach, destitute of vegetation with the exception of a few trees and shrubs. Although less than fifteen miles distant we were upwards of three hours in reaching the town, on account of the strong current of the river. About half a mile in breadth, stretching along the left bank for upwards of two miles, we saw an unwalled Chinese town, the houses low, small, and mean, not presenting a single attractive feature. The bank of the river in front was lined with crowds of Chinese, evidently viewing us with great wonder and curiosity.

At the upper end of the town we saw about a dozen one-story buildings, of mud and brick, surrounded by walls of the same material, which we afterwards learned was the foreign quarter. From the flag-staffs in the yards were floating the ensigns of three or four countries, indicating the consulates. We dropped anchor opposite the American consulate, some three or four hundred yards from the shore. Soon after anchoring the Consul came on board and was saluted with seven guns. From some of the visitors which came later in the day, I ascertained the name and condition of the place, and the cause of our coming here.

The foreign population numbers forty-five persons, the greater portion of whom are Americans. Only five of the number are females, and there are five or six children.

The town is usually called Newchwang, but the proper town of that name is several miles farther up the river, and this—Yingtse—is its seaport. The town, with everything about it, is built of mud, and when the weather is dry it is at times almost concealed by the clouds of dust which are raised by the wind, and which even enveloped us at times. The narrow point of land within the horse-shoe curve of the river above the city, is the only attractive feature in the landscape. That is fresh and green with the young paddy.

A band of robbers—"land pirates," they call them—have established themselves here, and go about the town and neighboring villages plundering the inhabitants of money and such other articles as they require. Their number is estimated at from fifty to two hundred. Their stronghold is located on the outskirts of the town, and the ruling mandarin either is powerless to break up this band, or is kept from doing so by sums paid him; the latter, I think, is the most probable. Their depredations have usually been confined to the Chinese, but a short time since they committed some outrages upon the Consul's boys, or servants, and upon his interfering, the pirates turned upon the Europeans, threatening to murder them, and carried off some articles belonging to them. To recover these, an expedition consisting of all the Europeans in the place, together with the sailors from the two or three merchant vessels in port, was formed under the command of Mr. Knight—the American Consul. But the expedition was defeated and obliged to retire with several wounded. Thus matters stood when we arrived here.

After thoroughly investigating the affair, Captain Townsend, about two weeks ago, told the Tau Tai—Chinese ruler of Yingtse—that if he could not break up this band of robbers, he, the Captain, would do so for him. The Tau Tai, apparently, availed himself of this offer with thankfulness, and gave the Captain full authority for doing so. After a day or two spent in making preparations, a little after midnight, Monday, June 25th, all hands were called, as silently as possible, and about a hundred of us armed and equipped for the expedition. We were landed in front of the Consul's, where we formed, and then moved forward in silence under the command of Mr. Philip, our object being to surprise them if possible. Mr. Knight, and Mr. Davenport, the English Consul, accompanied the expedition as interpreters. The Doctor, three or four of our officers, and a few citizens, also went with us.

After marching about three fourths of an hour we were brought to a halt at the lower outskirts of the town, before a low, irregular pile of buildings, surrounded by a high, thick, brick wall. This was the stronghold of the celebrated and much-dreaded pirate chief—Hu, "The Long Knife Man"—and his band. We were now deployed so as to surround the stronghold, and then, leaving the remainder to guard all points of egress, the ladders were brought and a party of us scaled the walls. In spite of the barking of dogs and the shots fired to alarm them, they were fairly surprised—probably never dreaming of such an expedition against them at such an hour, until we burst open the doors and took them prisoners. And well for us was it that we had succeeded in doing this, for in every apartment were found *jimgalls*, freshly loaded, with a great number of spears, swords, and two small pieces of cannon. For a short time it was rather warm quarters; but we soon overpowered them, with no injury to ourselves. When the prisoners were examined by the Consuls they said that the leader was not among them, but were confident that he was somewhere in the stronghold. At last two of us found him concealed in a small room under a pile of bedclothes. He made some show of resistance with a short sword which he had, but a blow from the butt of my musket soon put an end to it. The Consuls recognized him by a fresh bullet wound in his ankle received in the late encounter. In the same room we found a large quantity of arms concealed under a pile of bamboos.

The prisoners were taken to the street and then the building ransacked, and all the arms, of which there was a great quantity, removed. Only twenty-six were taken, the remainder of the band being away on one of their marauding expeditions. Having accomplished the object of our expedition, we set out to return, the prisoners carrying the arms and wounded upon litters.

By this time it was daylight, and as we returned through the town the sides of the streets were thronged with Chinese—the news of our midnight sortie and its success, having been circulated—and as we passed we were greeted with cheers, and there was an expression of joy on every face. After several halts for the prisoners to rest, we at length arrived at the American Consul's, and after " Splicing the Main Brace," we returned on board ship, bringing the prisoners and captured arms with us. In the afternoon the Captain paid an official visit to the Tau Tai, announcing the success of the expedition.

The following day the trial of the prisoners commenced, Captain Townsend and the Consuls sitting as judges with the Tau Tai. An armed party from the ship attended every day, so that we had an opportunity of witnessing some of the Chinese methods of torture and execution. In revolting cruelty some of them would rival any of those practiced during the dark ages. They are almost too horrible for narration. I had no idea that the Chinese could remain so firm and stoical under torture, as I saw them then; for, although suffering untold agonies, only two or three could be made to confess anything, and that was meagre and unsatisfactory. No person is condemned but upon his own confession. However, as torture is always used in all their trials, many innocent persons confess crimes they never committed, in order to escape the tortures. Nothing is gained by confession, unless it is immediate death instead of a lingering one.

The thumb-screw and whipping-machine were the most common instruments of torture employed. The thumb-screw is so constructed that after it is fitted the bones can be crushed by turning a screw—causing the most intense agony. The whipping machine consists of a wheel, in the rim of which strips of bamboo about four feet in length are inserted. This is placed so that in turning the wheel these strips are caught by a cross-bar and drawn back, so as to spring forward with great force. To undergo this mode of torture the victim is stripped to the waist, strapped to a board, and so placed that the bamboo strips will strike with full force upon him. The wheel is then turned until the flesh is lacerated to the bones, then a fresh spot is taken, and the operation repeated until the victim either faints or expires from pain and loss of blood. Beside these, I saw them cut off the nose and ears, and pull out the nails, to induce confession.

After witnessing these barbarities for a day, Captain Townsend said that he could and would endure the sight no longer, nor would he have anything further to do with the trial. Accordingly he delivered the prisoners up to the Tau Tai, leaving him to do with them as he might deem proper. They were all tried, and executed, with the exception of those that expired under the tortures. The whole trial was a mere farce, all the proceedings being an endeavor to force them to confess. Those who did so were immediately executed, while those who did not were executed just the same.

I witnessed the execution of two pirates, which took place in the square near the Tau Tai's. One of them was beheaded; but the other was placed in a case exactly fitting his body, and then commencing at the foot it was screwed up by inches. Very few of those condemned to death enjoy the privilege of being immediately executed; but are frequently made to endure days of lingering torments before death finally puts an end to their sufferings.

It is a lamentable fact, that while the Chinese have so many traits of character that would bear a favorable comparison with civilized and refined nations, they should practice barbarities which are no more than equaled by the most degraded and brutish savages. In defense, they say that it is "ola custom," and that the most stringent measures in the punishment of crime are necessary to preserve law and order throughout so extensive a country, with such an immense population. I am not sure but that in the main they are right, and that we cannot expect a different state of affairs, until the Gospel, with its enlightening rays, shall have penetrated their hearts and consciences, and thrown down the barriers of superstition and crime which idolatry has erected. Then, and not till then, can we expect that the milder and more human laws of civilized countries will take the place of "ola custom."

There are now lying before me on the table at which I am writing, several strings of dirty, green, greasy-looking copper coin, each one about the size of a ten-cent piece, having a square hole perforated through the centre, and with two or three Chinese characters on each side. The coin is called "cash," and about ten or eleven hundred of them make the value of one dollar. They are strung on bamboo fibres in masses of one hundred each, each mass called a "mace." This small coin, this, in value, infinitesimal coin, is a medium of currency among the Chinese, and is an index of the low cost of their subsistence. One hundred "cash" are considered a large daily expenditure among the Chinese, and instances are spoken of where only ten or fifteen are used.

The money we have served out to us from the ship is Mexican dollars, and as there is little or no fractional currency here, we have to take large bundles of these "cash" for change, or else cut up a dollar into small bits, which we sometimes do. In Macao I received for change chopped bits of a dollar, weighed, and then labeled with the amount, and from whom obtained. In large business transactions the Chinese use bars or ingots of silver stamped with the value in taels, each tael being worth about one and one-third dollars. They have had no gold currency for several centuries, and I have never met a person that has ever seen one of their gold coins.

Near the commencement of this letter I made mention of the strong current in the river, which at times runs as fast as six knots per hour. There is also said to be a strong undercurrent. As I was walking up and down the gangway on watch, Tuesday, May 15th, the quarter-master sang out— "A man overboard!" Running upon the poop, I found that a junk, in passing our stern, had run into the dingey, fastened there by a "painter," and had thrown Breems, the boat-keeper, into the water. A crew immediately sprang into the cutter which was lying there, but before they had proceeded a boat's length, Breems, although the best swimmer in the ship, sank with a cry, and was not seen to rise again. He was doubtless dragged down by the under-tow. Other boats were dispatched to different points along the beach in hopes that he might be found upon it, but he was not; and, although a rigid search has been kept up, his body has not yet been recovered. I have seen death in many forms, but never in so sad a manner as this—a ship-mate drowning alongside his ship in broad daylight, while the vessel was lying at anchor, and yet nothing that could be done to save him.

Breems was born in Germany, but the greater portion of his life was passed in France, where he received his education. He was about twenty years of age, fine looking, well educated, and in every respect an estimable young man. He was a good ship-mate, and much esteemed by all. For my part I have lost in him a dear friend, to whom I was much attached. I have also lost a good and kind teacher, who was ever ready to assist me in my French studies, and to whose abilities I owe my proficiency in the language.

A week or two later a boat containing two English sailors and three Chinamen was capsized alongside the ship lying at anchor below us, and not one of the number rescued. I have been told by an old resident that he never saw one rescued that fell in the river here, and he had seen a great many perish.

About two weeks of our stay here has been occupied in surveying the bar at the mouth of the river, and placing buoys to point out the channel. Three buoys have been put down with two anchors, the bearings and course of the channel accurately taken, and hereafter vessels going in and out of the harbor will be freed from the difficulties and dangers which they have hitherto encountered. Great credit is due Captain Townsend and the Board of Survey for their efforts, and the success which has attended them.

A few days ago the Tau Tai paid us a visit. He is a fine looking Chinaman, in rank a mandarin of the third class. The insignia of his rank are a sapphire and a one-eyed peacock feather on his hat, a peacock worked on the breast and back of his robe, and his girdle-clasp of gold. The title of Tau Tai is given to the ruler of a town or portion of a province. His retinue was similar to that of the governor of Canton, but consisted of less exalted personages. He thoroughly examined every thing about the ship with much curiosity and interest, and appeared quite pleased with his visit.

Among the interesting incidents of our stay here were the many boat expeditions and target practices which we had, making our long stay less monotonous than it otherwise would have been. In the early part of our stay the consul presented the captain with a large black bear, which has produced much diversion for all. He is a tame, playful animal, ever ready for a frolic with any one. Jocko sits and watches him for hours, sometimes, with evident dislike, but he has a rival now whom he can not annoy or injure.

Since we have been on the station we have had a great number of court-martials for different misdemeanors, the most common of which has been "taking French leave." The sentences have usually been light, such as the loss of a month's pay, or thirty days in the "brig."

Yesterday was more appropriately celebrated than was "Independence Day" of one year ago. We "dressed ship" at sunrise, as did also the few merchant-men in the harbor, and ashore the consuls' flag-staffs were gay with many-colored flags and streamers. At noon we fired a salute of twenty-one guns. All the messes had a grand dinner, and ales and champagne were abundant. In the evening I went ashore and fired off thirty-five bunches of fire-crackers—a bunch for each state. For the whole I paid about three *mace*. I wonder what the boys at home would think of purchasing fire-crackers at that price.

One of the chief unpleasantnesses of our stay here has been entire absence from mail communication. We have been unable to send or receive letters, and, for that reason, I am glad that to-morrow we are to leave for the southward. I hear that we are to proceed to Shanghai, making two or three stoppages on the coast on our way down.

LETTER XX.

U. S. S. WACHUSETT, Chefoo, }
July 20th, 1866. }

MY DEAR R.:

We did not leave Newchwang until Monday morning, July 7th, when we started, having Mr. Knight and Mr. Davenport on board as passengers. When I went on deck the next morning I saw that we were steering to the northward again. Upon inquiring the reason, I was told that we had passed the point where the Great Wall touches the sea sometime during the night, and that we were going back then, as the captain wished to see it himself, and give the officers and crew an opportunity for beholding it also.

About nine o'clock it was sighted from the mast-head, and, going up into the rigging, I beheld the world-renowned "Great Wall," some ten or fifteen miles distant, scaling the precipices and topping the craggy hills, which have along the coast a a most desolate appearance. It extends along the coast for several miles, and terminates near the beach in an old Chinese fortress. About noon we came to anchor in the lovely little harbor of Tungtse-kau, which marks its termination. By observation Mr. Grove ascertained our anchorage to be in Latitude 40° 4' North, and Longitude 120° 2' East. The cutters were immediately called away, and a party of us went ashore to examine it. The spot where we landed was near the gateway of the old fortress. Inside the fort we saw a fine building, where the emperor resides when he makes a fishing excursion to the bay of Tungtse-kau. Near the building is an old pagoda, built upwards of one thousand years ago. After seeing every thing worthy of interest there, we set out upon a ramble along the top of the wall.

"The Great Wall," called *Wan*-li-chang (*i. e.*, Myriad Mile Wall) by the Chinese, was built by Tsin-Chi-hwangti, about the year 220 B. C., to protect his domains from the excursions of the northern tribes. Almost every third man throughout the empire was drafted for its construction, and being but poorly supplied with provisions many died in the work. On this account the Chinese speak of it as "The ruin of one generation, and the salvation of thousands." The former may be true, but the latter will admit of some questioning, as the Tartars have several times invaded China, notwithstanding this barrier, and are now in possession of the empire.

"It is sufficient evidence of the solidity of its original construction, that it has remained so well-preserved in a region of frosts and moisture. Its entire length is estimated at twelve hundred and fifty miles, including all the doublings. The construction of this gigantic work is somewhat adapted to the nature of the country it traverses. In the western part of its course it is said to be in many places merely a mud or gravel wall, and in others cased with brick." The portion that we visited was composed of a mound of earth and pebbles, faced with brick masonry supported on a coping of stone, the whole being about thirty feet thick at the base, twenty at the top, and varying from twenty-five to forty feet in height. The top is terraced with tiles and defended by a slight parapet, the thinness of which may be taken as evidence that cannon were unknown at the time the wall was erected. There are brick towers at different intervals, some of them more than forty feet high, but the usual elevation is somewhat under that. They are independent structures, built against the wall instead of upon it, usually about forty feet square at the base, and diminishing to thirty at the top. In these towers guards were stationed and arms kept. On either side, as far as we went, the land is fertile and in a high state of cultivation. After walking along upon the top of the wall for four or five miles, we returned and found that the painters had finished putting our ship's name and the date of our visit, in ten foot letters, upon the wall. We then carved our names upon it with knives, and returned on board the ship. For mementoes each of us secured a brick, and I, in addition, took away a dog-like image from one of the many niches along the wall. As I looked over the bulwarks strange thoughts came over me, in comparing what must have been its former life and animation, with its present desertion and quietude.

Beside the name and date of visit of our vessel, there were those of a Prussian Frigate, an English Sloop, and a French Corvette. The Wachusett is the first American war vessel that has visited the spot, and I would not have missed of this pleasure for a large sum. It will be something worth boasting of—the visit to and ramble on the "Great Wall." It was about four o'clock when we returned to the ship, and half an hour later we were under way, standing to the southward.

At two o'clock on the afternoon of the following day, we came to anchor at Takoo, a small town on the northern bank of the Pe-ho river, near where it empties its waters into the gulf of Pe-che-le. On account of the shallowness of the water we were unable to approach within five miles of the shore. At anchor there we found five or six merchant vessels, a French, and an English Corvette. The country around Takoo presents a barren, sterile appearance. The scenery is said to improve as one advances up the river and approaches Tientsin. The size and importance of this city are owing to its being the terminus of the Grand Canal, and the place where the produce and taxes for the use of the Capital are brought. The mouth of the river is guarded by two strong Chinese fortresses, the first that we have seen that were not deserted. Takoo is chiefly noted as a stopping place for those going to and from the Capital, and as a point of embarkation. It is also worthy of note as the spot where the first interview between the English and Chinese plenipotentiaries was held, at the breaking out of the war in 1840 The most important feature of our visit to Takoo, my memory will ever assert to be those large, delicious peaches which two junks brought along side. They were the finest and most delicate-flavored peaches that I ever tasted. Our object in calling at Takoo was to land Mr. Davenport, and this being accomplished, we got under way again just before dark.

On the evening of July 10th, we arrived off the mouth of the harbor of Chefoo. Some thoughts were entertained of "lying off" until the following morning, but we finally concluded to enter. This we did, under the charge of the compradore who came out to meet us. As soon as we had anchored a boat was sent ashore to the Consul's for the mail, which had been forwarded there from Shanghai, and again we were rejoiced by news of our friends, and that we were held in continued remembrance by them.

The harbor here is nearly semicircular in form, about twenty miles in circumference, facing toward the north. Across the mouth, stretches a long, narrow, rocky island, adjoining which are two or three smaller ones, leaving at each side of the group but a narrow entrance, so that the harbor is nearly land-locked, and very secure. The view is shut in upon all sides by barren mountains; but at the foot of them, where the town, or rather towns—for there are two—stand, is a plain some three or four miles in width, curving around the bay on the southern and western sides. It is quite fertile and in a high state of cultivation. There is a large amount of shipping in the harbor, loading with silk, oilcake, and walnuts, which form the chief articles of export.

The principal town lies back, on a small bight, and consists of some thirty or forty unassuming European residences, and a large, unwalled, Chinese town. The English consulate occupies the most prominent site in the place—the summit of a small promontory which juts out into the sea, and is connected with the mainland by a low, narrow isthmus. The population is estimated at twenty thousand, of which only about one hundred and fifty are foreigners. The proper name of the town of which I have been speaking, is Yen-tai, the little village of Chefoo being on the western side of the bay, but the former is usually called by the name of the latter. Provisions here are very good and quite cheap, the climate delightful, and I should prefer remaining here during the summer months to going farther to the southward.

The third day after our arrival, the Consul, accompanied by a missionary, came on board, and told the Captain that there was some trouble at Tung-chow-foo, and wanted him to go up there with the ship and settle it. So we weighed anchor and went up there—about forty miles in a northerly direction—that same day, and came to anchor about a mile from the city. The cutters were immediately sent in shore to take soundings, and they found that the water was deep enough to float us within a few yards of the beach.

Tung-chow-foo is a pretty walled town, about three miles in circumference, and situated close to the beach, on the edge of a fertile, highly cultivated, and exceedingly picturesque plain, extending back some three or four miles to the foot of a barren, lofty range of mountains. The harbor is a mere roadstead between the mainland and a long, barren, mountainous island, some three or four miles removed. We were the sole occupants, not a junk or a boat being in sight. The following day three missionaries came on board, from one of whom I learned the difficulty. They, with their families, were the only foreign residents—a mission station having been located there for many years. Some time ago they purchased a piece of land from the Tau Tai, and now, after they had improved and built upon it, he wished to take it back, threatening to kill them if they should refuse. Besides this, the Chinese had desecrated the graves of the missionaries buried there.

Early Saturday morning, July 14th, "word was passed" for all those who were ashore on the expedition at Newchwang, to hold themselves in readiness to go ashore at Tungchow-foo. Accordingly we were provided with arms and ammunition, and at eleven o'clock about one hundred of us—sailors and marines—set out for the shore in the cutters and launches. As we approached the walls we found that there was an entrance to the city by water—there being a canal and water-gate at the northwestern corner, closed by two heavy iron-ribbed doors, and guarded on either side by two high stone towers, from which missiles that would crush anything passing could be hurled. Entering the city by this canal, we found a lovely sheet of water, occupying about one-half of the central area of the space enclosed by walls, crowded with junks and smaller craft. We landed at a little pier just inside the gateway, and leaving the boats under the charge of armed keepers, formed under command of Mr. Philip, on an eminence near which stands the principal temple of the city. There we were joined by the Captain, and one of the missionaries who was to act as guide.

Having formed, with fife and drum playing a lively air, we marched through the principal streets *en route* for the Tau Tai's. Every house, and the sides of the streets along our route were thronged with curious Chinese, it probably being the first time that the sound of the fife and drum and the tramp of armed men had ever disturbed their streets. I wonder what our government or our people at home would think should an armed body of foreigners thus land and march through the streets of some of their principal cities!

After marching through numerous dirty alley-ways, and a few fine streets, we at length emerged from the city through a strongly fortified gate into the western suburbs. After proceeding a few yards further, we came to a halt before a small chapel and the residence of the widow of one of the missionaries recently murdered by the Chinese. There we remained a few minutes to rest, and receive a glass of water which was kindly brought us by the lady's servants. Another half hour's march brought us to the Tau Tai's, in whose yard we stacked arms and broke ranks. Seldom have I seen more beautiful grounds than those of the Tau Tai at Tung-chow-foo. They are extensive, filled with large trees and beautiful shrubbery, tastefully laid out in charming walks, and everywhere is the tall, green grass. There we remained while the Captain and Missionaries transacted their business with the Tau Tai. And you may believe that we did enjoy ourselves! Could you have seen us rolling about in the grass, climbing the trees, and riding the mandarin's horses, you would have taken us for a troop of schoolboys instead of man-of-war's men, who are generally supposed to have natures utterly unable to take pleasure in any of those childish sports. Let that be as it may, we all were children for a time, in thoughts as well as actions, and for a time we had that perfect happiness which is said to belong to childhood alone. Large baskets of peaches were brought to us, and everything tended to make the remembrance of our visit there a delightful one.

After remaining about two hours, the business was all satisfactorily settled, and the "long roll" sounded for us to "fall in." A march of about fifteen minutes brought us to the residences and grounds of the missionaries, where we were agreeably surprised by finding an inviting supper awaiting us on tables underneath the fine shade-trees in the yard. To this we sat down, after stacking arms and breaking ranks. There was an abundance of everything that was good; the ladies anticipated and supplied our every want, and everything within their power was done to heighten our enjoyment.

The supper over, we had a look over the grounds. These comprise about ten acres, beautifully situated upon a slight eminence, and commanding one of the most charming and picturesque prospects that can be found. The missionaries raise the greater portion of their subsistence, and their crops are at the present time nearly ripe. The buildings are large, commodious, and Anglo-Chinese in architecture. Their school is composed of about forty scholars, which are instructed in both English and Chinese. Among the pupils I noticed several uncommonly bright and intelligent-looking ones, two or three of whom are to be sent to the States to finish their education.

At Tung-chow-foo there are four missionaries and their families; and, although they are deprived of many privileges and enjoyments, separated as they are from civilized and christian people, and surrounded by heathen Chinese, they can still draw much pleasure from the society of one another, and the many beauties of nature by which they are surrounded. Above all can they find comfort and happiness in communing with Him to whose service they are devoting their all, and who will comfort and sustain them through their many trials and privations, and at last fully reward them for all that they have done and suffered for His sake in this life.

I think that there was a feeling of regret experienced by all when the "long roll" sounded, and told us that we must bid them all "good-bye." This was done after "falling in," singing the Star Spangled Banner, and returning thanks for the pleasure that we had received at their hands. As we returned to the ship, all were revolving in their minds the deep pleasure they had received from the excursion into which our expedition had so happily turned. The following day we returned to Chefoo.

Tuesday the 17th, was spent by the crew in "coaling ship," and by a friend and myself in a ramble on shore. After a look at the town, which we found to be very mean in appearance, and very dirty in fact, we commenced to search for something to interest and amuse us. A Mandarin traveling in state was the first thing that rewarded our search. In front were two criers or heralds, crying out the Mandarin's rank, and also clearing the way. Following these were two executioners with black official caps, and behind them two torturers with red official caps, they as well as the executioners bearing the tools of their profession. Next came three or four musicians with gongs and cymbals, followed by two lads in official caps, bearing a crimson trunk containing a suit of criminal's clothes. These are borne to remind the Mandarin of his entire dependence upon the Emperor, and if at any time he receive a summons from his Celestial Highness, he is to don them and repair to his presence. The Mandarin was seated in a rich and magnificently trimmed and adorned sedan chair, which was borne upon the shoulders of six coolies. At his side walked one bearing a huge crimson cloth-covered umbrella, and bringing up the rear was a squad of soldiers without arms. This is the outline of the retinue of any mandarin or high official when traveling, the number and rank of the attendants being varied according to his rank or position.

We paid a visit to the grave yard, situated midway between the town and the village of Chefoo. This contains many antique monuments of stone, with curious carvings, and is the only thing worthy of note in the whole place.

The "general liberty" which we have been having for the past two days, has fully demonstrated the truth of what I said upon the subject in a previous letter. Men, after being confined on board ship for three or four months, and then permitted to go on shore in great crowds for a twenty-four hours' debauch, will have the tendency to outrage, which arises from the physical power of numbers turned loose for indulgence in a weak community. They are brought to this morbid condition by their long confinement; therefore I do not speak of their committing some slight outrages upon the citizens of Chefoo, during this liberty, as an unexpected event, but rather with wonder that this should be the first time that such an occurrence has happened this cruise. Of course there will be a number of courtmartials, and *some* of the guilty ones punished as it is but right and proper that they should be, but still I can but think that if there were more consideration paid to the fact that sailors have human natures, and they were treated accordingly, all possibility of such occurrences would be forever obviated, and the most beneficial results secured. While I would not seek to have the punishment withheld from the perpetrators of such outrages, I do hope that the lesson will not be unheeded, and that some plan may be adopted which shall not only improve and benefit all, but also add to the good name of the ship and those belonging to her.

A few days before we arrived here, great excitement was occasioned by the arrival of three fugitive French missionaries from Corea. The following account of their sufferings, and other interesting particulars, I copy from the *Shanghai, North China Daily News*, of July 16th.

CHEFOO.

"*From a Correspondent.*

"Most painful news has just been received from the Kingdom of Corea. On the 7th instant, a Corean junk with the French tri-color at one of the mast-heads, was observed entering the harbor. It brought the Reverend Abbe Ridel, Catholic Missionary, and eleven Corean Christians who have fled from that country on account of the persecution now raging there by order of the father of the King, against the Christian Churches. Mr. Ridel reports that, in the month of February last, the King received intelligence that the Russians had crossed his frontier, and that they were holding intercourse with his subjects. At the same time the Corean embassy in China informed their sovereign that the Chinese had murdered two Catholic missionaries, and that it would be well to imitate this example. Upon this, a general order was issued to apprehend all the Catholic Missionaries (there being no other missionaries,) and to exterminate the Christians. Two French bishops and seven priests were arrested, and after having been cruelly tortured, were beheaded. As a special favor, a request by some of the missionaries to be executed on Good Friday, was acceded to. Only three Catholic priests remained, and they managed to hide themselves in the mountains. They determined that one of their number should endeavor to reach the coast, and come to this port for the purpose of asking the protection of the French Government, for those who remained. Mr. Ridel was selected by his confreres for the task, and it was only in obedience to the united judgment of his brother priests, that he parted from them, and came on his present errand. He describes the devastation committed on the Christian Church of Corea as appalling. One town, nearly all Christians were ordered to renounce the faith. Many were martyred; others fled, and the greatest consternation prevailed. The Pagan population are averse to the persecution, but they are too weak to resist. There were at the beginning of this year about fifty thousand Catholic Christians in the kingdom of Corea. The two priests who survive, if they can escape the researches of the King's soldiers, will try to keep alive the faith until fresh missionaries arrive; but they have lost everything. The library which existed in the capital city, containing many Corean books, and especially two dictionaries of the Corean language, compiled by the French missionaries with the labor of twenty-five years continual application, together with the printing establishment and material for publishing books in the Corean language, have all been destroyed. The loss to the science of language incurred by the destruction of the above named dictionaries is, it is feared irreparable. All the sacred vessels for celebrating the holy sacrifice of the mass have been destroyed by the King's orders, and the Christian Church in Corea is threatened with destruction. At the time Mr. Ridel left, the persecution had momentarily ceased, as the King found that it interfered with the harvest of the crops; but orders had been given to resume the work of extirpating the Christians in the approaching autumn.

"Mr. Ridel left this port by the *Nanzing* for Tientien, in order to see the French Admiral, who is there present, and it is expected that a French vessel of war will be sent to Corea to demand reparation. The feeling in France when this sad news arrives there, will be so strong that the French government will hardly be able to decline assuming the responsibility of taking measures to prevent the recurrence of such cruelties. Such a wholesale massacre of French clergy by a Pagan monarch, without provocation on their part, will excite the strongest indignation not only in France, but wherever belief in Christianity exists.

"The Corean government is in a wretched state; the widow of the late king has adopted a youth for the sovereign, and it is the father of this youth who is the author of all these cruelties. Corea is completely undefenced. A gunboat could make its way to the capital without fear of resistance. The Corean army is a rabble unprovided with artillery or even muskets, and a very slight demonstration would suffice to induce submission. Mr. Ridel will most probably go to Pekin, and it is to be hoped that the British minister will not lose such an opportunity as this to ask, in conjunction with the French minister, for the opening of Corea to foreign intercourse. This will be the surest way to prevent the recurrence of such lamentable events. The Corean junk remains here during the journey of Mr. Ridel to Tientien and Pekin, and is a great [object of curiosity on the part of the inhabitants of this port."

LETTER XXI.

U. S. S. WACHUSETT, Shanghai,
August 17th, 1866.
MY DEAR R.:

Heat, sickness, and death, are the most noticeable events of the month which has elapsed since my last communication to you was mailed. It has truly been the saddest, most trying period of our cruise, and as I recall those sorrowful events, I can but be thankful that I have passed safely through them, and hope that I may never experience the like again. Having safely passed through them, I sit down to give you an account thereof.

We arrived here, from Chefoo, July 26th, after a very pleasant passage of four days, the only noticeable incident of which was, the washing of a man overboard while over the side putting the plugs in the hawse-pipes. He was subsequently recovered. Here we remained quietly until August 10th, there being little or no exercise or unusual work performed, except to take in coal and provisions. In fact it would have been almost impossible to have done anything, for the heat was excessive, (the thermometer seldom standing below 90° in the shade,) and the air dry and sultry—almost suffocating.

Friday, August 10th, we weighed anchor, and with Mr. Seward—consul-general—two American citizens, and some seven or eight Chinese servants, as passengers, we started for Hankow, a place about six hundred and fifty miles up the Yangtse-kiang River. It was late in the afternoon when we left Shanghai, so we did not proceed more than about twenty-five miles before we came to anchor for the night. The following morning we again got under way, and again anchored at dark, after proceeding about one hundred miles.

The Yangtse-kiang (*i. e.*, Son of the Ocean) flows nearly three thousand miles in all its windings. It is often simply called *Kiang* or *Ta*-kiang—the River or Great River. The basin drained by it is estimated at seven hundred and fifty thousand square miles, and from its almost central course, and the number of provinces through which it passes, it has been termed the "Girdle of China." Owing to the great width of the estuary, which extends about one hundred and twenty-five miles above its mouth, we were able to see but little of interest of the country through which we were passing. The surface for the most part is low and level, hills being but rarely seen. Wherever it is available, canals are dug and water let in upon the rice-fields; and, when this kind of grain is cultivated, it allows few or no trees to grow. The plains are divided by raised banks into plots of from one to ten acres each, the banks serving for pathways, as well as assisting in confining the water when let in upon the growing crop.

In the entire absence of fences to denote the bounds of the fields, a cultivated plain looks like a vast garden, in which the plats appear as beds. At intervals along the river are bayous and creeks, on which can be seen immense flocks of wild geese and ducks.

We started again at day-break Sunday morning, and after steaming a few hours, came to that point in the river where it leaves its estuary form, and narrows down to about a mile and a half in width. Just above these narrows is *Siung Shan,* or Silver Island, a beautiful spot, covered with temples and monastic establishments, surrounded by beautiful gardens and bowers. Massive granite terraces decorated with huge stone monsters are reached from the water by broad flights of stone steps; fine temples placed to be seen and yet shaded by trees, open pavilions and shaded summer-houses, give it a delightful air of retreat and comfort. On a little flat at the foot of the eminence on which these stand, picturesquely situated, and embowered with trees, stands a pretty European cottage, in front of which three small cannon are mounted, while from a tall flag-staff the American ensign was floating as we passed —the American consulate. About three miles above this island is the walled town of Chinkeang-foo, about half a mile from which we came to anchor. The gig was immediately lowered, manned, and sent after the consul.

A short distance above the city is *Kin Shan*, or Golden Island. A pagoda crowns its summit, and there are many temples and pavilions of various sizes and degrees of elegance. Golden Island is smaller than Silver Island, and has a more toy-shop appearance, from the crowd of temples, pagodas, and pavilions, which cover its sides, and glitter with green and yellow-glaced porcelain tiled roofs. These islands present by far the most picturesque scenery we saw on the river. The city of Chinkiang stands just below the junction of the Grand Canal with the Yangtse-kiang. Its position renders it the key to the country, being able to blockade both the canal and river. The scene at the junction affords a good exhibition of the industry and trade of the people. As Barrows says, "The multitude of war-junks, of burden and pleasure, some gliding down the stream, others sailing against it; some moving by oars, and others lying at anchor; the banks on either side crowded with towns and houses as far as the eye can reach, furnish a prospect more varied and cheerful than any we have hitherto seen." The country in the vicinity is well cultivated, and presents a pleasing variety. On the southeast the hills break into an undulating country clothed with verdure, while beyond stretch the lowlands, through which we had passed in ascending the stream. On the left bank of the river the land continues a low, swampy flat, with innumerable sheets of water separated by narrow mounds, so that the whole resembles a vast lake, intersected by causeways.

Willows grow along the sides of these causeways, and there are a few dwellings erected upon the elevations.

Chinkiang is quite a large city, its walls being about four miles in circumference. It lies between two quite high ranges of hills, extending back from the river, and meeting behind the town. There are a few elevations within the walls, upon one of which, at the farther extremity, stands an old pagoda, and near by the showy buildings of the Mandarin. The front wall is very high and thick, but the others are quite small. The city lies back about a mile from the river, but extending along the bank is a high, thick wall, about two miles in length, each extremity terminated by a lofty eminence, on the summit of which stand the ruins of what must have been formidable Chinese fortresses. Indeed, at the taking of the place by the English, on July 21st, 1842, the resistance on the part of the Manchoo garrison showed that the place was of uncommon strength, and that the Chinese were not entirely devoid of courage. It is said that "the Tartar general, Hailing, finding the city taken, seated himself in the midst of his papers, and set fire to his house, making it his funeral pyre. His ashes and those of his wife and grandson were afterward collected, and an honorary *fane*, or monument, was ordered to be erected to his memory at the public expense." At the upper side of the city stand a few European residences—the foreign section of the city. On the opposite bank is a large collection of low, mean-looking, bamboo, Chinese hovels.

Monday the thermometer varied from 95° to 104° in the shade. And such heat! It was not only exceedingly hot, but was a sultry, sickening, deadening heat. There was not a breath of air stirring, and one and all appeared, and in fact were, utterly powerless, caring but little whether they lived or died. Every few minutes during the day the decks were wet down, and the hose played upon the awnings. At such times the steam would rise, almost the same as if water had been poured upon a hot stove. From the sides of the ship and from such portions of the deck as were not protected by the awnings, the pitch could be seen oozing forth, and to walk upon the exposed portions with bare feet was little short of torture. At all hours of the day the men were seen lying about the decks, fanning themselves, and trying every method to keep cool.

In the morning, just after the "retreat" sounded, all were startled by the announcement that Mate Thomas Kelly had died while we were at quarters. The doctor pronounced the cause to be "congestion of the brain, brought on by the excessive heat." Early in the morning he was on deck, apparently in his usual health; his sickness and death all occurred in the space of about half an hour. Preparations were immediately made for his funeral. He was laid out in his uniform until a coffin could be made, which was done by Chinese carpenters on shore. Of the party that went ashore to dig his grave, four were prostrated by sun-stroke, and one of them is yet lying in a critical condition. Mate Kelly's funeral took place the following morning, and his body was followed to the grave, on Silver Island, by most of the officers and a firing-party.

I was awakened at 1.30 A. M., Wednesday, August 15th, by the corporal of the guard, and told that Captain Townsend had just expired. He was taken ill the evening previous, but his sickness was not considered to be anything serious until about midnight, when he commenced to grow worse rapidly, and so continued until he expired. A boat was immediately sent aboard the river-steamer, Plymouth Rock, for ice to place around the body and preserve it until we could reach Shanghai, whither he had given orders, a short time before he died, that we should proceed at day-light. At three o'clock Mr. Seward took passage for Shanghai in a river-steamer going down, so as to have a tug-boat meet us with a supply of ice. At four o'clock we got under way, and in passing Silver

Island we half masted the flag, and fired three guns to arouse the consul and inform him of the captain's death. In return he half masted his flag and fired three guns. The flag was kept at half mast all day, and all the vessels in the river half masted their colors out of respect to the dead. We arrived at Shanghai at 8 o'clock in the evening.

The following day, at 5 P. M., the remains were taken on shore for interment. A salute of seven guns from the decks of the Wachusett announced the lowering of the coffin over the ship's side; and shortly before 7 P. M. the procession left the Bund in the following order:

BAND.

Sixty sailors from the Wachusett under Lieutenant Philip, *Acting* Commander.

Captain Hewett,				Captain Bochet,
Mr. Dixwell,	4 sailors.	BIER.	4 sailors.	Mr. Seward,
Mr. Nye,				Mr. Grew,
Mr. Hayes,				Mr. Twombly.

MR. THORNE AND MR. TOWNSEND, Chief Mourners.

Officers of Wachusett.

Community.

The funeral service was most impressively read by Rev. C. H. Butcher, and after its conclusion three volleys were fired over the grave. It is said that a larger number of the community followed the coffin than ever had on any previous occasion—a mark of respect to the deceased which those who had the privilege of his acquaintance know well how highly he deserved.

The following obituary letter from Consul-General George F. Seward will meet with a hearty confirmation by all who knew him:

"My acquaintance with the decease was very brief, yet it was sufficient to enable me to appreciate somewhat the many excellent traits of his character. There are others I know who were equally attracted by his genial manner and rich conversation, and who grieve with me over his death. I feel it to be my duty to offer to such the information touching his life and character which I have been able to glean. I could wish that the service might be performed by another more familiar with his career and his high qualities.

"Commander Townsend's family has been long and honorably known in America. Some members of it served in the war of the revolution, both in council and in camp. It was represented well in the Mexican war, and during the late rebellion its old spirit of devotion to country was again exhibited. A brother of the deceased commanded one of the first regiments sent out by the state of New York at the outbreak of the rebellion, and did signal service. He has been widely known as adjutant-general of the state of New York. A nephew, barely twenty-three years of age, was killed in Grant's great march upon Richmond, while commanding the 106th New York Volunteers. Other members of the family were prominently active in various departments.

"The deceased graduated at Union College, New York, in 1835, and immediately entered the navy as a midshipman. His first cruise was in the Mediterranean. He afterwards took part in the siege and capture of Vera Cruz, and was otherwise actively engaged during the Mexican war.

"In 1851 Commander Townsend, then a lieutenant, having married, resigned his commission. At the outbreak of the rebellion he offered his services as a volunteer, and was accepted as an acting lieutenant. He served as such under Farragut at the passage of the forts and the capture of New Orleans. Still later he commanded the *Miami*, and did efficient service in the Sounds of North Carolina. Subsequently he was restored to the regular service with the rank of commander, and commanded the well known iron-clad, *Essex*, at the siege of Port Hudson. Still later he was division commander under Admiral Porter and upon the Red River—

campaigns of the most harrassing description. Just before the close of the war he was ordered to the East India Squadron.

"His career in China, though brief, was not an idle one. His conduct of matters at Newchwang was such as to afford a guarantee for the peace of the port, yet it was so considerate and careful, that no injury, but the contrary, was offered to the prestige of the native authorities. At Canton, he rendered some valuable service, and at Chefoo he put the difficulties of the missionaries in the way of settlement. Before his return from the latter place he received orders to proceed to Hankow, stopping at the ports, and it was at the first of these *en route*, that he met the hand of the Destroyer. His hard work and exposure to the malaria upon the southern Mississippi had implanted in his system the seeds of disease, and they were germinated readily by the fierce sun and the fresh water of the Yangtse.

"The deceased was somewhat exposed to the sun on Sunday the 12th, and to the night air on Sunday evening. On Monday evening, he had a slight fever, which increased on Tuesday. Yielding to urgent advice, and perhaps to a sense of impending danger, he concluded to return to Shanghai the next morning. No one dreamed that he was seriously ill, but the intense heat rendered it undesirable and unsafe for all that the voyage should be prosecuted. At 1.30, Tuesday morning, wearied with work and exposure, I went on board the ship, and as I passed to my cot I saw him quietly sleeping. In less than half an hour, I was awakened only in time to see him yield up his breath to its Giver. He had passed from sleep into a state of insensibility, and died without the opportunity to breathe a message to wife and children, and a prayer to the Mercy Seat.

"Favored by high social position, and inherited wealth, fortunate in his family and domestic relations, Capt. Townsend needed nothing which could make life dear to him. Neither his experience or active life nor his enjoyment of leisure had been unprofitable, but he had ever been a careful observer in the world, and there was stowed away in his capacious mind a vast fund of information.

"In character, he was benevolent and appreciative, yet just and firm. He was known as a fighting man on board his ship, and to the world, yet no one was more tender-hearted and considerate. His intelligence, his tenderness, his firmness, endeared him to his officers, while his manner was sufficient to ensure for him the affection of his men. The sorrow felt for him on board the *Wachusett* is deep and permanent, and forms the best testimonial to his qualities of head and heart."

GEO. F. SEWARD.

SHANGHAI, Aug. 17th, 1866.

The death of our Captain came most unexpectedly to us all, and never before have I seen such an expression of sorrow as has been manifested by the crew of the *Wachusett* since that sad event occurred. He was beloved and respected by all, almost as a father, and since his death scarcely a smile has been seen about our decks.

If anything can be wanting to perfect our respect for the deceased, we shall find it in the tenderness of the following lines to his wife and children, which are taken from the *Army and Navy Gazette*, and are evidently from his pen. The sentiments expressed in these lines has found a response in the hearts of most of us, as we thought of the loved ones, far, far away. We may not intrude upon the sorrows of his loved ones, but as we think of our own, we can but pause to think of the grief which will fall upon them, when the tidings of their loss reach their home.

A NEW YEAR GARLAND.

TO LOVED ONES AT HOME, FROM THE INDIAN OCEAN.

My own dear wife! dear boy! dear girls!
The wealth of love ye bear for me,

10*

Is richer than the fairest pearls
  That glisten 'neath this Indian Sea.
And gathered round our simple hearth,
  Breathing the atmosphere of love,
I ask no purer Heaven on earth,
  Nor dream a happier Heaven above.

Yet far away my treasure lies,
  Whilst storm-swept oceans roll between;
The Pole star reigning o'er those skies,
  Ne'er gazes on this alien scene.
But, as I pace the midnight deck,
  The Southern Cross is blazing high;
Ah! heart estranged I little reck
  The splendors of this Austral sky.

Only the glorious sun may shine,
  At once upon my home and me;
And, watching him at day's decline,
  Sinking beneath the tranquil sea,
My orisons instinctive break
  Upon the hallowed evening air—
I know his blessed beams awake,
  My darlings to their morning prayer.

Vicegerent of the God of Light!
  I cannot wonder that of old
The *Magi* worshiped, as the night
  Fled, vanquished by thy orb of gold,
Our purer faith—our hopes God given,
  Feel thy benignant influence still,
Raising the earth bound soul toward Heaven,
  Scatt'ring each brooding fear of ill.

Thus, upwards borne, my troubled heart,
  Reposes on the love Divine—
Far as the several poles apart,
  From those dear lives so linked with mine;
Long months away—for months no word
  To break the chaos absence brings;
My soul, beyond endurance stirred,
  Flies suppliant to the King of kings.

The good and gracious God will keep
  My loved ones in His holy care,
This yearning, anxious heart may sleep,
  Calm on the wings of trustful prayer;
And, strengthened, turn its wistful gaze
  To that sweet time of halcyon rest,
When, bathed in love's unstinted rays,
  'Twill be amid its treasures blest.

Up springing from the Tropic Sea,
  Again the glorious sunbeams shine,
Bringing your Vesper Hymn to me,
  Mingling your loving hearts with mine.
Dear wife! dear children! Orient sun,
  And sapphire sea, and pearly skies,
Beam with God's smile; the loving one
  Biddeth our downcast hearts arise.

                                    T.
U. S. S. WACHUSETT,
  Lat. 12° 44' S., Long. 99° 59' E., Jan. 1, 1866.

LETTER XXII.

U. S. S. WACHUSETT, Shanghai, China, }
Aug. 18, 1866.

MY DEAR R.:

When we returned here from Chinkiang, upwards of one-third of the crew were prostrated with fever, brought on by the excessive heat, and the unhealthfulness of that place. There were several quite critical cases of fever; but owing to the constant and excellent attendance of the surgeon, and his steward, all of the sick are in a fair way to recover, with the exception of a boy named Falvey, who probably has not many hours to live.

Come with me now, and we will finish that ramble about the native section of Shanghai, which we left incomplete on our former visit. We find that our former impressions as to Shanghai being a dirty city are confirmed, and that the houses are not as fine as those of some other Chinese towns we have visited. There are numerous fine shops, however, which present imposing fronts with their numerous and variously colored signs and lamps. The objects which most attract the notice of a stranger, are the silk and embroidery, cotton, and cotton goods, porcelain, chinese costumes lined with beautiful skins and furs, bamboo pipes four or five feet long, shops for selling bamboo ornaments, pictures, bronzes, specimens of old porcelain, and many other curiosities to which the Chinese attach great value. The most extensive trade, however, is in articles of food, and sometimes there is much difficulty in passing through the streets of the city owing to the immense quantities of fish, pork, fruit and vegetables which crowd the stands in front of the shops. Dining rooms, tea-shops, and bakers' houses are met with at every step. They are of every grade from that of the poor man who carries around his kitchen, or bakehouse, altogether hardly worth a dollar, to the most extensive tea-shop crowded with customers. For a few cash a Chinaman can dine upon rice, fish, and vegetables; nor does it seem to matter much to him whether his table is spread in the open street or in an elegant tea-house. Lying on the ground in front of the prisons, with their heads in the cague—a square board some three or four feet in length, with a hole through the center, through which the head is thrust, and then resting upon the shoulders like a collar—are seen criminals exposed to the rays of the hot sun, and the annoyance of the flies, as well as to the jeers and taunts of the passer-by.

But leaving these disagreeable sights, we will look for something more attractive. This we may find in the tea-gardens, a collection of artificial grottoes, miniature lakes and ponds, temples and pleasant walks, with picturesque little bridges leading to some temple or pavilion situated on an island in the miniature lake. The erection and construction of these evinces a taste for the beautiful and picturesque; but I am sorry to add that the same good taste is not displayed in keeping them in repair, neatness, or decency. We find the waters, green, stagnant pools, and the whole garden given up to fortune-tellers, gaming tables, conjurers, obscene show-men, and loafers. It presents a somewhat better appearance on one of their festive days, and at those times furnishes a characteristic scene of Chinese animation. The people that throng it are dressed out in their best garb; the fortune-teller, conjurer, show-man, and tumbler are engaged in their respective vocations, and the noise of gongs, cymbals, and crackers is terrific. We must not leave without having some tea, and signifying our desire to the guide, we are straightway conducted by him, over a picturesque little bridge to a tower on an island in the largest of the artificial lakes, where he tells us that we can get "No. 1, first chop, Mandelin tea." Ascending to the third floor, we seat ourselves in a rich and tastefully furnished room, which commands a fine view of the principal square of the gardens, and forthwith *tea* is brought us. We taste and forthwith exclaim, "this is *tea!*" I have never tasted its equal before." O ye afternoon New England tea-drinkers, could you but have some of this tea, methinks that that reputed flow of conversation for which you are famed, would resemble the rapid mountain torrent whose progress is not to be restrained by bond or barrier!

The Chinese have furnished us with tea as well as with cups, but few Europeans seem to understand the art of preparing the beverage, and are seldom seen to partake of it, for the sake of the pure taste of the tea. Tea-shops are everywhere to be seen throughout China, and a visitor is invariably presented with a cup of the beverage immediately upon his arrival. The Chinese seldom make " strong tea," and never add milk or sugar.

Tea marks the period of our departure from Shanghai for Japan to-day, and is a good word with which to close this letter. May we soon have a tea-drinking together in the United States, and if the article is not equal to that we had in China, there will be more than enough else to compensate for the mere loss of tea.

LETTER XXIII.

U. S. S. WACHUSETT, Nagasaka, Japan, }
September 22, 1866. }

MY DEAR R.:

As I feared, Falvey did not live a great many hours, but died that same evening before we reached Woosung. Accordingly we anchored there that night. The next morning a boat was sent ashore to dig a grave; but permission for doing so was refused by the Chinese authorities, and we were forced to bury him at sea. This is the first burial at sea we have had this cruise, and to me it was a very impressive and solemn occasion.

The headway of the ship was stopped; the flag put at half-mast; the body, sewed up in a hammock, with two thirty pound shot at the feet, was placed on a plank in the gangway, and covered with the jack; and all hands were assembled on the quarter-deck, and stood with uncovered heads while the funeral service of the Episcopal church was read. As the words, "we now consign the body of our beloved brother to the deep," were pronounced, the plank was gently raised, and the body plunged into the sea. After the benediction, three volleys of musketry were fired, the flag mastheaded, and we again moved on, leaving "our beloved brother" to remain there, until "the sea shall give up the dead which are in it." There may he rest, and

"Find pleasant weather,
Till he who all commands,
Shall give, to call life's crew together,
The word, to pipe all hands."

Thursday, August 23d, we arrived at Yokohama, having made the passage from Shanghai in about four days and a half, beating the mail steamer by twelve hours. Our passage was characterized by a smooth sea, little or no wind, and with no unusual incidents, other than that we had no exercise. We found the *Hartford* and *Wyoming* both lying at Yokohama, and immediately upon our arrival Mr. Philip went aboard the Flagship to report the death of the Captain, and to await further orders.

While lying there we had many Japanese visitors, representatives of the various classes of society, from the gentleman of rank to the meanest laborer. As a race they are far superior to the Chinese—the features more regular, and the complexion less sallow. If dressed in the garb, many of them would pass for Europeans. Instead of shoes, they wear sandals, with white or blue stockings, the sandal being retained upon the foot by a string passing between the great toe and its nearest neighbor—toe No. 2. Their remaining articles of dress consist of loose and baggy cotton trowsers, which are confined tightly about the ankles, and a short gown of the same material crossing the breast in intersected folds. The head is left bare, with the hair curiously arranged and decorated. The top from the forehead to the vertex, for the breadth of three or four inches, is clean-shaved. The hair is then gathered up from the back and sides of the head, and waxed into a smooth spike with the ends cut even. This spike is bound by a cord close to the head, and after making a short curve backward, is brought forward, and rests upon the middle of the shaven surface. This is the dress of the middle class. The lower class wear precisely the same costume, but of a cheaper material. Coolies are sometimes seen naked to the waist, and without stockings or sandals. The dress of a Japanese gentleman has not inappropriately been compared to "that of a plain, neat, but richly dressed Quakeress just attired for a street promenade." The pantaloons, with their loose, baggy legs, are of rich, soft-colored and figured silk, and meet at the waist a mantle of silk,—with large flowing sleeves,—which is brought across the breast in intersecting oblique folds, and secured about the waist by a girdle. Over this is worn a short frock or gown, of dark or dove-colored silk gauze, on each sleeve and shoulder of which is a white figure, enclosing the arms of the individual. The same device is also worked on the mantles of his retainers. A long, black-handled, black-scabbarded sword, with a similar short one, stuck through the girdle on the left side, completes the costume.

In their intercourse with foreigners, and with one another, I have ever noticed the most courteous and polished behavior. In manner and countenance they are intelligent and polished gentlemen. They are quiet and subdued, rather than demonstrative, in their expressions of courtesy, and seem to have their passions and emotions under perfect control, in this respect somewhat resembling the polished clergy of the Roman Catholic church. The smiles which constantly light up their countenances display beautifully white and regular teeth. Their mode of salutation when about to pass one another, is highly illustrative of their courteous deportment. "One rests his hands on his circumflexed knees, and with gracious smiles lowly bows his head forward; the other immediately does the same, and after repeating this they pass on. This mode of salutation is not confined to inferiors in saluting their superiors, but is employed to equals." By a close examination the Japanese may be observed to have a dual character, a fact which will perhaps account for the different reports which different writers have given of them. We see them in their official capacity, taciturn, suspicious, vindictive, cruel, while we again behold them in their social relations, communicative, trustful, kind, and hospitable. The character assumed during the time that they are engaged in their official duties, is all laid aside as soon as the business is over, so that we may behold them in the enjoyment of social intercourse with those who, but a short time before, they appeared to regard with enmity and distrust. Their honesty is remarkable; after a visit from any number of them no one would ever think of missing a single article; indeed, none could be induced to accept the most trifling present, and in all their dealings they are very exact. Cleanliness appears to be one of their chief virtues. Their modesty, however, is far from being equal to their honesty, for their cities are provided with public bath-houses, where all ages and sexes mingle freely, without any encumbrance of costume.

Before going on shore we will take a survey of Yokohama from the ship, to see if there is not something of interest to be noted, and, *sailor* fashion, we will commence with the harbor. In entering it a vessel turns to the northwestward from Yeddo Bay, and after proceeding in this direction for about a mile, the course is altered to nearly due west, in which direction the harbor extends for the remainder of its length. In all, it closely resembles a short boot in form, the entrance answering to the leg. There it is about two miles in width, and narrows down, irregularly, to a point at its inner extremity, some three or four miles distant.

On the southwestern side of the entrance is a high, rocky bluff, the scenery about which is exceedingly wild and picturesque. On its summit is a signal station, and close by are the English barracks, with the union jack flying in front. At the western, or inner foot of this bluff, are the French barracks. Further in is a canal, some seventy or eighty feet in width, which describes a rudè semicircle, about two miles in length, and terminates in a large bight, or cove, filled with junks and small Japanese craft. On the semicircular space inclosed by the canal, stands the town of Yokohama, facing to the northward, and at its greatest width measuring from half to three-fourths of a mile. The eastern portion is the foreign settlement, and the western the native portion, the two being separated by a wide street. Continuing on from the town, there are few houses seen until we cross a bridge, about a mile in length, at the inner extremity of the harbor. Then, going east on the opposite side, we come to the larger Japanese town of Kanagawa, facing to the southward, and nearly opposite Yokohama. On this side, near the centre of the town, we notice a large Japanese fortress, built of stone, mounting several heavy pieces of cannon, and comparing favorably with many a fort of European construction. In the harbor are a large number of men-of-war, steamers, and merchant vessels of different nationalities, besides the immense number of native junks and smaller craft. The surrounding country has in general a level aspect; beside the numerous fruit trees seen, a species of spruce, or fir, are the most common. And now, to complete the sketch—some forty-five miles in a northwesterly direction is seen the volcanic mountain, Fusi Yama, with its perpetually snow-clad summit of fourteen thousand feet high, celebrated alike in Japanese history and mythology.

While we are being rowed ashore in one of them, we can mark the difference of the Japanese boats from those of the Chinese. The most noticeable differences are the sharp, curving prows, somewhat resembling a skate runner cut off where it commences to curve over, and in their being propelled by two, three, and sometimes more scull-oars, resting on bars projecting from the sides.

We land at the little pier, or *hettlebar*, at the foot of the street which separates the two sections, and after proceeding about one hundred yards up this, turn off to the left, and find ourselves on Hamora street,—the Broadway of Yokohama. We pass up this street, cross the canal by a fine bridge, and ascend the bluff, from which we have a bird's-eye view of the city and the surrounding country. The town stands on a low plain, but farther back the country is very uneven, with, however, no considerable eminences. There is nothing about the foreign section of Yokohama to distinguish it from a town of equal size at home. Both that and the native section are laid out with much exactness, and have an appearance of neatness and comfort.

Now, descending the bluff, and taking a stroll around the town to the westward, there will be much of interest presented to us. A few steps bring us to the foot of a considerable eminence ascended by a long flight of stone steps, at the top of which stands a large establishment for drying and packing tea. We enter and find ourselves in a large room, filled with rows of earthernware or iron kettles set in arches. Before each kettle is a Japanese, busily engaged in stirring about two pounds of tea which is being dried by a slow fire. To each row of kettles there is one who from time to time passes along its entire length, taking a small portion of tea from each kettle, carefully keeping them separate from each other on a tray. This he bears to a little desk at one corner of the room, where sits the inspector, who tells at a glance if it is sufficiently dried. If it is, the tea is placed in baskets made for this purpose, carried to the packing room, and a fresh supply placed in the kettles. Further on we come to a number of temples, whose only attractions are the exceedingly picturesque situation, and the fine carvings in stone which are near. Then on, past a swampy tract, and we come to the Grand Cairo with its thousands of courtesans, a small city by itself.

As we again cross the canal, and enter the Japanese section at its western extremity, we find ourselves surrounded by entirely different scenes from those we have seen in Chinese cities. Although we are on the principal street—called Curiosity street, from the numerous curiosity and silk shops which line its sides—we find everything scrupulously neat and clean, and are not annoyed by the clamor and thronging of business which ever attend a walk through a Chinese city. There is activity and industry everywhere exhibited, but conducted in an orderly and subdued manner. The sides of the streets are not crowded with market stands, tea and cake shops, or those pursuing the various trades; but all have shops of their own.

Everywhere the push-cart, by which transporting is largely done, is met. This consists of a skeleton box resting upon two wooden wheels about two feet and a half in diameter. In front are two shafts with a cross-bar at the ends, at the projecting extremities of which, two push, and two more at the rear, resting their shoulders against bars projecting from the axle-tree, push also, all keeping time with a loud, guttural chant. These are the only wheeled vehicles to be seen throughout the Empire.

On or near all the bridges, priests and devotees are seen sitting, singing and tinkling a small bell. These have the entire head shaven, and wear a long black robe. In passing them, those so inclined gave them small amounts of money, or articles of food and clothing, receiving in return charms or blessings.

There are but two professions in Japan, doctor and priest. The doctor ranks with the privileged class, and is the most important man in a village or ward, of a city. Although the theory of their practice is Chinese, they follow the teachings of the Dutch to a great extent. Some of the more modern schools practice essentially the same as ourselves, but the greater number follow the blisterings, bleeding, and use of mercuriales, as taught by the most ancient Esculapians, and do infinitely more harm than good. A doctor never sends a bill. This would make him a trader, which all gentlemen scorn. The remuneration is left with the patient, and is usually a very small sum, but always accompanied with great ceremony in its payment.

Before leaving China for Japan, we all had great expectations of procuring some articles of lacquer bijou, for which the Japanese have been celebrated since they were first known to Europeans. Now let us turn to Curiosity street, from which we have been digressing. For shop signs we see large, globular, paper lanterns, suspended in front with Japanese characters painted upon them in gay colors. The shops themselves are entirely open in front, exposing as a prominent feature some splendid articles of lacquer work. We see them ranged along the open front sides, and piled away at the back on shelves to the roof. The articles consist of black and gold, black and inlaid, scarlet, maroon, gilded and inlaid boxes, and cabinets of various shapes and sizes, varying in value from a few cents to hundreds of dollars; lacquered cups and bowls, waiters, and a great variety of minor articles—whips, tops, poles, fishing-rods, turtle boxes, &c., of various sizes, shapes and colors, maroon, scarlet, green, and gold predominating.' There are also to be seen small collections of silks, porcelain, ivory studs and sleeve-buttons, with flies of bronze, curious chairs of bamboo, and turtles of bronze. With such an extensive and tempting variety before you, you hardly know what you desire the most, and provided your purse is deep enough you soon find yourself with a load that you are hardly able to carry, and .still not half satisfied. In this predicament I found myself every time that I went on shore at Yokohama.

Saturday morning, September 1st, the Hartford, Wyoming and Wachusett, left Yokohama and went up to Yeddo, some fifteen miles distant, our business there being to take up General Van Valkenburg, United States Minister to Japan, and Legation. Before we arrived there, the marines of the vessels had donned their uniform dress, and had everything bright and shining in readiness to go ashore, agreeable to orders received before leaving Yokohama.

Precisely at 1 P. M., the barge shoved off from the Hartford, bearing General Van Valkenburg, and wife, child, and female servant, his chief of staff and secretary, with Hon. Anson Burlingame, United States Minister to China. As

soon as they were clear, the Hartford thundered forth the ministers' salute of fifteen guns. Beside the barge another boat left the Hartford, one from the Wyoming and one from us, bearing the marines from the respective vessels.

A pull of about three miles brought us to the cordon of forts which stretched in a semicircular line at the head of Yeddo Bay, in front of the city, and about two miles distant from it. These forts—five in number—form a cordon of about four miles in length; are constructed of stone with thick, heavy walls; mount several heavy guns each, and taken as defenses are very formidable. On account of the shallowness of the water, vessels can approach but little nearer than three miles of these forts, and within the cordon the water is so shallow that the bottom could be reached, almost anywhere with a boat-hook. Approaching the shore, we found the banks too high and steep to land, to do which, we pulled up into a small cove and landed over numerous small boats. At the landing we were met by several Japanese officials and coolies with palanquins for the ladies. The marines were divided into two platoons, and the procession formed in the following order:—Fife and drum in front; first platoon of marines; ladies in sedan-chairs with the ministers and members of the Legation by their sides, on foot; and bringing up the rear, the second platoon of marines. By the sides of all walked the Japanese officials. Captain James Forney of the marine corps was in charge of the escort.

The procession thus formed moved forward through an arched way, and entered the city. The streets, as I have before remarked, differ from those of Chinese cities, in being a little wider and far more cleanly. All along our march these, as well as the houses, were thronged with the curious, wondering Japanese, male and female, old and young of every class and condition. Among the spectators were a great many females, the first that I had noticed with any particular attention. Their costume is similar to that of the males, except that the robe is shorter, and they have an addition of petticoats and bodices. The hair is arranged and decorated in a manner similar to that of the Chinese ladies. Fair, rosy-cheeked, dark-eyed, laughing-mouthed beings, the younger portion of them are almost as well formed and featured as European females, and of about the same size. Nearly all that we saw of a mature age, had their lips and teeth stained black. Their reason for so doing, I was not able to find out, other than that it is the custom for all married women to do so.

Every few rods along our route we would pass a fine collection of temples, situated in beautiful yards like the houses of the better class. These temples are the most costly and stately structures in the empire; in numbers far surpassing the churches of Catholic countries. They ever occupy the most prominent sites, are shaded by the finest trees, and in all their surroundings, there is more skill and beauty displayed than is elsewhere to be found throughout the country. In architecture, the Japanese are less proficient than in other branches of industry. Temples, gateways, and bridges are their principal works, and are the only edifices constructed of stone or brick. The reason of this is, that at any moment the city or town may be visited by an earthquake, and unless the edifice were very solidly constructed, they would be demolished. The houses are rarely more than one and one-half stories high, built of wood, and have tiled roofs. Occupying the most prominent and beautiful site along our route, and having the most charming surroundings, was an old tower, in which was suspended an ancient bell. This is covered over with ancient inscriptions, and is said to be over two thousand years old. The Japanese regard it with excessive veneration.

After marching about three miles, we entered upon a better street, lined with better houses, and with people more respectable looking and better dressed than we had previously seen. We proceeded but a short distance up this street before we turned off from it to the left, and, ascending a slight elevation, entered a courtyard, and found ourselves at the residence fitted up for the minister and family. Near it stood a tall flag-staff, from which floated the stars and stripes. As soon as we had stacked arms and broken ranks, we availed ourselves of the minister's kind permission and set out to explore his house and grounds. The latter are quite extensive, bordered on the front and left sides by a high, thick wall; on the right by a series of temples, and at the rear by a beautiful grove. They are finely adorned by many fruit and shade trees, and swimming in large earthen basins are numbers of gold and silver fish.

The residence is Anglo-Japanese in its style of architecture, as is also the furniture, although the greater portion of the latter is of European manufacture. The floors were all covered with fine white matting, the mats three feet by six, and two inches thick, almost too white and clean for the tread of our boots; indeed, the Japanese, as is their custom, put off their sandals in a small area before treading upon them. The peculiar, soft, white wood of which the posts, window-frames, and ceiling-joists were made, was unpainted. The latter were excedingly delicate, hardly thicker than the wrist. Bolts were extensively used in the construction of the building, and whenever they came through in sight, they were crowned with hexagonal or octagonal brass nuts. Light window frames covered with a silky, white, semi-transparent paper formed the windows. The whole was new and fresh, the timber a kind of satiny white pine, covered with dark paint when exposed to the weather, but otherwise left unpainted. The building was roofed with different colored tiles with ornamental edges.

This description will answer for that of Japanese houses in general. They differ of course, in some respects, but the main features are the same in all. The Japanese seem to excel all others in the art of ventilation, placing windows and partitions so that the air in entering the former, strikes against the latter and is diffused through every apartment. The partitions are not generally fixed, but so constructed that they can be shifted, and arranged at pleasure. After about two hours very pleasantly passed in looking about, we partook of some refreshments which had been prepared for us, and then set out to return, leaving the Minister, family, and Legation domiciled in a charming residence and with our best wishes for their happiness and success.

Yeddo, the capital of the Japanese empire, and the residence of the Tycoon, or Temporal ruler—lies on a beautiful and highly cultivated plain at the head of Yeddo Bay. The city is about five miles in length, and three in breadth, exclusive of the suburbs. It contains a population estimated at from one million and a half to two million inhabitants. With the houses constructed of such light material, fires are very numerous and very destructive. Thousands of the houses are annually laid in ashes, and it is estimated that the Tycoon's palace has to be rebuilt at least every five or six years. The most destructive fires are occasioned by earthquakes, when the conflagration caused by falling buildings, breaks out in almost every quarter at once. It is said that more than an hundred thousand people throughout the empire are annually buried under falling buildings. To protect their more valuable articles, many build stone houses under ground, or fire proof safes of clay and plaster. To the westward of the city is an extensive wild tract, which is said to be swampy. The view from our anchorage would not lead one to suppose that he was so near the second or third largest city in the world. Only a few houses can be seen, the vista being an almost uninterrupted plain, clothed with trees and verdure. There is no sound or hum of business to break the almost solemn stillness, nor any sign of that source of prosperity which is so dear to western nations, commerce. Apparently they have found happiness in seclusion—as the strenuous opposition that is made to foreign intercourse would indicate—and thus afforded an answer to the question as to whether it is to be more readily found in seclusion or in the active pursuits of life.

Wednesday, September 5th, we had muster, and Commander Robert W. Shufeldt, formerly captain of the Hartford, took command of the Wachusett. His address to us was short and to the point, and I can give no better description of him than to say that the address is characteristic of the man. He spoke as follows:

"I want you all to do your duty as men, and if you do, as such you shall be treated; and, so long as you conduct yourselves in a proper manner, you shall have every privilege that can be granted consistently, and no partiality shall be shown to officer or man, any farther than he is justly entitled to." Thus far we have found him to be everything that he promised, and one and all congratulate ourselves upon our good fortune in having Captain Townsend's place so well filled.

Among the incidents of our stay at Yeddo, was the convening of a general court-martial on board the Wachusett, for the trial of a number of officers and men belonging to the different vessels of the squadron. The charges against those tried were for more serious offenses than those usually brought before a summary court-martial, and some of the sentences were for two and three years in State prison at hard labor. September 9th we returned to Yokohama. There we remained till the 13th, taking in coal and provisions, and getting ready for sea.

Soon after Captain Shufeldt came on board, S—— suddenly discovered that his health was in a delicate condition, and that he needed a leave of absence in which to rest and recuperate. Accordingly, on our return to Yokohama, a sixty days' leave of absence was granted him by the Admiral, and he bade us "good-bye" for a time. One and all hope that he may never return, and it is confidently asserted that he never will, but that he will take immediate passage for the United States. He left us unregretted by a single one. His place is filled—and well filled—by Assistant Surgeon Page. He is a fine-looking, pleasant, gentlemanly young man, of about twenty-five years of age, and no novice in his profession. He came highly recommended from the Hartford, to which vessel he was attached.

We left Yokohama September 13th, for Nagasaki, having Mr. Burlingame on board as passenger. As soon as we emerged from Yeddo Bay and entered the Pacific Ocean, we found the sea to be very rough, and the vessel rolled and pitched about so much that many felt a little sea-sick. On the forenoon of the following day we were caught in a bit of a gale, which sprung one of the top-masts, tore up the sails, and played the mischief generally. In the afternoon, the wind increasing in fury, and the barometer falling rapidly, the Captain anticipated a storm, and so ran into the little bay of Oosima for shelter. Well for us was it that he did so, and we all have occasion to feel grateful to Captain Shufeldt for the exercise of superior judgment and precaution; for we had been anchored but a short time, when the anticipated storm commenced to rage with great fury. This kept steadily increasing during that night and the following day, and was then so terrific that we had to drop the sheet anchor, house top-masts, and keep steaming ahead, to avoid being blown ashore. About one o'clock Sunday morning when the gale was at its height, a bright light was seen in the direction of Yokohama, continuing until daybreak, and at times lighting up the decks so clearly that a pin could be seen anywhere about them as well as by daylight. The only explanation of this phenomenon that has been made, is that it must have been caused by an eruption of one of the many volcanoes which line the Japanese coast. Shortly after that time the gale began to subside, and before noon it was almost calm.

The harbor at Oosima is only about two-thirds of a mile in circumference, but one of the most secure and picturesque that I ever saw. It is completely surrounded by a range of high hills excepting at the little, narrow entrance on the southwestern side. The hills are in a high state of cultivation, and the scenery comprises much that is beautiful and picturesque. On the northwestern side of the bay is a small Japanese town, many of the inhabitants of which visited us.

As soon as the gale subsided we got under way, and the following morning entered King's Channel—the northeastern entrance of the Inland Sea, which body of water lies between the island of Niphon on the north, and those of Sikok and Krusur on the south. This entrance is very narrow, and guarded by two formidable forts. The sea is divided into several sounds, which take their name from the provinces whose shores they wash. As, Suwo Nada is the Sound-Nada—which washes the shores of the province of Suwo; and so on with Bingo Nada, Sima Nada, and the others. At the straits connecting these sounds, are erected strong stone forts, mounting many heavy guns, and in construction quite European. All the time that we were passing through the Sea, we had the battery loaded and everything ready for instant action. We took this precaution because the Inland Sea is not open to foreign passage; none but men-of-war attempt to go through, and they are sometimes fired upon. Only a few weeks ago a Sardinian man-of-war was fired upon and forced to turn back.

We were from Monday morning until Wednesday noon in making the passage, (coming to anchor on both nights,) and I can but say that it was the most delightful trip that I ever had. This feeling seemed to be common to all, and everything was laid aside to behold and enjoy the many objects of interest and beauty which were constantly presented to our view. In some places the sea is very wide, and in others so narrow that the shores are hardly a stone's throw distant; but at no point were we far from land, for the sea is thickly studded with islands throughout its whole extent. The shores are lined with neat and pretty Japanese towns and villages, at times so near each other as to appear like one vast continuous city.

This surface is, for the most part very mountainous, but the scenery beautiful and picturesque in the extreme, by far surpassing that of the Canton and Yangste-kiang rivers, of which I thought and spoke so highly. The sharp-pointed mountains are clothed with verdure to their very summits, and the steep valleys running up between these mountains together with the almost innumerable islands of every conceivable form and size, are neatly cultivated in terraces or shelves, rising one above another, and diminishing in breadth until they terminate in the deep angle of the nook of the former or in a pretty summer-house or pavilion on the latter. The picturesque beauty and richness of these valleys, which sweep down to the sea from the mountain interior is unsurpassed. From springs at their heads, water is collected in reservoirs, and then let out at pleasure, in winding channels which empty upon the rice fields along their course, or on the low lands at the foot of the mountains. The gentle slopes are devoted to upland grains, cultivated in small plots like garden beds, the beauty of their checkered appearance heightened by patches of snowy cotton. The farm houses and smaller villages usually occupy some sheltered ravine or sequestered nook at the foot of a wooded hill, or among forest trees and luxuriant shrubbery, so that one is frequently surprised by a village, when he is not thinking to be near a human abode.

The sides of the islands are usually very precipitous and laid out in winding terraces. On these terraces are cultivated grains, vegetables, shrubs and flowers. On the summits of many of the islands, the summer-houses and pavilions are embowered in beautiful groves of fruit trees. At points along the shores, and on some of the islands, the surface is ragged and rocky, and covered with beautiful shrubbery, as if by its loveliness it would hide all defects of nature, and in reality making the scenery ten-fold more lovely.

Wednesday night we anchored some fifty miles from the southwestern entrance of the Inland Sea. Soon after anchoring we were boarded by a Japanese official who imperiously demanded our business there, and by what right we had anchored. Capt. Shufeldt *politely* replied, "It suited us," and with this he was forced to be content. We got under way again soon after daylight, and at three o'clock in the afternoon we were at the entrance of the harbor of Nagasaki. This is guarded by a number of small batteries, located on terraces of the high eminences, which line either side. As we passed through it and opened the bay, the boatswain remarked, "I have been going to sea for more than forty years, and have visited almost every nook and corner on the globe, but I never saw a more beautiful harbor than this, nor one more secure!" It truly is a most beautiful and secure harbor. About six miles in circumference, it is almost completely land-locked—completely but for the narrow entrance, and surrounded on all sides by a chain of high hills. These are cultivated in the terrace form to their very summits, and covered with beautiful and variegated verdure.

The native town is very large and picturesquely situated upon the side of a hill at the southwestern side of the harbor. Separated by a narrow ravine, and also built upon the side of a hill at the western side is the foreign town containing a few fine houses of business and residence, which occupy prominent sites. Besides these there are the usual appendages of a few poorer houses, and a number of sailor-boarding houses and drinking-shops.

I have made no mention as yet of the Japanese currency.

Those denominations that I have seen in use are, one, two and a half, half, and quarter Itzabo pieces, and tempos. Excepting the last mentioned, these are square in form. The Itzabo piece is of silver, about an inch in length, two-thirds in width, and one-eighth in thickness. Value, thirty-three cents. The edges are bordered, and on each side are several Japanese characters. Similar in form and proportions and also of silver are the quarter Itzabo pieces. The two and a half, and half Itzabo pieces have the same form and general features of the others, but consist of silver coins covered with a thin coating of gold. The former are about one-third the size of the Itzabo pieces, and the latter about one-fourth the size of the former. The tempos are of copper, oval in form, and about two inches in length, by one and one-third in breadth. On the sides are two or three characters, and in the center is a square hole by means of which they are strung on bamboo fibres, like Chinese "cash," in masses of the value of an Itzabo. In the northern part of the empire this takes but sixteen or seventeen,—each one being of the value of two cents,—but here, twenty-five are given for one Itzabo. Besides those that I have mentioned there are Cobangs—of gold, of about the same size and form as the tempos, but thinner and without the square hole in the center. In value they are equal to twenty-one Itzabos. They are not now in circulation, and are sometimes worn as a mark of distinction or rank.

"I think that it would be much more pleasant to take a view of Nagasaki from horseback, than to go all over it on foot, and besides I would like to have a horseback ride, it is so long since I had one," said friend A—, to me soon after we landed the other day, the first time that we had been on shore since our arrival. I was of the same mind, so we set out for the stables, to procure horses. While they were preparing them for us, I noticed that the horses were included in the general fashion of wearing sandals; for instead of being shod, as is common with us, every time that they are used thick straw sandals are strapped upon each foot. These will last about one day, and effectually protect the hoofs from the small round stones with which the streets are for the most part paved. The horses being saddled, bridled, and *sandaled*, we mounted and tried their mettle in a race along the Bund in front of the town. This showed us that they were smart and active as well as easy riders. A ride of a few minutes brought us to the foot of the hill on which the native town is built. The streets of this we found to be unusually wide, neatly paved and clean. The latter is owing in a great measure, doubtless, to the great slope of the hill on which the town is built, so that all the dirt and filth is carried off by the rains. Stopping every few minutes to examine the many curious articles exposed for sale in the shops, also to witness several street theatrical and jugglery performances, it was at least three hours before we reached the summit at the back of the town, and from which place we had a fine view of it. When about to return, we found that riding down stairs, (there are so many steps in the streets that each one is like a long flight of stairs,) was a different thing from riding up; and, not having the same inducement for so doing that General Putnam had, we concluded that we would dismount and lead our horses. Notwithstanding this little inconvenience we enjoyed ourselves and our view of Nagasaki from horseback very much.

Before leaving Japan I must say a few words more regarding the Japanese. I have seen comparatively little of them, but still enough to say unhesitatingly, that they are by far the most intelligent, and farthest advanced in the civilized arts and sciences of any people of the East. Their intelligence may be noticed in that carefulness and understanding with which everything about an European man-of-war is examined, and in their construction of forts, from drafts which they themselves made of those in Europe and America; the

11*

forts being built by their own engineers, and comparing favorably with the models.

In the strict sense of the word the Japanese are manufacturers. They have no complicated machinery, and the turning lathe, though extensively used, is so rudely constructed, that it does not deserve the name of machine. However, it turns out many of the finest specimens in the world. The articles manufactured by them not only display great ingenuity and skill, but good taste in the form, color, and pattern; indeed, in these respects, they are hardly equaled by any. The Japanese swords have acquired a world wide celebrity, both on account of the fineness of the steel, and their superior finish; to the keenness of the edge of these swords, many foreigners as well as natives can affirm from experience. In inventions, the Japanese are more destitute than their general intelligence would seem to warrant. This may be accounted for by two special reasons; one is, that the government seems rather to discourage anything that tends to change old established customs; and the other is, that there is no protection given to inventions by patent rights, as there is at home. We are indebted to the Japanese, however, for two inventions; one, that of making masts for ships by binding together a number of pieces; and the other, the art of fastening false teeth to a plate. The Japanese are almost perfect imitators. With their imperfect means, they will from models make anything from a glass bottle to a telegraph or a steam engine. In their fine arts, they surpass the Chinese, and even excel other nations in their paintings of birds, flowers, and fishes. Their landscapes, and portraits of men or animals are badly executed. Some of their carvings that I have seen are truly wonderful, and their articles in bronze are said to nearly equal those of French manufacture.

As a nation, the Japanese are warlike and brave; they never ask for quarter, and never give it; they never shrink from danger, but rather seem to take pleasure in being placed in trying situations. Out of their army, of more than half a million, only a very few will use fire arms, preferring swords, and considering it disgraceful to fight in any way but at close quarters. Hari-kari or self-destruction for criminal offenses, is practiced only by the privileged classes. The word is derived from two others—*hari* bowels; and *kari* to cut. It is a privilege enjoyed only by the nobility, and then only for certain crimes. By putting himself to death, a person of rank not only saves himself from an ignoble end by the hands of the common executioner, but also saves his family from disgrace and property from confiscation. This is the only purpose for which the short sword is used, and the privilege of committing Hari-kari is sought as a great boon by offenders.

LETTER XXIV.

U. S. S. WACHUSETT, Hong Kong, China,
Nov. 2d, 1866.

MY DEAR R.:

We left Nagasaki September 24th, arriving here the 29th, having made the distance in the uncommonly short time of five days. With the exception of a little gale which lasted about eight hours, our passage was a very pleasant one, with strong, fair winds, and the sea quite smooth all the time. A total eclipse of the moon was the only unusual item of interest.

After a stay here of about three weeks, during which time we had five or six court-martials for trivial offenses, enjoyed general liberty, and " coaled ship," Saturday, October 13th we went up to Macao. The occasion of our going there was the *fete* held the 15th inst., upon the retiring of the old Governor and the arrival of the new one—the fifteenth of the Colony. The most prominent feature of the fete, was a ball given on the evening of the 15th, and which two or three of the officers attended.

We left Macao the following day, and, instead of returning direct to Hong Kong as was the general expectation, spent three days in cruising about the islands off the mouth of the Canton river, in quest of pirates, who of late have been growing to be very numerous, bold, and troublesome. These pirates originated during some of the early Chinese revolutions, and have always played an important part in every subsequent one. Merchant junks trading between the different ports carry guns for protection, and whenever a good opportunity offers itself, they turn into pirates. Imperial war junks, sent out to destroy these pirates, have in many instances become pirates themselves. Their latest great addition they had in the war junks of the late Taeping rebels, which escaped capture. Their junks do not differ in appearance from the merchant or war junks; in fact, the pirates follow whichever vocation is the most lucrative for the time being, and so it is almost impossible to distinguish them, unless taken in the very act of piracy. These junks are sometimes of three or four hundred tons burden, or more even, and are the largest vessels that the Chinese possess. They carry an enormous amount of sail, and from fifteen to twenty oars, and are armed with batteries of from four to twenty guns each, chiefly six and twelve pounders, with an occasional twenty-four. These might be quite formidable, but not one out of every fifty of the pirates understands the simplest principles of gunnery, and it is through chance alone that they are ever *guilty* of hitting an object.

Their usual time for attacking a vessel is when she is lying becalmed, at which time they can easily get alongside by means of their oars. The usual mode of procedure is to throw one of their "stink pots"—earthern pots, charged with offensive and suffocating material—on board, which drives every one below, and before they can again ascend, the vessel is in the possession of the pirates. They seldom kill any one, but after ransacking the vessel and taking what they want, leave her.

Of late many of the merchantmen trading with this part of the world have begun to carry a few small pieces of cannon, and a supply of small arms with which to defend themselves; these, the pirates seldom molest, and whenever they do they are sure to get worsted. They used to confine their depredations to native junks, and smaller craft, and it is only of late years that they have ventured to attack foreign merchantmen. Shortly after our arrival here from Nagasaki, an American bark sailed for the states. A week later she returned into port, telling the following sad story: The second day out she was becalmed, and toward evening, was attacked by pirates. Being without arms, the crew could make no resistance. After ransacking the vessel, and taking what they wanted, the pirate chief entered the cabin, where the Captain was sitting on the sofa by the side of his wife, and deliberately shot him dead; then without a word he turned on his heel, and with his band left the ship. The wife recognized the chief as one whom her husband, by some unknown means had made an enemy of while lying at Hong Kong. Our cruise after pirates proved an unsuccessful one, and October 20th we returned to Hong Kong, where we have since remained.

During our stay here, our band has received a valuable addition in an excellent bugler which we enlisted. All the calls are now done by the bugle, such as quarters, sick-call, boats' call, *reveille* and *tattoo*. The bugler also accompanies the other musicians in playing "colors" and "retreat."

The demoralizing and exterminating effects of the use of opium, are plainly marked among the Chinese. When the habit is once formed, it grows until it becomes inveterate; discontinuance is more and more difficult, until at length the sudden deprivation of the accustomed indulgence produces certain death. It is calculated that every opium smoker shortens his life at least ten years from the time that he commences the practice; one-half of his physical energies are soon gone, and his earnings rapidly diminished; then feeling strength and income both diminishing, he plunges into crime to obtain what he is no longer able to procure by labor, and drags down into the vortex of ruin his dependent relatives, and all within the sphere of his influence. It is no uncommon thing to see those that are no longer able to gratify the cravings of their appetites, hanging their heads by the doors of the opium shops, which the hard-hearted keepers, having fleeced them of their all, will not permit them to enter. Thus

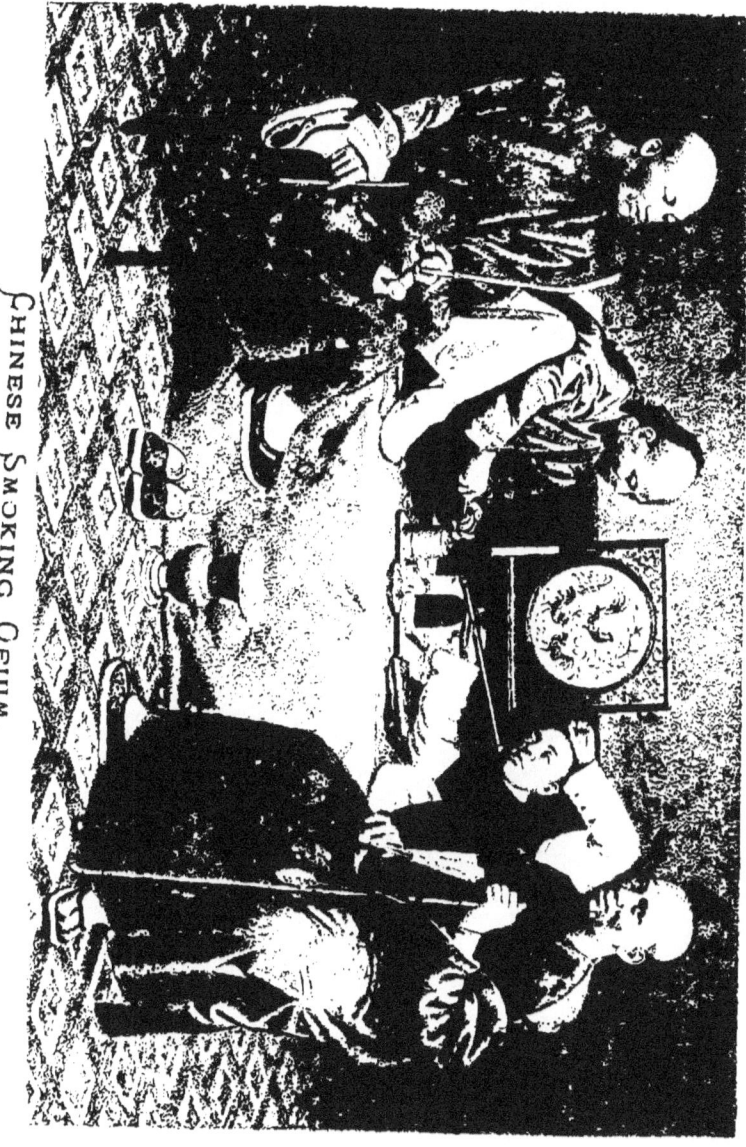

Chinese Smoking Opium.

shut out from their own dwellings either by angry friends, or ruthless creditors, they die in the streets unpitied and despised.

During one of my rambles on shore a short time ago, I paid a visit to an opium shop. Four or five rooms in different parts of a square court were occupied by men stretched out on rude couches with head-pillows and the apparatus for smoking opium. The latter consists of a glass covered lamp with a small circular opening at the top; a pipe consisting of a tube, somewhat resembling a flute—near one extremity of which is an earthen bowl, the circular cavity in which is barely one-sixth of an inch in diameter; a bent, knife-like instrument, for cleaning the bowl; a pair of scissors; a jar of opium, and a long needle. In one corner of the principal room stood the proprietor, with delicate steel-yards weighing out the prepared drug, which is of a dark, thick, semi-fluid consistency. The smoker places himself in the position for smoking, by reclining at full length on one side; then, gathers up a small quantity of the drug on the point of the needle and holds it over the lamp until it is sufficiently dried. He then forms it into an appropriately shaped roll, and inserts it into the bowl of the pipe. This done, he holds the bowl so that the blaze of the lamp can touch the opium and takes several quick, deep inspirations, until it is consumed, all the time retaining the smoke, and then allowing it to escape slowly from the mouth and nostrils. Some require as many as twenty-five pipes full, before they succumb to its intoxicating effects. In the shop could be seen those in every stage of intoxication, from those just experiencing its effects to those carried into an inner apartment, apparently dead, by the attendants which are appointed for that special purpose. The opium smokers formed a motley group of sallow, sunken cheeks, and glassy, watery eyes, all with an idiotic look, and vacant stare—the most miserable and abject beings that I ever saw. The intoxicating, exterminating, and demoralizing effects of opium are far worse than those of ardent spirits, more speedily and effectually destroying the mental, moral, and physical systems, and causing even a more premature death. The fumes are not unpleasant; in fact, they have rather an attraction, but after a short stay in the shop, I felt quite faint and sick from them, and was forced to leave.

"Old Sam." is an inveterate opium smoker, and when he was at one time on board of us for a few days, I used to watch him while taking his usual smoke. After some little difficulty, I at length prevailed upon him to let me have a smoke. I found it to have a soothing, pleasing effect, and no longer wondered at the pleasure which a smoker of opium derives from it, or that one so seldom breaks himself from the habit, when once it is formed. I took only two or three whiffs, but my head swam as if I had been whirled around and around in a swing. One time I asked Old Sam, if he did not know that opium was killing him, and why he did not leave off using it. He replied, "My sabee, he makee kill me, but suppose my no usee he, he makee kill me all de same." Again when I asked him what he would do if his son, of whom he is very fond—should begin to use opium, he replied, "My sooner see makee die than see he makee usee de opium."

Among the places of interest in Hong Kong, of which I as yet have made no particular mention, are the Public Gardens and Central Market. The latter lies between Queen's Road and the Bund, and is about five hundred yards in length by three hundred in breadth. There are upwards of twenty streets leading through it from Queen's Road to the Bund and these are all connected together by numerous cross streets. In one quarter are the meat and fish stalls, in another the vegetable stalls, in still another the fruit stalls, and so on an assortment and abundance of almost every conceivable article of food. The stall keepers are all Chinamen, and for the most part are also the proprietors. At any hour of the day there can be seen thousands making purchases, from the poor, wretched Chinese beggar buying a few cash worth of rice, fish, and vegetables, to the Captain or Purser making contracts for several thousand dollars worth of sea-stores.

The Public Gardens are situated on a sloping, uneven shelf of the mountain, back of the Governor's mansion and grounds. They comprise about twenty acres, beautifully and tastefully laid out in walks, terraced beds of flowers and shrubbery, and scattered here and there different species of trees. Everything there growing is quite young yet, it being but a few years since the Gardens were established, but in a few years they promise to become most charming. 'Tis pleasant to go there now upon a fine evening, when the wealth, beauty, and fashion of the city are out for a promenade, and the band is playing.

A pleasant sail of about twenty minutes, brought a friend and myself, the other day, to the opposite or Kowloon shore of the bay two miles distant from our anchorage. It is perfectly secure and safe now, but it is scarcely ten years since it was almost certain death for any *Fankwei* (i. e., White Devil, as the Chinese call all Westerns) to be found wandering there. Near the landing, where the chaingang have been at work getting dirt and stones from the steep ban to extend the Bund, we noticed several stone pillars, twenty or thirty feet in height, perfect cones and pyramids in form. They were evidently the work of Nature, but the art of man could scarcely produce any more perfect. The principal object of our visit was to search for shells, and in this we were rewarded by a few curious specimens.

Last Monday, October 29th, Mr. Knapp—Second Assistant Engineer, and Samuel Falstead—ordinary seaman, were sent aboard the American ship Powhattan, for passage to the States, they having been condemned by Medical Survey. The following evening Hong Kong was visited by a destructive fire; it was confined to the Chinese quarter, of which over three hundred houses were consumed. It seems strange that so large a city as Hong Kong should have no organized fire department; there is not even a fire engine, with the exception of a small one at the barracks. I have heard no expressions of regret for the fire, made by Europeans; on the contrary, they appear to rejoice at its occurrence, for the Chinese have by far the best locations in the city, and the Europeans have long coveted them for building purposes.

The weather is getting to be quite cool here now, the thermometer seldom standing higher than 75° above zero. This even, may seem quite warm to you to be called cool weather, but it is so much cooler than we have had in a long time, that it seems quite cold to us. The ship's company have not been in better health at any time during the cruise, and colds are the only sickness that any have. When we left the States we had quite cold weather for a time, but of late it has been an almost unvarying summer, the change of seasons being marked only by the change of names. It is now the general expectation that we will go to the southward before long to spend the winter around the East India isles, unless we receive orders to start for home; which, I am sorry to say does not look very probable at present. If it would do any good I would wish that we might start to-morrow, but wishes and desires I do not expect will be regarded.

LETTER XXV.

U. S. S. WACHUSETT, Hong Kong, China,
Dec. 6th, 1866.

MY DEAR R.:

We left Hong Kong, Saturday morning, November 3d, upon a cruise to the northward, stopping at several points along the coast, and going as far as Amoy. After remaining there a few days, we returned, arriving here the 29th, having had a very pleasant and interesting cruise.

While we were weighing anchor, and making the usual preparations for leaving here, a police boat from the shore came alongside, bringing two Chinamen who said that their boat had been taken from them by pirates a few days previous, and asked assistance from us in redressing their wrongs. As the principal object of this cruise was to search for pirates, their request was granted, and they were taken along with us, to point out where their vessel was seized, and to give such other information as they might be able. "Old Sam" also accompanied us for the double purpose of acting as interpreter and pilot.

After steaming about thirty miles, early in the forenoon, we dropped anchor in the pretty little harbor of Tsing Hoy. On the western side of it is quite a large Chinese city, having no foreign residents except two French Catholic missionaries. These, as is usual under such circumstances, have adopted the dress and most of the customs of the Chinese, and could barely be distinguished from the Chinese themselves. Lying at anchor there, were ten Imperial war junks, with the Admiral of which the customary salutes were exchanged. In the afternoon he paid us a visit, when the usual routine of parading, inspecting, and saluting had to be gone through with. After having heard their story he took the Chinamen which we had brought from Hong Kong away with him, and said that he would search after the pirates with his fleet. The signification of Tsing Hoy is "level water," and indeed the harbor is most appropriately named; for it is one of the smoothest and most beautiful sheets of water I ever saw.

We left at daybreak the next morning expecting to reach Swaton, one hundred and twenty miles to the northeastward, that same night; but, owing to a strong head wind which we had to encounter, we did not arrive until about noon the next day.

Swaton is situated about two miles from the head of a narrow bight which extends back from the sea some seven or eight miles. On the right hand side of the entrance is a small rocky island, upon which is an old, walled, Chinese town. From there, nearly up to the anchorage, the shores are for the most part rocky and barren. Near the town the bight widens a little, and the country grows less rocky and more productive. The southern side of the harbor is lined by a range of hills sweeping down almost to the edge of the water, upon the sides of which may be noticed patches of grain and vegetables. Stretching along the narrow strip at their foot are the houses and grounds of the Consulates and foreign merchants, some fifteen or twenty in number, and constituting the foreign section. Upon the opposite side of the bay is quite a large, unwalled, native city with a few stores of the foreign merchants. On this side for a long distance inland the land is low, level, and marshy, producing immense quantities of rice, which constitutes the leading article of export of the place. Having climbed with a friend to the summit of the hills, which stretch along the southern side of the bay, we were rewarded by a beautiful and extensive view. Beyond the hills the country was level or gently undulating as far as the eye could reach, and all in the high

in a good supply of these, and for nearly a month we lived almost entirely upon them, having them for breakfast, dinner and supper, until all were sickened at the sight or mention of sweet potatoes. Those which are raised in this part of the world are far inferior to those produced in the United States; in fact, those I have tasted in other places have been almost invariably watery, and stringy, and did not possess the same rich flavor. The sweet potato is the only one cultivated or eaten by the Chinese. Several attempts have been made to introduce the Irish potato, at least to produce a sufficient quantity for the supply of the European residents; but thus far all attempts have proved unsuccessful, such is the almost insurmountable difficulty of establishing any new thing in the favor of the natives.

Our stay at Tung Sang, like that at Amoa Straits, was characterized by boat expeditions, and target and other exercises, and of all these we had a sufficiency to satisfy the most desirous of us. And yet the majority are always ready for any such thing, not only on account of the present enjoyment, but also because by practice, proficiency is attained, and a true sailor ever takes an interest and delight in doing anything in his calling that will enable him to excel another. Without boasting, and with the strictest truth, I can say that the crew of the Wachusett have attained such a degree of proficiency in all exercises pertaining to a man-of-war as to be equaled by very few vessels in these waters, and to be surpassed by none, as many trials have shown to all.

We left Tung Sang November 17th, before daylight, and about the middle of the afternoon of the same day we arrived among the islands which at the distance of about eight miles from the city of Amoy stretch across the mouth of an extensive bay, formed by two projecting headlands of the coast. The harbor within enclosed extends for several miles, being open to the sea on the southeast, and having on the south the lofty hill of Lam-tai-too, situated on the mainland and est state of cultivation. A stroll along the beach in search of shells, and a short time spent in the little burying ground to the left and rear of the town, comprehended all that we found to interest us.

Our stay of five days was characterized by several interesting target and boat exercises, boat races, and drills on shore.

We left Swaton on the 10th, and continued our search for pirates. After proceeding about thirty miles we again dropped anchor in the Amoa straits, and sent armed boats to scour around the numerous small islands and deep bights in the coast. We hoped to find some piratical junks lying concealed there, as it was a notorious haunt of theirs; but not one did we discover. Circling around the inner extremity of a small deep bight was a small but pretty unwalled Chinese town defended by two large and quite formidable looking forts, upon two eminences near it, and the only ones in sight.

We remained there until the next morning, and then proceeded to Tung Sang, about fifty miles farther to the northward. The harbor there is nearly circular in form, about four miles in diameter, and with the exception of a very narrow entrance, completely land-locked. Lying at anchor we found the English gunboat Grasshopper, and a few large junks. The town is quite large, unwalled, and situated upon a barren, sandy plain, upon the side of the bay opposite to the entrance. It owes its importance to its numerous saltworks, and the inhabitants are chiefly engaged in salt making. This is done by letting the water from the sea into shallow basins, when it is evaporated by the heat of the sun. The salt thus made is of a very inferior quality, but forms the principal article of export. While lying there the messes got out of potatoes, so a boat was sent ashore with the caterers prospecting. They returned with a load of sweet ones, which they had purchased at the rate of about seventeen cents per bushel. As no others were to be obtained, we laid surmounted by a conspicuous pagoda. On the southwest lies an island with another conspicuous pagoda at the entrance of a river leading up to Chang-chew. On the east at a greater distance lies the island of Kinmun or Quemoy. The island of Amoy itself fills up the north and northwest of this circular range of hills, which rival each other in the bold grandeur of their towering cliffs, and the wild sterility of their scenery. Steaming along the southern shore of the island, which is here lined with an extensive range of batteries—now decaying and deserted, we at length came to anchor in the lesser harbor, between the city and the opposite island of Kulang-su, which lies about half a mile distant from Amoy. The harbor at Amoy is considered one of the best on the coast, and the scenery surrounding it, though quite barren, is varied and interesting. A day or two after our arrival, accompanied by a friend, I went ashore to see what there might be of interest. We landed on the Amoy side just below the city, and ascending the towering range of cliffs near by, and the huge rock which crowns the summit, we were rewarded by a complete and splendid view of the city and harbors, and the country for many miles around.

The island of Amoy, about forty miles in circumference, is, together with several lesser isles, situated within the before mentioned head-lands on the coast. Between these islands and the mainland is the harbor—or harbors rather; for it is divided into two portions called the inner and the outer harbors; the southern extremity of Kulang-su being the dividing point. The city of Amoy or Hiamun, (i. e., the gate or harbor of Hia) is situated on the southwestern side of the island of Amoy, at the mouth of the Dragon river. There is an outer and inner city, as one approaches it from the sea, or more properly a citadel and city, divided by a ridge of high, rocky hills, with an old wall extending along the top. A paved road, which we saw for the first time standing upon this rock on the cliffs, connects the two. The entire circuit of the city and suburbs is upwards of eight miles, and contains an estimated population of three hundred thousand inhabitants, while that of the island is estimated at one hundred thousand more. Amoy is further divided by the inner harbor, which extends in front and joins a large estuary running up some distance into the island, and skirting the northern side of the city. Thus it, in fact, lies upon a tongue of land, having only one-third of its circuit defended by walls, and these overlooked by the hills at its rear. The island of Amoy is said to contain one hundred and thirty-six villages and hamlets, the most of which could be seen from our standpoint. Like a stupendous citadel of natural formation, a range of towering cliffs extends over the whole, leaving, for the work of tillage, portions of low, undulating ground between their base and the sea, while upon the top of this range there are a few miles of highly cultivated land.

The western side of the harbor, here from six to seven hundred yards wide, is occupied by the island of Kulang-su, while away to the eastward is the island of Quemoy or Kenmun (i. e., Golden Harbor), presenting a striking contrast in the low, rice grounds on its southwestern side to the high land of Amoy.

Now to turn to our ramble, and what we saw and learned. Descending from our perch on the rock, we climbed the hills in the rear of the town. These have been its burying ground for centuries, and are entirely covered with graves; probably many millions have been buried there. In a previous letter I made mention of the graves of the mandarins, and the higher order of the Chinese. Those of the lower order are barely two feet deep, the sides and bottom being lined with a kind of cement. After the coffin has been placed in position, the grave filled up, and a convex mound raised over it, the top is covered over with the cement which in a short time hardens, forming a rock-like case. This effectually protects the body from the ravages of dogs, which are numerous and ravenous in China, and makes the hill appear at a distance, as if it were thickly studded with large rocks. We noticed several mandarin sepulchers, cut out of the solid rock, and finely ornamented with inscriptions and epitaphs. The Chinese seldom select as burial places for their dead, situations capable of agricultural use or improvement, but inter their dead on the hill-side or under the craggy precipice where little else could be made of the soil. In this manner are they forced in every way to economize the soil.

Decending into the city of Amoy at its rear, we found ourselves in a perfect maze of narrow, filthy streets, lined for the most part with houses of the poorest description. Upon an eminence commonly called "White Stag Hill," near the city, is a collection of temples, the only thing worthy of note that we saw. They consist of a cluster of buildings, perched upon overhanging rocks, and both in their situation and surroundings are exceedingly romantic and picturesque.

Along the water's edge, in front of the city, are a few European buildings, mostly stores and ship-chandleries. The residences of the Europeans are upon the Kulang-su side of the bay, which we reached after a few minutes sail. We landed upon a long stone causeway, which extends out into the harbor, and at which vessels load and unload. Ascending a succession of eminences, to a point where we could have a good view of the island, we found it to be about a mile in length, and the same in width in its widest part; we saw that, although partaking of the same general ruggedness of aspect as the main land, it possessed a picturesque and romantic beauty of scenery peculiarly its own, in the glens and deep, narrow ravines overhung with masses of rock of every imaginable form and appearance. In some parts little groves of banian trees encircle a few houses, and everywhere are to be seen plats of grain or vegetables. The northern side of the island is by far the most beautiful and picturesque, and of so high a degree of cultivation and beauty as to call forth the following description : " A series of gardens with their rich foliage rises gradually up the slope of a little hill, till they meet the odd jumble of chasms and boulder-stones, piled aloft or loosely scattered around." Scattered over the entire island are some thirty-five residences situated in beautiful gardens and fairly embowered in trees. Occupying a prominent site is the neat little chapel of the North Dutch Church.

There are upwards of five hundred European residents at Amoy, for the most part merchants and their families.

Among the interesting incidents of our stay were the usual number of boat-races and exercises, the visit of the Tau Tai, and upon Sunday the holding of service on board the ship by one of the missionaries, whose field is at Amoy. The majority of the crew attended, influenced in no small degree probably by the presence of the two pretty daughters of the missionary. To work good among sailors, I am inclined to believe that the missionary would find it advantageous to have some pretty and attractive female to accompany him, in order to induce them to listen to him, and to fix their attention. Then he might have better hopes of being successful in his endeavors.

The services were conducted after the manner of the North Dutch Church, and all seemed to be much interested, especially in the singing, in which the voices of the ladies made a great improvement.

We left Amoy Wednesday, November 28th, arriving here in the afternoon of the following day, after a very rough passage. Owing to a severe storm a day or two previous, the sea was very rough, and we rolled and pitched about so fearfully as to make many an old salt feel a little sea sick. We who were not sick were rejoiced at the roughness of the sea, for that precluded all idea of exercising, and we enjoyed a rest for two days.

The day of our arrival here, being the last Thursday in November, we decided was Thanksgiving day at home, and as such, those who were so disposed, celebrated it. I made an excellent Thanksgiving dinner upon two papers that day received from home, and a No. 1 repast gotten up to order at the hotel ashore, for myself and three or four friends. It would be hard to tell which part I enjoyed the most; but upon the whole, I think that it was the former, by as much as intellectual excels mere sensual enjoyments. You at home have no conception of the amount of pleasure which a home newspaper, even although it may be two or three months old, gives to a crew. As a choice treasure it is carefully preserved, and passed from one to another until all have thoroughly read it. If our friends at home had any idea how highly an occasional file of newspapers is valued, I am sure that more would be sent to those far away. Strikingly true in their case are the words of the wise man, "Like waters to a thirsty soul, so is news from a far country."

Since we have been here, the crew have been at work "setting up rigging," and doing other work aloft. The chief item of interest has been the losing of Dr. Page, who came to take Dr. King's place, and to whom one and all had become endeared. Nor were we less dear to him as was clearly shown in his affecting leave-taking. He took one and all by the hand, and bade them "good bye," while his face was wet with tears, and sobs almost choked his utterance. Few dry eyes were seen among all on board. Never was an officer more beloved by a crew, or a crew more saddened by the loss of an officer. Once only have I seen as much feeling manifested, and that was at the time of the late Captain Townsend's death. The petty officers asked the Captain if it was not possible to keep him, and when told that it was not, begged permission to "cheer ship" for him. But this was also denied them, as being contrary to the "Rules and Regulations for the better government of the Navy."

How much better and pleasanter it is for officers thus to have the best regards of the crew. Never did I hear of an instance where this was the case but there was joined to it the greatest respect for their authority. It perhaps may answer with other nationalities, but fear alone is not the wisest nor best mode of governing intelligent American seamen.

Yesterday a survey was held upon the Wachusett, and the board of Survey has reported that she needs to go into dock for repairs, so the admiral has ordered us up to Whampoa to-morrow for that purpose.

LETTER XXVI.

U. S. S. WACHUSETT, Hong Kong, China,
December 29th, 1866.

MY DEAR R.:

As we were ordered we went up to Whampoa the next morning, but did not go into dock for four days afterward, there being a vessel in there which had not finished making repairs. We were in dock about two weeks, and while there the vessel was thoroughly caulked both inside and out, new copper put on where it was needed, the decks were repaired, and a new yard and topmast made. The ship was most thoroughly overhauled, and from this many infer that we will remain on the station a much longer time, notwithstanding the many "well authenticated" reports that we are soon to start for home. It does not seem to me probable that the repairs would have been so extensive if we were soon to be "homeward bound."

For a few days the ship was in the greatest filth and confusion imaginable. One hundred Chinese caulkers continually hammering, made such a noise that one could neither read, sleep, eat, or even think comfortably; and for five whole days, the decks saw neither water nor sand, nor holy-stone, but everywhere dirt reigned supreme. After the caulking was all finished, and the signal was given, it was amusing to see the angry and furious onslaught made by the crew with their accustomed weapons upon King Dirt. After a short but vigorous conflict, he was completely vanquished, and really it did seem good to see the decks white and the ship clean once more. So long as I am not compelled to take part I will never again complain of the use of holy-stones and sand if it does not exceed three times a day; all feel so uncomfortable if a day passes without having the ship cleaned. The repairs were all made by the Chinese dock-laborers, and although they did their work better than was expected the same would have been performed by an equal number of European laborers in one-third of the time that it took them.

To add to the discomfort of being in dock, the crew were allowed to go ashore at pleasure, and with their usual propensity, the first place sought was where they could obtain liquor. As a consequence, the greater number would almost invariably return to the ship intoxicated, and there would follow the usual amount of shouting and fighting. A number paid dearly for some of their *antics* while in this condition, a summary court martial adjudging to each one the loss of three months' pay, thirty days solitary confinement on bread and water, and a sharp, cutting reprimand by the Captain before the whole crew assembled at muster. In this instance fear seemed to operate well in controling them, for after a few had been punished the remainder were more thoughtful and prudent.

Sadder than that of all the others, was the case of one of the firemen, who, in attempting to cross the narrow foot bridge which spans the creek back of New Town, while intoxicated, fell into the water and was drowned. He was not found until the following day, when his funeral took place and he was buried in a lovely spot near the summit of a small hill on Danes Island. He was a quiet, good natured fellow, well liked by all the crew, and all felt saddened by his death.

Although at times quite troublesome, yet on the whole the numerous curiosity dealers that thronged the wharves formed a pleasant feature of our stay in the dock.

Articles of every description that they thought could possibly attract were brought, from the richest silks and most costly boxes, to the small, cheap ivory buttons; and, in the

Whampoa, China.

lively competition which was occasioned, an excellent opportunity was afforded for making purchases. Of this opportunity all availed themselves, and purchases were made amounting, in the case of some who had an abundance of the "rhino," to as much as fifty dollars.

While we were lying in dock an opportunity was afforded me of witnessing the summary punishment of crime by the Chinese, the offense in this case being that of stealing. It required the closest attention, and most careful surveillance of all to prevent the Chinese from purloining the sheets of copper with which they were repairing the vessel, and despite our vigilance, one day four of the workmen with a sheet of copper each, passed the guard and were some distance away from the ship before they were suspected of thieving. Pursuit was immediately made, all of the copper recovered, and two of the thieves captured. These were taken before the Tau Tai of the district, who, upon hearing the facts of the case, immediately ordered them to be beheaded, and in less than ten minutes his command was obeyed. The condemned were let out into a court near the mandarin's house and there made to stand with the body inclined forward. Every mandarin of the rank of Tau Tai has an executioner in his suite, and this personage was then summoned and told to do his duty. The instrument which he used was a large, broad sword, which although it appeared heavy and clumsy, was as bright and keen as any razor. While the ease with which it was wielded, completely severing the head from the trunk, showed that the executioner was not unaccustomed to the duty. The bodies were removed, the heads placed upon stakes, and a placard posted up near by stating the circumstances of the execution as a warning to all offenders.

The crime of stealing is almost always thus summarily dealt with, and in Chinese law, ranks as the highest offense that can be committed. And this is necessary, for by less strict measures, where there is such a dense population, and where the mass are ignorant of those fundamental Christian principles of right and wrong, life and property would not be safe. It is truly wonderful how the Chinese, ignorant as they are of political economy, and destitute as they are of a knowledge of Christian ethics, manage to keep such a mass of people in order, and preserve life and property safe for a moment. Probably the secret of their success is in the establishment of the patriarchal system of government founded on the basis of filial obedience. The first principle in their moral code is the duty of children to their parents in all things, and the right of parents to dispose of their children. An idea of almost divine superiority of the parent over the child is cherished, and every disobedience of, or disrespect to parental authority is punished with the utmost rigor. No circumstances can arise in which a child is absolved from unqualified and the most implicit obedience to the parent.

This same principle forms the basis of their political code. The Emperor is considered as their parent, and to strengthen this assumption, the idea of divine right is superadded. Heaven and earth are considered the parents of all mankind, and the Emperor, as the Son of Heaven, is the next in authority and reverenced accordingly. Both parents and rulers are far exalted above children and subjects, and receive not only homage, but worship.

The parental prerogative has been the foundation of Chinese politics from the earliest antiquity, and is the source of the good order and peace which exist throughout the vast empire. For a heathen country, it may well challenge admiration for the wisdom of a legislative principle, which thus effectually unites and tranquilizes so great a nation.

The emperor's ministers are by him called his "hands and feet," "his ears and eyes," and are responsible to him for the exercise of the authority delegated to them, with their fortunes, and their lives. Any one of them, however high he may be in authority, can be submitted to the lowest indignity and made to undergo any punishment that a judgment or whim of the Emperor may determine upon.

The prime ministers of state are called the "inner chamber," or "cabinet," and are four in number—two Tartars and two Chinese. This same policy may be observed in all appointments of offices—of setting the two races to watch each other.

Under this cabinet are the six tribunals, which take cognizance of their several departments and report to the emperor for his decision and approval. The first is the tribunal of civil office, has a survey over the conduct of all magistrates, recommends persons to fill vacancies, and suggests the propriety of promoting or degrading individuals according to their respective merits.

The second tribunal is that of revenue; its members take cognizance of the amount of the population, the collection of taxes, the coining of money, the expenditure, the income, the payment of the various officers, and the maintenance of the state sacrifices.

The third tribunal is that of rites, having charge of all religious and state ceremonies, court etiquette, and astrological predictions; the introduction and arrangement of nobles at the levees, and the etiquette there to be observed and the clothes each one is to wear. The imperial astronomers who prognosticate terrestrial affairs, calculate celestial phenomena, and predict lucky and unlucky days, come under the superintendence of the board of rites.

The fourth tribunal is that of war, which takes the superintendence of the army, navy, and ordinance, appoints the number of troops assigned to each province, and attends to the management of all the defenses of the country.

Next comes the tribunal of punishments, which appoints and removes judges, takes cognizance of all judicial proceedings, and sees to the execution of the laws.

The last tribunal is that of works, to which is committed

the care of public buildings and construction of roads and canals. In addition to these tribunals there are various other officers; such as the Colonial Board or foreign officer, the public censorate, which is allowed to reprove the emperor or any of his officers without being liable to punishment, and the members of the national college at Pekin, to whom all matters with respect to literature, and many with regard to politics are referred, while the principal officers of state are chosen from among them.

The laws of China are numerous, minute, and circumstantial, and in speaking of them, the Edinburgh Review says, "There is nothing here of the monstrous verbiage of most other Asiatic productions; but a clear, concise, and distinct series of enactments, savoring throughout of practical judgment and European good sense; and if not always conformable to our improved ideas of expediency in this country, in general approaching more closely to them than the codes of most other nations."

Perhaps you may think my rather lengthy dissertation upon the Chinese political code, somewhat dry and uninteresting, but I thought it would interest you to know something concerning their principle of government, and have made it as brief as possible. Now we will turn to a ramble which I had with a friend about Whampoa and surroundings.

We took passage for shore in the bum boat, and while on our way, Old Sam's son invited us into the small room near the stern, which he calls his cabin. Immediately upon entering, he proffered us some mandarin wine, which we accepted. We found it to be superior to any of the many liquors manufactured from rice which we had before tasted, of a pleasant, spicy flavor, and, judging by its thick oily appearance, it must have been very old. He said that it was, and that it was very valuable, a pint of it costing upwards of eleven dollars. After partaking of the wine, he played for us upon his guitar, a commingling of weird and wild, yet strangely sweet sounds, which charmed us both. Hitherto, all the Chinese music which we had heard had been so characterized by an entirely unmusical noise, or frightful shrieks, as to disgust rather than please us, and we had concluded that the Chinese were an entirely unmusical people; but Young Sam's music excited both our wonder and admiration.

We landed at New Town, and after an hour's ramble over it, decided upon the following description : It is situated at the lower end of Whampoa Island, and as the name implies, is of recent construction—having been built since the opening of the river to foreign trade. Here reside many Chinese merchants, and the most of the Europeans resident at Whampoa. The foreign section is governed by a marshal under the direction of the United States Consul at Canton.

Our intention before we went ashore was to take a stroll back into the country, rather than to stay about the town; so, after this hour's look at it, we set out, armed with sundry refreshments, and with pockets full of *cash*. Just back of the town we came to the foot bridge which spans the creek where the fireman was drowned. The bridge is a rickety concern, and bad enough to cross when sober. After crossing, and passing a few scattered houses, we found ourselves fairly launched into the country.

How strangely good and refreshing it seemed to be for a time away from noise and tumult, with some congenial spirit, in the quiet of the country! Such a beautiful, delightful walk as we had! Oh, I would that I had the graphic pen of some to describe it! Our walk for a time was upon a wall or bank, between a branch of the Canton river upon our right, and a series of paddy fields upon our left. On the river could be seen the many interesting phases of boat-life, of which I have told you in a previous letter; and also, I have spoken of the rice fields, but I will add a few words here. These are laid out in from one to ten acres each; on every side is a ditch the dirt from which forms the raised wall or bank. Nearly every field has its threshing floor, which is simply a circular plot beaten hard. They have just finished harvesting one crop of rice, and are preparing the ground for another. Now to turn to the walk itself, some five or six feet high—it varies in width from six to fifty feet, and is for the most part covered with a luxuriant growth of vegetation—the sides being lined with beautiful shrubbery, and fine shade trees. Along this we continued our walk for two miles, until we were brought to a halt by a wide, deep, canal filled with water. To cross this we followed its windings for half a mile or more, when we found a regular crossing, with an old *sampan* for a ferry-boat. We went on board of this and were ferried over, for which the fare was one *cash* each. After ascending the opposite bank, we entered a charming grove of fine old teaks, and passing through it over a wide paved walk, we found a Joss tower situated on an artificial island, surrounded by a wide, deep moat, filled with water, and spanned by an arched, stone bridge.

Leaving this for a subsequent visit, we pushed on towards our destination—the old pagoda near the center of the island, and still some three or four miles distant. Our path after leaving the Joss tower was very winding and circuitous, in order to keep upon the banks between the soft, muddy paddy fields. The shade trees now changed, and were for the most part banana trees, which I, for the first time closely examined. After attaining to the height of five or six feet, they begin to put forth blossoms. These resemble an ear of green corn in form, and are of a reddish hue. As they grow the outer circlet of husks turns back, at the roots of which the young bananas are seen; and thus they continue, circlet after circlet, until sometimes the bunch attains four feet in length. I noticed some bunches where there were blossoms at the tip and ripe bananas near the butt.

When we had almost reached our destination, and were

congratulating ourselves upon the rest we were then to have, suddenly our path turned nearly about, and it took us an hour's quick walk to reach the old decayed village near it. The only redeeming feature of this place was the wide, paved, and beautifully shaded walk approaching the bridge which spans the creek at the commencement.

After passing through the town we ascended the eminence upon which the pagoda stood, and where arriving, we seated ourselves to rest, and enjoy the magnificent and enchanting view. In itself, the eminence is a beautiful, almost perfect oval, mound, the only one on the island, rising about one hundred feet above the level of the river, and being upwards of half a mile in circuit. It is covered with beautiful shrubbery, prominent in which are many rose-bushes, covered with variously tinted flowers. Scattered around are several mandarin sepulchres. Near the center of the eminence stands the pagoda, an octagonal brick structure, about one hundred and fifty feet high, and divided into nine stories. The top is conical in form, and surmounted by a cross. On the upper projecting roofs are growing several shrubs, quite trees, in fact. How they came there, I cannot say, but suppose that the seed was carried thither either by the wind or by birds, and in the decaying wood-work found a soil in which to take root and grow.

Leaving the eminence and turning to that beyond, before us and behind is a branch of the Canton river winding its way and covered with boats of every size and description. To the right Canton is dimly seen, while on the left is Old Whampoa, and all around both far and near, a beautiful intermingling of hill and dale, mountain and plain, bayou, river, and creek; so enchanting us that we stood for a long time admiring it, drinking in its rare beauties, forgetful of how short was our time before sundown. But nearer than all, right before us is the pagoda resting upon a stone base four feet high, supported by sixteen stone images. To the pagoda there are two entrances, one on the northern and the other on the southern side.

In entering I was surprised to find that the walls were of such enormous thickness, being no less than ten feet. At length we reach the inside and find nothing so very wonderful, after all, to be seen, merely a hollow shaft about twelve feet across at the bottom and tapering towards the top. The whole is entirely destitute of ornament. Upon two sides of each story are openings, and upon the others are niches, where once idols were doubtless placed. The walls are covered with the autographs of those that have visited it; one I saw from Bridgeport, Conn., 1842, but couldn't make out the person's name. Following the example of our predecessors, we placed our autographs upon the wall, and then with the sun an hour high, set out to return.

In returning, we took a different and more direct route, which led towards Old Whampoa, and after passing through a "City of the Dead" upon a knoll near the walls, we came to the gates of the city. In our walk through the town we found the streets to be unusually wide, and what is still more unusual, that shade-trees by the sides of the streets and pretty squares and ponds, were numerous. By the Chinese themselves it is regarded as one of their most pleasant and beautiful cities. In these a European seemed to be quite a curiosity, judging by the immense crowds that everywhere followed us, staring with open mouth and eyes; and not a single Chinaman did we meet that could speak a word of English. We wandered about there some time in the vain endeavor to find any one to show us our way, until at last a bright eyed little boy, dressed as one of the higher order of Chinese, seeing our difficulty, came up to us, and by signs signified his ability and willingness to conduct us out of the city; this he did, and refusing the offered reward, politely *chin chined* us off.

On our way to New Town we saw a Chinaman engaged in

ploughing. For a team he had a buffalo ox; the harness was not unlike a horse harness, and was attached by a whiffle to an English-like plough, not differing materially, except in having but one handle. Leaving him, without further adventure, or meeting with anything of more than ordinary interest, we reached the ship a few minutes after sundown, both of us considering that it had been one of the most interesting and pleasant days we had spent in China.

Another ramble a few days later presented us with much that was new and interesting. At a native apothecary's shop we saw a person grinding spices and other articles—learning the "rudiments" I suppose. The article to be ground was placed in a long, narrow, iron tray, and then a roller, fixed upon an axle-tree and exactly fitting the tray, was moved backwards and forwards upon the article—the Chinaman sitting down, and furnishing the motive power with his feet.

Near by was another person engaged in grinding wheat. The grain was placed in a hopper, and from it passed between two small mill-stones, which were turned by hand. In fact, all labor in China is performed without any aid from steam or water power, and all instruments employed are of the most primitive pattern.

Farther on we were attracted by a Chinese printer's establishment, and I think that some account of their mode of printing might be of interest to you.

The art of printing was known to the Chinese more than nine hundred years ago; for, by reference to Chinese history, it appears that, in A. D. 926, the ruler of Tang ordered the nine classics to be printed and sold to the people. In the time of Confucius, books were formed of slips of bamboo, upon which they wrote with the point of a style; in A. D. 150, paper was invented; in 745 books were first made, and in 926 they were multiplied by printing; so that the Chinese appear to have made early advances in civilization, while we only discovered the art of making paper in the eleventh, and that of printing in the fifteenth century.

Their mode of printing is of the simplest character, and although it discourages the compilation of new works, it has among its advantages those of speed and cheapness. Their language consists of a great number of characters, and instead of having an assortment of these, they prefer to cut the characters for each separate work, page by page. The first part of the process is to have the page written out in the printed form of the character, and is then transferred to the wood as follows: the smooth block is covered with a glutinous paste, the paper applied and allowed to remain until it is dry. When removed it leaves the inverted impressions of the characters upon the block. The engraver then proceeds, in a skillful and expeditious manner, to remove all of the wood around and within the letters. A page usually contains from four to five hundred characters, and will take a skillful and expeditious engraver from four to five days to prepare the block.

The block thus prepared, now passes into the hands of the printer, who places it upon a table, with a pot of ink and a brush upon the one hand, and a pile of dry paper upon the other, and before him a rubber. The workman now proceeds to business; first, to ink over the block; next, he smoothly places a sheet of the paper upon it, and then, after passing the rubber over it two or three times, the sheet is removed, and the same process repeated. An accomplished printer will in this manner make more than three thousand impressions in a day. The same process is gone through with other blocks, until the required number of copies of the whole book is completed; then come the arranging, folding, and stitching, and the books are finished. Their paper is very thin, but very cheap, ten sheets costing less than one cent; then, as labor is very cheap also, books in China cost almost nothing. The complete works of Confucius, with the commentaries of Choo-foo-tsze, comprising six volumes, and amounting to eight hundred octavo pages, can be purchased for less than twenty cents. Literature is thus brought within the reach of all, and it has been said with truth, that China has more books and more people to read them, than any other part of the world.

Leaving New Town, we took a *sampan* and crossed over to Bamboo Town, and from the summit of the beautiful eminence which rises immediately in the rear, we had a splendid view of the three divisions, the harbor, and the country for many miles around. This eminence is possessed by the Parsees, and by them used as a burying-ground—there being some fifteen or twenty of their square, box-like, stone sepulchres near the summit. In all its outlines and adornments the place is exceedingly beautiful, and it forms a prominent feature in all the Chinese paintings or engravings of Whampoa.

While we were up there we espied a native funeral procession wending its way along the foot of the eminence, towards a burying-ground some half a mile distant—and we, out of curiosity, joined it. The order of the procession was as follows: a man carrying a pole to which were attached many and variously colored streamers—Joss papers; one bearing dishes of food, drink, and fruits; one with a bundle of small Joss papers, which he scattered right and left; then the priest, beating a mournful march upon a pair of cymbals, and chanting an accompaniment; after him was borne the corpse upon the shoulders of four men; and then, mourners and friends brought up the rear. The chief mourners were dressed in sackcloth frocks and caps, while the others wore white sashes and caps. A crimson cloth covered the coffin. At the grave the collected Joss papers were burned, a prayer was offered by the priest, the articles of food were left, and the ceremony was over.

Other funerals I have seen where the whole procession is led by the loud and rapid music—if music it could be called—of gongs, cymbals, and flutes. Then, in a box suspended from poles and resting upon men's shoulders, is a pig roasted whole. After the priest, and slung on poles in the same manner as the pig, comes the coffin. Then follow five or six fancifully ornamented sedan-chairs, in each of which is some article of food, ornamented with wreaths and boquets of flowers. After these, come some dressed in white and wearing sugar-loaf hats, while behind all are the real mourners, dressed in sackcloth; the funeral is made a wedding by the substitution of a gaily dressed sedan-chair conveying the bride. And the friends for the mourners, sons and near relatives, wear white silk or cotton braided in their queues for mourning, for the two or three years following a death. Blue is used instead of white in some of the northern provinces.

After the funeral services were over, having three or four hours to spare before sundown, we crossed to Bamboo Town and visited the Joss tower back of the town, which we had passed a few days before. It is a hexagonal brick structure, about fifty feet high, divided into three stories, resting upon a granite platform five or six feet high and reached by a flight of stone steps on each side. The tower is surmounted by a conical-shaped, wooden roof. The grounds around are fine, and well kept. Across the moat is a brick house, where reside the priest and those having the care of the tower and grounds. A small present to the priest opened the doors for us, and we entered. The inside we found to be in good repair, with rich and gaily adorned idols placed in every story. A splendid and extensive view is to be had from the upper one.

Our stay at Whampoa had been characterized by so much interest and freedom of action, that all regretted the orders of the Admiral to return to Hong Kong, more especially as these orders were accompanied by others to get ready for sea as soon as possible, and start for the northward again. All dread the prospect of being farther north during the winter, for here we have to wear overcoats and mufflers during the night time, to keep comfortable. We left Whampoa the 23d, but, running aground, we were obliged to wait until high tide before we could get off, and consequently did not arrive here until the next day.

The convening of a general court-martial, and the arrival of the holidays, have been the prominent events of our stay here this time. Upon Christmas eve many of the vessels in the harbor, as well as houses ashore, were brilliantly illuminated. All our crew were quite noisy and jolly—heightened, no doubt, by sundry bottles of ale and wine sent forward by the officers—and the singing, dancing, and other sports, were kept up until a late hour. Christmas was a beautiful day, and was celebrated by us in grand style. I thought many times of the dear friends at home, and would have liked to have been with them to have spent the day; but as I could not, I contented myself with what I had, and can't say but that I enjoyed myself very much. It certainly was the pleasantest of the three that I have spent in the service. For more than a week preparations had been made for the dinner, and it was a perfect success—a complete triumph of culinary skill. I did not dream that the crew of a man-of-war could successfully conceive or prepare one, one-half as good. The bill of fare included: roast pigs, stuffed geese, chicken pies, roast beef and mutton, with puddings, pies, and fruits, for dessert. As an addition, the officers sent forward an abundance of ale and champagne to each mess, so that after dinner it was about as jolly a crew as one ever meets with.

Nature would affirm that this day has been a lovely one; for everything in it combined to make it so,—the air soft and warm, the sun shining brightly, undimmed by a single cloud, and everything so quiet and full of harmony. Yet it has been a sad and darksome day to many of us,—occasioned by the parting with ten of our shipmates, whose time had expired, and who were transferred on board of the *Supply*, to be sent home upon the first opportunity. Nature's bright face seemed but to heighten our loss. One there was among them who had been to me as a brother for two years, and parting with him seemed like parting with a brother. I had put off saying the parting words until the last moment, but when that came I could not speak, my heart was too full. I could only grasp him by the hand, and let the adieu be a silent one. For two years we have had everything in common—sharing all each other's joys, sorrows, and confidences, and thus weaving a bond of friendship which one can know or understand only by experience.

LETTER XXVII.

U. S. S. WACHUSETT, Chefoo, China,
January 22, 1867.

MY DEAR R.:

Immediately after the transfer and the sad parting attendant upon it, orders were given to make preparations for getting under way, and in less than two hours we were steaming down the bay, on our way for the northward. In Ly Moon pass we housed topmasts and sent down the yards, as we had a strong head wind to steam against. The two days following were very unpleasant,—the wind strong, the sea rough, and with nothing aloft to steady her, the ship rolled and pitched about terribly, making all more or less sea-sick.

The third evening out, the captain, apprehending a gale, with his customary forethought and prudence, put the vessel into Linchan Bay—a snug little harbor, formed by some barren, rocky islands off the coast, near Foo-chow. Fortunate for us was it that he did so; for we had been anchored but a short time, when the wind began to blow in fitful gusts, and soon increased in fury to a regular hurricane, or typhoon, as they are called here in China. This continuing, we remained there for two days, when the wind lulled, the sea calmed down, and we proceeded on our way to Shanghai. There we arrived January 6th, having been but a week in the passage from Hong Kong, including stoppages, which, at this season of the year, is considered a good passage.

Immediately after anchoring, money was served out, and the crew sent ashore on general liberty.

One evening, a day or two after our arrival, we were all startled by a loud explosion, and a few minutes later an

English brig, lying at anchor down the harbor, was seen to be on fire. The cutters were immediately manned and sent to her assistance, and in a short time succeeded in extinguishing the flames. When they returned to the ship they told the following story. Part of the brig's cargo consisted of powder, in kegs, and this they had been discharging during the day. Before sweeping up what had scattered from the kegs as they rolled them along, the mate lit his pipe, and while going about the hold with it in his mouth, he let fall some sparks upon the scattered powder, which communicating with a number of full kegs, caused the explosion. Considerable damage was done to the vessel, two Chinese laborers were killed, and several were severely injured and burned,—among the latter was the mate. The cutters conveyed the injured ones to the hospital.

For two or three weeks after the transfer I was terribly lonely, and would have given almost anything to have the transferred ones back again; or, better still, to have been with them. I miss my "chum" in everything, and it does seem like beginning a new life to get along without him,— so long have we been together doing and using everything in common. I shall be so glad when my turn comes to leave this far away, heathen country, and start for home.

There was nothing to occasion a long stay in Shanghai; so, after four days occupied in giving liberty and taking in coal and provisions, we again made preparations to proceed to the northward.

But I must not leave Shanghai without relating an incident which came under my notice while on liberty there, which, if it affects your risibility to such a degree as it did mine, I shall be amply repaid for the narration.

While walking along on the Bund my attention was attracted by an excited crowd of Chinese assembled in front of the Custom-house. Arriving there I found that the excitement was occasioned by two Chinese, engaged in what was to me a novel combat. They stood about two feet apart, and were lashing one another about the head and face with their long queues. These, they handled with such skill and fury that the face and arms of both were covered with blood, drawn by the force of the blows. It required no small amount of dexterity to strike an effective blow with these *queues*, grasping them as they did so close to the back of the head; and it would not have failed to make you laugh, could you but have seen how they would duck their heads at each blow they gave, in order to add more effect to it. The combat lasted for upwards of fifteen minutes, until both of the participators were completely exhausted. The spectators appeared to enjoy it very much, and frequently encouraged the combatants with cheering words. I have never before witnessed this mode of warfare, but I am told that it is very frequently practiced.

We were four days in making the passage from Shanghai to Cheefoo, the first two of which were quite warm and pleasant for the latitude and season of the year. The third day it was cold, stormy, and disagreeable, which increased rather than diminished on the fourth day, and making our visit to Cheefoo cheerless and dreary to begin with.

However, we had a warm welcome from the crew of H. B. M.'s Gunboat Insolence, whose hearts we gladdened with the two months' accumulated mail brought up from Shanghai—there being no regular mail communication with Chefoo during the winter season.

Notwithstanding the cold and dreary sensation which we experienced upon our arrival, our stay has been a very pleasant one. The Captain has done everything that he was able to make it pleasant for us—having no work done that was not absolutely necessary, and had hoods put up at the "break of the forecastle," underneath which the men were allowed to have a fire night and day, and where they could sit, smoke, make and drink their coffee.

Here game of almost all kinds is abundant and cheap, so that as regards the inner man all would be content to remain at Chefoo the remainder of the winter. Yesterday while on shore I amused myself for several hours in shooting wild duck, which in immense flocks lined the water's edge only a short distance back of the town.

After I had secured as much as I wished to take off to the ship, and having several hours left before the "sundown boat" would be sent in shore, I conceived the idea that I should enjoy a good skate on the little pond at the rear of the English Consulate's, which I had noticed was covered over with a sufficiently thick crust of ice. After racking my brain for a few minutes to think of a way and place to procure a pair of skates, I at length determined to go up to the Consul's and endeavor to procure a pair from him. Accordingly I went up there and stated my desire. He appeared to be much amused at my novel request, but after a few minutes' conversation he cheerfully loaned me the desired skates. I took them, went down to the pond, put them on, and skated away there hour after hour, with the deepest pleasure. At length the setting sun told me that it was time for the boat, so I unstrapped the skates and returned them to the Consul, with many thanks for his kindness. His name I have been unable to learn, but I shall ever think of him with feelings of gratitude for his kindness in cheerfully furnishing me with the means of an afternoon's deep enjoyment.

We expect to leave here to-morrow for Corea, to investigate the circumstances attendant upon the loss of the American schooner General Sherman, and the fate of the people on board of her, which vessel was wrecked there some time ago. It is feared that all on board of her at the time have perished—murdered by the natives. Our object in coming to Chefoo was to procure the Chinese pilot which was on board of the General Sherman a few days before her loss, and we are to take him with us to give such information as he may be able.

We are also to take with us the Rev. Mr. Corbett, an American Missionary at Chefoo, who is to act as interpreter, he being thoroughly acquainted with the Chinese written language. This is the same in China, Corea, and Japan, but the spoken language is unlike, and even entirely different dialects are used in different provinces of the same country. As my letter is not very long I will lengthen it by giving you some little account of their language, as far as I have been able to learn, feeling sure that any such information will be of interest to you.

The written language, as I have mentioned, is the same throughout the whole empire, and has been, for centuries, unchanged, while the spoken sounds vary in every province, and in almost every succeeding age. Both of the mediums of communication are of the most primitive order—the words monosyllabic, and the characters symbolic.

The earliest traditions of the Chinese tell us that events were recorded by means of knotted cords; their next advance was to pictorial illustrations; then hieroglyphics were employed; and then, their last and greatest improvement, was made in the invention and increase of arbitrary marks— forming their present written medium. They assert that the idea of employing arbitrary signs was first derived from the tracings of birds' tracks in the snow, and from the marks upon the back of a tortoise. These signs are said to have been invented by Tsang-këe, upwards of four thousand five hundred years ago.

Their characters are divided into six classes—the pictorial, the metaphorical, the indicative, the constructive, the derivative, and the phonetic. The first bear some resemblance to the object; the second derive their meaning from something else; the third convey their meaning by the formation of the characters; the fourth derive their meaning from the parts of which they are composed; the fifth are other characters slightly varied; and the sixth are those in which the form and sound harmonize. Their fullest dictionaries contain more than thirty thousand characters, but hardly more than one-tenth of that number are in common use.

Chinese characters appear complicated to one first observing them, but a careful examination will show that there are but six distinct strokes employed—the horizontal, the perpendicular, the right and the left oblique slanting, the hooked, and the dot. The whole number of the elements is less than two hundred and twenty; but of these no more than one-fourth are commonly employed, of which again one-fourth are most common.

Every character occupies an exact square, no matter of how many strokes it is composed, and a well written page appears divided into equal sections. They read from top to bottom, commencing at the right hand of a page, and at what would to us be the back part of the book. The paper is so thin that but one side of it is used, either in printing or writing. Eighty or eighty-five leaves form a volume, and are always bound in thin paper covers.

As the sound of each character is produced by a single emission of the voice, their spoken language is monosyllabic. Where two syllables appear to be, from the sound, it will be found upon examination that they are two characters joined, and where the pronunciation is written with a diaëresis, both vowels are, or should be sounded together. As their characters do not represent elementary sounds, the Chinese know nothing about spelling. However, every word is divided into an initial and a final. By the union of these, nine hundred and forty-six monosyllables could be produced; but less than one-third of this number are really extracted. At first it would seem impossible for the Chinese to converse with each other, with only three hundred monosyllables, but this is accomplished by giving to each syllable a variety of tones, easily discernable to the accustomed Chinese ear, but exceedingly difficult for a foreigner to acquire.

The tones are five in number—the high, the even, the departing, the entering, and a lower "even" tone. These make fifteen hundred distinct utterances; but no more than one-third of these are used. To prevent, in a great measure, mistakes from having several characters to the same sound, the Chinese combine individual terms in set phrases, which are used like our compound words; so that it is necessary to learn, not only the characters and tones, but also the collocation of phrases, which are very extensively employed.

With the exception of the United States, China takes the lead of all other countries in the number of its inhabitants which are able to read—it being estimated that at least one-half of them can do so. This is owing in part to the exceeding cheapness of all printed matter; but more, probably, to the great inducements offered for learning. The most of the titles and positions of rank are not hereditary, and are to be attained only by merit. In this, education holds a prominent position, and through it, as in the United States, almost any rank and title can be reached. They have a proverb, and a true one, too, that "while royalty is hereditary, office is not."

There has been so many strange things said about China, as well as other countries in the east, and so recently has it been opened to foreign insight and intercourse, that but comparatively few have yet received authentic accounts of the manners, customs, laws, and other points of interest about the people—that out of the many things said, one hardly knows how much or what to believe. The people, judged by our own standard, are a strange people; their customs are strange, and everything regarding their manners, dress, etc., are very strange. But they are a wonderful people after all, and their country is full of wonderful things.

Perhaps you may think that I digress greatly from the main intent of my letters, but I can but believe that anything relative to these strange people will be of interest to you, and so shall continue to give them to you as they are brought under my observation.

LETTER XXVIII.

U. S. S. WACHUSETT, Port Hamilton, Corea,
February 2, 1867.

MY DEAR R.:

Before wandering off into Chinese language and literature, we were about leaving Chefoo for Corea. Towards evening we started, with a good "beam wind," and under both steam and canvas. Early the next morning we sighted the high, ragged, rocky coast of Corea. The forenoon we passed in cruising about a large bay at the mouth of the Ta-tung river, engaged in taking soundings and bearings. The Ta-tung river empties its waters in Lat. 38° 04' N., and Long. 124° 50' E., into a large bay some ten or eleven miles in diameter, surrounded on all sides by high, barren, rocky hills. This bay has several openings to the sea, by one of which we came in; it is the largest of them all, being nearly a mile wide.

We at length came to anchor near the mouth of the river, under the lee of Nein-Fo, or Cow Island, in seventeen fathoms of water. Upon this island is located the chief one of a number of fishing villages, situated near each other. A visit from the inhabitants showed us none of the wildness and ferocity which the Coreans had been said to possess, in their looks and actions; instead, they appeared to be an inoffensive, unarmed race, yet very rude and barbarous. At first sight they might be taken for Indians, or, nearer still, Japanese, but they do not closely resemble either—being about midway between the latter and the Chinese. Their skin is dark, almost copper colored; they do not shave the head at all, but collect the hair all together and fasten it in a knot upon the top of the head; their features partake of the characteristics of both races; their clothes are, for the most part, of skins, and made up for comfort, regardless of looks. They use stockings and sandals similar to those worn by the Japanese, but with no separate place for the great toe. Altogether, their appearance is inferior to that of either the Chinese or Japanese.

The next day the chief's son was sent by us with a communication to the king of Corea, and also with a letter to the presiding officer of the province, Chang-Yuen-Heen. The following is a copy of the latter:

(Copy.— Translation.)
UNITED STATES STEAMER WACHUSETT,
Mouth of the Ta-tung River, Jan. 24, 1867.

SIR:

The Commander of the American Armed Vessel Wachusett sends greeting to the presiding officer of the Province of Chang-Yuen-Heen, and wishes to inform his excellency that he has come to the borders of Corea, not to engage in war nor any unlawful business; but is anxious that harmony and peace should exist, as heretofore, between America and Corea.

"He respectfully requests that you forward the accompanying document to your king with all due dispatch. It is hoped that the answer to the accompanying document will be returned without delay, that he may depart without delay, in peace, from where he is now lying at anchor in the harbor of Ta-ping.

Very Respectfully, &c., &c.,
(Signed)   ROBERT W. SCHUFELDT,
Commander of the United States Steamer Wachusett.

His Excellency the Presiding Officer of the Province of
Chang-Yuen-Heen.

The following is a copy of the communication sent to the king:

(*Copy.—Translation.*)

"UNITED STATES ARMED VESSEL WACHUSETT,
Harbor of Ta-ping, January 24, 1867.

To His Majesty, the King of Corea:

The Commander of the American Armed Vessel Wachusett begs to inform your Majesty, that he has come to the borders of your kingdom, not to engage in war, nor any unlawful business, but in obedience to the command of the officer commanding the American armed vessels stationed in these seas, who has learned with great pleasure and thankfulness of the kindness of your Majesty's officers and people to the shipwrecked crew of the American vessel in the month of June last, on the west coast of Corea; how your Majesty had them transported to the confines of China, from whence they safely reached their friends. The whole American people cannot but feel thankful, and praise your nation, for this act of brotherly love.

The officer commanding the Armed Vessels of America has since learned with pain and surprise, that the people of another American vessel, wrecked in the Tai-tong river, in the Province of Ping-Yang, in the month of September last, were all put to death and the vessel burned, and he has ordered me to ask of your Majesty if this be true, and if true, to ask of your Majesty what evil these people had done that they should be made to suffer such treatment. But if any or all of these people are still living, the officer commanding the Armed Vessels of America has directed me to ask of your Majesy that they may be delivered to me on board of the Wachusett, now lying in the harbor of Ta-fung, near the Nein-fo islands, or at any more convenient port your Majesty may select. This is especially desired, that the peace and friendship, which has hitherto been uninterrupted for many years, may still continue between America and Corea. A speedy answer is requested to this communication in order that I may depart in haste.

Very Respectfully, etc., etc.,

ROBERT W. SHUFELDT,

Commanding United States Armed Vessel Wachusett."

His Majesty, the King of Corea.

While awaiting the replies to these communications, a survey of the bay and adjoining inlets was made, as there had none been made before. To the bay we gave the name of the vessel, and called the various inlets after our officers. Attempts were also made to establish and cultivate friendly relations with the natives. The inhabitants of the fishing villages appeared to be kindly disposed towards us, but in great dread of their government, and came as little in contact with us as possible. We saw no iron in use; the boats were constructed with wooden pegs for fastenings, or bound together by coarse seaweed cordage.

One afternoon the old chief came on board, accompanied by several of the natives. His costume did not differ from that of the others in style or material, with the exception of having a covering of fine wire network for his "top-knot." Upon seeing it an old sailor remarked, "That ar's the old feller's winter cap, he has a cooler one for summer." He examined everything about the ship with the deepest interest, and seemed to be much pleased with everything he saw.

Like the Chinese, the Coreans appear to regard filthiness as a virtue; and if they are right in such a belief they are the most perfect race of people that I ever met with, for they are certainly the most filthy. Their appearance would testify that water was unknown to them; and then such lice as they had—ugh! It makes me crawl to think of them; and a certain old salt—noted for confining his yarns to the *strictest bounds of truth*—said that he "saw them jump from the clothes of the natives into the rigging, run up it, and perch themselves upon the to'gallant mast truck, where they could be plainly seen laughing at and making comments upon us down below." Was he not so well known as a person of undoubted veracity, I could hardly credit the whole of his story. Be this as it may, it is certain that the Coreans are filthy and covered with vermin beyond description.

All the natives to whom anything was said about the *General Sherman*, spoke with great reserve, but told the same story;—that the vessel was burned last September, up the Ping Ying river, and that all that were on board of her at the time, amounting to twenty-seven persons, were killed in a *melee* with the natives on shore, and not by order of the mandarins. The river will not be clear of ice for two months yet, and then a vessel cannot ascend more than half way to Ping-Yang-soo, the principal place on the river.

The Coreans say that frequently the Chinese pirates make a descent upon the coast with their junks, and rob the inhabitants; and that ten of the crew of the *General Sherman* were of these pirates. This report was confirmed by our pilot. Mr. Hogarth, an English subject, who was on board the *General Sherman* when the disaster occurred, was well known throughout China for his reckless character, and his acquaintances think that if a disturbance was created, he took a prominent part.

Tuesday morning, January 29, an officer who said that he came from Hai-Chow-Poo, the capital city of the province, fifty miles up the Ta-ting river, was brought on board by one of our boats for which he had signaled. The manner of this officer was haughty and imperious, and he presented in his appearance the most perfect type of a cruel and vindictive savage. His presence seemed to inspire the greatest fear and dread, and it is feared that the old chief, and the messenger, his son, will pay for their friendship towards us, by the loss of their heads. It is thought that he was either the governor of Hai-Chow-Poo, or some high official in his confidence. The interview with him, as usual, was carried on by writing—Mr. Corbett acting as interpreter—and resulted in a most unsatisfactory manner. He professed to know nothing concerning the *General Sherman* affair, and told us that we had better leave the coast. The main answer to all of Captain Shufeldt's questions was, that it did not become us to remain longer in the place, and earnestly hoped that we would depart and return to our own country. So all hopes that there would be found some peaceable and satisfactory solution of the *Sherman* affair, as well as to have discovered some of the crew still living, and rescued them, have proved futile, and the matter remains as before. With this conviction, and thinking that it would be useless to remain longer, we got under way that same day and started for the southward, our parting words being that "we should come again with more ships."

Three days' steaming brought us to anchor at Port Hamilton, (Nanhoo,) among the islands off the southern coast of Corea. It is situated in Lat. 34° 01' 23" N., Long. 127° 20' W., and about three hundred miles from Wachusett Bay; but in the passage we logged four hundred and fifty-five knots.

In connection with our visit to Corea for the purpose of inquiring into the *Sherman* affair, we were also directed to inquire into the advantages of Port Hamilton as a rendezvous and sanitarium for the squadron, and also as a harbor of refuge in times of danger, for American commerce in these waters.

The harbor is certainly a secure and lovely one. It is about two miles in length by one in width, oval in shape, and formed by two long narrow, and one small triangular islands. To this basin there is an opening, accessible to the largest vessels, on the southeastern side. It is also open to the sea for some distance on its northwesterly side, but a sand-bar prevents any but small boats from passing through this channel.

The outside appearance of these islands is exceedingly bold, rocky, and precipitous, romantic and picturesque in the extreme—nearly perpendicular for from one to two hundred feet; afterwards rising into peaks six or eight hundred feet high; then gradually sloping inward to the basin, and all forming a large natural fort, which might with a trifling amount of labor be rendered impregnable. Doubtless the whole is the top of a sunken volcano, and the spot where we are now lying at anchor, was once an active, burning crater. On account of the steepness of the outer side of these islands, only the inner, or those that surround the basin, can be brought under cultivation. These comprise about two-thirds of the entire area. The arable portions are in an exceedingly high state of cultivation, acquired only by an immense amount of labor, for the land is naturally very rough and stony. They are divided into small, rectangular patches, extend about two-thirds of the way up the mountains' sides, and are already green with the wheat sown last fall. There is but little that can be called terracing, such as is seen in China and Japan. Wheat and millet are the principal products. In general the climate and vegetation are similar to those of China and Japan.

The islands being separated on the northwest and southeast, the breezes from the sea have free access to the basin, and must render the air cool and healthy in summer, thus making the place an admirable location for a sanitarium.

The inhabitants live in four villages, two on the eastern, and two on the western islands. They informed us that they numbered five hundred families, and reckoning five persons to a family this gives us two thousand as the total population—a rather low estimate. Their villages are very compact, and each house is surrounded by a thick, high wall, of small stones, laid up without mortar or cement. A door is made in this wall, and a small house built near it, together forming a sort of " compound."

Their houses are all very low, and have walls built of small stones, or a framework of wood with the interstices plastered with clay. The roof is a coarse thatching of straw, fastened down with ropes of the same material. The rooms have wooden floors, but are so low one cannot stand up in them. Through the open doors and a few small paper windows, a scanty light is admitted—sufficient, however, to show a complete dearth of any kind of furniture. In front there is generally a rude piazza, where the people seem to pass most of their time when at home. Their streets are mostly very crooked and filthy, and narrower even than those of Chinese towns.

They all dress with the greatest uniformity, in garments of the same pattern as those of the Chinese. White is universally worn, and since we have been in Corea we have not seen a colored article of clothing.

The government is patriarchal, the oldest men being the heads of the villages, and each village being distinct from the others. We have seen no animals of any kind during our stay, and the only trees in sight are a few small pines. Our intercourse with the natives was carried on by writing. Mr. Corbett acted as interpreter and scribe, and to him am I indebted for such facts and incidents regarding the place as did not come under my personal observation during my rambles on shore.

I have been particular in describing all that I have seen and heard regarding Corea, as I am firmly convinced that shortly it will be a place of great interest to foreigners; and my slight acquaintance with the country and people has created a strong desire to prosecute this acquaintance much further.

LETTER XXIX.

U. S. S. WACHUSETT, Shanghai, China,
February 24, 1867.

MY DEAR R.:

We arrived here the 5th, having made the passage from Port Hamilton, Corea, a distance of four hundred miles, in forty hours. We found a mail awaiting our arrival, and were gladdened by news of friends at home. For the first time since we have been in China, I have not heard of this mail's bringing sad news to any one—one and all wearing smiling faces as they perused the contents of letters from friends near and dear. I would that it could ever be thus, it would make all so much happier and more cheerful. But so long as the world stands will there be sad partings and losses, nor can we reasonably expect that we should not have our share of all.

When we left Hong Kong, our orders were, that after we had fulfilled our mission to Corea, we should return to Shanghai, communicate with the Admiral, and there wait his orders. So we have been here ever since, our time employed with the usual port routine of cleaning up the ship, exercising, and taking in coal and provisions—yet finding a great amount of leisure for rest, and for doing whatever else our minds desire. Having myself little or no work to perform, and not being in a mood for reading or study, I have spent the greater portion of my time when not on duty, on shore, with one or two " congenial spirits " for companions.

Rambles now about the Chinese quarter present us with new features in their customs, it being their New Year's holidays. These commenced the latter part of last month, and properly ended on the 10th of this, in what is called the "Feast of Lanterns," but they are usually kept up for two or three weeks more. During this time the Chinese perform no labor except what is absolutely necessary; but, apparently forgetful of their usual thirst for gain, give themselves up wholly to the pursuit of pleasure.

Upon the last day of the old year all are very punctillious in balancing their accounts and settling the debts of the year, saying that they could not enjoy the festivities unless they had previously done so.

A custom prevalent at this season of the year deserves special notice, and almost seems to have been derived from the command found in Deut. vi: 9. The entrance to every Chinese dwelling has depicted on the door and doorposts, as well as upon the cross-beams above, two or more antithetical sentences, chosen with great care from their most approved writings. The New Year's holidays are the period for removing the old sentences and substituting new ones in their places. The paper upon which these sentences are written is of various colors, but the general color is a deep red. White paper denotes that the inmates have lost a parent during the past year. The second year's mourning requires blue for a father, yellow for a mother, and carnation for a grandparent. A light red indicates the third year's mourning, after which the dark red is again resumed.

During the entire holiday season the shops and houses are all open—fitted up for the new year's callers. Those that we visited had the walls hung round with favorite views, which are only used during these holidays, and which are then laid away till they come round again. At the farther extremity of the room stood a table upon which were placed the family idols and the ancestral tablets. Upon another were various adornments and refreshments, and near it the host was seated. One calls—he is met at the door by the host, greetings are exchanged, and then he is led to a seat;

he then partakes of some refreshments, chats a few minutes, and after exchanging greetings again, he passes out.

In walking through the streets you would think that the whole Chinese world was out of doors, not hurrying along intent upon their business, but leisurely promenading, with a smile and greeting for all. They appear to have wholly given themselves up to enjoyment, and to have forgotten that there is in the world a Fankwei whom by their religion it is their first and highest duty and pleasure to cheat, if no more than to the value of a single "cash." All were dressed in their very best costumes, and there was a profusion of the richest and most costly silks, satins, and furs—some valued as high as two or three thousand dollars. Such a costume will last a man a lifetime, and as there is no changing of fashion, he does not hesitate to put one-third or one-half of his fortune upon his back.

In their dress, however, the Chinese are very anxious to economize the soil. Barrows says, "that an acre of cotton will clothe two or three hundred persons," and as the cotton can be planted between the rice crops, and thus vary the productions and relieve the soil, they prefer such clothing as they can raise at the least expense of ground and labor. Cotton is thus the most common article of clothing worn—garments of silk, satins, and furs, being substituted for it only on great occasions.

A few days ago we had a visit from two French Catholic missionaries,—the sole survivors of the late massacre of missionaries and Christians here. While we were at Chefoo last fall a boat came in there from Corea, bearing these same two missionaries, who then reported the massacre that had taken place. They proceeded to Shanghai, and communicated the intelligence to Admiral Rosa, commanding the French squadron in these waters. The French are ever prompt and ready to avenge any wrongs done to their religion or to its ministers, and he, with characteristic vigor, immediately organized a force and proceeded to Corea. He left Yokahama with his squadron in the latter part of August, but the expedition proved to be an unsuccessful one, the Coreans repulsing the French with considerable loss. They now have the coast blockaded, and are making preparations for another campaign,—this time with a greater force.

Besides my rambles on shore, I have done an immense amount of ship-visiting since we have been in Shanghai this time, going on board of the men-of-war of the different nationalities, and on three or four American merchantmen. Of the former, the pleasantest and most interesting visit was to the Prussian Frigate Vineta. She is a clumsy-looking, old-fashioned, single-banked frigate, but everything about her was so scrupulously neat and clean, and her crew so intelligent and courteous, that one could but enjoy a visit there.

Of the latter I formed some very pleasant acquaintances in the officers and their families, and I have enjoyed myself very much in the numerous visits that I have made. We leave here to-morrow for our second trip up the Yang-tse-kiang, and, this time, I hope that it will be without any of those sad events which so painfully characterized our former one.

LETTER XXX.

U. S. S. WACHUSETT, Hankow, China,
March 13th, 1867.

MY DEAR R.:

Six hundred miles into the interior of China! As far away from salt water as those living in Ohio! If sight-seeing was our *only* object in view, we could not be much more favored.

The summary of places we have visited and sights we have seen during the past year, is a very varied, extensive, and interesting one. We have twice been the entire length of the coast of China, and several times over large portions of it, visiting all but two or three of its open ports, and many that are not yet opened to foreign intercourse; been in many of its cities and towns, and up several of its rivers; seen its great wonders, in fact, everything worthy of note, getting a good insight into the appearance, manner, and customs of its inhabitants; visited the principal places in Japan—seeing nearly everything worthy of note there, and getting an insight into the appearance, manners, and customs of the Japanese; passed through the inland sea (a trip in itself worth no small sum to sight-seers); explored somewhat the much talked-of, and, at present, interesting Corea; and, at last, we find ourselves six hundred miles in the interior of China.

The weather is quite warm for this season of the year, but far different from what it was upon our trip last summer. On the whole, it is as pleasant as we could expect, and the trip has been all that one could have desired. All of our traveling has been done in the day-time, anchoring every night, and, as the weather has been clear and pleasant all of the time since leaving Shanghai, every opportunity has been afforded for sight-seeing.

We left Shanghai Monday afternoon, February 25th, under the charge of the captain of the Fire-Queen, with Dr. Toute (who has been appointed American consul at Hankow) and an English marine, as passengers. We arrived at Chinkiang the 27th, and there remained two days, receiving visits from the consul and family, and also from several of the citizens from shore. With the exception of the weather we found that little change had taken place since we were there before.

In passing by the point where the Grand Canal connects with the Yang-tse, the engines were stopped and we had a good view of China's second greatest wonder. I think that the Grand Canal, or *Chah-ho* (*i. e.*, river of Flood-gates), called, also, *Yung-ho* (*i. e.*, Transit river), in many respects reflects more credit upon its constructor than the Great Wall, and, at the time it was constructed, it excelled all other works in usefulness. By means of its connection with the rivers, there is a greater inland communication than any other country possesses. A large portion of the canal is constructed by high banks an hundred feet or more in width, and faced with stone. Such was that which we saw. Stretching along its banks as far as the eye could reach were villages, or rather one continuous city, so close are the villages to each other, and crowding the canal were innumerable small craft.

After leaving Chinkiang we anchored six times before arriving at Hankow, arriving here the 6th, but as we made no lengthy stay at any point, I will leave particular descriptions until we go down, when we expect to call at all the principal places, and will now confine myself to the general appearance of the country.

For the entire distance cities and walled towns are very numerous, and it is estimated that we passed within sight of more than one hundred and fifty of them. A great sameness exists in all. A stone wall encloses all towns of any size, and frequently the suburbs are larger than their *enciente*. The streets are not usually over six or eight feet in width, but the lowness of the houses makes them appear less like mere alley-ways than they would in western cities. Villages have a pleasant appearance, viewed at a distance, usually embowered in trees, among which the whitewashed houses look prettily.

The Chinese delight in light and ornamental architecture, and in this they display great taste. They are also very skillful in laying out their grounds, and improving all the natural features of the landscape. Their summer villas, generally on the banks of some stream (they are very numerous on the Yang-tse) or on the border of a picturesque lake, are sometimes extremely fanciful, even bordering on the grotesque; but often delightfully airy, comfortable, and luxurious. The situation is almost always skillfully chosen and artistically improved. The top of some rugged eminence, the slope of a jagged rock, or a wooded island is sure to be occupied by some fairy-like or fantastic structure, surrounded with flower-gardens and shrub-trees, with arbors and lookouts perched on the prominent points or nestled in the quietest nooks.

These may be seen in almost every part of China, scattered here and there; but the scenery at intervals along the banks of the Yang-tse river, near large cities, may well be represented as perfectly elysian. The wealthy mandarins have taken up every spot of land down to the water's edge, and appropriated them for villas, palaces, temples, pleasure-grounds and gardens. The water, too, may be seen thronged, day and night, with barges and pleasure-boats of every grade.

On the lowlands rice is almost universally cultivated. The terrace cultivation renders the acclivities of many of the hills beautiful in the highest degree. The finest and most pleasing example of the terrace cultivation may be seen where a valley or wide ravine runs up to the top of a range of hills, growing narrower as it ascends, so that, in the distance, it looks like a mammoth staircase for the gods. On these terraces, as well as on the unterraced acclivities of the hills, grains and vegetables are cultivated; sometimes rice is grown on them, and by means of reservoirs at the tops, the terraces are flooded by the water let down from them.

And yet for all that I have said, elegance or ornament, orderly arrangement or grandeur of design, cleanliness or comfort are almost unknown in Chinese houses, cities or gardens. Everywhere the finest and most commanding situations are chosen for temples or pagodas, which are not only the abode of priests and senseless idols, but also serve for inns, theatres, etc. A lofty solitary pagoda, an extensive temple shaded by trees in the opening of a vale or on a hillside, or boats moving in every direction through narrow creeks or on broad streams, are some of the peculiar lineaments of Chinese scenery. No imposing mansions are found on the skirts of a town; no tapering spire pointing out the village church; nor towers, pillars, domes, or steeples in the cities, pointing out the public buildings, rise above the walls or the low level of tiled roofs. No meadows or pastures containing herds and flocks are seen upon the hill-tops of China, nor are coaches or railroad-cars ever observed hurrying across its landscape.

The right bank of the river is more picturesque than the left, on account of the chains of hills rising behind each other, covered with rich and varied foliage, and in many places sweeping down to the banks of the stream. Nearly as far as the eye can reach on the left bank, and also in many places on the right, the land is low and level and devoted to the culture of rice. The farther we proceeded up the river the more varied and picturesque we found the scenery, and the villages and towns appeared cleaner and more thrifty. The width of the river varies greatly, in some places being two or three miles, and in others narrowing down to less than half a mile. It is now at the time of high water, and many places that we passed over, the pilot says, in the course of the summer will be dry land.

One new feature in Chinese boat life we noticed in our passage up the river, in the large rafts floating upon it covered with earth and having grain and vegetables growing; while in one corner of each would be seen a snug little house. Some of these floating farms would have half an acre of good land upon each, from which sufficient was raised to support a large family.

We passed, on our way up, several high, conical-shaped islands in the river, apparently inaccessible on every side, but whose summits were crowned by exceedingly picturesquely situated temples and pavilions.

Hankow is situated on the left bank of the river, on a low plain about forty feet above the present level of the water. There is said to be fifty-seven feet difference between the high and low water marks, and that sometimes the inhabitants of the city go about the streets in boats. I was surprised to find so much of a foreign settlement here, when it is hardly five years since the first house was built. It is about as large as the English Concession at Shanghai, which, in general appearance, it closely resembles. Extending along in front is a fine wide " Bund," which, as we came up, was well lined with ladies and gentlemen who were out for an evening promenade in accordance with their daily custom.

The town is upwards of one and one-half miles in length, and one in width, and never did I see a city with houses so uniform and so uniformly first-class as they are here. Most of them are two stories high, built of brick and painted. The streets are wide, and the town is very neatly and regularly laid out.

Above this, and joined to it, is the Chinese quarter, about one and one-half times as large as the foreign. Extending around all but the river side of both sections is a wall and moat, constructed only two years ago. The wall is about thirty feet high, fifteen feet thick with a sloping, earthern embankment thrown up against it on the inside, and is the only good defense that I have seen in China. Upon the top cannon are mounted, and the tents of the garrison or guard are pitched along its entire length. Outside the walls, about seven miles distant, is another detachment of Imperial troops, numbering ten thousand. These are necessary to ward off the attacks of the rebels who are very numerous in this province.

• At the upper end of the city the Han river, a stream about one-third of a mile in width, empties into the Yang-tse, and on the opposite bank of the Han is the small, walled town of Han-yang. Across the Yang-tse from the last mentioned city is the large, walled-city Wuchang—the capital of the province of Huph, and the residence of the military governor. It is said that "these three cities probably present, with the shipping before them, the largest assemblage of houses and shipping, inhabitants and sailors, to be found anywhere in the world." The number of junks of the largest class is estimated at ten thousand, while the smaller craft number several times that.

One day after a ramble about Hankow with a friend, we found ourselves on the banks of the Han, about a mile above the point where it empties into the Yang-tse. A glance up and down the river presented us with a scene of the greatest animation. In both directions as far as the eye could reach, the river was one living mass of boats. I had thought that the scenes in boat life in the river about Canton were almost too marvelous for narration, but those would bear no comparison with the one before us, and, in my mind I could think of no more fitting comparison than that of a swarm of bees.

Out of curiosity we took a sampan and started down the river, and there found ourselves in a business thoroughfare, exceeding in noise, bustle, and confusion, any of our large cities.

One that has ever been in the midst of a frightened multitude endeavoring to escape from some imminent danger, can form some idea of the situation in which we found ourselves. The river was fairly choked by the dense mass of junks and smaller craft of every size, form, and hue, and engaged in almost every conceivable occupation. There were shops, restaurants, silk lacquer-wares, and ivory stores; cobblers, menders of old brass, iron, and chinaware; fruit and market stalls, and flower boats, besides those bearing burdens and passengers; then the talking, shouting, and fighting of the men, the shrieks and cries of the women and children, and the crashing of boats, were such, that in comparison Babel would appear as quiet as an English grammar school.

In such a crowded and busy thoroughfare, there seems to be but one law of the road, and that is, that the smaller boats keep out of the way of the larger ones, or else suffer the consequences. There is no such thing as giving half of the way. If a boat is upset no attention is paid to it by any one, but the occupants are left to right their craft and look out for themselves. Several times our boat was nearly upset by larger ones, but not the slightest attention was paid to us, further than a smothered curse for being in the way. Once when an old woman's market boat was upset by ours, our boatman was passing on without the least attention to the accident, and appeared to be much surprised and very indignant when we compelled him to turn back and assist her in righting her boat and collecting her wares. Full an hour and a half were we in proceeding this mile, and when we reached the quiet waters of the Yang-tse we felt as if we had just escaped from some desperate encounter for life.

In crossing the river at Wuchang we were overtaken by a storm which well nigh swamped our boat, and drenched us to the skin. Ascending a short flight of stone steps from the landing, we found ourselves on a prettily flagged Bund, about thirty yards wide in front of the city walls. These are very massive, full forty feet in height and from thirty to fifty feet thick, built of huge blocks of granite, some of which would measure twenty feet in length, by ten in width and thickness. I wonder where they got the power to move or place them! Upon the top cannon are mounted and guards armed with spears, swords, and bows and arrows, are stationed. The walls are five miles in circumference, and the city does not differ in general appearance from other cities which I have visited. The inhabitants seem to be if possible rather more primitive in their manners and habits, and evidently regard Europeans with the greatest wonder and curiosity. Everywhere that we went we were followed by a great crowd of both sexes, and of all ages, and occasionally the muttered word "*Fankwei*" could be heard.

Two or three days ago the crew of an English and a French Gunboat, together with our own men, engaged in a variety of athletic sports on shore, which were witnessed by nearly all of the European residents and by an immense crowd of Chinamen. The English took the first prize in running and took the watch from the top of the pole; the French excelled in leaping, took the prize in the sack race, and one little boy with his mouth caught the greased pig by the tail; the Americans were victorious in the hurdle-race, in throwing the cricket ball and putting the shot, and took the second prize in running. It was a beautiful day, everything passed off pleasantly and in good order, and one and all seemed to enjoy themselves very much. To-morrow morning we start down the river towards Shanghai again.

LETTER XXXI.

U. S. S. WACHUSETT, Shanghai, China, }
April 2d, 1867. }

MY DEAR R.:

The right bank of the river from Hankow to Kieukiang—a distance of one hundred and fifty-six miles, (and, indeed for some distance below) was lined with thousands and thousands of men, women and children, with their movable effects—refugees from depredatory excursions of rebels to the towns and villages on the opposite bank, on the evening of the day we left Hankow, and but a short distance above Kieukiang, I counted no less than eighteen large cities and towns in flames, while the glare of many more could be seen in the distance. At those near us the rebels could be plainly seen engaged in their nefarious work, and the shrieks and cries of their unfortunate victims distinctly heard.

The founders, as it were, of this band, were a number of unpaid soldiers who commenced a series of depredations out of revenge. From time to time they have received large additions in escaped convicts, outlaws, and adventurers, until now they have become a formidable body, and are dignified by the title of rebels,—"Land pirates" would be a more appropriate name; for they have no revolution in view, and belong to no especial party, but commit their depredations alike upon all that come in their way—plundering and burning towns and villages and murdering all but the able-bodied men, whom they compel to join them. They are nearly all mounted, well-armed, and have many European adventurers among them as leaders. I will mention an incident of which I was a witness and which will convey some idea of their cruelty. A junk load of refugees was just preparing to cross over to the other side of the river from one of the burning cities, when they were surprised by a body of these human fiends, and every one of the number brutally murdered. The junk was then plundered and set on fire. Thus far these marauders have confined their depredations to the left bank of the river; but they are rapidly increasing in number, and flushed with their recent successes, there is no knowing what they will do next.

We intended to make but a short stay at Kieukiang, but the foreign residents, apprehensive of a raid from the rebels, so earnestly requested Captain Shufeldt to remain, that he finally concluded to do so, and our stay was lengthened out to the 23d, when we were relieved by an English gunboat. During the entire time immense crowds of refugees were constantly arriving, and it was estimated that there were more than fifty thousand of them encamped about the city walls. The many strange, sad, and even amusing incidents connected with the arrival and disposition of these refugees, the movements of the Imperial troops, and the patroling of the river by the Chinese gunboats, furnished us an abundance of excitement.

The glare of burning villages could be seen nearer and nearer each night, and before we left the marauders had approached within six miles of the city. There they made a halt and seemed undecided what to do next. I have not the remotest idea that they will venture to make an attack upon the city, so long as they know that there is a well organized and armed body of Europeans to defend it. There are upwards of two thousand Imperial troops garrisoning the city walls, but they are worth absolutely nothing; for besides being poorly armed and equipped, and without any discipline, they lack the one thing essential to a good soldier—*courage*. In fact they are the most abject cowards imaginable. With a thousand well armed European or American soldiers, one might march from one end of China to another in spite of all that the Chinese could do to oppose them.

It was very amusing to take note of the movements of the Imperialists—both the land and the naval forces. The gunboats in great numbers were constantly moving up and down the river, beating gongs and firing blank cartridges from their single cannon in the bow. Similar movements might be observed among the land forces—the same beating of gongs and firing of guns, with the addition of a great display of flags, and of lights when the "grand rounds" of the city and encampments were made in the night-time. They intended to keep entirely aloof from all danger, and usually did so, but, one day when a body of them were patroling the river bank opposite the city, they unexpectedly encountered a body of rebels, and, as there was no means of avoiding it, battle was joined with them. This was certainly the most amusing thing which I saw in China, surpassing in noise and gesticulation any theatrical performance, but bearing thereto a most striking resemblance.

The majority of the combatants sat down to drink tea and smoke their pipes, while the remainder, relieving one another from time to time, kept up a continual beating of gongs and tom-toms, firing of jingals, shouting, and waving of flags and banners. The contending armies were fully one-fourth of a mile apart, and during the entire engagement not one was killed on either side. At last, the imperialists, having displayed the greatest number of flags and made the most noise, were supposed to win the victory, for the rebels retreated in the wildest confusion, after an engagement of about two hours. The imperialists immediately pursued, and put to death all the stragglers that fell into their hands, the number of these being counted as the number killed in battle. The greatest excitement prevailed throughout the city and encampment during the progress of this engagement, and the wildest enthusiasm was manifested when the result became known. I should not wonder if it was dramatized, and the whole recorded as a brilliant feat of arms. It is said by those of good authority that this is a fair sample of the Chinese mode of warfare.

A few words now about Kiukiang, and then we will go down the river about one hundred and fifty miles to Nankin, our next stopping place. Kiukiang consists of a large walled Chinese town, some four miles in circuit, with a small European town at its upper side, all located on a beautiful and fertile plain on the right bank of the river. The town enclosed within the walls is old and fast going to decay, but the suburbs are surpassed by few cities we have visited in the wideness of the streets, the size of the buildings, and the richness and variety of articles exposed for sale in the shops. The foreign section numbers but few houses as yet, but it is fast growing. The chief exports are porcelain-ware and tea, Kiukiang being the center of the most noted districts in China for the manufacture of the one and the growth of the other.

The manufacture of porcelain commenced with the Tang dynasty, A. D. 630, and although of late the Europeans have made advances in the whiteness of their porcelain, and the brilliancy of their colors, to the Chinese are we indebted for a knowledge of the art, and, even now, they excel in the compactness of the material and the fineness of the ware.

A visit to a porcelain manufactory presents one with much of interest. First we notice a man preparing the paste from *pĭh-tun*, "white clay." This is done by mixing the clay with a powder, a bluish-white stone, to which is added the glaze-ashes, prepared from a kind of fern—all forming a thick paste. Another workman, by means of a lathe, fashions this into cups, vases, or such article as may be required, and then fits it to the mold. The excrescences are pounded to a milky consistency, and used by the painters, to whom the work next passes. Here we see two more employed, one engaged in drawing the outline, and the other in putting on the colors.

The glazier sometimes does his work by means of a brush, but it is now nearly superceded by the blow-pipe. This consists of a tube about nine inches in length, covered at the end by a thin gauze, through which the workman blows a certain number of times, according to the size of the vessel or the consistency of the varnish. After the article has been committed to the furnace and burned for some time, the process is finished, and the ware ready for packing and shipment.

China has not only furnished us with the cups, but also with the tea. Its first use is not known definitely, but was at a very early period. Before coming to China I was wont to hear that the only difference between green and black teas was, that the former was dried on copper plates, and the latter on iron ones. This is not so, for both are dried in earthen basins, and the process I have described to you in a previous letter. To those who have passed any great length of time here, there is no doubt that they are produced from entirely distinct shrubs, and in different parts of the country. However, there are many persons who are inclined to believe that they are both produced from the same shrub; that the difference is owing in a great measure to the stage of the leaf when it is picked, to the difference of climate, and to the manner in which it is prepared. Be it as it may, there are in all thirteen kinds of tea—seven of black and six of green—occasioned by the causes just mentioned. The process of making tea has many times been minutely delineated in pictures, and described in books, but best authorities here in China say that the exact manipulations of the leaf is a secret known only by the Chinese.

A few days ago I was shown a small quantity of tea which cost fifty taels (sixty-six dollars) per pound. This may seem incredible to you, but when I have explained the matter a little you will not wonder so much. The main cause of difference between the different brands of the same kind of tea is owing to adaptation of the soil and the age of the leaf when picked. This brand of tea (green) is produced on a plantation near Nankin, and can be grown nowhere else in China. The leaves are picked immediately after the plant is out of blossom, and the leaves when cured are as small as the finest gunpowder. It is estimated that leaves sufficient to produce one pound of this tea, would make over thirty pounds if allowed to mature. It is all for the exclusive use of the Emperor and Governors of Provinces; unless it might be in a case like this, where one is allowed to obtain a small quantity, and is a rare token of great favor. The usual price here for the choicest brands of black tea is fifteen cents per pound, and green tea seventeen cents.

Kiangning-foo, better known to you as Nankin, is the capital of the province of Kiangsee. It was once the most celebrated city in the Empire in regard to the extent of its buildings and the character of its inhabitants. There are now to be seen the remains of an outer wall, which has been traced for thirty-five miles, but how much of this space was occupied by houses, is not known. The walls are now only about half as extensive as formerly, and hardly one-half of the space enclosed by them is occupied by houses.

From where we lay at anchor I landed at a small walled village in front of the town, near which are three or four houses occupied by foreigners, the only ones at Nankin. The city lies back from the water about two miles, and is overlooked by high hills on the east, from which I had a good view of it. The northern, or river wall, is formed by a thick embankment thrown up against and overtopping a high stone wall, and this is also true of the western face. The others are the customary brick walls, but of uncommon height and thickness. On the eastern face are two gates, and on the northern two. The city contains an estimated population of 450,000, all of whom reside within the walls.

The land towards the river is marshy, and the approaches

to the gates are over stone causeways, but on all the remaining sides the country is beautifully diversified by hill and dale, hamlet and field, and is in a high state of cultivation. Nankin is the center of one of the most fertile as well as the most beautiful portions of the Empire, and I can conceive of no reason why the Emperor should have wished the capital removed to Pekin.

In my walk through the city I found that it was very regularly laid out, and in all respects well built. It consists of four wide and parallel avenues, intersected by others of less width. The part occupied by the Manchoos is separated by a cross wall from the Chinese town. Nankin has extensive manufactories of fine satins and crapes, and the cotton cloth which in European countries is called "Nankin," derives its name from this city.

Paper and ink of superior quality, and beautiful artificial flowers, are also produced. I would have visited all these manufactories, but my time on shore was so limited that I could only take a passing glance at all the places and points of interest. Besides the manufactories of the above mentioned articles, Nankin is also celebrated for its scholars and literary characters, and for being the residence of the governor-general of these provinces.

Outside the southern walls of the city are the ruins of the celebrated Porcelain Tower, called by the Chinese, "Recompensing Favor Monastery," and which, probably as much as anything, has made Nankin noted abroad. But a faint idea of its former grandeur and magnificence can be formed from what is now remaining. From the description of it when in its pristine beauty and splendor, one can judge how much it surpassed all similar buildings in China in completeness and elegance, the material of which it was built, and the embellishments of its interior. Williams thus describes it: "Its form is octagonal, divided into nine equal stories, the circumference of the lower one being one hundred and twenty feet and gradually diminishing to the top. Its base rests upon a solid foundation of brickwork twelve feet high, up which a flight of twelve steps leads into the tower, whence a spiral staircase of one hundred and ninety steps carries the visitor to the summit, two hundred and sixty-one feet from the ground. The outer face is covered with slabs of glazed porcelain of various colors, principally green, yellow, red, and white; the body of the edifice is brick. At every story there is a projecting roof covered with green tiles, and a bell suspended from each corner. The saloons are more gaudy than elegant, and are filled with a great number of little gilded images placed in niches. This unique structure was completed A. D. 1430, having been nineteen years building, and at an estimated cost of three million three hundred and thirteen thousand nine hundred and seventy-five dollars."

The same afternoon that I paid a visit to the city I witnessed a sham battle between divisions of the Imperial troops stationed at Nankin, which numbered about 60,000. All were armed with English muskets, and in addition they had several heavy pieces of ordnance. One division was resisting the attempts of the other to cross over a shallow ravine; but after being repulsed several times they at last succeeded in crossing. The manœuvres were admirably planned, and the movements and firing were executed in as good order, and with as much regularity, as those of the best disciplined European troops; and yet in actual fighting these soldiers are good for nothing, for their bodies control their minds, and will run away from all danger.

The 27th we left Nankin for Chinkiang, arriving there the same day. We intended to remain at the latter place a few days; but quite unexpectedly got under way on the morning of the 29th and started for Shanghai, having on board Mr. and Miss Sands, and a Mr. McGowan—agent of the projected Russo-American Telegraph Company, as passengers. We arrived here the next day, having been gone on our trip thirty-four days and logged twelve hundred and thirty six knots. It has been a trip full of interest and pleasure from beginning to end, with nothing to mar our enjoyment.

LETTER XXXII.

U. S. S. WACHUSETT, Ningpo, China,
April 22, 1867.

MY DEAR R.:

We remained at Shanghai only a sufficient time to take in coal and provisions, and then, agreeable to previous orders from the Admiral we left there April 3d for Foo-chow, where we arrived the 6th. We went down by what is called the Inland Passage—having the main land on our starboard, and the Saddle Islands and the Chusan Group on on our port, and coming to anchor every night. We were in sight of land during the entire passage, but not until the morning of the 6th did we have a glimpse of anything except high, rocky, and barren ridges of hills.

The scenery improved as we entered the northeastern of the two mouths of the Min River, which are formed by the large island Kin-pai-mun, some forty miles in circumference. In a short time we crossed the bar, and entered a fine circular basin six or seven miles in diameter. Passing through this, we came to where the river suddenly narrows down to less than half a mile in width, and is overshadowed on either hand by ranges of hills from fifteen hundred to two thousand feet in height, defended by numerous batteries. Beyond these the river widens to about three-fourths of a mile, which remains the uniform width until *Lo-sing-tah*, or Pagoda Anchorage, some twenty-five miles from the mouth of the river, and nine below the city of Foo-chow, the place where all the foreign ships and large junks usually anchor, is reached. nothing that we have yet seen in Chinese scenery can excel the wild beauty and imposing grandeur of the river Min in

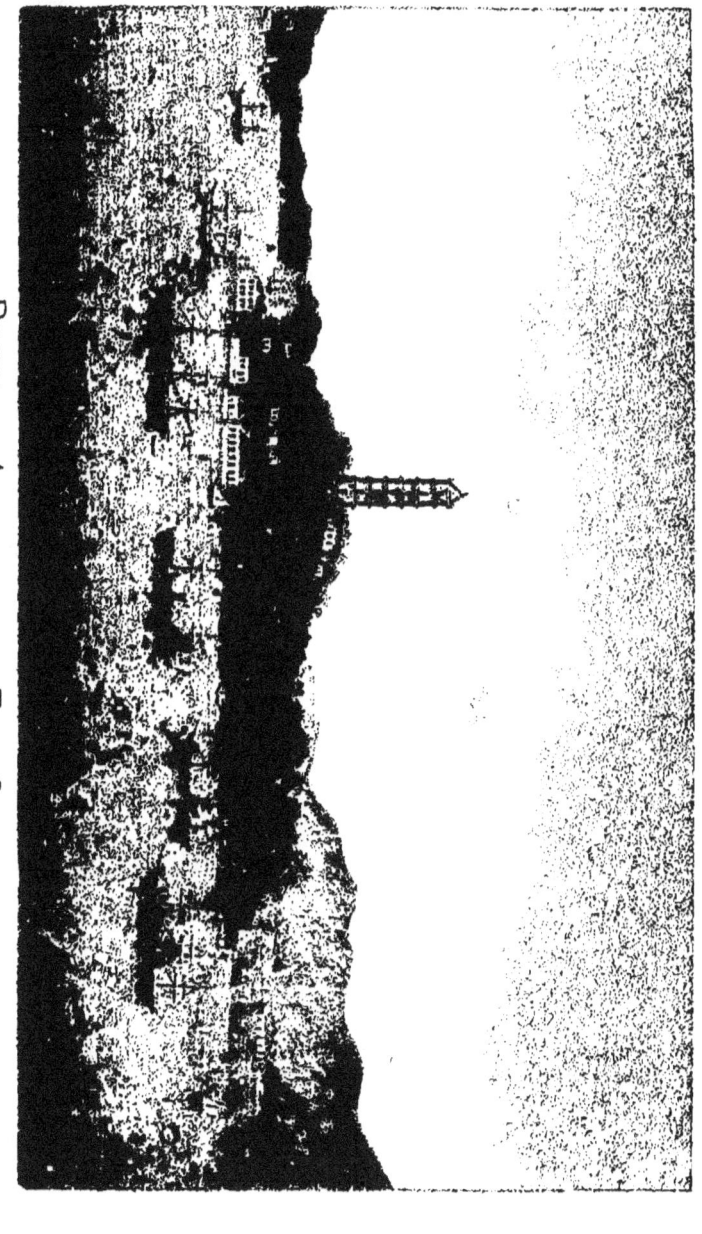

Pagoda Anchorage, Foo Chow.

approaching Foo-chow. On either hand is a lofty mountain chain indented with deep gorges or ravines down which ran beautiful rivulets leaping and dancing, the clear waters flashing in the sunlight through occasional openings in the pine groves with which the ravines and gorges are usually lined. Although exceedingly rough, with immense granite knobs jutting forth, these hills may be said to be clothed with verdure from the base to the summit. The less rugged are laid out in terraces rising one above another, sometimes to the number of forty or fifty.

On nearly every hill were to be seen orange, lemon, and mulberry groves with varied and beautiful patches of shrubbery. Of cultivated products wheat and barley were the principal. Although of a different composition, the scenery of the Min is said to bear a favorable comparison with that of the Hudson.

"Pagoda Anchorage" is a lovely basin some eight or ten miles in length by six or seven in width, formed by the widening of the river. For some little distance inland the surface of the country is low and level and devoted to rice culture; it is there all enclosed high, picturesque hills, and has been admirably likened to a vast amphitheater. During our stay there were quite a large number of merchant ships engaged in loading with tea and silks, which form the principal articles of export. Presenting an interesting feature in the native boating-life are the boats decked out in evergreens and flowers, and many of the boat-women wear head-dresses of beautiful flowers.

Pagoda Island, situated on the northern side of the anchorage, and about two miles in circumference, is for the most part an oval eminence, rising about three hundred feet above the level of the river. With the old Pagoda near its summit, the rustic cottages, grand old trees, fine shrubbery and luxuriant growth of vegetation, it forms an exceedingly wild, beautiful, and picturesque spot. On the southern side are some eight or ten quite fine European buildings, and scattered all over the island are about one hundred Chinese houses. Just above Pagoda island the river unites from the division which occurs above Foo-chow, enclosing a fertile and highly cultivated tract of land.

The old Pagoda, from which the island and anchorage derive their names, rests upon a stone dais seven or eight feet in height. It is an octagonal stone shaft about one hundred and twenty feet high and divided into seven stories. It is ascended by staircases passing through the pagoda from one side to the other, and opening upon a narrow platform or coping at the base of the story immediately above. Upon this coping one has to walk half way around the pagoda to reach the foot of the staircase of each succeeding story. The upper copings are much narrower than the lower ones, being barely eighteen inches wide, and are in a very dilapidated condition. At such a great height one is apt to feel giddy, and unless one has a strong nerve, the ascent is a dangerous undertaking; it might easily prove a fatal one, as there is nothing to lay hold of, and a fall from such a height would be certain death. From the appearance of the top I should judge that formerly its height was one or more stories more than it now is, and I have been told that at the time of its construction there was a tower, increasing its height fifty feet. From the summit I had a magnificent view of the surrounding country; the river wending its way between lofty mountain ranges, and bordered by green paddy fields, beautiful groves, pretty hamlets and villages, and nine miles in the distance the large city of Foo-chow, with its celebrated stone bridge of forty-nine arches, its teeming river population, and two-thirds of a million of inhabitants.

During our stay at Foo-chow, the ship was thronged at every meal-hour by peddlers, with their boat loads of soap-stone carvings. Boxes, plates, dishes, vases, and a great number of ornaments, were among the articles noticed, and many of them were very prettily designed and skillfully carved. So little compensation was demanded for them that nearly every one made purchases, varying in value from a few cents to a number of dollars.

Our object in going to Foo-chow was to meet the United States double-ender "Ashuelot," which vessel had lately arrived on the station, and had brought up stores for us from Hong Kong. Having taken these on board, we left there April 13th, for Ningpo. About noon, the 16th, we arrived off Square Island—a small but lovely island off the mouth of the Yung or Tahiah river—on which Ningpo stands. About three miles nearer the coast we passed another small island, (Tiger's) on which was a light-house and signal-station; and then, after proceeding a few miles further, we dropped anchor off Chinhae, a district town at the mouth of the river, and some ten or twelve miles from Ningpo.

Chinhae is so situated and possesses such natural advantages that, with ordinary fortifications, it might be made to completely command the passage. On the northern or left bank of the river, immediately below the town, is a high, rocky and precipitous bluff, accessible only by a narrow foot-path, which leads up from the sea. On the summit of this hill are the ruins of what must have been an extensive and strongly-fortified citadel. From the number of Joss temples within its walls, the eminence doubtless derives its name of "Joss-house Hill." At the time of the assault upon and taking of the place by the English in 1841, there was a greater loss of life than in any previous engagement, excepting that at Chinkiang; indeed, after several ineffectual assaults, it was at last taken by stratagem.

The town is connected with this eminence by a stone causeway, and with the eminence occupies a long, narrow tongue of land, having the river on one side and a deep bight of the sea on the other. Upon this latter side, some three or four miles in length, is a dyke, built of large blocks of hewn granite, which affords a good protection from the waves. The city walls are about twenty-five feet high and thick, and three miles in circumference, and the suburbs are upwards of one-half the extent of the *enciente*. The variously-colored tiles on the roofs of the houses; the many fine, large trees; the tall masts of the junks gliding along a small branch of the river which flows through the town, and the numerous pagoda spires, give to Chinhae an exceedingly gay and picturesque appearance. The country immediately around it is very mountainous and broken, but nevertheless very fertile and in a high state of cultivation, partly in the terrace form.

After remaining at Chinhae two days, we, with a beautiful day and a trusted pilot, started up the river for Ningpo. Above Chinhae the hills gradually recede, so that Ningpo lies in an extended plain, stretching away some fifteen or twenty miles and uniting with the high, blue hills beyond. With the exception of the hills in the immediate vicinity of Chinhae, the view on that side presents nothing but the ocean. It all forms quite a varied and extensive prospect; and the eye, in roaming over it, catches many a pleasing object. Landward it sees villages and hamlets, smiling cottages and family residences, pleasant fields and snug farm-houses; temples, canals, and water-courses; monasteries and family tombs, and numerous resting places of the dead. Seaward, a vast plain, stretching away to the ocean; but the river is fairly alive with boats, and the banks are lined with ice-houses. These ice-houses are quite a novelty in themselves, stone walls rising some eight or ten feet, and thatched over with bamboos and straw. At the rear of each one are large, shallow vats, where the ice is collected during the winter season. An hour's steaming brought us to anchor just below the city, where the river is about one-third of a mile in width.

Ningpo-fu (*i. e.*, " Peaceful City,") is next to Hanchow, the most important city in the province of Chinkiang, and bears the deserved name of being the finest city on the coast open to foreign intercourse. It is situated on the left or northwestern bank of the Tahee or Ningpo river, just below its junction with the Tsz-ki, which flows in from the westward, so that two faces of the city are defended by the river. The others are defended by a moat, nearly three miles in length, and in many places more than one hundred feet in width. By means of this the city is surrounded by water, and its site is often called an island. The city walls are about five miles in length, from twenty-five to thirty-five feet high, and so wide that three carriages can easily be driven abreast upon the ramparts. They are very solidly constructed, and are strengthened by huge square buttresses. There are six gates, besides two sally-ports for the passage of boats which ply on the canals within the city. On the triangular tongue of land, on the northern bank of Tsz-ki river, is the foreign quarter, containing many fine buildings and upwards of one thousand inhabitants.

But, come! we will row our boat ashore, and see what of interest a ramble will present us. We land at a rickety wooden pier at the foot of the principal street in the foreign quarter. We make no stay here, but are brought, by a few minutes' walk through the extensive northern suburbs, to the floating bridge which crosses the river separating them from the city. This bridge is two hundred yards long and five wide, made of planks firmly lashed, and resting upon sixteen huge lighters, chained together, but which can be opened to admit of vessels passing up and down the river. Crossing this bridge through numerous market stalls, and amid peddlers and tinkers of every kind, we come to a toll-gate at the opposite end, and have to pay four cash each to the Frenchman who has charge, for the privilege of walking over. We are first attracted by a fine stone monument, not ten yards away. From its inscription we learn that it was erected to the memory of the officers, seamen, and marines of the French and English squadrons, who lost their lives in the attack on Ningpo, May 10th, 1862. It stands upon the spot where the rebel battery was planted. An hundred yards further on, upon the eastern side, and we arrive at Bridge gate, by which we enter the city, between two massive stone towers, more than fifty feet high. Here we are saluted by the Chinese guard, who are armed with old English tower muskets.

As the first thing, we decide to visit their Tein-fung-tah, or "Heaven Conferred Pagoda," that being considered the greatest wonder and principal item of interest about Ningpo. With this in mind we make our way through several streets, and the court-yards of a neighboring Buddhist monastery, and are at length brought by our guide to the open space in which the tower stands. This space is overgrown with a thick herbage, and in it are several ancient tombs. Everything surrounding it bears a decaying and deserted appearance, and the tower, in many spots, is fast crumbling away. It is hexagonal in form, has seven stories, and is more than one hundred feet high. Upon the projecting roofs, around the openings, and upon the roofs of the tower which surmounts it, plants take the place of ivy in decorating the aged walls, and give to the old tower an exceedingly picturesque appearance. The guide tells us that it was built nine hundred years ago, during the How-Chow dynasty, but that since that time it has suffered much from the elements, and many changes made in the repairs of it. Extensive repairs were made about twenty years ago, both inside and out. One marked feature in this tower is, that it leans so much that a line let fall from the top would strike the ground at least ten feet from the base.

We have seen the outside, and now we will enter. This we find is impossible, until we have unlocked the door of the priest's heart with a handful of "cash," then he opens the door of the tower with his huge, rusty, iron key. In the lower story is a large collection of images, adornments, and the usual paraphernalia found in temples, but the upper ones are bare. A succession of rickety wooden stairs, two flights in each story, conduct us to the top; and, as we gradually ascend the view is increasingly extensive, grand, and magnificent, until, at last, reaching the summit the entire city of Ning-po lies at our feet, and we have a complete view of the suburbs, rivers, and much of the surrounding country. The many and variously-colored tiled roofs of the temples, the grotesque styles of architecture, the curiously sculptured arches, the various emblematic signs of civic authority, and the vast populace of a city teeming with busy toil, form the foreground of the picture, while the city walls, their dull monotony relieved by the high watch-towers, the suburbs beyond, the river fairly alive with its numerous, busy population, and the verdant country stretching away as far as the eye can distinguish, dotted with villages and hamlets, snug farm houses and country residences, temples, grave-yards and monasteries, all combined form a view varied, beautiful, and grand. 'Tis a scene over which we might with pleasure spend hours drinking in its wondrous beauties; but the shortness of our time forbids more than a passing glance, and half satisfied we are forced to leave it and descend.

Our next visit is to the Mahommedan mosque, near the centre of the city. The building is not extensive, but has an air of peculiar neatness. We cannot fail to admire some flowers that are tastefully arranged in the principal court, into which two or three dwellings open, and at the upper end of which the mosque is situated.

We tell our guide that we do not care to remain here long, and request him to take us to a place of more interest. A few steps more and we enter a "sing-song house" and a temple combined. The entrance to it is by the usual triple doors, under arches and through two or three courts, but everything is on a more elaborate and magnificent scale than is usually met with in Chinese cities. We find ourselves in a court about twenty yards square, entirely surrounded by a range of two-story buildings of the most approved style of Chinese architecture. Like the generality of the better class of Chinese houses, the one story is raised above the other by pillars, and each has a separate tiled roof, with many projecting cornices from which bells are suspended. The pillars upholding the roofs, and also the tripods, braziers, and other utensils employed in their worship, and ofttimes seen in court yards, are curiously and elaborately sculptured. The entire lower floor is open, facing the court, and the walls are hung with fine paintings of favorite Chinese scenes. From the roof of the first story on one side a balcony projects, where the orchestra is located and the scenes enacted. The three other sides are open towards the court, and seats placed around, much like the dress-circles of our theatres at home. There are upwards of three thousand persons present, wholly absorbed in the representation of some ancient deed of prowess. For the theatre in general, we are obliged to acknowledge, that the orchestra is far superior, the costumes more gorgeous, and the acting much better than any before seen in China.

Upon the side opposite the stage and adjoining the theatre is a joss temple dedicated to the goddess Kwan-Yin, and, although quite small, it well-nigh dazzles one by the splendor and magnificence of its adornments. As a woman the most beautiful in form and feature that the Chinese mind could conceive of, the goddess occupies a central recess on one side of the building. Two other images similar in form but of inferior size occupy recesses on either hand, and these three are the only images to be seen. Offerings of almost every conceivable kind cover the large, curiously carved table in front of the idols. The walls are hung with rich paintings in the greatest profusion, while from the ceiling are suspended upwards of fifty large Chinese lamps with their sides of stained glass of almost every hue. In the midst of these hangs a golden chandelier, having sixty burners. The sunlight is purposely excluded from the interior of the edifice, and by the continual light of the lamps, the real beauties and gorgeousness of the temple are ever seen greatly heightened.

The Confucian temple at Ningpo is somewhat celebrated the guide tells us, so we conclude to visit it next. Arriving there we find a large, plain, neat temple, and upon entering we see no idols, but in their stead some tablets, and a room very plainly furnished. The Confucian religion is the most honored, both by the government and by the learned, but as it has little or nothing to do with theology, and is merely a scheme of ethics and politics, from which things spiritual and divine are uniformly excluded, it seems almost a misnomer to call such a system a religion. He compares the government of a country to that of a family, and bases the whole upon a due control of self and the right management of the heart. He lays down the golden rule of doing unto others as we would they should do unto us; and lays the foundation of moral conduct in feeling for and excusing others, as we would for ourselves. According to his school, the five cardinal virtues are righteousness, benevolence, politeness, wisdom and truth; and the duties of the human relations, those which should exist between parents and children, husbands and wives, princes and ministers, friends and companions. Of all these, filial piety stands foremost; respect and reverence to parents are required not only in youth but even until the latest period of life are they to be treated with honor, and after death they are raised to the rank of gods. This feeling, they say, is necessary to insure fidelity to one's prince, affection for one's brethren, kindness to one's domestics, or sincerity among friends. This feeling, if conceived in the heart, and embodied in the life, will lead to the performance of every duty, and the entire renovation of the whole man. It is not to be confined to time and place, but is to be maintained, whether the object of our respect be absent or present, alive or dead; and thousands of years after their death ancestors are still to live in the undiminished affections of their descendants.

It is strange that while Confucius teaches such excessive veneration for parents, he should have entirely omitted the reverence due to the Father of our spirits. But thus it is, and, although from some expressions about "heaven" and the "Supreme Ruler," we might infer that the Chinese had some knowledge of the Creator and Ruler of the universe, and honored Him as such, their constant propensity to materialism, proves that the system is destitute of the main truth which lies at the basis of all truth, viz., the being of a self-existent, eternal, and all wise God. In some of their earlier writings there are allusions which would seem to imply that at one time the Chinese had some idea of an universal Sovereign, but the belief if it ever existed has since been eradicated by philosophy, or flung aside by vain conceit.

This sect acknowledges a material trinity, called heaven, earth, and man. By the latter a few sages only are meant, and of these Confucius ranks foremost. By the Chinese he is often referred to with the expression, "equal to heaven." They even pay him divine honors; for it appears, by reference to the recent translation of a native work, that there are upwards of one thousand six hundred temples in the empire dedicated to Confucius. At the semi-annual sacrifices, in the spring and autumn, there are immolated to the manes of Confucius about sixty-five thousand animals, and at the same time are presented nearly twenty-eight thousand pieces of silk. All these are provided by the government—and are in addition to the numerous offerings of private individuals.

Instead of believing and teaching that the Great Spirit was the maker of all things, the Confucians hold that spirits are far inferior to the visible and material heavens, and even rank below sages and modern rulers. Confucius acknowledged that he knew very little about them, and therefore preferred speaking about other things. His universal maxim was, "Respect the gods, but keep them at a distance;" that is, "show them all due honor, but have as little to do with them as possible." It is customary with the Chinese to attach a presiding spirit to each dynasty and kingdom, to the land and grain, to hills and rivers, wind and fire; while the four corners of the house, with the shop, parlor and kitchen of every dwelling are supposed to be under the influence of some tutelary divinity. Confucius thought it necessary to honor these, but was averse to what he called flattering the gods by constant services.

With regard to the future state the Chinese seem to be wholly in the dark. They speak of the intellectual principle as distinct from the animal soul; but do not say anything about its existence after death. The idea of retribution is not connected with the invisible world at all; but they imagine that the rewards of virtue and vice are confined to the present state, and if not dealt out in the lifetime of the individual, will be visited upon his children and grand-children to the latest generation. There seems to be nothing to allure one to goodness but the principle of pursuing virtue for its own sake. The Confucian doctrine in regard to human nature is, that men are born into the world free from sin or wickedness, but by intercourse with others they become corrupt and vicious; but the sages, by their instructions awaken and renovate mankind when they revert to their original purity. Such is the outline of the honored state religion of Confucius. Of the other two religions of China I will make some mention in a future letter.

After leaving the Confucian temple, and as we walk the entire length of Tung-mun-keae,—East-gate street, the principal one within the walls, there is much that is new and interesting presented to us. The streets are for the most part uncommonly wide, well-paved, and quite clean and neat. The houses are better than the generality of those in Chinese cities. Those of the better class are situated within small courts, the latter finely flagged, and ornamented with flower-beds, shrubbery, and shade-trees. In many of these courts are placed large vases, in which can be seen swimming gold and silver fish. The shops are unusually large and fine and well stored with rich articles. The chief curiosities to us are the many and various rich silks, and the picture-frames curiously carved from a species of soft, satin, white wood. But stop! Close by the gate, as we are going out of the city, is the greatest wonder and curiosity we have seen to-day;—a little Chinese boy with blue eyes and golden hair.

Last Sunday we had the rare treat of having divine service, held on board ship. The pastor of the Congregational church here officiated and gave us an excellent discourse. But the treat to the greater portion of the crew, consisted, for the most part, in the addition made to our singing by several exceedingly attractive ladies who attended from shore.

Soon after our arrival at Ningpo, a crack four inches long was discovered in our crank-pin. Since that time there has been much excitement over the many rumors about its hastening our return to the States. We expect to leave here for Shanghai this afternoon, where a survey will be held, and we shall then know something more definite concerning our future movements.

LETTER XXXIII.

U. S. S. WACHUSETT, Shanghai, China,
June 24, 1867.

MY DEAR R.:

We have made the tour of China; so I do not dislike the prospect of remaining here for a few months while repairs are being made on our engine, with the almost certainty that we shall start for home soon after the repairs are completed. There are some two or three more places that I would like to visit, but they hardly offer sufficient inducements to remain longer in China, away from home and friends.

We arrived here April 24th, having been about fifteen hours in logging the one hundred and forty-one knots from Ningpo. The evening after our arrival we had a boat race between our second and third cutters. The distance was about five miles, for a purse of $70. The second cutter came in one and one-fourth minutes ahead, having made the distance in thirty-one minutes.

Although we have had considerable racing since we have been out, I have neglected to make any mention of it until now. We have two boats, a cutter and a gig, with which we intend to challenge and beat every boat of that description in these waters. The gig was built to order last year, and in every respect is a superior boat. In practicing, the racing crew man the boat and go on shore whenever there is an occasion for so doing, and we have daily practice besides.

On the evening of the second day after our arrival here, the bells in English Concession commenced ringing the alarm for fire, and were almost immediately followed by those of American and French Concessions, and the firing of an alarm gun by H. B. M.'s sloop Pelorus. Our fire company was immediately called, and dispatched to the scene of the fire, taking with them the fire-engine belonging to the Americans. It seems that the fire originated in some Chinese shops at the rear of the Danish Consulate, and spread so rapidly, that only the timely arrival of assistance and the most energetic endeavors prevented its becoming a very disastrous conflagration; as it was, very little damage was done.

The next morning the store ship Supply anchored near us, having been seventeen days from Hong Kong. She brought the promotions of several officers; and smiling faces, and a greater display of brass have since been noticed on our quarter-deck. Furthermore, the crew have benefitted somewhat by the promotions, in the increased privileges which they have enjoyed, and the smaller amount of unnecessary duty required of them. Soon, however, the satisfaction derived from the knowledge that they in reality possess the long coveted grade, will be superseded in the minds of our just-fledged officers by the wish to exercise the new and increased authority, and then our benefits will be past.

The first thing after our arrival here, the crew were set to work in making everything about the ship as neat and trim as possible. The task was completed Tuesday, May 7th, with the exception of the crank-pin, upon which the engineers are still engaged. The next morning the captain mustered the crew, and made them a little speech. He was glad that the men came off from their last general liberty in an unusually creditable manner, and so long as they continued to do so, he should give orders that they might go on shore whenever they could be spared from the ship. He said also that he had made arrangements for having divine service held on board the ship, so long as we should remain here, which would be several months at least; and, as it would do no harm and might do some good, he hoped that all would attend. His promise has been fulfilled and we have had good preaching, and in all respects exceedingly interesting services every Sunday since we have been here this time. We have a different minister nearly every Sunday, but so far we have had none that we did not all like very well. Rev. Mr. Yates, who is at the head of the Methodist missions here, has held service more frequently perhaps than any other divine, and is rather better liked. It is really quite refreshing to see our ship when everything is prepared for the morning service. Both ship and crew are in their cleanest and best attire, and the quarter-deck is fitted up with seats and tastefully decorated with flags. Our church is getting to be quite fashionable, too, as may be seen in the increased number of ladies and gentlemen who come from shore every Sunday. The American consul, Mr. Bradford, has brought his melodeon on board, so that we have excellent music and singing, and the entire services are conducted in the same manner as in churches on shore.

The spring meeting for the Shanghai races was held May 8th, 9th, 10th, and 11th, and, with beautiful weather and an attendance of upwards of five thousand Europeans from all parts of China, was the most successful meeting that has yet been had. Several tickets were sent to our executive officer for distribution, one of which I was fortunate enough to obtain. The first day I set out alone for the race grounds, which are located about two miles back of the English concession; but, being unacquainted with the locality, I was more than two hours in reaching them, and succeeded in doing so only after numerous inquiries and double the necessary amount of travel. I found that I was early, the ponies just being saddled for the first race.

While waiting for them to get ready, we will have a glance at the grounds, etc. The course is a rude pentagon in form, one and one-fourth of a mile in circuit, divided off by tall white posts into fourths of a mile. A portion of the track has recently been ploughed up, and the rest is turfed over. Just inside this course is a second about one mile in circuit, on which, at short intervals, are fences, mounds, and ditches, for steeplechasing and scrambles. In the center of the grounds is a fine cricket field. Only a low fence surrounds the grounds, so that a good view of the races may be had from the outside; but policemen are stationed all around to prevent any one from coming in, except through the main gate, where tickets are required. The enclosure where are the grand stand, stables, and promenades for the spectators is a fine grassy plot of about ten acres to the westward of the course. The stand itself is a fine, large, two-story building. On the lower floor is a restaurant, and the place where the riders are weighed. The second story is reached by a flight of stone steps, running the entire length of the building. It is open in front, with the seats slightly raised toward the rear, and now filled with the wealth, beauty, and intellect of Shanghai and other foreign towns in China. At the rear of these seats the band is placed. The top of the building is graded, and comfortable seats placed there. Over the front steps an awning is placed, and from staffs in front float the English, American, French, and Prussian ensigns. To the right of the stand is a fine two-story hotel, on the upper balcony of which are many spectators. In the rear of the stand are the stables for the horses, and in front is the judges stand. Close by, on a pole, is suspended a scale, with the number of the horses which are about to run. Both ladies and gentlemen have their betting books out, and almost every one stakes something.

"They are off!" says some one close by me, and turning around I see some fifteen or twenty horses dash past, with riders dressed in tight buckskin trowsers, and different colored jackets and skull-caps. The English flat-races are all new to me, but it is certainly a splendid and exciting sight to see so many horses with riders thus gaily dressed, start off together, with whip and spur urged forward to their utmost speed. And great is the excitement as one gains, then loses, another gains, loses, and so on until at last they reach the gaol. The race over, the victorious horse is led in front of the grand stand, and whilst the band is discoursing some favorite air, the prize is given. That day there were seven races, all of them close and exciting. The last one was the most exciting of all, because the greatest sums were staked upon it, and the horse against whom the greatest odds had been given won the race. Many were the sad, woeful faces noticeable in consequence.

I went again the 10th, accompanied by a couple of friends. One of them had been told that he could go by water to the race-ground, and not feeling very well, he concluded to do so, while the other one with myself decided to take the surer land route. Leaving him to scull his sampan up the creek past the English consulate's, we landed, and after a pleasant walk arrived at the grounds, some time before the race began. Just after the second race our missing friend made his appearance, looking decidedly heated and dusty for one just off from an aquatic trip. After a few good wishes for his Chinese boatmen, he cooled down sufficiently to inform us that the lubber had taken him a long way into the country, and that finally he had to walk a much greater distance than he would had he come with us. The first four races of the day were flat races with Chinese ponies, close and exciting, but not differing materially from those of the previous day. The fifth race was a steeple-chase for all horses—distance three miles around the course, with six fences and six ditches to be leaped each time around. Only two horses started, *Kangaroo* and *Miss Mowbray*. The former took and kept the lead, doing the leaps beautifully and making the three circuits in nine minutes. On the second circuit he fell over the last hurdle or fence, turning a complete somersault and throwing the rider, but inflicting no injury other than barking his nose slightly. However he quickly recovered and finished the race without further accident.

The last race was a scramble for all ponies—distance, twice around the course for steeple-chasing. Eighteen ponies started, and for a long time it was impossible to conjecture which would be the winner. Did one lead between two hurdles, he would get to the ditch just in time to be at the bottom of all the others, and so it would continue, first one and then another taking the lead, until finally, contrary to the expectation of everybody, *Potshot* came in first ahead of half a dozen competitors. The race was intensely exciting and amusing from beginning to end, and seemed to be enjoyed by all more than any other race of the day.

Friday, May 17th, the several fire companies of Shanghai had a grand parade and collation. Our fire brigade manned the Hong Que steam engine. The following account I clip from the *Shanghai Recorder* of May 8th:

"The trial of the fire-engines yesterday evening on the Bund, though possibly not quite so successful, in a purely mechanical point of view, as might have been wished, afforded much amusement and attracted a large number of spectators. As we mentioned in a previous issue, the nature of the trial was to ascertain which engine could throw water the farthest, both perpendicularly and horizontally. Two boat's crews from the *Wachusett* were in attendance, who, after the preliminary arrangements of stationing the engines and adjusting the hose, set to work with energy upon Shanghai engine No. 1, which was under the direction of Mr. Holcomb. It soon, however, became apparent that the energy of the sons of Neptune was far more than the hose, which has withstood for a lengthened time the enervating influences of the climate, could bear. . From time to time shouts of laughter arose in different directions, as length after length of the hose gave way, treating the spectators to a shower-bath which, however cool and refreshing, was nevertheless a shade stronger than was expected by them. The hose in fact showed unmistakably that it was not unaffected by the hardness of the times and had a most decided tendency to "burst up." The results of the throwing of water, though satisfactory in one or two instances, the stream having gone considerably higher than Messrs. Dent & Co's flagstaff, cannot, on account of the defectiveness of the hose, be taken as a sample of what the engine, under more favorable circumstances, would have performed. It was not until the whole of the available hose had been tried that it was decided to replace No. 1 Engine by No. 2, when the men of the *Wachusett* moved her off from the Custom House jetty in earnest and rapid style, No. 2 Honggur being pulled down with energy and rapidity to take her place. Indeed she was tugged along with such speed that it required as much energy to stop her before she got to the end of the jetty.

"The Chinese coolies worked away at her with pluck; but unfortunately the same results to the hose soon became apparent, as it "burst up" in one or two places. She threw the water notwithstanding to a good distance; but it is of course quite impossible to form any estimate of the relative powers of the two engines on account of the defectiveness of the hose in both instances. The Chinese will, we think, require some little drilling before they are able to turn their powers to proper account, or compete with the gallant sons of Neptune. The Municipal band were in attendance on the Bund and enlivened the proceedings by playing several pieces; and a large number of spectators assembled to witness the trial.

After the trial, all repaired to the Imperial Hotel, where we found awaiting us an inviting repast furnished by the generosity of the citizens of Shanghai.

In a ramble within the walls of Shanghai a few weeks ago I met a French priest, called Father Valleur, with whom I formed a very pleasant and interesting acquaintance. Nearly twenty years of his life had been spent among the Chinese, and he had adopted their costume and spoke their language fluently. He was able therefore to penetrate almost any part of China, and learn almost everything regarding the manners, laws, customs, and religions of the people. I found him to be a man very willing to converse upon any subject, and give answers to all my numerous questions. The few hours that I passed in his society were full of interest to me, and I really believe that in that time I learned more about China than I ever did before in as many weeks, while depending upon my own observations alone. To his cordial request that I would call upon him at his home, I replied that I should by no means deny myself so much pleasure and profit, as to neglect to further cultivate his acquaintance.

You will doubtless remember my giving you a short description of the Confucian or State system of religion—the first of the three sects into which the Chinese are divided. I then intended to give you some account of the other systems whenever a good opportunity should offer itself. In passing a pile of temple buildings near the southern gate of Shanghai, Father Valleur remarked that those belonged to the second sect, which is called Taou. Upon expressing a desire to learn something regarding their origin and tenets, he gave me the following account :

The original meaning of the word Taou is, a *way* or *path*, a *principle*—and the principle from which heaven, earth, man, and nature emanate. *Le* is the latent principle, and Taou is the principle in action. It also means a word, to preach, and to say ; and is very like the Logos, or the "eternal reason" of the Greeks. The founder of this sect was Laou-tau, who was cotemporary with Confucius ; but the Taou, or Reason itself, they say, is uncreated and underived. The votaries of this sect speak a great deal about virtue, and profess to obtain a greater degree of it, by abstraction from the world and the repression of every desire. By the mortification of every feeling, they claim to obtain perfect virtue, and to this end some of its votaries leave the busy haunts of men, and alone upon the mountain tops pursue their studies uninterrupted. They affect to despise fame, wealth, and posterity, claiming that at death all benefits and distinctions arising from them cease, and the labor bestowed upon them is thrown away.

Great attention is paid by them to the study of alchemy and the transmutation of metals ; and by the combination of various elements, they endeavor to produce the philosopher's stone, and the elixir of immortality. Some claim to have discovered an antidote to death, and when the administration of the heavenly potion does not produce the desired effect, they assert that the victim has only gone to ramble with the genii, and enjoy that immortality above which cannot be found below.

It is narrated that a certain emperor, having procured the elixir at an immense expense, ordered it to be brought before him. But while it was on its way from the compounder to the throne, one of his officers drained the contents of the cup. This so enraged the emperor that he immediately ordered the offender to be put to death. He, however, coolly replied, that having drank the elixir, he was immortal ; either all their efforts to terminate his existence would be in vain, or else the whole system was false. After a few minutes' consideration the minister was pardoned, and the pretender banished from the empire.

While the Confucians have hardly determined whether spirits exist or not, the Taou sect, is founded mainly upon their existence, and they profess to have intercourse with, and control over the demons of the invisible world. Chang-teen-eze, the principal of the Taou sect in China, is supposed to be immortal, like the Lama of Thibet, (or rather the place is supplied with a new occupant as soon as the old one dies,) and assumes an authority over Hades. As the emperor appoints officers over certain districts and removes them at will, so does this demon ruler appoint and remove deities, and no tutelary deity is to be worshiped or is supposed to have power to protect his votaries, until authorized by him to exercise his functions in the particular region.

From the power which this individual is supposed to possess, everything coming from him is considered to be efficacious in counteracting all noxious influences, and is sold at an enormous price.

The Taou priests issue charms, or amulets, consisting of small scraps of yellow paper, with a few enigmatical characters written upon them, from the sale of which they realize large sums of money. These charms are efficacious for only one year, and new scraps have to be obtained to frighten away the imps of the new year.

After a death, the house in which it occurred has to be purified, and, as this ceremony is attended by considerable expense, it is no uncommon thing for lodgers and strangers, when dying, to be turned out into the streets. The purification of houses is done by the prayers and sacrifices of the priests. A district is usually purified by the votaries of Taou, going barefoot over ignited charcoal. But the anniversary of the birth of the "high emperor of the sombre heavens" is an occasion most worthy of notice. The introductory ceremonies consist in chanting of prayers, ringing of bells, the sprinkling of holy water, the blowing of horns, and the brandishing of swords. A large fire, some fifteen or twenty feet in diameter, is made before the temple of this imaginary being, and the performers strike and beat this with the swords in order to subdue the demon. They then dash through the flames, barefoot, preceded by the priests carrying the gods in their arms. The entire affair presents a scene of the wildest excitement, and all the participants act more like madmen than rational beings.

The Taou sect worship a variety of idols, some of which are imaginary incarnations of Eternal Reason; and others, rulers of the invisible world, or presiding divinities of various districts; among the rest are the "three pure ones," who are first in dignity; the "pearly emperor," and "supreme ruler," the most honorable in heaven; the god of the north, the god of fire, with lares and penates, genii and inferior divinities without number.

My first introduction to the Cremorne Gardens was one pleasant evening in June when a number of us took a horseback ride thither. These are situated about three miles back of French Concession, and to which we have since usually extended our almost daily rides. Immediately after landing we sent "boys" after some horses and a few minutes later they appeared with them. Horses! did I say? Like the old saying about tailors it would take at least nine of them to make one. Small, poor, scraggy, blind, lame,—well, not worth the space I am devoting to their description. But it was too late to wait for any better ones, so we concluded to take them and do the best we could. G. got the best one, D. the next best, and I by far the poorest. Well! mounted and armed with good cudgels away we started. G. was off like an arrow, D. close after and I—I couldn't make my horse go faster than a walk, and sometimes not that even. At last we got the better of him, G. took position ahead, D. behind, and with all our combined efforts, we finally got him "under way," and thus proceeded to Cremorne Gardens. The ride was amusing, if not pleasant, and exciting if not interesting. The night was dark, so that we saw comparatively nothing of the country, and the gardens were closed, so that after resting our horses a few moments, we returned with a repetition of the amusing and exciting ride, that we had when going out.

Not satisfied with this visit to the much talked of Cremorne, a few days later another and larger party was organized to go out there. As before, we sent out for horses, which were speedily brought us. They did not, however, suit our exact *tastes* and remembering the experience of the former night, we determined to go to the stables and choose for ourselves. Arriving there first, I selected, as I thought, a fine, high spirited animal, and with a glance at the girths I mounted. But very few horses are seen in China and all these are owned by the more wealthy Europeans, who import them solely for their own private use. Still there are a large number of native ponies seen everywhere. These are small, but smart, capable of enduring an immense amount of fatigue, and will go like the wind. They are quite cheap riding too, a good one, all equipped, costing less than a dollar per day.

Well, after some little difficulty and delay, all were suited. We mounted, and with the ponies' noses turned Cremorne-ward, away we started upon a race over as fine, level, smooth and pleasant a road as I ever saw. The way was skirted on either hand by beautiful, smiling fields of rice, cotton, grains, and vegetables, and the entire country was evidently in the highest state of cultivation. The landscape, dotted with pretty villages and towns, snug farm-houses and rural hamlets, monasteries, temples, and graves, stretched away in one vast continuous plain, some eighteen or twenty miles, and melted into the high, blue hills beyond.

Upon leaving the city and passing the old tree near the northeastern corner of the walls, my mind would dwell upon the train of thought which this same tree called forth from a distinguished writer twenty years ago :

"There is a delicious, eloquent communion, to be held with one of these single old trees standing in a vast plain, and you and he entirely alone—no fellows of his kind, and none of yours. I have enjoyed it on this day as I did in other regions. Just as the sun is setting, and you are hurrying on your way to escape the shadows and wanderings of the night, the old fellow beckons to you with a long and giant arm. Your heart turns to him, but your eyes are on the big falling sun, and you think you will push on; but there is so much beseeching in his moving arms, he is so lonely you rein up your horse to have a talk. He tells you of his chronology—of the vast and wavy sapling herds which stood around him in his green youth; how man and storm and disease had taken all but himself; how he had looked down upon race changed for race—plain for city, and city again for field. While you are thus absorbed by his eloquence, the shades of night are around you both, and he grows more animated as they fall around him. You bid him good-bye, and he waves you such a farewell, as his arms pass into the night shadows, as seems to dismiss you into eternity, while he promises to wait there and tell the same story, and yours, too, to some traveler of a future age, who may stand in your place. There are few places where an old tree could tell more than one of these standing on the plains of China, on the banks of the Yang-tse-Kiang, and near the walls of Shanghai."

Now, to return to the race. G—— led at first, but I soon passed him and was going at the "rate of sixteen knots per hour," when away went the *starboard* stirrup-strap, and was compelled to "haul up" for repairs. By the time I had completed them I was left far behind; but, as the others were riding slowly I soon caught up, and away we went again. A break-neck pace for about a mile and I had passed them all but D., and for a long time we were "neck and neck." I don't know how the race would have terminated, for, after a few minutes' riding thus, away went my other stirrup-strap, and again I had to "halt" for repairs. A moment after J. came up, and just after passing me his pony wheeled around (as they ofttimes will, unless a strict look-out is kept) and he "hove to like a fillyloo bird on a fence;" or, in common *parlance* was unhorsed as prettily as I ever saw any one, and plunged head foremost into a pool of dirty water, without, however, injuring him in the least. So long was I in making repairs this time that I was the last to reach the Gardens. Giving my pony into the care of a "boy" I went into the house, where I found the others enjoying themselves at the billiard table.

Whenever you feel very thirsty on a hot, sultry day, if you have the ingredients at hand, just mix a mint-julep after Delcour's receipt, and see if it don't refresh you as nought ever did before. To one-third of a glass of milk he added a little wine and a lump of sugar, then filling the glass up and putting in some bruised leaves of fresh mint he told me to "taste it." Nectar, egad. I thought I had never tasted drink before so delicious and refreshing.

Leaving the others to amuse themselves in their games, I lit a cigar and went out for a look at the house, grounds, and views. The house is quite a large, one story structure, divided up into bar, billiard, sitting, and dining rooms. Running entirely around the building is a fine, deep verandah, protected by rolling blinds, or shades, and finely fitted up with card-tables and lounging-chairs. It stands upon a slight but beautiful eminence (the only one in sight) near the centre of the grounds. These comprise about ten acres, tastefully laid out in walks and drives, ornamented by fine shrubbery, and plants, and beautiful flowers, and with charming little summer-houses scattered all over them. It is but a few years since the Gardens were laid out, consequently the shrubbery and vines are quite young and small yet; but, in the course of time this will be the most beautiful place about Shanghai. Even now it is a favorite place of resort on hot summer days for many of the citizens, and those visiting Shanghai. There they sit on the wide, deep verandah, enjoying the cool breezes in quiet, or admiring the beautiful prospect on every side, or engaging in games and socialities with one another; or, perchance, they ramble about the lovely grounds with a rest and a chat in one of the summer-houses or arbors, and food and refreshments in the house.

I was startled out of a little reverie, into which I had fallen in one of the summer-houses, by one of the party's coming in and bidding me wake up and get ready for a ride to Sek-a-wai—a place some three miles farther back, and the site of a Roman Catholic college and nunnery.

Our horses were led out, all equiped, so we mounted and rode leisurely along, the better to enjoy the beautiful scenery, and the many items of interest. Among other things we noticed on our way several low, square towers with a hole near the top on one side. These are houses built for the reception of the bodies of dead babies who are found thus or are put to death by their parents. Female infants being of less value than males make up the great mass of those with which these towers are filled. These, with a provincial Wei-Kwei, may be noticed near every place which we have visited. The latter is the council hall of those who belong to another province, but reside for a time at Shanghai, and is also used as a place of deposit for their dead until they can be moved to their own province. The way side resting places for travelers, provided by the authorities, I have noticed before, but think that I, as yet, have given no description of them. They consist of merely a low tiled roof supported by a brick or stone pillar at each corner, and covering low stone benches.

Nothing of special interest occurred to the party on the ride out, with the exception of breaking an occasional stirrup-strap or saddle girth, and a harmless unhorsing. My absorption in what was about me was broken several times by the curious capers of my pony, who, on two or three occasions rode down others of the party. Finally, when I was busily engaged in admiring the tiled roofs of the one-story cottages, with peaked and carved gables rising just above the line of high hedge fences, the eccentric animal coolly walked over the edge of the high bank of the canal along which we were passing, and rolled with me to the bottom. Fortunately there was no water in the canal at the time, so I escaped with a few slight bruises, and the soiling and rending of my clothes. There was no need of examining the pony to discover if he was hurt, for they are like India-rubber; and really, I have no doubt but that the whole affair was viewed by him as a fine frolic. It certainly was by the whole party, anxiety for my preservation not being able to repress their mirth and uproarious laughter. I think my mind suffered most by the roll, for it had soared high in contemplating the picturesqueness of my surroundings, and the fall was as great as it was abrupt.

At Sik-a-wai, according to the usual custom, we were cordially and politely received by the French and Italian priests, and by them shown over the college buildings. These are quite fine and commodious, and kept in admirable order. There are at present upwards of five hundred children under instruction there; and, as I watched them at their various amusements I could not help acknowledging that they were a very bright, happy body. They are generally the children of Roman Catholic parents, although there are some orphans whom they have taken. I was greatly struck and much pleased by the many articles of modeling, sculpture, and painting, which I saw about the buildings, executed by the teachers and students.

After about an hour spent in a survey of the buildings and grounds, we returned to the gardens where we found the dinner, which we had ordered, awaiting us, and to which we did ample justice after our long ride. After a game or two of billiards we returned to the ship.

This synopsis of one day's enjoyment, which I have given, will answer for many others which we have had, and anticipate having, during our stay at Shanghai, and by which we lessen what would otherwise be an almost unendurable longing for home and friends. The effects are seen in the spirit of happiness and contentment which pervades the entire crew, as evinced in their looks and demeanor towards one another;

in the almost entire absence of quarrels and fights, and in the lightness of spirits which nightly bursts forth in choruses that make the ship fairly tremble and can be heard for miles. It is evinced, too, in the alacrity and dispatch with which any required work is performed, and in the many sports which have been revived and inaugurated. In arriving at this desirable state of affairs many thanks and much credit are due, to the officers, who, in striving to lessen the hardships and unpleasantness of shipboard existence in avoiding all unnecessary work and exercise, and in the privileges bestowed, cannot fail to have added greatly to their own happiness. It seems strange to me that this state is so seldom reached, but in almost every man-of-war in our navy, man is considered but little better than a brute or a mere machine, and is treated thus, according to the "ola custom." Let us hope that at no distant day those that man our war vessels will be treated more like men, and then will be seen a more efficient Navy than has heretofore existed.

LETTER XXXIV.

U. S. S. WACHUSETT, Shanghai,
July 27th, 1867.

MY DEAR R.:

At last the repairs upon our engine are completed, and our pleasant and interesting stay of three months and a half at Shanghai is about to be brought to a close. I as yet have heard no definite announcement as to whither our future movements will tend, but the general expectation derived from the many rumors is that we are soon to start for home, returning by nearly the same route as we came out. I am not very particular by what route we go, but I do hope that we may start very soon.

A few months ago an American bark was wrecked off the coast of the island of Formosa, and most of the crew, consisting of the captain and wife, two mates, and four European and seven Chinese sailors were murdered by the natives. One Chinaman escaped and also the captain's wife, who is said to be still a prisoner in their hands.

The Ashuelot, after parting company with us last April, proceeded to Formosa and in conjunction with H. B. M.'s gunboat Cormorant landed an armed party to learn further particulars of the affair if possible. In this, however, they were unsuccessful, and being fired upon by the natives they concluded to postpone investigations until they could communicate with the Admiral, who was then in Japan with the flagship Hartford, and the Wyoming. He arrived at Shanghai, with both these vessels in the early part of June, and about the middle of the same month he left for Formosa. We should have accompanied the expedition, if our engines had been in a condition to admit of our doing so, but they were not. About a week after their departure, they returned, and considerable excitement was caused by the news of their movements, and deeds while away. Although I have heard many versions of the affair from actual participators, I know of no more concise and truthful account, than the following which I copy from the Shanghai Recorder of June 20th, and which is regarded as semi-official.

"THE AMERICAN ARMS AT FORMOSA."

"A few days since the U. S. Ship Hartford, bearing the flag of Rear Admiral H. H. Bell, accompanied by the U. S. steamer Wyoming, Lieutenant-Commander Charles Carpenter, left the port of Shanghai for the south point of Formosa, to punish the Natives who inhabit that part of the island, for their murder of the crew of the American Bark Rover, which was wrecked there in March last; and if possible to destroy any of their settlements which might be found in the vicinity, and to clear the country of the dense jungle which enables the savages to attack shipwrecked parties, and to conceal themselves when attacked. On their way down the vessels touched at Takao for an interpreter, and received on board Charles Carroll, Esq., H. B. M.'s Consul, who had expressed a desire to go with the expedition.

" On the morning of the 13th inst., the ship anchored off South Cape, and a party of sailors and marines, numbering in all one hundred and eighty men, were landed under command of Commander G. E. Belknap of the Hartford, the object being to destroy lurking-places, houses and cattle of the Natives. After landing, the force in two detachments marched into the interior, and burnt a collection of huts which were found. Here the savages manifested an intention to dispute the march of the column, by firing from every hill-top and jungle. The men of the squadron were seldom able to get a sight of the enemy, and only knew of their proximity by the discharge of their muskets from the jungle and the gleaming of their gunbarrels above the foliage.

"The savages by quick marches were driven from every hiding-place, and by 3 P. M. were forced three miles into the interior. The sun now began to tell upon the men, the thermometer standing at 92° in the shade, and several suffering severely from sunstroke, it was concluded to return to the ship. While at a halt, a party of the enemy fired a volley from ambush, at short range into the column. Lieutenant Commander McKenzie, chief of staff, who had volunteered for the expedition, immediately led a charge against them, and while at the head of his men was shot, dying almost immediately.

"After driving the enemy again into the interior, and being unable to penetrate it further, and there being no further object to be gained by remaining, the column returned to the ship, carrying with them the body of Lieutenant-Commander McKenzie, and several of the officers and crew, who were dangerously ill with sunstroke. Having burned their huts, and the jungle being too green to burn, the following day the vessels returned to Takao, where the remains of Lieutenant Commander Mc Kenzie were interred with military honors in the private burying grounds of the British Consulate, the use of which had been kindly offered by Mr. Carroll."

There are various opinions and rumors concerning this affair and many conjectures as to what is to be done in the future; but all seem agreed that as soon as it is cooler weather, and the undergrowth dry enough to burn, another and a much larger expedition will be formed against the Formosans, and every precaution taken to ensure success.

"Three pirates were condemned to be executed about a week since, and if you would learn another mode of Chinese executions, you can do so by going within the walls to the city prison," said a citizen friend to me some time ago.

Having business within the walls that same afternoon I determined to go to the *prison*, and arriving there I witnessed a mode of execution, at once the most shocking and barbarous, and beyond what I thought it possible for the human mind to conceive. The victims were placed in cages, some three feet square and seven feet high, made of stout bamboo splints. The head of each one was thrust through a hole in a board, or rather placed between two sections of a board, so fashioned that when joined together one edge was in the mouth and the other pressed against the lower and back part of the head, both sections meeting at the extremities. By these boards, they were triced up so that their toes barely touched the bottom of the cage and then left without food or drink under the guardianship of merciless Chinese soldiers until released by death. When I saw them they had been in that situation for nearly six days. Two died the day before, and the other was dying then. The look of agony which I saw portrayed on their countenances I never care to witness again; it was horrible beyond anything the mind can conceive of, and utterly defies description.

In returning from witnessing this horrible sight I was joined by friend A—— who, like myself had never seen a small foot, uncovered, and upon the subject being mentioned we determined to gratify our curiosity in that respect that very afternoon. For this purpose we secured the services of a little Chinese boy who said that he could guide us where we could see one. He took us to a house near the walls, where resided his mother and sister. For a long time both persistently refused all our entreaties, arguments or proposals, but at length, for the promised reward of half a dollar, the sister consented to uncover the foot. The shoe and stocking having been removed, several layers of bandages had to be unwound before our curiosity could be gratified. Then we saw an ugly, ill-shapen mass, no toe excepting the great one in sight, that stunted and deformed, and the others turned under and grown into the bottom of the foot; the heel about one and one-half inches long, and the bridge of the foot pressed up into the ancle, and there forming a large bulb. The foot thus compressed takes a shoe only about four inches long and two wide at the instep, terminating in a point at the toe. When a child is quite young the foot is encased in iron shoes, and kept there until the foot is stunted in its growth.

The current statement of the origin of the custom of cripling ladies' feet is that Ta-ke, a wicked empress in the third century before the Christian era, during the Tsin dynasty, influenced her husband to issue an edict, obliging the Chinese ladies to make the Empress club feet the standard.

The custom is less prevalent than it was a century ago, and is slowly falling into disuse. Probably not more than one-fourth or one-third of the ladies of the present day contract their feet, and those belong to the aristocratic class.

When sitting down their feet do look quite cunning and pretty, encased in those cunning little shoes prettily embossed and embroidered; but when they attempt to walk, or lay bare the foot, admiration instantly changes to pity or disgust.

The "glorious Fourth" was duly celebrated here, and although quite rainy, it was well-enjoyed by the participators. All the vessels in the harbor crossed to 'gallant yards and dressed ship with the American ensign at the main, the flag-staffs of the Consuls and other leading men of Shanghai were also dressed, and from many a balcony the glorious Stars and Stripes were flung out to the breeze. At sunrise and at sunset the American Consul fired a salute of thirty-seven guns, from four little pieces of cannon which he had mounted in front of his office. Murphy, "the Irish Consul" did likewise, and a continual firing of guns, crackers, etc., was kept up from morning till night, with a fine display of fireworks in the evening. Notwithstanding it was contrary to port regulations the Admiral fired a national salute at noon, having sent word to the authorities, beforehand, that he intended to do so, and would not be responsible for broken windows nor any other damage that might be occasioned by so doing. The dinner was in every respect a success, an advance even on that of last Christmas, and everything was done by "the powers that be" to make the day a happy and a joyous one. By an order from the Admiral no one was allowed to go on shore, as so many English sailors were on liberty, and on this particular day, the chances were in favor of there being rekindlings of the old revolutionary spirit.

The great excitement and principal topic of conversation during the day, as well as many preceding and following it, were the boat-races between our vessel and the Hartford. After the many challenges, acceptances, backing outs, &c, the following three races were decided upon and rowed: Our gig, against the Hartford's second cutter against the barge, and dingey against dingey. The distance for the first two was about five miles, and the starting point our gangway. At 4 P. M. the first race, that of the gigs, came off, for a purse of $150.00. As the gun was fired our gig started off splendidly, but one of the Hartford's crew at that moment took a cramp and threw two oars out of the rowlocks. Before they could get righted, our boat got at least three lengths ahead. The water was a little rough but our boat being heavy in build, paid no attention to that, and kept gaining steadily, while the Hartford's (like that of the Spanish Consul's, which we raced a short time ago,) would fairly jump ahead at every stroke, but would lose her headway when the oars were lifted from the water. Our boat turned the stake nearly half a minute first, and came in full four ship's lengths ahead, making the distance in twenty-nine minutes and twenty seconds. As the gigs came in both ship's crews "manned the riggings" and the buglers struck up our boat's call, "The Mocking Bird." The barge and cutter, both twelve-oared boats, were already manned, and immediately took up their position, the Hartford's getting the choice. The race was for a purse of $120.00. The ships had now swung so that it was an exceedingly bad position for starting, between us and the Hartford. Just as the gun was fired for starting, the barge put off her helm, tossed her port oars, and riding our starboard oars broke three of them; then, immediately clearing herself made it appear as if it were all done according to previous intentions. Cheer after cheer went up from the Hartford over this maneuver; but even with our boat thus disabled, the barge came in only forty seconds ahead, and then had the race declared "foul" by both umpires. The dingey race came next. Distance about a mile for a purse of $20.00. Nearly every one bet on the Hartford's and was certain that it would win, but ours came in full half a ship's length ahead. Three days after the Fourth, the race between the barge and cutter was tried over and our boat won by nearly a minute. In all our racing we have never yet been beaten once, but still fly the game cock with no one able to take it from us, and freely sing our chorus,

> For any amount you name
> Up to a thousand pounds,
> We'll pull any boat, in a Shanghai port,
> Or a thousand miles around.

The most intense excitement prevailed during all the races; riggings were manned from the tip of the flying jib booms to the royal-mast trucks; cheering, throwing overboard old caps, etc, were freely indulged in, and the decks of the vessels as well as the Bund were thronged with eager spectators. All seemed to regret the foul race, for, with that exception everything went off in splendid style.

Since we have been in Shanghai this last time I have attended church nearly every Sabbath eve, at the Episcopal chapel of the Americans, at Hong Que. There are many reasons why I enjoy going there very much; the church is almost always full of American citizens, and it makes me feel for the time almost like being at home and among friends. The singing and chanting could hardly be surpassed anywhere, and the beautiful service of the Episcopal church is most impressively read by the rector, while the discourses which he gives are ever full of good, plain, practical truths. Two or three Sabbaths ago he gave us a very interesting discourse on the subject of "Missions in China."

Commencing with the earliest accounts he said that Assemanus assures us that Thomas the Apostle, having done much for the establishment of the Christian faith in India, passed over to a country in the East, called China, where he preached the gospel, and founded a church in the city of Pekin. In the Chaldee ritual there is an office for the celebration of St. Thomas, which says that "by him the Persians, Hindoos, and Chinese were converted to the Christian faith." In confirmation of this he spoke of the early intercourse which subsisted between China and the West, stating that a Chinese general, who flourished before the close of the first century, extended his conquests as far as Arabia and Judea, and that the famous Kwan Yunchang had left in writing an account of the birth, death, resurrection, and ascension of a Saviour which must have been derived from some indistinct traditions of gospel history.

Chinese history further mentions, that about A. D. 150, an extraordinary person arrived in China, who taught a doctrine truly spiritual; and drew the admiration of all by the virtues he possessed and the miracles he wrought.

The next intimation of the introduction of Christianity into China, he said was the celebrated marble tablet which was dug up in 1625. This tablet was between ten and eleven feet long, five and six broad, and surmounted by a small cross. It contains an inscription in the Chinese and Syriac languages, describing the principal doctrines of the Bible as contained in the first five books of the New Testament, and the history of its introduction into China. The inscription states that this occurred in A. D. 636, and under the reign of two emperors, the preaching of the Christian religion was authorized and supported. Then the Buddhist priests, jealous of the success of the new religion, instituted a persecution against it, which for a time diminished the number of the faithful; but after a time, two able advocates were raised up, who soon brought the new religion into notice and royal favor once more. The emperor, Suth-tsung founded several churches; and in order to perpetuate his good deeds the tablet was erected A. D. 782.

Since that time the church has many times been bitterly persecuted in China, and all apparent evidences of the existence of Christianity been rooted out; still, persevering efforts have been made, and Christianity has had a foothold since the latter part of the sixteenth century. This has been slight at times, and held by the Jesuits alone until the commencement of the present century, since which time the Protestant missions have been gaining in numbers and strength, especially during the past few years. Instead of beginning at the top of society, he said they proposed to commence from the bottom, and aim to influence, first, the extremities, and then the heart of the empire. With the love of Christ for their motive, and the salvation of souls for their end; employing Christian benevolence and Christian intelligence as the means, and depending simply and solely on God for His blessing; all true Christian workers may hope and believe that, though slow their work will be sure, and finally effectual.

Another visit to Father V. gave me an insight into the laws of China. These are numerous, minute, and circumstantial, and are more worthy to be compared with those of civilized nations than it would seem possible that those of a heathen country could be. To a foreigner it does not seem hardly possible to have such an immense population united under one government. The secret of their success lies in the establishment of the patriarchal system, grounded on the basis of filial obligation. The first principle in their moral code is that parents, having brought their children into the world, have a right to dispose of them as they think best; and a child is never released from duty and obedience to its parents until death.

This principle forms the basis of their political code. The emperor is considered as the great father of the Chinese races, and as such has absolute power over all.

As he cannot attend to the administration of all the affairs of the empire in person, he employs ministers which are designated as his "feet," his "hands," and his "eyes," but there is no one so high in authority but that he can be degraded and bambooed at the pleasure of the emperor.

There are four prime ministers forming what is called the "Inner Cabinet." Two of these are Tartars and two Chinese, the usual way in which appointments are made so that one party may watch the other.

Under these are six tribunals answering somewhat to our Heads of Departments; the Tribunal of Civil Office, of Means, of Rites, of War, of Punishments, and of Works. Under these tribunals are officers appointed all over the country who report to them, and they in turn to the emperor and cabinet.

Such is an outline of the government of the immensely peopled empire of China. I have given you but the outline, because I felt sure that a more lengthened account would be wearisome to you. It is now the "kite season" in China and in closing this letter, I will say a few words about kite-flying.

While in most things the Chinese are no farther advanced than they were ten centuries ago, they are far ahead of all young Americas in the kite business. They have many strange customs, and not the least funny of them all, is the one they have of the old men flying kites while the boys look on. But then a Chinese kite is an elaborate affair in comparison with the tasteless sexagons and octagons with which our urchins besprinkle the atmosphere. Centipedes, sixty feet long, composed of split bamboo hoops, covered with light paper, and furnished with legs, immense moths, birds, and quadrupeds of all descriptions, fishes, snakes, and amphibious animals hover in the skies of China during this season. Yes, kite flying is a grave affair in this country, and the solemnity is greatly heightened by the fact that grave yards are almost universally selected as the spots to fly them.

LETTER XXXV.

U. S. S. WACHUSETT, Pootoo, China, }
August 20, 1867. }

MY DEAR R.:

We left Shanghai Monday, July 29th, with the express purpose of passing away the hottest weather in a cruise about the islands off the eastern coast of China, and recruiting the health of the ship's company. Our stay there of three months and a half with the thermometer standing at more than 100° above zero much of the time, had not been without serious effect on the crew, and before we left nearly one-third were under medical treatment. We had no prevailing epidemic, and but few serious, with no fatal, cases of sickness; but there seemed to be a general weakness and utter prostration, that required a change. Indeed it was mainly upon the advice of Dr. Jenkins of Shanghai, that the cruise was made. In a sanitary respect it has proved successful beyond the highest hopes and expectations of all. At no time since we left Boston have the crew been in as good health as now, and a more robust or cheerful body of men could hardly be found. In addition to this, all will agree with me in saying that it certainly has been the pleasantest and most interesting month we have spent in China, or Chinese waters.

Among the interesting incidents of our last few day's sojourn at Shanghai, were the sums contributed and presented to the representatives of the Catholic and Protestant Missions located there, thus showing that we were not unmindful of their exertions for our enlightenment and edification during our stay, nor ungrateful for them. One hundred dollars were raised for each, and placed in the hands of our Consul for presentation to them, accompanied by our most hearty thanks for their many kindnesses, and our best wishes for their future success.

The moment we had cleared the mouth of the Whang-po river, and felt the cool, refreshing sea-breezes, uncontaminated by contact with the low, pestilence breeding swamps which surround Shanghai, a new life and vigor seemed to be infused into all the crew, and from that moment the health and spirits of all began to mend rapidly. The next morning we anchored at the Ragged Islands, which lie to the southward and eastward of the city, and distant about eighty miles. There we remained nearly twenty-four hours while we had our quarterly target exercise with the battery, and the next day after steaming about sixty miles we dropped anchor off Square Island, which you will doubtless remember as being five miles from Chinhai at the mouth of the Ningpo river.

By the steamer of the next morning from Shanghai, we received orders from the Admiral to proceed up to Ningpo, and there await the arrival of Vice Consul General Mangum and wife, and Mr. Thorne—nephew of the late Captain Townsend—who were to accompany us on our cruise. They came down the 2d, and came on board the Wachusett the following morning. A further addition to the party was made in the persons of a son of Dr. Jenkins, and two or three Chinese compradores and pilots.

Everything being in readiness we weighed anchor a little after noon of the same day and started down the river. At Ningpo we had found the air, if possible more sultry and deadening than at Shanghai, and as we passed Chinhai and met the pure and refreshing sea-breezes again, I thought that they never seemed so good and life-giving as then. Our general course, after clearing the mouth of the river, was easterly, but very winding and circuitous, in order to pass between the many islands which extend along the coast. It was about 5 P. M. when we dropped anchor at Tinghai, having logged forty knots since leaving Ningpo.

The Chusan Archipelago belongs to the department of Ningpo, and forms the single district of which Tinghai is the capital. It is divided into twenty-four *chwang*, or townships, whose officers are responsible to the district magistrates. The southern limit of the whole group is Quesan, in Kiu-shan island in Lat. 29° 21' N. and Long. 120° 10' E, consisting of eleven islands. The northernmost is False Saddle Island in Lat. 35° 50' N. and Long. 122° 41' E. The total number of islands in the archipelago is over a hundred.

The town of Tinghai lies on the southern side of *Chan Shan*, or Boat Island, from which the entire group derives the name of Chusan. This island is twenty miles long, from six to ten wide, and fifty-two in circumference. The general aspect of this as well as of the neighboring islands, is that of steep ridges of hills, occasionally running into peaks, but seldom exceeding twelve or fifteen hundred feet in elevation. Up these hills extend cultivated tracts, separated by fine, even hedgerows. Between these ridges, running from the centre of the islands to the sea, are fertile, well-watered, and highly-cultivated valleys. Across the mouths of many of the valleys, a wall extends, so that in process of time they have been raised several feet by the deposits washed down from the hillsides. In most of the valleys rice is cultivated; while some of the hills are covered with tea-plantations, others with fields of sweet potatoes, barley or yams, and those that are not susceptible of cultivation are covered with the cypress and the tallow-tree. On the more elevated plains are seen growing fruits, cotton, sugar-cane, and vegetables of various kinds. The population of the entire group is estimated at three hundred thousand, of which Chusan alone contains over two hundred thousand. Those of the natives we have met with present an uncommonly healthy, cheerful and vigorous appearance; while beggars and persons diseased, which are so numerous in China, are seldom seen here.

The harbor of Tinghai is on the southern side of Chusan

Island, and is formed by it together with five or six smaller islands. In form it is nearly circular, about three miles in diameter, surrounded by a cordon of hills, with four or five openings to the sea through which are received the refreshing sea-breezes. The town lies back some distance from the beach, on the inner side of the harbor, so that we are obliged to go on shore if we would see anything of it. I went ashore there several times: but the explorations of the first day, when I was accompanied by two or three friends, were so thorough that no subsequent visit revealed any new thing worthy of note.

We landed at the suburb of Ta Tautau, a small village where are the custom house and principal landing-place. Along the beach, in front of this suburb, extends a heavy stone wall covered with earth, and nearly grass-grown; on its summit, on rickety carriages several old pieces of ordinance are mounted. At the eastern extremity of this embankment is a high, rocky eminence, its summit crowned by a strong Chinese citadel, called Pagoda Fort, from a joss tower there located. From this fort the English received the greatest opposition at the time of their capture of the island in 1843.

The valley of Yung-tung, in which the district town of Tinghai lies, is about two and one-half miles wide, and is one of the most beautiful that I ever saw, particularly that half-mile of its length which intervenes between the town and its suburb, Ta Tautau. There everything in nature and art seems to be blended to make it beautiful. Two canals, large enough for boats, lead from the harbor to the city, and we might have gone up by water, but preferred walking over the fine stone causeway which extends from Ta Tautau to the south gate. A delightful walk of a few minutes brought us to the bridge which spans a moat, some thirty feet wide and ten deep. This moat entirely surrounds the city, with the exception of a portion of the western side, and enters it, near the South gate.

Entering the city by this gate and rambling about there a while, we at length ascended Cameronian Hill, which is crossed by the western wall. A pagoda of some pretentions is the only building upon the hill, but there are several fine groves of trees. As it appeared to us, the city is of an irregular, quadrangular form, about two-thirds of a mile in extent from north to south, and about the same from east to west. A solid wall about twenty-five feet high and fifteen wide surrounds it, and through this four gates, named respectively from the four cardinal points of the compass, open upon the surrounding country. The houses are low, built of brick, and having variously colored tiled roofs. The streets are from ten to twelve feet wide, paved with granite, with sewers underneath, but the general appearance of the town is decaying, deserted, filthy and mean. The only really fine building that I saw was a Confucian temple, the walls of which were composed of very beautiful mosaic work. The hills on the northern side of the city are covered with tombs, showing that the town is very ancient and at some time must have been very populous. Some ten or fifteen years ago, when used as a supply depot by the English, there were many European residents at Tinghai, but at present there are none; and the only European articles that I saw in all my rambles, were a few panes of glass and two Catholic portraits.

Among the more important and most interesting events of our stay at Tinghai were a number of charming picnic excursions in large junks to several of the surrounding islands, and the serving out of chickens instead of fresh beef. As I have before mentioned, in most parts of China it is almost impossible to procure beef, and here we found it quite so. As the crew had been living on salt rations for some time and no beef was to be procured, the purser decided to furnish the messes with chickens, which were both good and cheap. All agreed that the substitute was an excellent one. Those huge pot pies were beneficial as well as palatable, and not very expensive for Uncle Sam.

The principal excursions were to the sacred island of Pootoo, some fifteen or twenty miles distant, and the captain finally concluded to go there with the vessel. Accordingly Thursday, August 15th, we got under way, and, after two hour's steaming between high, mountainous islands, all in a high state of cultivation, and presenting such beautiful and picturesque scenery as is rare even in China, we dropped anchor on the southern side of the sacred island, so famous in the annals of Buddhism.

The legendary account of the island is, that a Japanese priest, in returning from a visit to the celebrated temple at Tein Tai, south of Ningpo, found his vessel unaccountably obstructed by vast quantities of water lilies and shell-fish in the water. He immediately prostrated himself before an image of the goddess Kwan-yin, and implored her protection. His vessel was at once drifted towards the shore of Pootoo. He landed and narrated his marvelous deliverance as vouchsafed by the goddess. He fixed his permanent abode on the island and consecrated a building to the goddess. This was about a thousand years ago, but the goddess Kwan-yin has ever since been honored as the patron deity of the place. The island soon became famous; large and costly temples were built; pilgrimages were made to its shrines; even the emperors were impressed with the deepest veneration, and the whole of Pootoo with portions of the neighboring islands were granted to the priests. The island itself is about five miles long, and from one to two broad.

At 5 P. M. "the word was passed" for all those who wished to go in bathing to "lay aft on the quarter deck." I with about sixty others did so, and set out for the shore in the cutters. We landed at a little pier, near which several junks were engaged in unloading rice, brought from some of the neighboring temple lands. A party of us concluded that we preferred having a ramble over the island, to going in bathing, and so we separated from the others.

Close by the landing is the How-sze, the second monastery in point of importance on the island, containing about ten temples, several of which were sadly out of repair. Still there are left many remains of former grandeur and magnificence. From the How-sze a finely flagged path, shaded on either hand by large, noble old trees somewhat resembling our elm, but covered with a flower much like that of the locust in form, color, and perfume, leads to the top of a high eminence. Besides these, here and there is a garden tastefully laid out, and the walks lined with aromatic shrubs, which together with the flowers of the China tree fill the air with a delicious and exquisite perfume. Ascending the eminence by the path, at every corner and turn, we encountered a temple or a grotto, an inscription or an image, until at last we reached the summit and seated ourselves in the pretty pavilion there located. This was open on all sides and from it an extremely beautiful prospect was spread out before us. To be seen were numerous islands, far and near, rock and precipice around and below, here and there a monastery, temple or grotto; and down before us, the finest, most interesting sight of all, a great collection of temples with their yellow tiles indicative of imperial distinction, in the loveliest of lovely little valleys. All the aid that could be collected from Nature and Chinese art had been here concentrated to render the scene enchanting.

The descent to the valley is quite steep, and there being no steps, and our shoes being very slippery, we had many an amusing, (and some not so much so,) tumble on our way down. This valley is very quiet and retired, and in all respects is one of the most beautiful spots I ever saw. As we walk along, we see fine hedgerows, separating cultivated tracts, the hedgerows themselves covered with the woodbine, and the surrounding hills covered with luxuriant shrubbery, or clothed with verdure.

We now find ourselves in the precincts of the temples, but to enter the enclosure we must pass through a small tower, covered with tiles of the imperial yellow, showing that it was a present from the emperor. Passing through this we cross a fine, arched, stone bridge with a small octagonal tower in the middle, thrown across a miniature artificial lake, covered with lotus plants of immense size. We now pass through one of the buildings, enter a large court, and before us stands the principal temple. Crossing the court, and entering the temple, or large hall, we see before us, in the elevated shrine, the three precious Buddhus—the past, the present, and the future,—gaudily gilt and painted, while ranged up and down at each end of the hall are eighteen other images—the god of war, the protectress of seamen, the goddess of wealth, &c. The three Buddhus are represented half naked, with woolly hair, and in a sitting posture; one holding the mundane egg in his lap; one adorned with the sacred thread; and one with his finger upraised, as if for the purpose of instructing mankind.

Before their altar are ranged the ornaments of worship. A large table is covered with vases filled with flowers or fruits offered to the gods; and, near the centre of the hall, are the censers in which incense is burned, and the large iron caldron for burning gilt paper. In one of the front corners of the hall is placed a huge bell covered with antique inscriptions, and in the other a huge drum or gong whose grave and sonorous sounds are mingled with those of the bell to arouse the attention of the gods when important personages come to adore him. Then there are the bamboo which holds the little bits of wood by which the purposes of fate are interrogated, and the sacred books which not even the priest understands. From the ceiling hang enormous circular lanterns, like the sides of the altars covered over with inscriptions in honor of the gods ; and on the floor in front of the altar are a few cushions and mats on which the worshipers kneel. With some slight exceptions or additions the furniture of every Buddhist temple is the same.

The priests are at their devotions. The smoke of incense rises from the huge censer, and, round in front of the altar, stand fourteen priests, erect, motionless with clasped hands and downcast eyes, a posture which with their shaven heads and flowing robes gives them the appearance of the greatest solemnity. The low and solemn tones of the slowly moving chant, might awake religious emotions, but for the hideous idols. Three priests keep time with music, one by beating on the drum, another on the bell, and the third on a hollow wooden sounding piece about the size and form of a human skull. Continuing the chant for some time, they suddenly, at a signal from a small bell in the hand of their leader, kneel upon low stools covered with straw matting, at the same time bowing low, and striking their foreheads against the stone pavement, then slowly rising they face inward towards the altar, seven facing to the right and seven to the left, and immediately resume their chant. At first they sing in a slowly moving measure, then gradually increase the rapidity of the music until they utter the words as fast as it is possible to articulate, after which they return gradually again to the slow and solemn measure with which they commenced. Again a signal from the little bell changes their movements and they march slowly in procession around the shrine while one of their number takes a cup of holy water, and pours it upon a low stone pillar at the temple door. Thus they continue their prostrations, chanting and tinklings of bells for half an hour or more. Some of the old monks appeared to be exceedingly devout, but some of the younger ones did not hesitate to joke and laugh.

This is their daily service, but beside it they have matins, morning and evening prayers. They have no Sabbaths, or periodical seasons of rest, but observe the new and full moon with particular solemnity; and keep, on the whole, one hundred and sixty-two fast days every year, beside the matins and vespers of each day. But all their chanting is only what you may see written on every corner of the temples, at every turn of the roads, on every scrap of paper, on the bells, on the gateways, on the walls, what every priest repeats while counting his rosary, answers your questions; indeed, the whole island seems to be under the spell of this talismanic phrase, and devoted to recording and re-echoing O-me-to-Fuh (i. e., Precious Buddhu.) The following extract from one of their works will serve to show to what extent they carry their vain repetitions, as the commands therein embodied may be seen carried out to the utmost.

"Swear then, that you will henceforth repeat the name of Buddhu, and seek to live in that western world of joy. Give up books and classics for others to fag at; leave the thousand roads for others to toil in. Beyond this sentence, 'O-me-to-Fuh,' you need not a single word. Let each seek a retired room, and sweep it clean; place therein an image of Buddhu; put incense and pure water, with a lighted lamp before it; whether painted on paper, or carved on wood, the figure is the same as the true Buddhu; love it as your father and mother; venerate it as your prince and ruler. Morning and evening worship before it with reverence; on going out inform it; and on returning do the same. Wherever you travel, act as in the presence of Buddhu. Whether you eat or drink, offer it up first to Buddhu. Raising the eye or moving the lips, let all be for Buddhu. Let not the rosary leave your hands, or O-me-to-Fuh depart from your mouths. Repeat it with a loud voice and with a low one; in lines of four words and six words; quickly and slowly; audibly and silently; with clasped hands and bended knees; when fingering the rosary, and when walking in the road; when in a crowd and when alone; whether at home or abroad; whether at leisure or in a bustle; whether sitting or lying; repeat it even in your dreams. Thus to repeat it will make the tears flow; thus to repeat it will inspire the celestial gods with awe, and the terrestrial demons with reverence; thus to repeat it will make heaven rejoice, and the gods be glad. At the sound of Buddhu's name the debt of gratitude to parents, princes, superiors, and benefactors, will all be paid. If you realize behind you the boiling caldron of hell, and before you the lotus pools of heaven, though all the world should try to prevent you repeating the name of Buddhu, their efforts would be entirely vain."

Besides this they have other prayers, understood by only a very few of the priests, and repeated by the great mass without a single word being intelligible to them. Yet, such an efficacy is attached to one of these, that they teach that after repeating it two hundred thousand times the intelligence of the deity begins to bud within him who repeats; when he has repeated it three hundred thousand times he may expect a personal vision of the god O-me-to. The following is a specimen:—

"Nan-mo o-me-te po-zay to-ta-küa to zay, to-te-zay-ta, o-me-le-to po-kwan, o-me-le-to, sech-tan-po-kwan, o-me-le-to, kwan-küa-lan-te, o-me-le-to, kwan-kia-lan-to, kea-me-me, kea-kea-ma-cheh-to kea-le, po-po-ho."

There are two accounts of the introduction of Buddhism into China. One is that the Emperor hearing of Christ sent embassadors to invite him to pay a visit to China. The embassadors went as far as India, and there meeting with some priests of Buddhu, whose religion was then astonishing the heathen world with its wonders, they thought that they had found the object of their embassy, and with a number of Buddhist priests returned to China.

The other is, that the Emperor sent to India, having heard that there was a religious personage in the west, of the name of Buddhu, to inquire into his doctrines, obtain his books, and bring some of his priests to China. It is certain, however, that the religion was introduced into the country about the year A. D. 66.

A prominent doctrine of the Buddhists is that the spirits of departed ancestors may inhabit the bodies of animals. Hence, the strictest kindness towards the entire brute creation is enjoined upon all true believers, and around every Buddhist temple may be seen an immense number of fat hogs and lazy dogs, who are sustained until they die of obesity, or perish by scurvy. But their kindness is confined to the brute creation and to ghosts, while they utterly neglect the miserable among men. Their bractice of providing for hungry ghosts is somewhat singular.

On the anniversary of their ancestor's death, and at the annual feast of the tombs, all persons must present offerings to the manes of their progenitors. This is done for their support, and as the food is not diminished in bulk after being feasted upon by the spirits, the Chinese imagine that they take away only the flavor; indeed, they contend that there is no more taste in that which is left than in the white of an egg. Thus, those who have left children, are well provided for, but woe to those who have died without having left any! They must wander hungry through all eternity.

They have instituted a ceremony which is usually held after the seventh moon, for the relief of those wretched ghosts who have left no posterity to provide for them. The funds for the procuring of the necessary provisions are raised by subscriptions, and on the appointed day they are placed upon a stage erected for the purpose. Upon another stage the priests stand and by means of prayers and the movement of the fingers in a peculiar way the gates of hell are opened, and then by the sound of gongs and drums the hungry ghosts are assembled to the banquet prepared for them.

In the spirit land, according to the Chinese belief, money and clothing are as necessary as in this life. Hence those who wish to benefit the dead must transmit them not only food, but money and articles of clothing. The money is represented by pieces of paper about four inches square, with a patch of tin foil or gold leaf near the middle, by burning which the real bullion is supposed to be transmitted. Miniature houses with all the necessary furniture are constructed out of paper, articles of clothing are delineated on paper, and then burnt; and thus transmitted to friends in the spirit land.

The Buddhist priests, although honored by their immediate adherents, are treated with the utmost scorn by the *literati* of China. Probably the great mass of the Chinese population profess the Buddhist faith; but these are of the lowest classes, while those in authority, and the men of learning espouse the Confucian religion, which is that of the State. As a class the Buddhist priests are indolent, subsist by begging, and do nothing towards the improvement of the world or for the benefit of posterity. Whatever may have been the case in the past, at the present day the Buddhist priesthood is in a most degraded state, and their temples in a most dilapidated condition. These circumstances would seem to indicate the speedy downfall of the system, and when this happens, a brighter day will dawn for China.

After leaving this temple we visited the smaller and inferior temples of the God of War, the God of Good Cheer, the God of Wealth, and several other less noted divinities. The temple of the goddess Kwan-yin, the patron deity of the island, was smaller than any of the others, but the interior was fitted up with much greater splendor and magnificence. The image of the goddess, although as fine as the Chinese mind could conceive and their art execute, was not attractive enough to excite the devotion of any of the party on personal grounds.

Leaving the temples and crossing over to the opposite side of the lake, I endeavored to persuade one of the priests to wade in and get me one of the lotus plants; but the only answer he made me was "O-me-to-Fuh," as he stood motionless counting his rosary. Meeting with no success in this quarter I waded in myself disregarding their forbidding looks, tones, and gestures, and procured one of the white and one of the red flowers, but not without getting a good ducking. These lotus blossoms, or "Sacred Flowers of China" as they are called, are very large, full eight inches in diameter, have four rows of leaves, with a bunch in the centre, somewhat resembling a student's cap. There are two varieties, the white and the red, and the odor is so powerful, that it is almost suffocating to walk near the bank of the lake.

From the valley we went up upon the hill to the rear of the village where is a genii's well, some thirty feet deep, cut out of the solid rock. The descent to the water is by twenty-two stone steps also cut out of the solid rock, and done, as the Chinese affirm, by the celestial gods. The waters have a sweetish but very pleasant taste and are as cold as ice water. The Chinese have a tradition concerning them which says that for every bowlfull drank by a mortal, a thousand years will be added to his life in the spirit land. If there be any virtue in them I have added greatly to my life there, for I drank several bowls-full.

It is estimated that there are more than one hundred monasteries, temples, grottos, and pavilions on the island, in which at least two thousand priests chant the praises of their gods. In fact there are no buildings on the island but sacred ones, and no inhabitants except priests and boys training for the priesthood. These are supported by the products of the island, and by the contributions of those making pilgrimages hither, or coming to worship. Like all the priests of Buddhu, they profess to renounce all family connections, take a vow of celibacy, shave their heads, dwell in temples, and abstain from animal food, liquors, and tobacco.

Descending the eminence upon which the genii's well is

located, crossing a narrow valley, ascending and descending another slight eminence and you are upon the northern side of the island, where is as fine a spot for surf-bathing as can be found anywhere in the world. To many of us surf-bathing is a novelty and at first we got roughly handled by the breakers, but the semi-daily exercise of our week's stay here has made us nearly as expert as the oldest surf-bathers.

As I said in the forepart of my letter the benefits are plainly visible in the crew, and there has not been a more pleasant period in the cruise. I have no idea how much longer we shall remain here; but hope that our next port will be Hong Kong, there to fit out for the homeward bound passage. Even for that, the crew are not anxious to bid Pootoo "good-bye," so much are they charmed by this lovely spot, and so pleasantly and swiftly do the days of our stay here pass by.

LETTER XXXVI.

U. S. S. WACHUSETT, Hong Kong. China, }
September 11, 1867. }

MY DEAR R.:

The same evening that I finished your last letter a junk arrived at Pootoo from Ningpo, bringing dispatches from the Admiral ordering us to proceed to Shanghai immediately, and as soon as we could take in the necessary coal and provisions to go to Hong Kong, and make the necessary preparations for the "Homeward Bound Passage." The wildest excitement was caused by these dispatches, and a joyous activity has since pervaded every duty.

We got under way the next morning at day-light, anchored just inside the light-ship at dark that evening; got under way at day-light the next morning, and a little after noon we were at our old anchorage at Shanghai. We found the Flag-ship there, having returned the day before from Chefoo, and heard it rumored that the Wyoming and Supply were with us to start for home as soon as possible. The Hartford left for Hong Kong Friday morning, August 23d, and that same afternoon we commenced coaling ship. By working all night we finished the next forenoon.

Saturday and Sunday the ship was fairly thronged with friends from shore, paying us their farewell visit. All seemed loth to have us leave the station, but wished a speedy and prosperous passage home. The citizens of Shanghai are having a "Homeward Bound" pennant manufactured for us, but felt disappointed that it was not finished in time for us to fly when we left there. In my last ramble on shore there, and as we got under way and started down the river Monday forenoon, bidding Shanghai "good-bye" for the last time, it seemed almost like leaving home, and parting from home friends. We have certainly spent a great many pleasant days there, formed many pleasant acquaintances, and I think that we left with the best wishes of all—of whatever nationality.

Shortly after passing Woosung the wind commenced to blow very fresh from the south-east, accompanied by squalls of rain. The pilot said that it would soon clear off, but the captain said "Mr. Pilot, you don't take me out to sea in a gale, I want you to understand," and with his customary prudence he brought the ship to anchor. The pilot's prediction proved to be correct, for it cleared off beautifully during the night, so the next morning early we got under way and started for Hong Kong. We went down by the "Inland Passage," anchoring nearly every night, and with steam and all sail set, logging eight and ten knots per hour each day; so we made the distance of eight hundred and seventy miles in six days.

At Hong Kong we found the Hartford, Ashuelot, Monocacy, Unadilla, and Aroostook. That same evening the supply arrived from Japan, and a day later the Wyoming from Shanghai. There are therefore eight U. S. war vessels now in harbor, the largest fleet of ours that has been seen in China for many years. By all it is conceded to be as fine an assemblage of war-vessels as was ever gathered in these waters—and likely to prove as *effective*. The Monocacy is double-ender like the Ashuelot, only she has a jib-boom and is square-rigged forward. The Unadilla and Aroostook are small gunboats of four or five hundred tons burthen, and built after nearly the same model as the Wachusett. They were sent out here for the express purpose of running up small rivers, and cruising about the numerous bays, islands and inlets, on the Chinese coast, after pirates.

Tuesday, September 3d, our executive officer, Lieutenant Commander John W. Phillip, was transferred on board the Hartford, and Lieutenant Commander Browar was sent from her in his stead. Some few feel rejoiced at the change, but the majority of the ship's company are sorry to lose Mr. Phillip. For all those who have endeavored to conduct themselves as *men*, he has treated as men should be treated. What higher commendation could be given of an officer than that? Still I have no fault to find with our new executive officer, for thus far, he has been just and kind in all of his dealings with the crew.

As yet little or nothing has been done in making the necessary preparations for home, but with scarcely anything to do, the crew are celebrating the prospect of soon being returned to their homes and friends near and dear, once more. This is done in true sailor style by singing, dancing, and various sports on board ship, and by debaucheries on shore. Some exceptions there are, of course, to this rule, but very few. As a general thing a sailor lives a whole cruise in the anticipation of the enjoyments which he intends to have at its end. And yet the realization gives but a few days, or a few weeks at the most, of unlimited sway to his passions and desires, and then he starts on another cruise, only to have the same thing repeated. This will continue to be the case until some plan is devised by better treatment to keep the men ever mindful of their being men, and of their duties and privileges as such.

There seems to be a general wish that we may not start for home for a week or two yet, as it is now the time of the changing of the monsoons, and consequently the "typhoon season" on the coast of China. The word typhoon, comes from the Chinese *ta-fung*, or "great wind." Typhoons are produced by the increased temperature with other causes not fully understood. They annually occasion great losses to the native and foreign shipping in the Chinese waters, and

Hongkong, China.

more than half the vessels lost on the coast, are from them. They are now understood to be whirlwinds whose fury is exhausted within a narrow tract, lying in no uniform direction other than from north to south, at a greater or less angle.

The principal phenomena indicating the approach of these hurricanes are the direction of the wind, which commences to blow softly from the north without assuaging the heat, or disturbing the calmness of the atmosphere, and the sinking of the barometer. The mercury usually commences to fall several hours before the typhoon begins, and not unfrequently is known to fall below 28°. The wind increases as it veers to the northeast, and from that point to the southeast, it blows with the greatest fury in fitful gusts.

The Chinese dread these gales, and in some parts have erected temples to the Typhoon Mother, a goddess whom they supplicate for protection against them.

Monday, September 9th, the harbor of Hong Kong was visited by the severest typhoon that has been known on the coast for ten years. Indications of its approach were given the evening before, so that all the vessels in our squadron were well prepared for it and sustained little injury. The same was true of the men-of-war of other nationalities in the harbor, but the merchant vessels did not escape so luckily and many of them were roughly handled. About a dozen were piled up together near where the English hospital-ship Malvern is at anchor, there beached on the Kowloon shore, and a great number lost masts and yards. Several small craft, among which is the American schooner Fowler, are reported sunk, and such is the fate of many junks.

The saddest case of all, however, was that of a Spanish bark which was lying at anchor near the Chinese quarter, without cargo or ballast. At 8 P. M., Sunday evening, she commenced dragging her anchor, and in about two hours she had got between the Hartford and the Wachusett, and was then dancing about in such a threatening manner, that all hands were called, in case she might bear down upon us. Before all were fairly on deck, she got foul of the Hartford's cable, and after two or three attempts she finally capsized and sank. It is thought by some that a hole was made through her bottom by the Hartford's cable. It was truly sad and sickening to hear the heartrending cries of the poor wretches on board of her. The third cutter was cleared away for lowering and a crew volunteered to go to their relief, but the captain said that it was madness to lower one of our boats and would not let them do it. We were all rejoiced the next morning to know that the Hartford's barge had picked up fifteen of the crew, yet saddened to learn that two of the crew and a little son of the captain's were drowned.

Ashore, houses were unroofed and blown down, and much damage done. It is estimated that one hundred vessels were wrecked along the coast and twenty-five hundred lives lost. Yesterday H. B. M.'s ship Pearl came into port in a deplorable condition. She was caught in the typhoon, lost all her boats and five men, threw eight guns overboard, and was so badly strained that she had to keep her pumps going constantly, night and day, to prevent her filling and sinking. This afternoon the Monocacy came in, after an absence of only three days. She too was caught in the typhoon, and lost her top-masts, smoke-stock and three of her boats. It is almost a miracle that she was not lost. How soon we may start, I am sure that I am unable to tell. Anxious as I am to see home and friends as soon as possible I do not wish to leave Hong Kong until the weather becomes more settled, and this seems to be the feeling of all.

"Homeward Bound!" How often and with what anxious longing have I looked forward to the time when I could in reality say that, and again be united to friends near and dear after so long a separation, and after experiencing so many dangers and privations. Although we have upwards of eighteen thousand miles of sea to sail over, taking at least four or five months; yet if we once get started, it will seem almost as if we had home in our grasp. God grant that we may soon start and have a speedy and prosperous passage.

LETTER XXXVII.

U. S. Flagship Hartford, Hong Kong, China,
October 9, 1867.

My Dear R.:

I can imagine your look of surprise as you read the heading of this letter, and find that I am in another vessel and still in China, instead of being on the Wachusett and "Homeward Bound." In fact no one was more surprised at the transfer than myself, for up to the day in which it was made, I had not dreamed of such a thing.

Verily we know not what a day may bring forth, for, within that short time all my hopes and expectations of soon starting for home were dashed to the ground, and now the prospect of their being realized is less than it was a year ago. Transferred just as I thought that I had home in my grasp, and then to leave a home, too,—certainly what has been more like a home than I thought it possible to find in the service! Then, still more than all this, to part with old shipmates and friends, one especially who seems almost more than brother to me, so long and close has been our friendship for more than two years, sharing each other's joys, sorrows, and confidences. In every respect it seemed like leaving home, to leave the Wachusett.

Thursday morning, September 12th, the excitement about transferring commenced, and before night one and all knew that there was to be a transfer of all those on the Wachusett and Wyoming whose time did not expire prior to January 1st, 1868, to take the place of those on the Hartford whose time did expire before that date. Of the marines, four were to be transferred from each vessel to take the place of those were to be invalided home. The question then arose, "Who is to be transferred?" I certainly did not expect to be of the number until late Friday evening, when the Sergeant told me that he had received orders to make out my accounts with those of three others. Of course I stormed and raved over it, even going to the Captain and Admiral to see if there was no possible way of avoiding the transfer; but I derived no hope from them.

Well, there was not much sleep for me, as well as for many others, that night, but when I arose the next morning, it was with the conviction that nothing was to be gained by giving way to sorrow and regret, and with the determination to make the best of what I had. Accordingly I set to work, packed up my things, and made the necessary preparations, and after signing accounts, receiving grog and ration money, I, with one hundred others, set out bag and baggage for the Hartford.

Clambering up the Hartford's side and stepping over her gangway, I found the spar-deck in genuine "Guard O" order— crowded with men and bundled up with bags, boxes and baggage, with noise, dirt, and confusion everywhere. Some of the "Guard" kindly lending me a helping hand, I soon had all my things snugly stowed away, and sat down to dinner at noon with a good appetite.

After dinner, I paid a short visit to the Wachusett to get some things which I had forgotten, and to bid those that I had left behind "good-bye." All were busily engaged in taking in stores, and were working with a *will*, as they expected soon to start for home. The following evening friend A—— came on board the Hartford to see me—paying his farewell visit. Although in some respects the occasion was sad and painful, yet I spent a very pleasant evening with him. As far as he is concerned personally, he would not under the circumstances have objected to being transferred, too. In bidding one another "good-bye" we exchanged best wishes

17

for each others prosperity, success, and happiness, and promised, if our lives and health were spared, to meet one another in the United States.

At 5 P. M., September 18th, the Wachusett was reported to be under way and all hands were sent up into the rigging to "cheer ship." As she crossed our bows the order was given for cheering; but I must confess that the Unadilla's crew of forty-three men gave a heartier, louder response than did ours of four hundred. Still it was a stirring sight to see the Wachusett slowly moving down the harbor, her "long pennant" flying, the riggings manned by those who returned three hearty cheers for those given by the different vessels as she passed them, the Bugler playing "Home, Sweet Home," "Auld Lang-Syne," etc. It was with feelings of sorrow and regret that I saw her go out, leaving me behind, but still I gave her three hearty cheers, and sent forth a fervent wish that she might have a speedy and prosperous passage home. The Wyoming left the following morning, when the same routine of "cheering ship," etc., was gone through with.

By the English mail steamer, which arrived here yesterday from Singapore, we learned that the Wachusett was thirteen days in reaching that place, and in the passage was caught in a typhoon, in which she lost boats and top-masts and sustained much other damage. The Wyoming went to Batavia, where she arrived one day later.

And now for a glance at the Hartford — my new home. She is a screw propellor of 1,900 tons burden, ship-rigged, carrying royals. She carries a battery of twenty-one guns; nine nine-inch and one one hundred pound Parrot rifle on a broadside with a thirty pound Parrot on the forecastle, besides two boat howitzers. The battery, with the almost continuous line of hatches stretching fore and aft through the middle of the deck, and the boats and booms amidships between the foremast and smoke-stack, occupy so much of the spar-deck, that although of much greater beam, there is in reality less room than there was in the Wachusett. The forecastle, too, is quite small and contains but little room underneath. The poop extends nearly to the mizzen-mast, and affords ample space underneath for the Admiral's and Captain's cabins, reception rooms, Secretary's office, pantry, printing office, closets and lockers.

The berth-deck is flush fore and aft, and is as fine a one as is often met with. The forward portion, nearly as far aft as the main-mast, is partitioned off from the rest for the "sick-bay," and is fitted up with swinging cots, and with every convenience and comfort that could reasonably be expected on board of a man-of-war. Just abaft the fore-màst is the galley and Admiral's stove. From there aft to the main-mast is the space occupied by the messes, but the sleeping billets extend through the steerage country to the ward-room bulkhead, about midway between the main and mizzen-masts. The Guard occupy about twenty yards of the after portion on the port side. Around the main-mast is a rack and row of pegs for the Guards' muskets and belts. Going aft on the port side are the Issuing, Sailmaker's and Carpenter's rooms and Engineers' steerage. On the starboard side are the Forward officers' mess room, Gunners' and Boatswain's rooms, and starboard steerage or "Gun-room," leaving between them a "steerage country," from thirty-five to forty feet wide. The ward-room is the largest and finest I ever saw, and is well furnished.

Underneath the "Bay" are the Yeoman's and Painter's rooms. Abaft them is the Fore-passage, some forty feet in length, where are the sergeant's store room, bread and sail rooms, and two armories. Extending from there to the fire-room are the fore and main holds and chain-lockers. The fire and engine rooms, coal bunkers, and sheet chain-lockers extend nearly as far aft as the ward-room bulkhead. Underneath the ward-room is the cockpit or Orlop deck, where are the spirit rooms, more sail rooms, and some seven or eight store rooms. Underneath this still are the magazines.

Such is the Hartford, as seen by me after a stay of nearly one month on board of her. Mrs. Admiral Farragut's "The dear old Hartford," and the crew's "The Pride of the Ocean," were well earned by her glorious career during the late rebellion; and on that account she ought to be, and doubtless is, dear to every true American, and the pride and glory especially of all American seamen.

My mess arrangements are somewhat better than they were on the Wachusett, for here four of us non-commissioned officers have a separate mess, with a table, camp-stools, and many conveniences. The remainder of the Guard are in two messes, each of twenty-three men. In taking the place of one who was sent home, his term having expired, I take his place, not only in duties and mess arrangements, but in the chumship of one whose friendship is certainly worth cultivating. He is an easy-natured, good-tempered, openhearted fellow, with an unmistakably merry, fun-loving disposition; a splendid yarn-spinner, and an ardent admirer of "Artemus." He never complains at any misfortune, and I never yet have seen or heard of any strait that he was in from which he did not come out successfully. I am sure that we shall get along famously together.

As there are four of us to stand watch, we have twelve hours off and much easier duty on the whole than I have been used to. There are more sentries to attend to, and the duties are somewhat different, but when I get thoroughly established, I am sure that I shall like the new duties as well as the old ones. At first I had some difficulty in finding the right man; but I had a good assistant in a prominent member of the "guard," a man of a genial countenance, a nimble tongue, an obliging disposition, and an uncertain age, who knows everything about everybody in the ship, and takes delight in posting up any one else. When I get puzzled, I go to him and soon get set to rights. The Guard has no gun to attend to, and at general quarters some are stationed in the tops to act as sharp-shooters, others over the magazines, seven to act as " color-guard," and the remainder to "fall in" at the rear of the boarders, and to be ready for such duty as may be assigned them. My station is to take charge of the " color guard."

Ten men with a non-commissioned officer are detailed every day as " quarter-deck guard," and scarcely a day passes but what they have to be paraded to receive some distinguished visitor.

We have a Chaplain on board, and have divine service every Sunday. I have attended regularly when not on watch, and so far have enjoyed the services very much. Yet, with the exception of the apprentice boys and some of the officers, but very few attend.

We have had another typhoon, and a worse one, it is said, than that of September 9th. Monday evening, September 30th, the wind commenced to blow quite fresh, accompanied by light squalls of rain. All that night, and all the following day, the gale kept steadily increasing until about 10 P. M., when it was at its height. Although the force of the wind was much greater than it was during the previous typhoon, less damage was done to the shipping in the harbor, as the preparations were more complete. However, several small vessels and boats are reported lost, and when the gale was at its height, the Supply parted her moorings, drifted over near the Kowloon shore, and only saved herself from being beached by throwing her guns overboard, with hawsers fastened to them. On shore more houses were unroofed or blown down, and much more damage done than before. The early part of October is the time laid down for the close of the typhoon season in the southern part of China, and we all hope that this may prove to be the last visitation. The English line-of-battle ship Rodney was out in the gale, and was roughly handled. She lost yards, masts, and boats; and, incredible as it may seem, the wind was so strong that it burst holes through her strong oaken sides large enough to throw a hammock through.

An American ship, the Rattler, lately arrived from San Francisco, and having a large amount of specie on board, in silver bars, was beached on the Kowloon shore. Several days were occupied in getting the specie out, and during that time a strong guard had to be kept on board of her, with loaded muskets, to prevent the thieving Chinese, who thronged the beach like hungry birds of prey, from taking possession of the vessel and murdering the crew.

The work of the crew since we have been lying here has been to get up the anchors, which were fastened to buoys at the time that the Spanish bark got foul of the cable during the first typhoon, and paint the ship and put it in the finest possible harbor trim. All agree that the appearance of the crew, the cleanliness and comfort, as well as the general appearance of the vessel have greatly improved under the executive management of Mr. Philip.

October 5th the Great Republic arrived here from San Francisco, deeply laden with California products. She brought our mails and home news up to September 3d. On her return trip she takes out a large cargo of tea and silks, with about seven hundred Chinese steerage passengers, besides about one hundred Europeans in her cabins.

Dame Rumor's to-day's edition hath the report that we leave here in a day or two for Japan. We all hope it may prove to be the case, for if we are to remain any length of time longer on the station, it will be much more pleasantly and profitably spent in Japan than in China. In the latter place we have seen nearly everything worthy of note that we would be apt to see by making a longer stay, while in Japan we have barely commenced "seeing the sights." Yes, I hope we may shortly depart for Japan.

LETTER XXXVIII.

U. S. Flagship HARTFORD, Nagasaki, Japan, }
December 2d, 1867. }

MY DEAR R.:

With Mrs. H—— and two daughters — Admiral Bell's sister and nieces — on board as passengers, we left Hong Kong Thursday, October 10th, and arrived here after a very pleasant passage of ten days. The pleasures of the passage were heightened by the fact of our having ladies on board, and never did I see more life and animation exhibited by a body of men than was displayed by our crew during those ten days. Sports of every kind were prompted and carried on, and in music, both instrumental and vocal, the Hartford's men fairly surpassed themselves.

I was surprised at the steaming qualities of the Hartford, having always understood that no dependence could be placed upon her engines; but, although the fore part of the passage was against a strong head-wind, we logged over a hundred miles each day; and then, when she got a wind so as to be able to carry sail, we easily sailed treble that distance. When we left Hong Kong, many of us expected to have a rough, disagreeable trip, but it was a remarkably pleasant one, and most of the time the ship was as steady as if at anchor. With this comfort, there is still another thing that tends greatly to reconcile me to the transfer; and that is, having here a good comfortable place to eat my meals, read, write, or study, in the warm weather, and especially when under steam. Poorer fare taken in comfort, I think, is equal to better fare taken in misery.

At the date of my last letter the weather was warm, but it is getting to be quite cool now, the thermometer standing as low as 44° above zero on some of the nights, — real wintry weather. Yes, everything betokens that winter is at hand, and we all find that overcoats and mufflers are comfortable, even in the day time. The Hartford's berth deck is quite cool in warm weather, and cold in cold weather. It is uncomfortable here without extra clothing on, and there is seldom any one een lying about the decks. But there is more of dancing, skylarking and other sports going on, beside a daily drill or exercise in something; so that the time, on the whole, passes about as pleasantly and quickly as it did when the weather was warmer. Then we are having such good nights for sleeping that there is genuine comfort in one's hammock.

The fleets of the different nations are assembling here, and about the middle of this month all expect to go to Osaca, to be there at the opening of the port, which, according to the provisions of the treaty of one year ago, is to occur January 1st, 1868. Of late rumors have been afloat that trouble is apprehended about the opening of this and one or two other ports specified in the treaty of January 1st, 1867. The rumors are based upon the strong spirit of opposition manifested by several of the leading daimios or princes of the empire; but the ministers of the several powers have received instructions to delay no longer than the time specified; and then, unless the ports are opened willingly, to open them by force of arms. A few remarks now about the government of this Empire, with its population of 30,000,000, I think might be interesting to you.

According to the Japanese mythological account of the Creation, after the world was created, it was for a long time the abode of spirits, before our first parents appeared. These gave birth to a daughter named Ten-she-o-dai-gin, from whom heir spiritual emperor or Mikado is descended. About the year 600 B. C. their authentic record begins with the accession to the Mikadoship of Gimutenon, who conquered the various tribes and founded the Japanese Empire. Such was the origin of the Mikado or spiritual emperor.

A successful military chieftain, named Yorotomo, was confirmed by the Mikado, about the close of the tenth century, as the first Tycoon or temporal emperor. Since that time Japan has had a dual form of government, with two emperors. Although the Mikado is acknowledged to be the chief ruler of the empire, his power is only nominal, while the Tycoon, in administering the civil and military affairs of the State, is in reality the emperor. Once raised to the Tycoonship, pretending to be desirous for the ease and dignity of the Mikado, he strips him of all power, by supporting him in idleness, and in furnishing him protection and the necessaries of life.

The religion and patriotism of the Japanese are closely allied, for the basis of both is found in their considering it their highest duty, while they believe in the divine origin of their Mikados, and the infallibility of their ancient records, to preserve inviolate their Mikadoship and its lineal succession. To some extent, the Buddhist faith has been grafted on; still this principle is never lost sight of, but is regarded as the basis of their religion, as well as that upon which their national existence depends.

The present dynasty, with its political condition, was founded by Gongensama, who attained the Tycoonship about two hundred and fifty years ago. There were eighteen feudal lords, or princes, who were not subdued by him, but still hold their ancient titles and estates. Besides these there are about two hundred and forty other princes, who hold greater or less sway over their own estates; but their titles, estates, and lives even are subject to the Tycoon. Not so with these eighteen, although to a certain extent, they acknowledge the authority of the Tycoon.

In the administration of the government, the Tycoon is assisted by two hereditary bodies of nobles, and two that are elective and legislative; thus in some respects resembling the Parliament of Great Britain. The aristocracy, or privileged class, of Japan is very large, and its members may be known by the long and short swords, which are thrust in the belt on the left side. Birth alone can entitle one to be a member of this class; for there is no transfer, however great may be the wealth or merit of the individual.

In my rambles on shore during our stay at Nagasaki, I have gained a tolerable insight into their penal laws and the severity of their punishments for crime. Counterfeiting is regarded as the highest offence that can be committed, and is punished by the crucifixion of the individual; arson is punished by burning at the stake, and theft and adultery by decapitation. No person is punished until he has confessed his guilt; but all investigations and trials are accompanied by tortures, and while many guilty ones doubtless escape, it is equally probable that many innocent ones confess crimes they never committed, preferring immediate death to the lingering one so frequently resulting from torture and confinement in loathsome dungeons. In respect to witnesses, the Japanese have a law, that if by one's testimony an innocent man is punished, the witness must suffer the same penalty. Private disputes, if not arranged among those interested, are usually settled by friends of the parties at their expense.

A slight sickness has prevented my going on shore as much as I otherwise should; so I have not made thorough researches into as many points in Japanese customs and manners as I would like and intend to make. The whole country, as well as everything about the people, is full of interest, and daily do I become more and more cognizant of this fact, and desire to push my researches further.

Thursday, November 21st, all were saddened by the death of Horace L. Peterson, Admiral's Secretary. For a long time he had suffered almost untold agonies from one of the worst forms of rheumatic complaint, and in his case death did seem to be a relief. All that knew him have a good word to speak in his behalf, and Admiral Bell says, "that as a man and as a Secretary, he had few equals." At 2 P. M., the following day, all hands were called to bury the dead, and the funeral service of the Episcopal Church was read by the Chaplain. The remains were taken on shore, accompanied by the Marine Guard in full uniform, and the officers of the Hartford, Supply, and Ashuelot, and were interred with military honors. Several boat-loads of English officers were in the funeral cortege, and the last tribute paid to the memory of the departed was as imposing as it was sad.

The arrival of a shipwrecked party here yesterday from the western coast of the island of Niphon, and their account of their treatment by the Japanese, leads me to say a few words regarding piracy in these waters. Piracy, so great a scourge on the Chinese coast, is unknown in Japanese waters. The severity of the law against dishonest wrecking, and the faithfulness of its execution, are well worthy of imitation by more civilized nations. Property wrecked on the most thinly inhabited or hostile coasts of the Japanese group is more sure of recovery than on the coast of New Jersey. The C—— was wrecked on the coast of one of the most hostile princes, yet the officers and crew say that they met with the greatest kindness and hospitality. The Japanese rescued them at the utmost peril to themselves. They even went so far as to put up a bathing place and an apparatus for heating water, as a daily hot bath is almost a religious duty with "*Jap*," and they could not refuse to undergo a daily evil, for fear of giving offence to their hosts. Every article, however insignificant in value, floating ashore from the broken vessel was returned to its owner. The wrecking was done under the direction of a government officer, and some insignificant articles were brought here several days after the arrival of the shipwrecked ones.

LETTER XXXIX.

U. S. FLAG-SHIP, HARTFORD,
HIOGO, JAPAN, January 20, 1868.

MY DEAR R.:

I would commence this letter with "Glory, Glory, Hallelujah," over the good news which I have to communicate concerning the satisfactory and peaceable opening of the ports of Osaca and Hiogo, January 1st, and the prospect of soon starting for home, did I not also have to narrate the melancholy fate of our Admiral, Flag-lieutenant, and ten shipmates. Certainly no period of our cruise has had more interesting, joyful, and sorrowful moments than that which has intervened since the date of my last letter to you. But to return to Nagasaki, and the narration of the events in the order of their occurrence.

We left Nagasaki, Tuesday, December 16th, and on the evening of the following Thursday dropped anchor off the exceedingly beautiful and picturesque town of Simonosaki on the northern or Niphon side of the straits of the same name at the entrance to the Inland Sea. I have seen many lovely sites, in our rambles about China and Japan, but I have never seen any whose natural beauties, and the natural beauties heightened and perfected by art, were equal to those of Simonosaki. On one knoll is to be seen a group of fine temples overshadowed by a beautiful grove of trees, on another a noble palace with its handsomely terraced gardens and grounds, in the ravine between them a collection of neat farm-houses—these with many other beautiful, and tastefully conceived features, go to form a *belle vue*, which will ever remain stamped upon my memory.

The Japanese are passionately fond of flowers, and the dwarfing of shrubs and trees is carried by them to a high state of perfection. Of the latter I saw some of the finest specimens at Simonosaki. I saw a number of perfect oaks, upward of fifty years old, that were scarcely more than six feet high, and fifteen in circumference at the point where the branches were most wide spread. I also noticed several pines, dwarfed in equal proportion, and with the additional interesting feature that the branches were trained to grow out in a nearly horizontal direction, instead of having an upward tendency as is natural. Other trees and shrubs I saw, dwarfed, and with their trunks tied in curious knots, or with their branches pruned and trained so as to represent some desired profile or character.

At Simonosaki the straits are less than a mile in width and the shores on both sides present admirable natural advantages for fortifications, which would effectually command this entrance to the Inland Sea. Simonosaki is included within the province and is the favorite residence of Prince Negato, a very wealthy and powerful Daimio, and one the most bitterly opposed to foreign intercourse. We remained there nearly two days and took in about fifty tons of miserable coal. It was brought there from a native mine near by.

When about fifty miles from Osaca, we were joined by the Iroquois, and with her anchored a few hours and had target practice with the battery. We then continued on in company, and just before dark, dropped anchor at Hioga, about seventeen miles distant from Osaco, and across the bay from it.

Hioga, a small, but quite pretty little town, situated on the northwestern side of a fine large bay at the head of Harrima Nada, the eastern section of the Inland Sea, is the seaport of Osaca. There all the shipping lay, and the foreigners will doubtless reside. On each of the projecting points of land which form the semicircular harbor, is located a small stone fortress, each mounting six or eight heavy guns. Along the western side of the harbor for about a mile, the town stretches at the foot of a range of low hills. The houses which compose it are low, mostly built of wood, and the town itself has no prominent feature worthy of special note. In front is another circular, stone fortress, the largest and finest of the three. Upon the left or eastern side of the harbor is a low, sandy tract, about a mile square, which has been set apart for foreign residents, and is now partly covered with rude buildings in the process of construction.

I hope that you had a merrier Christmas than we had. It was a cold, disagreeable day, and there was nothing to show that it was one of our most joyous holidays. Aside from this, and tending to make it a peculiarly sad and unpleasant day for all, was our consigning to his last resting place the highly educated, refined, gentlemanly, and universally beloved Dr. Page. For several months he had been confined to his room, in the last stages of consumption, and for more than a week, his life had hung by a single thread, liable to be severed at any moment. For a long time he had suffered greatly, and Death to him was a welcome visitor. He quietly breathed his last, on the morning of the 24th. His final resting place is in the midst of a small grove of pines on the left of the town, where two or three seamen had been buried before. The ceremonies, customary upon such occasions, were performed on the ship and at the grave.

During the month of December, there was everywhere about us the greatest excitement, kept up by the various rumors that were in circulation. At one time we would hear that the ports would be opened peaceably at the appointed time, and then again the report would be that the Japanese would oppose the opening by force of arms. We all knew that the Tycoon was favorably inclined to foreign intercourse, and consequently to the opening of the ports, but opposed to him were several of the most powerful Daimios.

The first of January finally came, and not the first sign of difficulty came with it; but with apparent readiness and good will the ports of Osaca and Hioga were opened to foreign trade and residence. At 8 A. M. that morning the vessels comprising the English and the French squadrons " dressed ship " with the Japanese flag at the main, and at 9 A. M. were followed by those of our squadron. From the flagstaffs of the forts, as well as from the mast-heads of the Japanese war vessels Fusiamma and La Place the Japanese colors were also floating. Exactly at meridian the Hartford fired the first gun of a national salute, which was immediately accompanied by every man-of-war in the harbor. This, with the booming of the guns of the forts, and those of the Fusiamma, (American flag at the fore answering our salute, and the La Place, English flag at the fore answering their salute,) made a sight more imposing and more impressive than the natives had ever before witnessed, and one in my experience only equaled by the ceremonies observed when the Emperor of Brazil passed through the fleets lying at anchor in Rio. In the afternoon two steamer loads of adventurers were landed and before evening there were to be seen the American, English, French, and Dutch Consul's flags flying from newly erected flag-staffs. Our nation was represented at Osaca by the Shenandoah, Commodore Goldsboro, and the booming of her eleven-inch guns could be distinctly heard across the bay, fifteen miles distant. Notwithstanding their apparent readiness to open the ports, the Japanese do not seem to entertain as kind and cordial feelings towards us as were hoped for. Thus far they have furnished us those articles which we required, with much apparent reluctance, and at almost fabulous prices. With this, everywhere and in everything it is to be noticed, that the dislike to foreigners and foreign intercourse is gaining ground daily and unless some change is soon made for the better, it will terminate in open rupture. Still we are all hopeful that our fears may prove groundless, and that our intercourse may grow more close and friendly every day.

I consider that one of the most important and interesting subjects connected with this empire, and our visits to it, is its reestablishment to foreign intercourse, after its ports have been so long hermetically sealed to the world, or at least the greater portion of it. The success of Japan in maintaining her long seclusion is difficult to understand, especially when we take into consideration the never ceasing encroachments of European nations, and their unscrupulous exercise of power in extending their commerce to every quarter of the globe. We can see that the re-opening of the country has been the inevitable result of currents of commercial progress of modern times, setting in from different quarters, and finally uniting here, after having reached China on the one hand, and California on the other. However, the Japanese are a progressive people, and but for the conservative tendency of the feudal system, would now have been much farther advanced. Probably the government of the Tycoon is the more progressive branch, but this is not liberal in the highest sense, and makes use of its absolute power to prevent any but the higher class from receiving the advantages of the higher grades of education made accessible by the opening of the country. However we have great occasions for rejoicing at the progress that has already been made, and must still, and the more earnestly strive to further on the work begun.

Early Wednesday morning, January 8th, the Shenandoah, (which had returned from Osaca, the day previous,) Iroquois and Aroostook were signalized to make the usual preparations for getting under way. About an hour later we all weighed anchor, and started for Osaca, where we arrived after about two hours sailing; anchoring about a mile from the beach. In form the harbor there is much similar to that of Hioga, being a wide semicircle, but the water is so shallow that vessels are forced to lie a long distance out from the shore. In fact, there can hardly be said to be a harbor there, inasmuch as it is exposed to all but the easterly winds, and in any but the most pleasant weather affords a very insecure anchorage. No shipping (more than one or two vessels at a time on extraordinary occasions) will ever lie there, but will lie at Hioga, which, as I have mentioned, is the port of Osaca.

Emptying into the bight of this roadstead is the Osaca river some eight or ten miles up which the town of Osaca stands. The river is about a mile wide at its mouth, and is guarded by a large stone fortress mounting twenty-five or thirty heavy guns. The city of Osaca stretches along the left bank of the river for upward of six miles. Its population is estimated at 865,000,—the second city in size in the empire, and the first in commercial importance. Several fine arched stone bridges can be seen spanning the river at short intervals, approaching, and along in front of, the city, while on either side of the stream, as far as the eye can reach, is a perfect forest of masts, belonging to the almost innumerable number of junks by which the commerce of the city is carried on. But the most important feature in the river, is the Tycoon's palace, which occupies a prominent site on a bend in the river, near the upper end of the city. This is variously estimated as being from one and one-half to three miles in circuit, and its walls are full thirty-five feet high, and twenty wide at the top. It is constructed of huge white stones, the walls having a sloping outer face. It is considered by all to be the finest and strongest fortress in this part of the world, and very few there are anywhere that can compare with it. The Osaca river takes its rise in Lake Binake, about forty miles to the northeast from its mouth. On the southern side of this lake is situated Miaco, the residence of the Mikado.

Saturday, January 11th, will ever remain a dark day in the calendar of all the Hartford's crew, for upon it transpired the most saddening event of our cruise, the drowning of Admiral Bell, Flag-Lieutenant J. H. Reed, and ten of the barge's crew while attempting to cross the bar at the mouth of the Osaca river. The three days that we had been lying there, the wind had been blowing very strong from the northward— causing the surf to run very high on the bar, and preventing us from holding communication with our minister at Osaca. Before breakfast that morning the Admiral, doubtless anxious to finish our transactions so that we could return to Hong Kong and prepare for home, went upon the poop and looked long and anxiously at the bar over which the heavy seas were breaking. For a few minutes he stood watching some junks going in with a fair wind; then turning to the quartermaster on watch, he asked him if he thought it would be safe to venture over the bar that morning in the barge, He replied that he did not think it would be safe. "Why," says the Admiral, "those junks' seem to go over well enough and why can't the barge do as well? I think that it can." To this the quartermaster replies, "Yes, sir, but those junks are entirely differently constructed boats from the barge, and are peculiarly adapted to going through the surf before a fair wind." With no further remarks the Admiral went into the cabin again, and soon after sent word to Mr. Reed to get ready to go ashore with him. About 9 A. M. he ordered his barge to be "called away." Mr. Reed then remarked to some of the officers in the wardroom "I would like to see a subscription started for a monument for us, before we go ashore," and again as he was going over the gangway he said "stand by to save us."

The ill-fated boat left the ship at about 9.30 A. M., and a pull of about ten minutes brought them to the first line of breakers on the bar. Nearly every eye in the ship was watching the progress of the boat hopefully and prayerfully; but soon after entering the breakers, the barge was plainly seen to "broach to," and shortly to capsize. A cry of horror burst forth, thrilling every one, as such a cry can do, — "The barge has capsized!" Capsized! and on such a day as this!

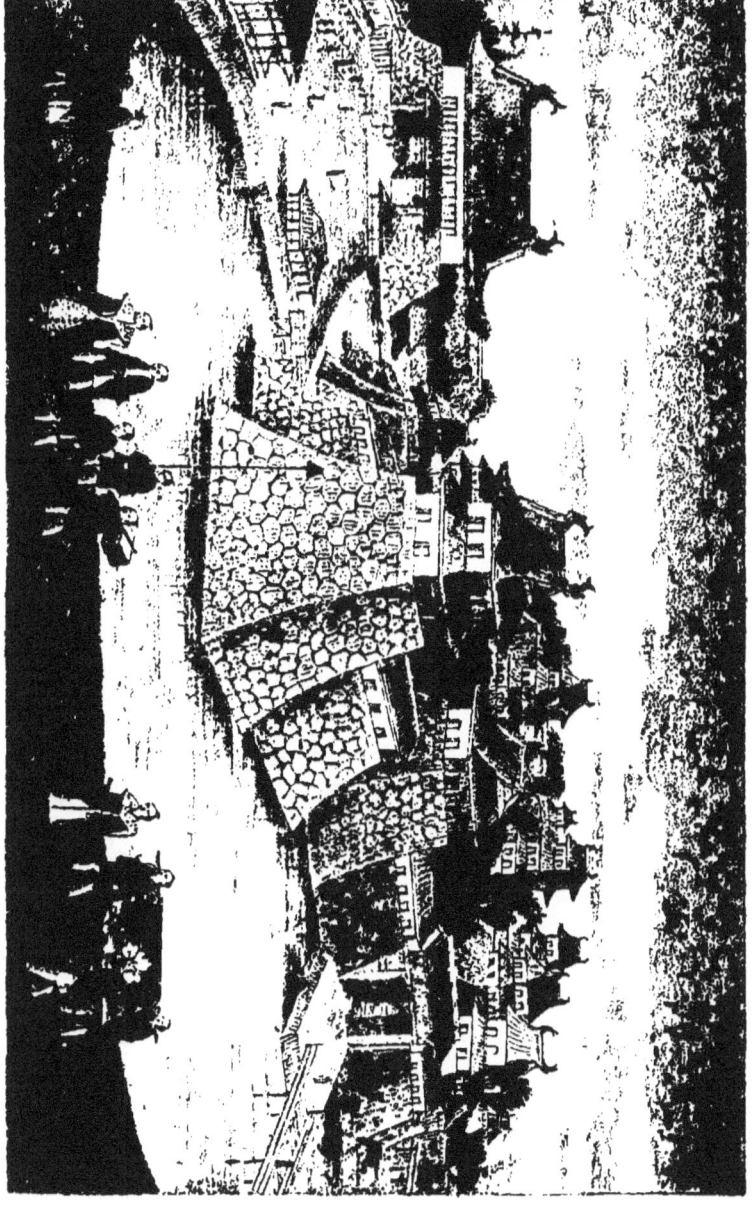

The Taicoon's Palace.

Why, a man would certainly be chilled through before assistance can be afforded him, with the thermometer standing away down below the freezing point! Surely they can never survive it;" were the thoughts if not the words of all. However, the boats were immediately lowered and manned and signals made that the barge had capsized. The fourth cutter, which had been kept manned in case there should be any accident, swamped alongside the ship, but in a moment after, the third cutter, under the charge of Lieut. Sands, gallantly pulled to the rescue. This was soon followed by the first cutter, under the charge of Lieut. Comdr. Higginson and Boatswain Long, and boats from the Shenandoah, Iroquois, and Aroostook.

Although the third cutter was only four minutes in reaching the scene of the disaster after leaving the ship, and barely ten minutes after the barge capsized, even this short time proved too long for the poor wretches in the water, and when the boats came up only three were to be seen—Patrick Deveney, clinging to the bottom of the barge; John Churo, clinging to an oar near by; and, some fifteen or twenty yards off, Samuel Van Vleet, who being unable to swim, had had the precaution to lash himself to three oars with his neck-kerchief. The first two mentioned were picked up by our boat, and the third by the Aroostook, and immediately brought off to the ship, in a very low condition. Restoratives and good care soon made them as well as ever again. When last seen, Mr. Reed was trying to assist a seaman that could not swim. He saw the boats approaching, and called out to the Admiral, then seen on the bottom of the barge, to hold out a few minutes longer, as help was coming; but both were forced to succumb to the chilling effects of the water.

At 1.30 P. M., the third cutter went in the second time, under the charge of Lieut-Comdr. Higginson and Boatswain Long, with a steering oar. They returned two hours later, bringing off the body of Admiral Bell, which was found on the beach near the fort. They immediately went in again, and this time returned with the body of Peterson, also found on the beach. The Shenandoah and Iroquois sent boats in shore to remain all night, and the next morning they returned, bringing the bodies of Flag-Lieut. Reed, Ernest, Redmond, and Nichols. At 1 P. M. that same day we got under way, and in company with the Shenandoah, returned to Higoa; and on the following day the Iroquois came over bringing the remainder of the dead bodies.

The following is the list of the drowned: Rear Admiral H. H. Bell, Flag-Lieut. J. H. Reed, Coxswain Harry Ernest; Seamen, John Peterson, Moses Redmond, Charles Baldwin, Orlop Holmburg Thomas Davis; Ordinary Seamen, Bernard Reddy, Edward Nickols, William Rickett, and John U. Small.

Thus ended our long talked of and much anticipated visit to Osaca — unpleasant and sorrowful in the extreme from beginning to end. I do not think that one of the crew will ever forget our sad sojourn there in January, 1868; and it seems to be the universal wish that we may never visit the place again. Ever since the disaster all the flags have been kept at half-mast, as also the Rear Admiral's pennant.

In Admiral Bell the country has lost one of its best and most polished representatives, the Navy one of its ablest officers, the crew of the Hartford a true friend, the circle of his friends and acquaintances one of its brightest ornaments. No one could know him but to admire and respect as well as love him, and all feel sad at his melancholy fate, peculiarly so since the sorrowful event occurred when he was about to retire from a long career of usefulness, to enjoy for the few remaining years which in the ordinary course of events might be spared him, the society and intercourse of those dear ones from whom he had so often and so long been separated. For all his friends there is left this comforting thought, that he had lived a good Christian's life and was fully prepared to die. What is our loss is his great gain.

Lieut. Comdr. Reed, although very young when he met with his untimely end, had distinguished himself in several instances, and proved himself to possess more than ordinary abilities, intrepidity, and courage.

Charles Baldwin was the only one of the old Wachusett's crew in the barge at the time it was capsized, and the only one with whom I had any extensive personal acquaintance; but so far as I have been able to learn from their messmates and acquaintances, the men lost were, without exception, good thorough seamen; and among the best and most estimated messmates, Moses Redmond's story is the saddest one of all. For the last eleven years he has been endeavoring to get home from China to the States. Eight different attempts had he made — getting shipwrecked each time. The last time, he reached Mauritius, and was there again shipwrecked. At that port he shipped on board the Wyoming when on her way out, hoping thus to get home eventually. When told that he was to be transferred on board of the Hartford, he exclaimed, "I have been trying to get home for eleven years, and I shipped on board of the Wyoming hoping to get home in her; but from the Hartford I shall be transferred to the Shenandoah, and from her to some other vessel, and — my God! it does seem as though I was doomed to die out here!" Alas, poor fellow! his forebodings have proved too true.

Our carpenter's gang, with assistants from the Shenandoah, Iroquois, and Oneida were occupied for two days and one night in making coffins for the dead; and go where you would, our ship, more than I thought it possible for a man-of-war, looked like a House of Death. The entire after portion of the berth-deck was screened off, and the barge's crew were laid out, dressed in white. The cabin too, and wardroom had their dead; and all around, above and below, scarcely anything could be seen going on but preparations for the funeral. Seldom was there a smile on any countenance, the thoughts as well as the labors being with the dead.

Never again do I wish to see, or have an occasion for seeing, such an universal mourning.

The day following the disaster, the crew were mustered, and "General Orders Nos. 1 and 2" read from Commodore J. R. Goldsboro. No. 1 spoke of the death by drowning of Rear Admiral H. H. Bell, Lieut. Comdr. J. H. Reed, and ten of the barge's crew, at Osaca. No. 2 said, that in consequence of the death of Admiral Bell, Commodore Goldsboro assumed command of the Asiatic Squadron, but that all orders of the late Admiral should continue in force. Then followed directions for the funeral.

At 9 A. M. Tuesday morning, January 14th, the marines from all the vessels in the squadron assembled in full uniform on board the Hartford, and were from her landed on shore to form, and receive the bodies when they should be landed. A 10.30 A. M. the boats began to assemble at the Hartford, and then after prayer by the Chaplain, the bodies were hoisted over the side and placed in the boats prepared for them. Precisely at 11 A. M. the boats formed in procession and started for the shore. The English joined in the ceremonies, and in the procession their boats occupied the left flank. The marines were drawn up in line on the beach, and came to a "present," and the music gave "three rolls" as each body was borne past. In the procession from the boats to the grave the marines under command of Captain Forney, with reversed arms, took the lead; next came the fine band of H. B. M.'s Ocean which had been kindly tendered for the occasion; then our Chaplain and the Chaplain of the Ocean in front of the bodies, which were borne along in the order of their rank. By the side of the bodies of Anmiral Bell and Flag-Lieut. Reed walked some of the highest officers in the American and English squadrons. By the side of the barge's crew walked the three survivors, and behind them came the sailors in two columns of four abreast, ours one the right and the English on the left, while a vast concourse of citizens and natives brought up the rear. As we were marching along thus, with no sound to be heard save the heavy tramp of the thousands and the band playing the solemn " Dead-March in Saul," the untimely fate of our beloved shipmates was so vividly presented to our minds that many an eye was moistened with tears. At the grave the usual ceremonies were performed, and the Admiral, Flag-Lieut., and ten men of the barge's crew buried, side by side. As the boats "shoved off" from the Hartford she commenced firing a salute of thirteen minute guns. As the echo of the last one died away the Shenandoah took up the burden and was followed in turn by the Iroquois and Oneida, each firing the same number, thus prolonging the salute and making it more solemn, if that were possible. Returning to the boats from the grave the band played the beautiful and appropriate air, "A Life on the Ocean Wave." At sunset, the late Admiral's pennant was saluted with thirteen guns, and then hauled down, thus completing the ceremonies of tribute to his memory and to that of the brave ones who perished with him.

A day after this, a friend and myself obtained permission to go on shore on business. We were landed at the little *hettle-bar* in front of the central fort. To transact our business was the work of but a few minutes; and then, as we had the greater portion of the day before us, we determined to provide horses and ride around to Osaca. To procure horses we found to be no easy matter: but after fruitless search of half an hour, we met our compradore who easily obtained two fine ponies for us. Mounting these, and with a truly native guide, we took the road leading from Hioga to Osaca, riding slowly so as to examine and admire the country through which we passed.

After leaving Hioga the country is gently undulating all the way to Osaca. We passed some fine groves on our way, but saw nothing extraordinary, horticulturally speaking, except some fine shrubs and plants. At points along our route we saw the farmers preparing the ground for the next crop. In this, as well as in cultivation, an instrument like a garden spade, fixed to a handle like a hoe, is almost exclusively used. A plow is rarely met with. Almost everything in Japan is planted or sown in drills, and the whole system of husbandry is more like horticulture than agriculture. The productions are nearly all those belonging to the temperate zone in other countries. Tea, cotton, and silk are the principal products that find a foreign market. Tea, for their own use, can be seen grown by all the farmers in their own yards. The tillers of the soil are held in high estimation, but are generally poor (or appear to be so,) in consequence of the enormous draft made on the product of their labor by a numerous indolent, non-producing, privileged class.

At the entrance of villages and towns, and at prominent points by the wayside I had frequently noticed bright tablets posted up, and containing several Japanese characters. Noticing one on our way to Osaca, I asked the guide what it was for. He told me that these tablets contained the inscription naming the fearful and certain punishments for any one who may profess Christianity. He further said, that about three hundred years ago, a number of Jesuit priests came to this country, and for a time were very popular, and converted many of the natives. After about fifty years of unparalelled success, they began to thirst for temporal power and to lay plans to obtain it. The Emperor, alarmed, issued a decree of expulsion, and under the stringent laws made against the profession of the Catholic faith, a most fearful persecution followed. Ever since that time it has been obligatory for everybody to subscribe himself at some Buddhist temple, at the risk of being thought a Christian, which is worse than death, as it would include the sacrifice of his family and nearest relatives as well as himself. Until the government repeals these laws our missionaries will not make many converts.

As we entered the little village about midway between Hioga and Osaca, we saw that a large crowd was collected. They set up yells and shouts as we approached, but when we charged upon them with our horses, the "small-fry" scattered in every direction; but as soon as the horses went on again, the shouts became more vigorous. It was only by the aid of a *yacumin* that they could be brought to reason. The way that he managed was simple in the extreme. A mere wave of his fan was sufficient to produce silence among more than a hundred people, many of which wore two swords. Verily, the Japanese police is perfect! A more convincing proof of their efficacy could scarcely be found.

Arriving on the outskirts of Osaca, we saw one of the most picturesque bits of architecture imaginable. In the centre of a large quadrangle rose a wooden pagoda, with dragons and other devices painted on it, and the Chinese curly roof. It was surrounded by temples and situated in a beautiful park. We went into the inn, and after lunch, we had a walk around the courtyard of the temple. This was made lively by the policemen and soldiers sitting in groups, smoking and talking. The horses were enjoying their meal and we our cigars, so we were loth to leave so quiet a scene. But the interior of the inn was equally curious; folding screens in all directions, forming rooms, in which *yacumins* were writing accounts, others eating dinner, others again smoking pipes; and servants were running about bringing such articles as were wished. The kitchen presented a wonderfully animated scene. There were charcoal fires, and boiling and frying were going on in all directions. There was a great clapping of hands to call domestics, the responding "*He!*" answering to our "Coming, Sir!" Here we were waited upon by young girls, much to the annoyance of the *yacumins*, who seemed to show themselves particularly solicitous for our morals. With the aid of the guide, we had a few minutes' very pleasant chat with them, and the damsels bowed their heads gracefully as we bade them "good-bye."

Leaving the guide with the horses at the inn, we set out for a short ramble about Osaca, the Paris of Japan. We crossed the *Iodoga-wa* or Osaca river in a native boat, and entered the northern part of the city. In many parts of the city, and especially in the southern part, we saw many fine palaces and temples. A large canal supplies the southern part of the city with water, and several small channels cut from the larger pass through the chief streets, deep enough to float small boats, which bring goods to the merchants' doors. More than a hundred bridges, many of them extraordinarily beautiful, span these channels. The city is very populous, and the Japanese boast that it can raise an army of eighty thousand men.

We both wished that we had had more time to spend in looking about the city, and especially to visit the Tycoon's palace. As it was, what little time we did spend there we had but little opportunity to see anything but the people. Everywhere that we went we were followed by an immense throng of every age and of both sexes, who viewed us with the greatest wonder and curiosity. Evidently the most of them had seen but little of Europeans if they had ever seen one, and many times we had difficulty to force our way along.

Soon after entering the city, we made the startling discovery that we had but one *tempo* — two cents — left, and that we had either lost our purses or left them on board the ship. The latter we afterwards found to have been the case. This was to us a very serious state of affairs; for without money, we could neither recross the river nor obtain our horses from the inn. For a few moments we were puzzled enough to know what was best to be done, and were upon the point of endeavoring to make a sale of some article, when B——'s ever fertile brain ushered into existence a feasable plan to extricate us from our difficulties; and shouting "Eureka!" he straightway proceeded to put it into execution. Taking the *tempo*, he went to a small stand at the side of the street, and purchased with it a *rude* flute. Several times during the cruise he had attempted to play the fife or flute, but had never succeeded in making more than a noise. But taking the flute, we proceeded up the street until we came to a small square. This was thronged with people anxious to see us. B—— now took the flute, and mounting a stone dais near the center of the square, proceeded to *make a noise*, accompanying the music by an occasional "step," which, like the music, was a decided "*brakedown.*" However, the "*Japs*" appeared to enjoy it mightily, judging by the way they laughed, shouted and cheered, — doubtless not knowing but that B—— was playing some choice American airs. My part in the programme was to "pass round the hat" occasionally, which I did; and in a very short time we had a load of *tempos* — sufficient for our wants. But the "*Japs*" were not content to allow us to stop there, but kept us performing for half an hour or more, until we, by signs, made them understand that we were tired and could perform no more. I leave you to imagine how ludicrous we appeared. Every time that I call it to mind I am nearly convulsed with laughter, as are all that have heard our story.

The "*Japs*" seemed loth to part with us; but as it was getting late, we made them understand that we must return. Having partaken of food and *saki* with them, we crossed the river, mounted our horses, and started for Hioga. Nothing worthy of note delayed us on our return, but with the horses put to a gallop, we were in about two hours at the Compradore's. Leaving the horses there, we took boat for the ship, and escaped a reprimand from the Captain for our disobedience and imprudence in going to Osaca, by narrating our day's experience.

LETTER XL.

U. S. Flag-Ship HARTFORD, Hong Kong. China, }
March 30, 1868. }

MY DEAR R.:

After the funeral we remained quietly at Hioga, until January the 21st, when the Shenandoah signalized us to get under way and proceed to Nagasaki. In less than twenty minutes afterward we were steaming down the harbor. We anchored nearly every night, and on account of a strong head wind which we had to steam against, did not reach Nagasaki until the 26th.

At Nagasaki we remained until February 1st, engaged in taking coal and supplies out of the store ship Onward, in giving liberty, and transferring. Fifty-four men were transferred to the Shenandoah in place of fifty-five men sent from her to the Hartford; and on Friday evening, January 31st, Commodore Goldsboro transferred his pennant from the Shenandoah to the Hartford.

We were just one week in the passage from Nagasaki to Hong Kong, and under sail alone most of the time. As we were leaving Nagasaki the Shenandoah and Onward "manned the riggings" and "cheered ship" for us, which compliment was returned. Loud, ringing cheers they were, and given from the bottom of our hearts. During this passage the moments, and especially the evenings, were enlivened with good "homeward-bound" songs, and it really did seem as if we were going home without further delay. When we arrived at Hong Kong, however, and received our mail and dispatches from home with the news that we might have to remain some considerable time longer on the station awaiting the arrival of our Relief, the Piscataqua, somehow the songs changed or entirely ceased.

From February 8th until March 4th, we were engaged in taking in coal and provisions and "fitting ship" for home, the labors being interspersed with several grants of money and plenty of liberty; so that, although longing for the period of our departure, the time passed quite pleasantly and quickly, Two interesting features in China life came under my notice in my rambles on shore, and I must tell you about them. One was revealed by a visit to some gambling houses with an acquaintance, and the other is what is known as "The Feast of Lanterns."

Since I have been in China I have witnessed many different modes of gambling, and the Chinese seem to be perfect slaves to the vice under one form or another; but this time we met with a species entirely new to us. It is, however, the one most general and the favorite one with the Chinese. By them it is called *Fanton,* or "Game of Fours." Crowding through a throng of Chinamen around a large table at one extremity of a spacious hall, we watched the game for a few minutes and soon gained an insight into its mysteries. Near the centre of the table is a metal plate, some six or eight inches square, the sides of which are numbered one, two, three, four, — No. 1 being toward the teller. Between this plate and the teller is a large pile of checks, about the size and form of "*cash,*" and numbering some ten or twelve hundred. An unknown number of the checks are separated from the pile and instantly covered. Now is the time to make bets; and in doing so, a person may bet on any one of the four sides, or on two or three of them, and lays the money down on the side or sides chosen. When all the bets are made, the cover is removed from the pile of "cash," and the teller proceeds to draw them in with a long needle, four at a time. Whatever number remains the corresponding numbered side of the plate wins, and whoever has bet on that side receives his money back, and in addition three times that amount, minus fifteen per cent., which goes to the bank. All those that have bet on other sides lose and their stakes go to the bank. About a year ago the English licensed those gambling houses that are situated within their jurisdiction, and by so doing *have brought* them into more general notice; and now they are becoming a favorite resort for Europeans as well as Chinese.

While speaking about these establishments, I will narrate an adventure which two of us had during our visit to Whampoa. One pleasant afternoon while we were lying there. S——, who by the way is one of the most noted gamblers I ever knew, and the most passionately fond of gambling came to me and asked if I did not wish to go up to Canton with him that afternoon. I had intended to have gone up the day previous, but a headache prevented me; and wishing very much to visit the city again, and not caring to go alone, I thankfully accepted his invitation. We employed one of the many boats which thronged the ship's side, and with both wind and tide favorable, in less than an hour and a half we were ascending the steps of the little pier in front of the "Tactorris." We spent an hour or so in examining the many wonderful and attractive articles of ivory, tortoise-shell, sandal-wood, and lacquer displayed in the "shops" along Curiosity street, and making a few purchases, we then entered the city through a gate near the head of the street, and walked along some two or three miles without seeing anything unusual to attract our attention. Finally S—— proposed entering the gambling house near where we then were, saying that he "must play a little,"—something that he had not done for two whole days! Not caring to go about the city alone, and being desirous to understand better a game which is now of so much interest to all visiting China, I went in with him and watched the play. While the Chinese would almost invariably stake their money on the last winning number, S—— would bet on the same number every time, mak-

ing each successive bet double the preceding one, until his
"number" should win; then he would begin low again —
usually making his first stake ten cents. Under ordinary
circumstances his number would win once in four times, and
by the doubling process, he would continually gain. All of
his playing that day was an unbroken series of successes; and
we both became so much interested in the game, — he in
playing, and I in looking on, — that we "took no note of
time," until finally the "bank" closed, and we found to our
dismay that it was nearly midnight. It certainly was anything but pleasant to be conscious that we were in the heart
of a hostile city alone at midnight, with a large sum of
money — something over two thousand dollars — about us,
and this known to about one hundred greedy, avaricious, evil-looking, unscrupulous Chinamen with which the gambling
house was thronged. We would willingly have given all of
the ill-gotten gains then to have been safely on board of the
Hartford. However, we each of us had a revolver, and, determining to do the best we could, we took good care to display them, taking them from our belts and recapping them in
their presence, all the time taking care to appear happy and
unconcerned.

With the money done up in handkerchiefs and these carried in our left hands, with our right we grasped our revolvers and started. The streets of Chinese cities are not lighted
in the night time, nor are persons allowed to be out in the
street after about ten o'clock. After this hour the streets are
barricaded by wooden barriers placed across them at intervals
of about a third of a mile. At each one of these five or six
soldiers are stationed. Although there was some slight show
of opposition on the part of these guards, yet we passed the
first five barriers without anything worthy of note taking
place — a full moon enabling us to see our way almost as
well as if it had been daylight. We had no difficulty in finding the way, our previous knowledge of the same trades being

confined to the same street aiding us, and we noticed that when we went up we passed only clothing and shoe stores. In passing through the dark alley-way which connects the two streets lined with these stores, about twenty of our acquaintances met at the gambling house, armed with knives, rushed out from a recess and attacked us. We immediately cocked our revolvers and fired upon them, taking care to hit them in the legs. Their *courage* about this time suddenly evaporated, and they scattered in all directions, leaving their wounded — four in number. We did not stop to examine them, but pressed on as fast as our legs would carry us, until we reached the gate. This we found to be closed and guarded by about twenty-five soldiers. They had heard our shots, and were not disposed to open the gates for us; but we presented our cocked revolvers and intimated that we would fire if they were not opened forthwith. They doubtless saw that we were in earnest, and not caring to contend against us with their bows and arrows and rude *jingals*, they reluctantly allowed us to depart. But we took good care to keep under shelter of the buildings until we were at a safe distance from the gate, fearful lest they might fire upon us. It may seem strange to you to think that we could have such an affray in the midst of so large a city, and then get away without accident; but then you must remember that the Chinese are the most veritable cowards, (or, in the words of "Old Sam," "Chinaman's heart allee same cow: too much fear; makee lun away;") also that no one is allowed in the streets at night time; and so common are noises and disturbances in the night that even the noise of our firing aroused no one. Arriving at the river's edge, we endeavored to hire a boatman to take us down to the ship, offering him the fabulous fare of five dollars. But he refused, and we finally were compelled to resort to our revolvers and *compel* him. We did not go directly on board but landed at New Town, and sent the boatman back. As soon as he was out of sight we took another boat and went on board. We did this to avoid being mixed up in any disturbance, of which we did not fear the result, but only the possible delay. However, we never heard anything further from it. Not all the money in Canton could induce me to run the same risks the second time, nor do I desire to ever enter a gambling house again.

"The Feast of Lanterns" takes place on the last of the New Year's holidays, and varies in different years from the middle to the latter part of the month of February. This year it occurred on the 13th. It was shortly after sunset that I explored the various streets and public places of resort, amid a continual discharge of fireworks, the frequent assemblages of play actors, the noise of gaming tables, the universal signs of feasting in the families, and a profuse display of lanterns of every imaginable pattern and design. Some were made of glass, others of glue, and some of paper, in the shape of birds, beasts, fishes, and dragons, all so arranged as to be carried around by a current of rarified air, and thus represent different kinds of animals and junks in motion. In all the principal temples, and in the houses of the wealthy, were to be seen huge candles, some of which measured more than two feet in circumference. Bands of pipers, with sounds of gongs and cymbals, were to be heard in all directions. The principal table in each temple was covered with huge cakes made in the form of a tortoise—the sacred symbol of Buddhist mythology. Some of the fireworks, especially the larger pieces, were finely executed and very curious and interesting in design.

At all the principal temples during the New Year's holidays theatrical performances and other sports are kept up by the wealthy, partly for the benefit of the poorer class and partly for their own spiritual advancement. During this season the temples themselves are beautifully decorated and brilliantly illuminated, and not unfrequently the sports are kept up for two or three weeks after the " Feast of Lanterns."

Thursday, March 5th, we got under way, and in company with the Unadilla, went up to Whampoa. There we remained six days while the Commodore and several of the officers and crew paid a visit to Canton in the Unadilla, and during which time my visit and adventure occurred. Meanwhile the crew had almost semi-daily exercise with the sails, battery, or small-arms — fully as much as if we were just in commission. It does seem as if the officers considered doubly precious the short time that remains to them to hold authority, and were more than ever loth to lose any opportunity for displaying their powers. Day after day we exercised for hours at a time, with no profit to us and with no apparent object or result save the gratification of this official longing for the exercise of authority.

Among the purchases that I made at Canton were two or three Chinese books. To a "Western" these are quite a novelty in more respects than one. Before attempting a description I will say a few words about printing. While this art was known to the civilized world in the fifteenth century, it was known to the Chinese more than nine hundred years ago; but, on the other hand, while Europeans have made rapid advances since the discovery of the art, the Chinese seem to have stopped at the invention; for as yet they have no movable type. All their printing is done by cutting the characters for each work, page by page, by hand, on blocks of wood, and the impressions are taken without aid from machinery. It is quite interesting and not a little amusing to see them print and manufacture books. First the engravers mark out the page upon blocks of wood, and then by means of their tools cut away the superfluous wood from the characters. A good engraver will get through with about one hundred characters in a day, for which he receives ten or twelve cents.

The block is now ready for the printer, who places it upon a table or stand, with a pot of ink and a brush upon one side, a pile of blank paper on the other side, and a rubber in front. After inking the block, he takes a sheet of the paper, places it smoothly upon the block, passes the rubber over it once or twice, and the impression is produced, the sheet removed, and another placed upon the block. In this manner a workman will throw off from three to four thousand impressions in a day. The whole apparatus of a printer are his gravers, blocks, and brushes, and with these he may travel from place to place, purchasing ink and paper whenever it is required. The paper is cheap, there being but one cent's worth in a book of eighty pages that I purchased, and the whole cost being but three cents. However, the paper is so thin that it is printed only on one side. Their books are wonderfully cheap, as may be seen from the price of the one that I have mentioned; and one of their most popular works, containing fifteen hundred leaves, may be purchased for half a dollar. This is accounted for in part from the fact that very few new works are published, and there is not much variety. But reading is within the reach of all; and it is maintained by good authorities that there are more books in China and more people to read them than in any other part of the world. Eighty leaves constitute a volume, which always has thin paper covers, and has the number of page and title on the side instead of the top of the page. Their most noted works are those of Confucius and his disciples — the "five classics and four books." These are all about the size of the New Testament; but if every book of this kind was destroyed, there are *more than one million people in China who could repeat it word for word!* They have several other works, one of which I have seen translated into English, and it is certainly a very readable book.

They are enabled to labor for very low wages on account of the small amount that is required to procure the necessaries of life. The diet of the common people is generally a little rice, salted fish, or vegetables and tea. As such, a laboring man can, in many parts of the empire, maintain life on from one to two cents per day. This diet is sometimes varied by a little pulse or millet, or occasionally a few ounces of pork is stewed in with the vegetables. The common food of the poor people in some localities is sweet-potatoes or yams, rice, and the universal bowl of tea. Occasionally a pork meal may be had, and on great occasions a little poultry. I have mentioned in a previous letter the horror which they have to the use of beef. Instead of beef and mutton they have resource to the flesh of dogs and cats, whose flesh is equal in price to that of swine; or in default of this to the most disgusting vermin.

The evening after we returned to Hong Kong from Whampoa I was invited to a tea-party at the house of a noted Hong Kong Chinese tea merchant. Shanghai and Foochow are the most noted ports in China for shipping tea, but still there are some large tea merchants at Hong Kong and other places along the coast. Our host told us that there were more than one hundred and twenty millions pounds of tea exported from China in a single year, and that full twenty times as much was used by the Chinese themselves.

The guests numbered twelve in all, half of which were English gentlemen. One that is unacquainted can hardly form any idea of the elaborateness of a Chinese tea-drinking. All of the Chinese gentlemen present, as well as the host, were arrayed in their best apparel, and we were met by the latter with the blandest smiles and the most cordial and courteous greetings. We were almost immediately led to the dining-room where refreshments had been prepared for us, consisting of some delicate cakes, fruits, hot wine and tea. For the latter a cup for each one was placed on the table with a dish of tea in the centre. This was passed to each one, and hot water poured by servants, so that each one enjoyed the privilege of making his own tea. In the numerous bowings that precede the drinking one has to be very careful lest he may violate a rule of decorum and spill his tea; and on this account the cups are but half filled. The Chinese drink the beverage in short, quick sips, taking care to empty the cups and set them down at the same time. The tea is always taken very warm, and as the weather was quite warm upon this particular evening, the perspiration started very freely. It is a breach of etiquette to notice this; but in order that no one may be unnecessarily uncomfortable, the host immediately says, "I invite you to take your fans." As we were so unfortunate as to be without any, the others desisted from the use of theirs out of compliment to us. After the refreshments we were all treated to the Chinese luxury of having our faces bathed with napkins, dipped in hot water. After this ceremony upward of half an hour was passed in conversation, the principal feature in which were the compliments passed. In these each one appeared to be zealous in debasing the first person and elevating the second, all of which were made known to us by an interpreter. Finally the highest in rank among the guests arose and said, " We have been troublesome to you a very long time," and immediately took leave of us. His example was followed by all, in the order of their rank.

It was all enjoyed by me only as an interesting feature of Chinese life, and in itself was almost torture from beginning to end. It seemed strange enough with our " Western ideas " of tea-drinkings, thus to attend one ungraced by the presence of ladies. With its almost solemn formalities, the poetic effusions so aptly descriptive of ours, could in no sense be termed appropriate in China; —

> "How they chitter, chatter,
> O'er a cup o' scalding water,
> O'er this one's death or that one's marriage;
> Of A's new dress, or B's new carriage."

This is probably the last letter I shall send you from China; but before I bid China " good-bye," I must say something regarding its history, size, population, etc. However, as my letter is already quite lengthy, I shall be as concise as possible.

In commencing with the early history of China, it might be well to correct the error into which many have fallen in regard to the faulty and extravagant chronology of the Chinese. Many suppose that they maintain such antiquity as to be at variance with the Bible and such records of the foundation and duration of the human race as we have been wont to consider as authentic; so that if we believe the one the other must be disbelieved. This is explained by the fact that they have a mythological as well as a chronological period, the former of which relates to their gods, extends through myriads of ages, and even by themselves is considered fabulous. In this they speak of their celestial emperor, who reigned forty-five thousand years; of their terrestrial emperor, who reigned eighteen thousand years, followed by their human emperor, who reigned as long; without condescending to enlighten us as to the names, characters, events or circumstances of these wonderful individuals, or their still more extraordinary reigns; nay, without so much as telling us whether their dominions were established in heaven or earth, or whether they referred exclusively to China or included other nations. In short, the vague account they furnish us of these fancied emperors shows that they were merely the figment of the imagination, introduced to supply a deficiency and to amuse the credulous.

After these, come portions of history which are based upon indistinct traditions of the creation and the flood. It is probable that immediately after the dispersion of the great human family, the founders of the Chinese race wandered off to the far East and settled down somewhere on the banks of the Yellow River. Their most noted historian, Foo-choo-tsze, commences at about this period, entirely passing over the mythological period as not worthy of note. This historian places the foundation of the empire at one hundred and four years after the flood, when Yu began to reign, and is the first real character made mention of. During his reign the lands were drained, and wine discovered. When Yu tasted the wine he is said to have rejected it, and remarked, " This wine is sweet, but at some future time it will occasion the ruin of the country."

Since that period China has been shaken by many revolutions, subjected to foreign invasion and internal commotions, dynasties have changed, and even now China is subjected to the Tartar yoke; yet China is China still. Her language and customs remain unaltered through all. Those who are accustomed to attach veneration to antiquity cannot fail to do so when they consider the patriarchal character of the Chinese, as it existed not centuries but milleniums ago; and the modern kingdoms of Europe are but as yesterday in comparison.

Upon tracing Chinese history one finds four distinct dynasties previous to the Christian era. The first I have already spoken of, and in the second nothing worthy of special note occurred more than the continuance of the work begun by Yu — the founder of the empire. In the third dynasty their great philosopher, Confucius, was born. He laid the foundation of the Chinese literature, and the history of his own time is as much depended upon as the recitals of Greek and Roman historians. The fourth dynasty commenced about 250 B. C., and was called *Tsin*, from which the modern name of China is derived. The ruler of Tsin conceived the insane idea of establishing a dynasty which should extend from the beginning to the end of time. To accomplish this, he collected and burned all the records of previous ages that he could obtain possession of, and buried alive all the wise men of the country, thinking thus to obliterate all remembrance of antiquity, or but that he was the first universal emperor of China. Fortunately, however, his plans were frustrated by the discovery of the works of Confucius in the wainscot of an old house.

Doubtless you have studied geography and are quite familiar with the location of every prominent country in the world; so as you refer to the atlas of your memory with your mind's eye, you will see China bounded on the south and east by the China Sea and Pacific Ocean; on the west, by Thibet and the Desert; and on the north, by the Great Wall. At the first settlement of the Chinese in their patriarchal regions on the banks of the Yellow River, the lands were divided into nine shares, the eight outer allotments of which were cultivated by eight separate husbandmen, while the middle one was wrought by the whole for the service of the state. As the population increased they extended their boundaries, until in the time of Tsin, they occupied all their present limits between the Great Wall and the Yangtse Kiang river —all south of this river not being added for several ages.

Thus far China had extended her boundaries by conquering; but all subsequent extension was by being conquered. The Tartars, after gaining possession of the country, instead of altering its institutions and maxims, conformed themselves to the laws and customs already existing, and were in fact subdued by the Chinese.

In addition to China Proper, which with its eighteen rich and fertile provinces (each of them equal in extent and population to some European kingdoms,) covers an area of one million three hundred thousand square miles, it is swelled by the annexation of Chinese Tartary, a thinly peopled but outstretched region extending from the Sea of Ochotsk, on the east, to Bukaria, on the west, and from the Altai and Nenshink mountains, on the north, to the Great Wall, on the south, and covering an area of over three million square miles. The Chinese empire occupies no inconsiderable space on our map, and fills up nearly the whole of their own. No wonder then that they should consider their country as the

"Middle Kingdom," and speak of their empire and the world as synonymous terms.

Probably nothing relative to China has been the subject of more controversy or is more interesting to the politician than the question of its population. It is stated that the country, already over-populated, is doubling its population every twenty-five years, and that in time she will press her enterprising, though not warlike, teeming myriads upon neighboring countries. Now let us examine this question closely and see what conclusion we may arrive at. The latest census gives China Proper (by far the most thickly peopled portion of the empire) a population of three hundred and sixty-six millions to her area of one million three hundred thousand square miles, an estimate which no one who has paid any attention to the subject will deny. But allowing that there are so many people in China, it leaves over two and one-fifth acres for the support of each individual (though competent judges maintain that one acre will support five persons;) so for a long time there is no danger of surrounding nations apprehending that their welfare or their peace will be disturbed by the influx of a mass of shrewd and hungry invaders driven out from their own country for want of subsistence. In comparing China with other countries, we find that it is not more thickly peopled than some other regions, and even less than some; for while Belgium has nearly three hundred and fifty persons to every square mile China Proper has less than three hundred, and the whole empire less than one hundred.

Still China has an immense population, and every means has to be employed to economize the soil. This is very fertile, and probably there is no country in the world as extensively cultivated as China, or to as good advantage. From a late estimate it appears that more than three-fourths of the surface is owned and tilled by man, and the greater portion of this is laid out in arable land. The principal animal food is pork, which is home-fed, and on this account there are no grazing farms, no meadows, and but once in all my rambles about China have I seen cattle grazing in a pasture; and almost every acre is turned up by the spade or plough to afford sustenance for its teeming inhabitants. With the Chinese the art of agriculture is carried to a very high state of perfection, as may be seen by the rotation of crops, the cultivation of products best adapted to the seasons and soil, and the use of fertilizers. The skill of the husbandman may be seen in the irrigation of his rice fields, and they may be considered adepts in the system of terrace cultivation.

The past week has been spent by the crew in taking in coal and sea-stores and in making all the necessary preparations for the "Homeward Bound Passage;" and this, Dame Rumor says, will begin to-morrow. This afternoon the citizens of Hong Kong presented us a Commodore's pennant, eighteen feet long, and a Captain's pennant, two hundred and twelve feet long. This evening the crew are very enthusiastic and very happy over the prospect of so soon bidding these shores "good-bye." Every face wears a smile, and every thought and action seems to centre on the conviction that

"We are homeward-bound!"

LETTER XLI.

U. S. FLAGSHIP HARTFORD, Singapore, East Indies,
April 26, 1868.

MY DEAR R.:

With the deepest pleasure I resume my pen to write you my Homeward-bound letter No. 2, this time feeling sure that "We are Homeward Bound" in good earnest. The month, nearly, that we have been delayed here at Singapore while awaiting the arrival of our relief, the Piscataqua, has been anxiously and impatiently passed, and all feel rejoiced that our waiting is now at an end.

Saturday, March 21st, was as beautiful and bright a day as could be desired on which to start for home; and those that interpret or put confidence in signs and omens, augur from this that our passage will be a pleasant and prosperous one. At 8 A. M. we "broke the stops" of the Homeward Bound Pennants, unmoored ship, and got up our anchor before dinner. During the entire forenoon the ship was fairly thronged with people making their farewell visit to the Hartford. At noon all hands shifted into white clothes. Old Sam completely unloaded his boat in presents to all; and after bidding every one in the ship "good-bye," he was "piped over the side," ten petty officers taking the place of "side boys." At 2 P. M. the "word was passed" for all visitors to leave the ship, and a few minutes later we heard the long looked for and anxiously awaited word, "All hands up anchor for home!" It would have done your heart good could you but have stepped on board the old Hartford at that moment and seen the excitement that prevailed there The crew really seemed like so many wild men in their actions than anything else, and the way the anchor came up, to the tune of "Homeward Bound," beat anything I ever saw, while cheer after cheer rent the air. In less than ten minutes we were under way, everybody was sent up into the rigging, and a salute fired. This was answered by the battery on shore, H. B. M.'s Rodney and the U. S. S. Ashuelot. As we slowly steamed down the harbor, cheers were given for the port and those given us by the different vessels. And what cheers they were, too! Four hundred were cheering with a will — such cheers as' make one's pulse beat faster, and crowd a little lifetime into a minute! As we passed the different flag-ships, their bands struck up "Hail Columbia," and we gave them in return a "tiger." During the cheering the air was darkened with the caps and old shoes thrown overboard, — for luck I suppose, — and if there is any virtue in so doing, we ought to have a remarkably pleasant and prosperous passage. Then from each royal mast truck a game cock was thrown, crowing as it went, and one of them alighted on board the Rodney. Old Sam, the bum boatman, Atee, the compradore, and several other Chinamen that we have extensively employed since we have been on the station, kept up from their boats a continual racket of fireworks and crackers and burning of joss sticks and papers, so long as we were within sight or hearing. On the whole it was a very exciting time and by all will long be remembered with pleasure. The Aroostook and Unadilla accompanied us until we were at the Ly-mun Pass, and then started for the northward, giving and receiving three hearty cheers before parting company. The last seen of them, they were racing, the Unadilla ahead.

We steered easterly all that night and the next morning altered our course to the southward, which course we kept with some slight variations until we reached Singapore, March 31st. This passage was an exceedingly pleasant one; for aside from the good spirits of all, the wind, though light, was favorable, the sea smooth as glass, and the ship most of the time as steady as a house. We sighted points of land almost daily, among which were the islands of Banca, Pennang, Timour, and Ara. Sunday, March 27th, we passed a small island in 80° N. lat., situated about thirty miles from the main land, and called Pulo Zapato, from the native Pulo, signifying "island," and the Spanish Zapato, signifying "shoe," from the fancied resemblance of the island to a shoe whose toe points towards the north. Viewed from the forecastle a few hours after passing it, when the heel only could be seen, it bore a striking resemblance to some enormous castle rising out of the sea. The next evening we sighted the light-house at the entrance of Singapore Straits, thirty miles distant from the city, and "lay to" over night. The next morning after taking on board a Malay pilot, we started up the straits, which are dotted on either hand with large and small islands, exceedingly picturesque in appearance and in a high state of cultivation. About noon that day we dropped anchor about two miles out from the town.

The city of Singapore is situated on the southern side of the island of the same name, which lies a short distance off from the southern extremity of the Malay Peninsula. Any one who will look at its geographical position and its relations to the commerce between the East and West, passing through the Straits of Sunda and Malacca, will not greatly wonder how a thriving city of eighty thousand inhabitants has been planted in the jungle in so short a time. Although the papers record that in the surrounding thickets of Singapore island the tigers destroy an average of one person daily, we found its harbor floating the models of all nations, from great, lumbering, red-painted, goggle eyed Chinese junks, to the beautiful clipper of the States; and among the flags of Europe and America we saw the white elephant banner of Siam and the gaudy-hued flags of other eastern nations.

We had barely anchored when the ship's sides were fairly

thronged with boats, bringing compradores, washermen, peddlers, etc. There were a few Chinese *sampans*, but a majority of the boats were narrow, sharp, flat-bottomed things, roofed over the middle with matting, and rowed by three or four natives. The natives are for the most part Mahometans, with a few Malays and Chinese.

The Mahometans, or Mussulmen, have the entire head shaved and covered with close-fitting, many-colored straw or rush plaited caps, or crimson or white turbans. White or red striped petticoats or sarongs fall from the waists of some, and a few wear bright colored jackets, but many are encumbered with no more clothing than is needed to satisfy the demands of decency. These are the only faces new to us met at Singapore. Our compradore we find to be a more important personage than those we have been accustomed to having. He is an uncommonly fine looking, intelligent, Mahometan, and named Mahomet. All of his boatmen, with the exception of a single Chinaman, are also Mahometans. The Chinaman is employed to handle swine's flesh or anything appertaining to it, the Mahometans having a religious horror of so doing. We were not a little amused a few days ago at a trick played upon one of the Mahometan boatmen by one of our crew. He placed a piece of pork in a jar among some other articles, and then when a boatman was bringing it over the gangway, showed the pork to him. With a look and cry of horror and disgust, the jar was dashed down and broken into a hundred pieces, while all its contents rolled into the water.

When I was upon the forecastle a few days ago, conversing with an acquaintance who has been in business at Singapore for a great many years, among other things I spoke of the islands in sight from our anchorage. He told me that the Alabama used to lay behind them and get her mails, provisions, coals, and whatever she wished, and at the same time the U. S. S. Iroquois would be lying at anchor in the harbor.

If by chance the Iroquois should learn of her whereabouts and start out in pursuit, by the time she could get around there, the Alabama would be behind some other island far away. Ofttimes a false telegram would come to the Iroquois, stating that the Alabama had been seen committing depradations off Hong Kong, Calcutta, or some other distant place, when of course she would immediately start off in pursuit. All this time the Alabama would be lying concealed behind one of the islands, and as soon as the Iroquois was gone, she would slip in, take in a load of coal, and be off before her enemy returned. All this could be easily carried on, as nearly all the foreigners resident at Singapore are English, and all were rebel sympathizers.

We have been in few places where a ride or ramble on shore would develop more of interest and pleasure than Singapore affords. I have been on shore almost daily, and have always enjoyed myself very much. The usual landing is at a stone pier near the mouth of a small stream which separates the foreign quarter, with its stylish residences, fine gardens, charming drives, and pleasant promenades, from the long, narrow, close-crowded, opium-smoking, toddy and bang-drinking streets of the pounding, blowing, sewing, stitching filing, laboring Chinamen. The river is crossed at several points by bridges, and the streets which run along its banks are lumbered up with the products of the East, and with buffalo carts and laborers carrying the various articles to the neighboring shops and store-houses. Rising above all, to the height of five hundred feet, is the foliage-covered "government hill" with the British ensign flying before the buildings which crown its summit. From this hill is to be had a charming view of the town, harbor, and nutmeg groves of the surrounding country.

As you go up from the landing, you see ranged along in front of you several sagacious looking little ponies, harnessed to the *palki-garis* or "palanquin-carriages," low, square, close vehicles, with a front and back seat, and with an attendant driver and interpreter. Up in front is a seat for the driver and other attendant. No one thinks of walking through the dusty streets of Singapore, under the rays of the hot, burning sun, when one of these establishments can be had for a long drive for a shilling. Nothing can be more pleasant and interesting than to take one of these carriages and drive out among the palatial residences situate in beautiful and extensive gardens in the suburbs, or among the nutmeg groves of the surrounding country. If the ride is taken in the latter part of the day one will meet the wealth, beauty, and fashion of Singapore in elegant turnouts, enjoying a drive in the cool of the day.

Quite an excitement was recently occasioned by a lorcha which was endeavoring to leave the harbor. When about a mile distant, the English Corvette Persius fired a shot to bring her to, but without paying any attention to it, the lorcha kept on. Seeing this, the Persius commenced firing at her in good earnest, and also sent an armed boat in pursuit. As the wind was blowing up the bay, and the lorcha compelled to beat her way out, we all thought she would be easily captured. But she would have made her escape, defying the shots of the Persius and the armed boat, had she not been "brought to" by the powder hulk down the harbor. Dame Rumor first informed us that it was a pirate endeavoring to make his escape, and after that, a smuggler; but the last edition with the correct statement showed that it was neither pirate nor smuggler. It seems that a Chinese servant of the captain of the Persius, having stolen a large sum of money, a revolver, and several other valuable articles from him, and having got possession of the lorcha by a forged order, hired a Malay crew, and boldly set sail for China. H undertaking proved a failure; but he displayed more pluck and daring than is usually credited to the Chinese. He is now confined on board the Persius awaiting a trial.

Although we have had but little drill since we have been lying here, we have had several days of "humbugging" and "petticoat ruling" with a vengeance. Our present captain was formerly executive officer of the Shenandoah, and succeeded Captain Shufeldt in command of the Hartford. When on his way out, he became acquainted with, and married the daughter of Mr. Prescott, U. S. Consul at Ceylon. While we were in China she resided at Hong Kong, but when we started for home the Captain obtained permission for her to take passage to the States in the Hartford. Although much inconvenience was occasioned by her presence, and some new rules were laid down, no murmurs were heard until the "humbugging" commenced in this port.

When we first came in, Mrs. B. went ashore to board during our stay. A few days afterwards she came on board accompanied by a lady friend, and nothing would do but that "George" must exercise the crew at general quarters for their amusement. He, a perfect slave to her every wish, thought it nothing if four hundred men were made to run about, haul, and over-exert themselves in every way for two or three hours, in the hot, burning sun, so long as *she* was *pleased;* and then the four hundred victims, with no word of thanks or commendation, only received for their exertions a subsequent damning and had their privileges taken away for not doing better! But to return; the men were given but half an hour for breakfast and smoking, and then set to work making preparations for the *grand* performance. The exercise of four hundred men for the gratification of an idle, thoughtless wish was bad enough; but we were further kept for over an hour with everything in readiness, and all "standing by," prepared to jump at the first tap of the drum, waiting for the spirit to move our visitors, and the *murmurs* began to grow loud and deep. At last the chairs were taken from the cabin to the poop, and the visitors escorted there. The "quick beat," "cast loose and provide," then "All ready for Action," is reported to them, and the performance commenced. All that was ever done at general quarters before, and some things never previously heard of, were gone through with, and the particularly interesting movements several times repeated before they said " enough " and the " retreat " sounded. Then came batalion drill for half an hour or more; and it was dinner time when they thanked " George " for his pleasant entertainment and withdrew to the cabin. Dinner time, but no dinner — and it was late when we did get it, and then but half cooked!

But the end was not yet. After dinner there was an accession to the party of four gentlemen who wished to be "tickled," too. So we "manned and armed all the boats" for them, and kept supper waiting for more than an hour' until they could find it convenient to look at the berth deck.

Exhibitions similar to those I have mentioned have been repeated several times since we have been in Singapore, and the crew made to exercise when no benefit resulted, but rather detriment was done to the service. Aside from this, these many repetitions have a tendency to lessen if not entirely destroy that high regard, worship almost, which is so natural for a sailor to entertain for woman. When Mrs. B. came on board at Hong Kong, all were prepared to like her in advance, and she certainly is quite pleasing and attractive at first sight; but more intimate acquaintance has weakened and almost entirely destroyed the good opinion of all. Yet I would not attribute to her more than the sin of thoughtlessness, for I cannot believe but that, had she fully understood and realized all, she would have sought amusement from some other source. The Captain knew better, and occupying his high position, he should never have suffered this thing to have been done. Nor would it have required, in my opinion, more than an honest statement of the true facts to have had all requests for such displays withdrawn. How many more such days we will have I can only conjecture, yet I can but feel thankful that the cruise is fast drawing to its close, and that the greater portion of it has been passed under different circumstances.

The cause of our extended stay at Singapore was the non-arrival of our relief, the Piscataqua. Of course all were impatient at the long delay, but there was no help for it — we were obliged to wait. So many times had we been deceived by rumors of her speedy arrival, that when an American steamer was announced from the signal-station as being off the mouth of the harbor, day before yesterday morning, no one would venture to say that it was our long looked for relief. But just after we had assembled at quarters, the coming steamer displayed some signals which were soon made out to be the Piscataqua's numbers. Retreat was immediately sounded, the guns run out and loaded for a salute, and for a time the wildest excitement prevailed, officers and crew alike cheering, shouting, shaking hands, and on the whole acting like so many happy school boys.

When the Piscataqua was about two miles distant from us, we fired a salute of thirteen guns for Admiral Rowan, which she returned with eleven guns for Commodore Goldsboro. The Persius then saluted Admiral Rowan with thirteen guns, which were returned gun for gun. As the Piscataqua came up and rounded our stern, she dipped her Admiral's pennant; cheers were given and returned, her band struck up "Home, Sweet Home," and then, crossing our bow, she came to anchor just outside us. The barge was immediately called away, and Commodore Goldsboro went on board the new-comer to pay his respects to Admiral Rowan, and turn over the command of the Asiatic Squadron to him. The Piscataqua, therefore, and not the Hartford, is now the "Flag Ship of the Asiatic Squadron." We shall probably remain here two or three days longer until the several departments have turned over their respective commands; and next Thursday, April 23d, is the day fixed upon when, in good earnest, we are to start upon our "Homeward Bound Passage."

Although there has been much tending to make our month's stay at Singapore a long and unpleasant one, there has also been much to make the stay pleasant, — certainly much more so than we at first anticipated. There has been a great amount of excitement, and much to be seen that was novel and interesting; and last, but far from being least, we have all had an abundance of the most delicious fruits that the world produces. Fruits of almost every kind common to a tropical clime can be had in any quantity by simply going on shore after them; but all prefer to buy them of the boatmen who bring them alongside at prices so low that it does not seem as if they could make fair day's wages. It is low to say that one thousand pineapples have been consumed by the crew every day during our stay here, besides an immense number of oranges, cocoa-nuts, bananas, and other fruits.

But in a few days we leave all these, and soon our relations with the Asiatic Squadron will be ended. Many, no doubt, will still continue to wander about strange and foreign shores, but still there are some, who with me, remember with pride that we are citizens of a country whose grandest influences are found at home, in the ways of peace and humanity, and to which we return and cling with strengthened affection.

LETTER XLII.

U. S. S. HARTFORD, Cape Town, South Africa,
June 19, 1868.

MY DEAR R.:

Nearly two months have passed away since the date of my last letter, and here we are no more than half way home. We had hoped to be nearing the States by this time, but He who controls the wind and the waves has seen fit to order it otherwise. We murmur over the light and baffling winds that so far have characterized our passage; but no good results from so doing, and all are made more uncomfortable and depressed in spirits.

Thursday morning, April 23d, I was awakened just in time to get on deck to participate in the parting cheers with the vessels in Singapore harbor, when much the same ceremonies were observed as characterized our departure from Hong Kong. As passengers we had on board, besides Mrs. Belknap, two little sons of Rev. Dr. Dean of Singapore, who were going home to the States to be educated.

Pleasantly but slowly steaming down the Rhio and Banca Straits, Sunday night we passed into the Java Sea, and the following afternoon sighted Anjer Point, a long, narrow point of land which extends out in a northwesterly direction from the island of Java, with high mountains rising behind it. About dark we dropped anchor there, a mile from the shore.

Anjer Point lies in Lat 6° 03' S., Long. 105° 56' E., and is well known to all those interested in maritime affairs. For the world-wide notoriety which it has attained, it is a small, insignificant place. Only three or four mean looking houses are to be seen, with the Dutch flag floating over them. The country around is exceedingly wild and picturesque, covere with forests and a luxuriant foliage. Along the beach are large groves of fruit trees, and in full view from our anchorage was one of the noted banyan trees, which is said to cover more than an acre of ground. We stopped for coal; but when the Paymaster went on shore the following morning, he found that none was to be had without first sending to Batavia and getting permission from the Governor, which would detain us three days at least. The Commodore decided not to wait; so after taking on board a quantity of fowls and fruits, and making some additions to our already large number of monkeys and other pets, we set sail from Anjer that same day.

For three or four days we pursued a southerly course, hoping to get fair winds. On the evening of May 6th a musk-cat fell overboard, and the old sailors predicted and prepared themselves for a "blow." Sure enough, we did have a blow, which came upon us without a moment's warning. The "light sails" were soon taken in and the topsails reefed. A squall of a few minutes, and then the wind settled down into a good, steady breeze, so that we stopped the engines, triced up the propeller, and proceeded under sail alone. But the wind was not long steady, and soon we had another squall, worse than the first. Through some carelessness or mismanagement of the man at the helm, the ship was laid in the trough of the sea, and then commenced some of her *antics*. She rolled and pitched about terribly, throwing hen-coops, ditty-boxes, and other loose articles into glorious confusion on the spar-deck, and mess-chests, kettles, and other utensils on the berth-deck. To make matters worse, she at the same time took in a heavy sea over the entire length of the weather side, completely flooding both decks. To the more fortunate it was amusing to see the various articles washing backward and forward about the decks, and to witness the almost frantic attempts of some poor unfortunate to recover treasures which had got adrift. That morning we were content with a pint of half made coffee and a cracker or two for breakfast, because it was more than we for a time expected.

We had three or four such unpleasant days at different times; but the passage on the whole was an exceedingly quiet and pleasant one, although the wind was so light that we could not make as rapid progress as all desired. The Hartford displayed her sailing qualities in overhauling and passing a great number of vessels — fast tea-clippers and all. Not a single vessel did we encounter that showed sailing powers equal to those of our good craft. Yes! it certainly was a very pleasant passage; and as the weather was mild and comfortable most of the time, there was but little work to be done. Drills were suspended, and all had abundant opportunities to prepare their "homeward bound" suits, spin yarns, and talk over and plan about home matters.

Early June 1st, we sighted land which later in the day we found to be a point on the coast of Southern Africa, called Hole-in-the-Wall. This is so called because there is a large hole in the rocky ridge of hills which line the coast. It is a bleak and barren point, but possesses an unusual amount of wild and romantic scenery. There are many curious formations beside the one that I have noticed, some of them bearing a striking resemblance to familiar objects. Among the most noteworthy of these are the profile of a lion and a fort of gigantic proportions. Four high peaks towered above the others, so that the inclosed apex seemed the magazine; the precipitous, angular sides frowned destruction at every point, like bastions; an immense ravine formed the fossé, or moat, and the sloping glacis down to the plain was equally well represented.

As we altered our course from the westward to the southward, and sailed along the eastern coast side, nothing could be seen but barren rocks; or, as a French voyager says, "It appears as if just having suffered from the effects of great fires. The naked rocks, that are heaped in disorder one over the other, and cut off and rent by fantastic fracture, rise from the bottom of the sea and mount to the clouds." It is not thus, however, by the best accounts, in the valleys and along the hillocks of the interior, where abundant moisture sustains vegetation, and the tropical plants display their rich fruits beneath an eternal verdure. In these places, I have been informed, there are some of the finest and most productive tracts in the world.

After we left Hole-in-the-Wall, we were a week in reaching Simon's Town. There we were gladdened by news from home, and the usual ceremonies of an arrival in port were performed. No change worthy of note had been made since we were there two and a half years ago. We remained there a week, and then, not being able to procure what coal and provisions we wished, came around here. The first intention was to transport the necessary supplies over land to Simon's Town, as it is dangerous lying here at this season of the year. Of the insecurity of Table Bay for shipping I informed you at our previous visit. The breakwater which I then mentioned as being constructed has been extended out about half a mile, and the chain gang are still kept at work upon it. The earth used in its construction is all taken from the space between the breakwater and the town, where is to be made an Inner Harbor, large enough to accommodate forty or fifty vessels. We are lying behind the breakwater, and although we have had one day of windy, unpleasant weather, we were not in the least affected by it, and continued taking in coal all day. Most of the time, however, since we have been here, the weather has been remarkably calm and pleasant.

We finished taking in coal and provisions to-day, and to-morrow we leave here for St. Helena. All are lively and merry this eve and anxious for the morning, praying for good, fair breezes to favor us and speedily bear us to our loved ones at home.

LETTER XLIII.

U. S. S. HARTFORD, St. Helena,
July 7, 1868.

MY DEAR R.:

With everything on board that we required, Saturday noon, we again heard the welcome words, "All hands up anchor for home." With alacrity every one took his position at the "bars," and when the order was given to "heave away," all seemed to be striving to vie with the fife in liveliness. Since leaving Hong Kong, every successive occasion for weighing anchor has been attended with increased animation. There has been no need for any one to hunt up the "skulkers" and drive them to their stations, but upon the first signal all promptly respond, and work with a will, anxious to be nearer and nearer to those loved ones from whom we have been so long separated.

We have on board as passengers, in addition to those we had before, Judge Pringle, — U. S. Commissioner to Africa to investigate the slave trade and aid in its suppression, — a deserter, and a destitute seaman.

After the customary salutes had been fired and we had "cheered ship," we moved slowly out of the harbor, with the long pennant flying and all hoping for fair and favorable winds for the remainder of our "homeward bound passage." And yet there was a feeling of regret experienced by many, as they stood upon the forecastle and felt that they were beholding for the last time Good Hope, with all its peaks and promontories, and the charming little city of Cape Town, with its picturesque surroundings. The view was certainly beautiful in the extreme and one long to be remembered.

19*

The wind favored our passage from Cape Town throughout; and along with steady strong breezes, we had charming weather, a smooth sea, and all hands in the best of spirits. Every day there was an exercise of some kind — sometimes two or three exercises; but there was always time and inclination for sports in the evening. With the work and sports, the two weeks occupied in making the passage, flew by very pleasantly and quickly.

At daylight on the morning of the "Fourth," St. Helena was sighted — then some seventy or eighty miles distant. As we approached, it appeared like a huge rock — as it is in reality — rising out of the sea. As we then viewed it, there was little or nothing offered to the eye but an assemblage of lofty and barren hills, intersected in all directions by deep and narrow valleys, in many places little better than ravines, and generally devoid of vegetation, except here and there patches of prickly pear and profitless weeds. The shores on all sides are lined with almost perpendicular cliffs running down to the sea, and frequently rising to a height of more than five hundred feet. A mere glance shows St. Helena to be volcanic, belonging most probably to the secondary period. The island cannot fail to be of considerable interest from its solitary position in the South Atlantic, as well as from its marked and peculiar character. Well was the spot chosen, not only for the safe keeping of Napoleon, but also for soon wearing out a man with such an active and soaring mind as his, in this dreary and rocky prison.

Sailing along close under the eastern side of the island and rounding Sugarloaf Summit, we dropped anchor on the northern, and leeward, side, about two miles distant from Jamestown. This is the principal collection of houses on the island, and lies at the foot of a gently-sloping valley, which runs down to the sea from the interior, and which is the only one in sight from the sea that has any signs of vegetation. It is narrow and winding, extends back about one and one-half miles from the beach, and is bordered on either hand by perpendicular walls of rock, more than six hundred feet high. The beach along in front of the town affords the only good spot for landing on the whole island, and is strongly fortified by a fine stone battery, extending along its entire length, two or three batteries perched upon the eminences to the eastward, and the fine fort on Ladder Hill, which overlooks the town.

Ladder Hill takes its name from the ladder, or flight of steps, six hundred and sixty-two in number, by which its summit is reached from the town. Upon the eminence back of the fort are the ruins of the "Alarm-house," near which are located the Artillery barracks.

Immediately after anchoring we "saluted the port" — English ensign at the main — which was answered by the fort. Then when we had received visits from the health officer and one or two other officials, several bumboat-men and washerwomen, we "dressed ship"; and as a compliment to us, the few vessels in the harbor did the same. The afternoon, as usual, was given to the crew, and was celebrated by them in the customary manner. At sunset a salute of twenty-one guns was fired, both by the Hartford and the fort.

Many of us were hoping to be able to obtain permission to go on shore; but upon the first application, the Commodore gave orders that no one except officers was to leave the ship.

Yesterday, however, I was sent on shore on duty, and then obtained permission to spend the day as I chose. I landed at the little pier at the eastern end of the broad walk which extends along the beach in front of the battery. Between these there is a wide, deep moat, in which the ditches — dug along the base of the hill on either side of the town — discharge the waters which run down their sides during a rain storm. By this moat the water is carried to the sea.

After having passed along the greater portion of the walk,

I crossed over the moat, passed through the gate in the battery wall, and stood in the square on the inner side. Upon either hand were barrack buildings and guard-rooms, before which sentries were pacing to and fro. Farther on, and bordering on the Square, there were, on the right hand, two or three hotels; on the left, a mansion and grounds, and at the head, a church.

In the first place, while waiting for a friend, I decided upon ascending Ladder Hill. The hill is only six hundred feet above the level of the sea, but the Ladder is more than seven hundred feet in length. For the first fourth of the ascent, I experienced little or no fatigue; the second, I began to feel tired; the third, I had to rest every few steps; and by the time I reached the top, I was completely exhausted. The satisfaction of having performed the feat, and the splendid view that I had of the town and harbor, more than repaid me for my exertion and fatigue. As I was about to visit the fort, I saw my friend approaching the shore, and made haste to descend and join him.

After leaving the Square, we went up a small, narrow street, lined on either hand with stores — the business quarter of the town. We branched off from this street, passed through the market, and came to a small square, on two sides of which were "stables." Our officers were before us and had selected the best of the horses, so we were forced to be content with two as "sorry nags" as man ever rode. For the use of them we were compelled to pay in advance fifteen shillings, which was in reality four times what the beasts were worth. I do not doubt but that the owners would have thought they had made a satisfactory bargain if we had killed or made away with the horses, and they had never received any compensation more than the sum we paid for a day's use of them.

Leaving the town, we took the road to the westward, and at a brisk canter started to ascend the hill. As we advanced the harbor, town, and valley were spread out before us, forming one of the most picturesque and charming panoramic views that it was ever my good fortune to behold.

About a mile above the town, we came to "The Briars," a beautiful spot and intimately connected with the Emperor Napoleon during the earlier part of his captivity. It was here he resided while Longwood House was being prepared for his reception. The property is now owned by Messrs. Solomon & Moss, the wealthiest ship chandlery firm in Jamestown. Hitherto our road had been bordered with barren rocks, with no other vegetation than a few creepers and a species of cactus. The principal varieties of rocks met with on the island are soft Limestone and what is called the blue-gray Lava Stone. The hardest and best qualities of Lime Stone are found nearest to the water's edge; and in practice, it is said that it will yield lime rich enough to bear being mixed with an equal quantity of sand, measure for measure. The Lava Stone is very abundant, and is the most durable rock found on the island for building purposes. It is nearly as hard as granite and of considerable density, although "honeycombed," like most lavas. It is often traversed by dark veins of exceedingly hard, flint-like stone, which is very difficult to work and ruinous to chisels not well tempered.

I said that the "Briars" was a beautiful spot. We had not thought it possible that such a charming place existed or could exist on such a barren island,—a huge rock it appeared to us in approaching it from the sea. The house is quite a plain two-story building; but the grounds,—comprising some twenty or thirty acres, situated in a lovely little valley,—are very finely laid out and adorned. They are surrounded on three sides by a chain of mountains, five or six hundred feet high, their sides almost perpendicular, and ragged with huge calcined boulders, which look almost as if they had been at no remote period vomited from the fiery mouth of some volcano. These mountain sides are rendered exceedingly picturesque and charming by the luxuriantly growing Scarlet Geranium, and the large quantity of furze and scrambling brambles; while their beauties are farther enhanced by a pretty little cascade, which comes leaping down behind the house.

Just beyond this point our road took a sharp turn to the left, and then after a few steps, to the right, in which direction it continued for about one-fourth of a mile, between rows of willows. These are said to thrive exceedingly well, and aside from being valuable for firewood, are now quite ornamental and pleasing to the eye, being covered with their yellow catkins. At the end of this walk stands the half-way house, called "Willow Cottage," from the fine grove of willows in the midst of which it is situated. Here we stopped and partook of some refreshments — "cakes and beer."

From the cottage to the "Alarm House," the road, still ascending, has for its shade-trees a species of Ebony and Redwood, while scattered here and there, may be seen a few specimens of the Cabbage-tree. This is not a remarkably graceful tree, the odd bunches of leaves and flowers at the head of its branches looking at a little distance not unlike a cabbage, whence probably its name. With the exception of Diana's Peak, the hill on which Alarm House is situated is the highest point of land on the island. The former is 2,70 feet high, and from it a fine view of the whole island may be obtained.

Leaving Alarm House and ascending gradually, we soon came in sight of the "Devil's Punch Bowl," a circular ravine, sloping towards the northward, near the head of which is the Tomb of the Emperor Napoleon. Passing through the gateway on our left, and descending by a bridle-path, a few minutes' ride brought us to the outer enclosure of the Tomb Near the entrance is a little house, against the outside of which hangs a board bearing a request that "All visitors will dismount, uncover their heads, and behave with respect and reverence in entering the inclosure."

At the gate we were met by the French Sergeant in charge of the Tomb, who showed us about and gave us such information as we desired. The space enclosed by the outer fence is about half an acre in extent, and is surrounded by a fine wooden fence, five rails high. Within the inclosure are ten cypresses, and overshadowing the Tomb is the largest and finest weeping willow that I ever saw. Near the upper side is a spring of water, the stones around the sides of which were placed by Napoleon's own hands.

Near the centre of the enclosure is the Tomb surrounded by an iron fence, about twelve feet in length on each of its four sides. The plain marble slab which covers the grave is nearly concealed by geraniums — the only plants there growing. This spot was a favorite resort of Napoleon, and it was at his request that he was buried here. He was brought to the island October 9, 1815; died May 5, 1821; and his remains were removed October 9, 1840.

On the upper side of the inclosure is a small cottage where resides the Sergeant and his wife, and close by this is another building, used as a sort of sitting-room for visitors. We went up to the latter and registered our names in a book kept there for that purpose, and which, when filled, is sent to Paris. This done, we purchased some views from the Sergeant, picked a few leaves from the geraniums around the Tomb, and took our departure.

Returning to the road, we continued on towards "Old Longwood House." After proceeding about a mile we came to Hutt's Gate, where is located a small Chapel and a house where refreshments can be procured. From thence to Old Longwood House the distance is about a mile, over nearly a level road. On the right hand this road is bordered by a plain which stretches away a mile or more, while on the left are the heads of two deep, picturesque ravines, both of them

terminated by rocky bluffs, three or four hundred feet high. As we rode along the edge of these bluffs or precipices, and looked down into the giddy depths below, our heads swam, and my companion had some difficulty in keeping his saddle. I then felt that —
"It is a fearful thing
To stand upon the beetling verge, and see
Where storm and lightning from that huge gray wall
Have tumbled down vast blocks, and at the base
Dash'd them in fragments, and to lay thine ear
Over the dizzy depths, and hear the sound
Of winds, that struggle with the woods below,
Come up like ocean murmurs."

The better to enjoy the sublime view, we rode slowly, so that it was nearly noon when we arrived at Old Longwood House. Two little boys took our horses, and through a small gate we entered the grounds. These comprise about two acres, laid out as they were by Napoleon — the same shrubs and plants growing, and the same kind of vegetables and flowers being cultivated in the garden.

The house stands near the centre of the grounds, and is a range of one-story buildings in the form of a cross. Entering by the front door, or foot of the cross, we stood in the reception room. We passed through this, and entered the most interesting room of all. It is called "Napoleon's room," and is the one in which he breathed his last. In the spot where the bed stood is now a marble bust of the Emperor, surrounded by an iron railing. The "cast" was taken after his death, but the bust is certainly a very fine and interesting piece of sculpture. Beyond this room is the dining-room, which, with a stairway, occupies the middle of the cross. In the right wing are a bed-room, library, and bath-room, and in the left wing are two or three spare apartments. In the head of the cross are the kitchen, pantry and store rooms. None of the rooms are now furnished. The wall-paper was removed a few years ago, and new put on of the same color and figure as the old. As at the Tomb, everything at Old Longwood House is under the constant supervision of a Sergeant in charge. Here also the name of every visitor is registered, and the book of names, when filled, is sent to Paris.

A few rods to the northward is Longwood New House. This was built by the British Government for the Emperor's accommodation, but was never occupied by him. It is a very fine looking building and contains fifty rooms. The grounds are extensive and very tastefully laid out and adorned. We wanted to make a visit there, but as it was late in the afternoon, thought best to return to Jamestown.

In returning, my companion was thrown from his horse striking within two feet of the edge of the precipice near Hutt's Gate, and only by grasping a willow bush saved himself from being dashed on the rocks, two hundred feet below. At Hutt's Gate we were met by a lady who had some ferns, mosses, sprigs of cypress, flowers, and sample grains produced on the island, fastened on the leaves of pamphlets, and which she offered for sale. Some of these, with the views, were the only desirable curiosities we procured or saw.

The extreme length of St. Helena is ten and one-half miles; extreme breadth, six and three-fourths miles; circumference, twenty-nine miles; superficies, thirty thousand and three hundred acres. Diana's Peak is the highest point of land on the island, and has an elevation of twenty-seven hundred feet. The population is estimated at six thousand, exclusive of the Garrison. The inhabitants are a mixture of every shade, color, and nationality, and the theory of miscegenation can be seen put into practice to its fullest extent.

Well, I have been ashore at St. Helena, and I am now ready to start for home at any moment, and wish for no further delay or stoppage anywhere. There has been a fine and favorable breeze blowing ever since we have been lying here, and it does seem almost too bad that it had not carried us on — nearer to home and friends; but we expect to leave this evening, and hope that the same breezes may befriend us.

LETTER XLIV.

NEW YORK, August 15, 1868.

MY DEAR R:

Home again! and now I sit down to finish the account of our voyage home, and the putting of the Hartford out of commission. I left you in my last letter at St. Helena, uncertain as to what we would do. However, notwithstanding the "well-authenticated" report that we were to "move nearer in shore" and give general-liberty there, the following day saw us take our departure from St. Helena. The order given there was, "All hands up anchor for the United States!" Willing were all at the "bars" there, and it did not require the fife's enlivening numbers to aid in

"The groaning capstan's turning 'round,"

for all were desirous to devote their entire energy to doing anything and everything that should shorten the time and space between us and the loved ones there. As soon as the anchor was up, the sails were loosed and filled by that fair and strong breeze which had been blowing for several days, and which lasted us close up to the Line. Then, as the breeze was too light to waft us on with the desired speed, we let down the propeller, steamed two days, and were again blessed with a strong and favorable breeze, which we held almost up to Sandy Hook.

Every spare moment of this passage was employed by all in perfecting ourselves in our various duties, and in putting the ship in the most attractive trim for visit and inspection. In the evenings, when the labors of the day were over, here and there about the decks might be seen knots of "congenial ones," talking over home matters and speculating upon them.

As our thoughts would dwell upon those loved ones there, from whom we had been separated for so long a time, we could speak of but little else, and none seemed to tire of planning and conjecturing, as well as wishing for the manner and circumstances of their meeting with those friends. While the most of us have had our fondest hopes and desires realized, there are some of our number that have had them all dashed to the ground. Yet we could not reasonably expect that it would be otherwise; but still we may extend to them our most heartfelt sympathy and trust that in His own good time and way the cup of sorrow may be changed for one of happiness, better for having undergone their present trials and sorrows.

Thursday, August 6, 1868, will long be remembered by us all as being one of the brightest days of our lives; for it was then, after an absence of forty-one months, we were permitted once more to behold the shores and people of our own country, and once again grasp by the hand and exchange greetings with friends near and dear. Then our hearts all echoed the sentiment expressed in C.'s favorite song:

"I have roamed over mountains, and crossed over flood,
   I have traversed the wave-rolling strand;
Though the fields were as green, and the moonshine as bright,
   It was not, no, it was not my own native land.

Then here's to Columbia, the land that we love,
   Where flourishes Liberty's tree;
'T is the birth-place of freedom, my own native land,
   ''T is, yes, it is the land of the free."

How different from those we had forty-one months ago, as we steamed down Boston Harbor, bidding country and friends "good-bye," not knowing as we should ever behold them again, were our emotions as we sighted the Highlands of Neversink that morning, passed Sandy Hook and the vessels lying there that forenoon, and slowly steamed up the Bay, and at noon dropped anchor off the Battery. Pen hath not power to express the joy that we felt, as we beheld old, familiar home-sights once more, and realized that we were really

"Home again, from a foreign shore."

As soon as we had anchored, the ship's sides were thronged with would-be visitors — friends and relatives of those on board. No permission, however, was granted to any one to come on that day, but the whole crew were employed in completing the preparations for the final inspection. Many were disposed to murmur at this order, but the more sensible ones saw the wisdom and fitness of it; for, upon the inspection's being a satisfactory one, depended our more speedy release from the ship, as well as honor and praise for all. This the order would further, and soon we all saw it thus, and choked down all rebellious feelings and eager desires, so far as we were able, longing, however, for that time soon to come.

Nor were we compelled to wait a long time; for the following day we were visited by the Commandant of Brooklyn Navy Yard and the other members of the Board of Inspection. I will not weary you with the details, and will only say, that the Board was highly gratified with the appearance of everything about the ship, and with the various exercises of the crew; so that, after an inspection of more than four hours, the Commanding Officer complimented us by saying that we "excelled in every particular any ship or crew ever before inspected by him."

After the inspection, we remained at our anchorage off the Battery until the 10th. During the intervening two days, the ship was fairly thronged with visitors — many to behold and speak with their friends and relatives once more after the long separation, and not a few desirous of seeing the vessel which by its career in the late war had won the merited title of "The Pride of the Ocean." " What a magnificent ship!" exclaimed one and another of a boat load of visitors in whose company I returned to the ship from shore one day, " How majestic and graceful!" (and those who spoke were no ordinary land-crabs;) and all felt that she was a beautiful object to look upon. From her immense but symmetrical form rose her gallant-masts, and throughout her rigging, her tapering spars, and delicate blocks, each part seemed to lend and gain a charm from every other; and, as Jack Fid said of the Rover, when he stowed into his cheek a lump that resembled a wad laid by a gun-slide, "I care not who knows it, but whether done by honest men or done by knaves, one might be at Spithead a month, and not see hamper so light, and so handy as is seen aboard that flyer. Her lower rigging is harpened in like the waist of Nell Dale, after she has had a fresh pull upon her stay-lanyards, and there isn't a block among them all that seems bigger in its place than do the eyes of the girl in her own good-looking countenance." We all have good reason for being proud of our ship, and therefore may be pardoned for mentioning anything that might be said in her praise.

Monday morning we were towed up to the Navy Yard, and moored alongside the wharf. Three days were occupied by the crew in removing the ammunition, stores, and running rigging from the ship, and then they were allowed to go on shore and remain until their accounts should be returned from Washington. These were received Thursday evening, and yesterday morning the Paymaster began to pay them off and give them their discharges. The work was accomplished about noon, and after a delay of about two hours the Guard and the Officers assembled on the quarter-deck, while the Captain read the papers placing the ship out of commission; then, at the third roll of the drum, the Guard presented arms, and the Officers uncovered their heads, the colors and pennant were hauled down, and the Hartford was "put out of commission." The Guard then formed, under command of Captain Forney, to march to the Barracks. Our fine appearance, dressed as we were in showy " uniform " and white pants, was heightened by our elegant silk flag which we had had made in China and brought home with us; so that as we marched through the principal streets on our way, their sides were lined by thousands who had assembled to see us.

There is now no more a " Hartford's Crew." Our corporate life is extinct. Once more we are citizens. Some there are among us whose future life will be but a repetition of the past three years. They have no home but "on the rolling deep," nor do they desire any other ; and they will be content to pass the remainder of their days upon the ocean and in visiting foreign climes, desiring no more than a month on shore in their own country, in which to spend the accumulated earnings of the cruise. It may perhaps be well that the larger share of us have reasons to remember with pride that we are citizens of a country whose grandest influences are to be found in the ways of peace, and to which we will henceforth cling with strengthened affection, after the many trials and privations which we have endured. But these latter belong to the past, only to be remembered in the future as a background the more clearly to set forth the blessings that may be in store for us.

APPENDIX.

LIST OF OFFICERS OF THE U. S. S. WACHUSETT, FROM MARCH 5, 1865, TO SEPT. 14, 1867.

Comdr. Robt. Townsend, †	Captain.
Comdr. Robt. W. Shufeldt,	"
Lieut. John W. Phillip, ‡	Executive Officer.
Lieut. E. T. Brower,	"
Master T. G. Grove,	Sailing Master.
W. B. Newman,	Master.
J. C. Pegram, §	Ensign.
W. C. Wise, ‡	"
C. R. Haskins,	"
Thomas Kelly, †	Master's Mate.
Reuben Rich,	"
Jas. Moran,	"
Wm. M. King, §	Surgeon.
Thos. Penrose,	Passed Asst. Surgeon.
E. H. Sears,	Assistant-Paymaster.
E. B. Latch,	First Asst. Engineer.
M. H. Knapp, §	Second " "
Edmund Lincoln,	" " "
J. H. Lewars,	Third " "
Jefferson Brown,	" " "
Jas A. Barton,	" " "
A. Forbes,	" " "
Paul Atkinson, §	Boatswain.
T. Russell,	Gunner.
Mr. Townsend, §	Captain's Clerk.
Mr. Shufeldt,	"
Mr. Thomas,	Paymaster's Clerk.

† Died of Disease.   ‡ Transferred.   § Sent Home.

APPENDIX.

LIST OF OFFICERS OF U. S. FLAG SHIP, HARTFORD, FROM SEPT. 14, 1867, TO AUGUST 14, 1868.

Rear Admiral H. H. Bell, ‖	Comdg. Asiatic Squadron.
Commodore J. R. Goldsboro,	" " "
Comdr. Geo. E. Belknap,	Captain.
Lieut. Comdr. J. W. Phillip,	Ex. Officer.
" " F. J. Higginson,	Sailing Master.
Lieut. J. J. Read, ‖	Flag Lieut.
Lieut. W. W. Maclay,	"
A. S. Crowningshield,	Lieutenant.
Jas. A. Sands,	"
W. C. Wise,	"
W. M. Folger,	Master.
Horace Elmer,	"
Joseph Beale,	Fleet Surgeon.
Washington Irving,	" Paymaster,
Andrew Lawton,	" Engineer.
G. W. Dorrance,	Chaplain.
Capt. Jas. Forney,	Fleet Marine Officer.
Wm. Watts,	Midshipman.
C. H. Page, †	Assistant Surgeon.
F. A. Wilson,	First Assistant Engineer.
D. Smith,	" "
O. W. Allison,	Second " "
J. A. Smith,	" " "
G. McAllister,	Third " "
Robt. Muir,	" " "
Jas. Mellon,	" " "
Wm. Long,	Boatswain.
R. H. Cross,	Gunner.
R. A. Williams,	Carpenter.
Jacob Stephens,	Sailmaker.

† Died of Disease.   ‡ Transferred.   § Sent Home.   ‖ Drowned.

COMPREHENSIVE SUMMARY.

Of a Cruise in the U. S. S. Wachusett, Continued in the U. S. Flag Ship Hartford.

ASIATIC SQUADRON,

COMMENCING AT BOSTON, MARCH 5, 1865, ENDING AT NEW YORK AUG. 14, 1867.

PORTS VISITED.	ARRIVED.		No. of Days in Port.	DEPARTURE		No. of Days at Sea.	Distance Sailed in Knots.
	Month.	Day.		Month.	Day.		
	1865.			1865.			
Boston, U. S.	March	5		March	5		
Port Royal, Martinique,	"	16	16	April	1	10	1,944
St. Pierre, "	April	1	3	"	4		12
Porto Grand, Cape Verde,	"	29	11	May	9	24	3,530
Porto Praya, "	May	10	17	"	27	1	165
St. Catharine, Brazil,	June	28	6	July	4	32	4,066
Rio Janerio, "	July	7	66	Sept.	20	3	472
Simon's Town, S. Africa,	Oct.	20	7	Oct.	27	29	4,006
Cape Town, "	"	27	27	Nov.	23	1-2	60
	1866.						
Batavia, Java,	Jan.	10	17	Jan.	27	49½	5,710
Ambnng, Borneo,	Feb.	5	1	Feb.	6	8	1,120
Manilla, Luzon,	"	13	15	"	28	7	719
Hong Kong, China,	March	5	10	March	15	5	692
Macao, "	"	15	18	April	3	1-2	40
Canton, "	April	3	12	"	15	1-2	83
Hong-Kong, "	"	16	2	"	18	1	107
Shanghai, "	"	24	5	"	29	6	892
Yingtse, "	May	4	64	July	7	4	699
Great Wall, "	July	8	1-4	"	8	1	151
Takoo, "	"	9	1.6	"	9	1	145
Chefoo, "	"	10	2	"	12	1	161
Tung-Chow-foo, "	"	12	3	"	15	1-6	40
Chefoo, "	"	15	6	"	21	1-6	40
Shanghai "	"	25	16	Aug.	10	4	530
Chinkiang-foo, "	Aug.	12	3	"	15	1 1-2	207
Shanghai, "	"	15	3	"	18	1-2	107
Yokohama, Japan,	"	23	8	"	31	4 1-2	1,054
Yedo, "	"	31	7	Sept.	6	1-4	15
Yokohama, "	Sept.	6	6	"	13	1-4	15
Oosima, "	"	14	2	"	16	1 1-2	235
Nagasaki, "	"	20	4	"	24	4	489
Hong-Kong, China,	"	29	14	Oct.	13	5	1,037
Macao, "	Oct.	13	3	"	16	1-4	40
Hong-Kong, "	"	20	14	Nov.	3	4	50
Tinghoy, "	Nov.	3	1	"	4	1	46

444 APPENDIX.

PORTS VISITED.	ARRIVED.		No. of Days in Port.	DEPARTURE		No. of Days at Sea.	Distances Sailed in Knots.
	Month.	Day.		Month.	Day.		
	1866.			1866.			
Swatow, China,	Nov.	5	5	Nov.	10	1	144
Tungsang, "	"	12	4 1-2	"	17	1-2	34
Amoy, "	"	17	11	"	28	1-2	63
Hong Kong, "	"	29	8 1-2	Dec.	7	1 1-2	260
Whampoa, "	Dec.	7	15½	"	23	1	82
Hong Kong, "	"	24	5	"	29	1	82
	1867.						
Shanghai, "	Jan.	6	4	Jan.	10	4	885
Chefoo, "	"	14	8	"	22	2 1-2	486
Nein-fo, Corea,	"	23	6	"	29	1 3-4	154
Port Hamilton, Corea,	Feb.	1	2	Feb.	3	2 1-2	455
Shanghai, China,	"	5	20	"	25	2 1-2	408
Chinkiang-foo, China,	"	27	1 1-2	March	1	1 3-4	162
Kiu-Kiang, "	March	4	1	"	5	1 1-2	300
Hankow, "	"	6	7 1-2	"	14	1	156
Kiu-Kiang, "	"	15	8	"	23	1 1-2	156
Nankin, "	"	24	2 1-2	"	27	1	255
Chinkiang-foo, "	"	27	2	"	29	1-3	45
Shanghai, "	"	30	4	April	3	1	162
Foo-Chow, "	April	6	7	"	13	3	444
Chinhai, "	"	16	2	"	18	3	320
Ningpo, "	"	18	5	"	23		12
Shanghai, "	"	24	95	July	29	1	142
Ragged Islands, "	July	30	1	"	31	1	75
Ningpo, "	Aug.	1	2	Aug.	3	1	60
Tinghai, "	"	3	11½	"	15	1-4	40
Pootoo, "	"	15	6	"	21	1-4	40
Shanghai, "	"	22	4	"	26	1	150
Hong Kong, "	Sept.	2	17	Sept.	19	7	870

Summary Continued, in the U. S. Flag Ship Hartford.

Hong Kong, China,	Aug.	29	41	Oct.	10	6	984
Nagasaki, Japan,	Oct.	19	58	Dec.	17	9	1,120
Simonosaki, "	Dec.	18	1	"	19	1	150
				1868.			
Hiogo, "	"	21	18	Jan.	8	2	160
	1868.						
Osaca, "	Jan.	8	4	"	12		13
Hiogo, "	"	12	9	"	21		13
Simonosaki, "	"	25	1	"	26	4	160
Nagasaki, "	"	27	5	Feb.	1	1	130
Hong Kong, China,	Feb.	8	27	March	5	7	1,160
Whampoa, "	March	5	7	"	12	1-2	70
Hong Kong, "	"	13	9	"	21	1	70
Singapore, Malaysia,	"	31	22	April	23	10	1,550
Anjer Point, Java,	April	27	1	"	28	4	520
Simon's Town, S. Africa,	June	8	6 1-2	June	15	41	5,622
Cape Town, "	"	15	5	"	20	1-2	60
St. Helena Island,	July	4	3	July	7	14	1,896
New York, U. S.,	Aug.	6	8	Aug.	14	30	5,260
TOTAL, 81 PORTS VISITED.			887			383	Knots. 53,888, or 62,196 Miles.

www.ingramcontent.com/pod-product-compliance
Lightning Source LLC
Chambersburg PA
CBHW022100300426
44117CB00007B/524